Shy Children,
Phobic Adults

Shy Children, Phobic Adults

Nature and Treatment of Social Anxiety Disorder

SECOND EDITION

Deborah C. Beidel
Samuel M. Turner

American Psychological Association
Washington, DC

Published by
American Psychological Association
750 First Street, NE
Washington, DC 20002
www.apa.org

To order
APA Order Department
P.O. Box 92984
Washington, DC 20090-2984
Tel: (800) 374-2721
Direct: (202) 336-5510
Fax: (202) 336-5502
TDD/TTY: (202) 336-6123
Online: www.apa.org/books/
E-mail: order@apa.org

In the U.K., Europe, Africa, and the Middle East, copies may be ordered from
American Psychological Association
3 Henrietta Street
Covent Garden, London
WC2E 8LU England

Typeset in Minion by World Composition Services, Inc., Sterling, VA

Printer: Maple-Vail Book Manufacturing Group, Binghamton, NY
Cover Designer: Minker Design, Bethesda, MD
Technical/Production Editor: Tiffany L. Klaff

The opinions and statements published are the responsibility of the authors, and such opinions and statements do not necessarily represent the policies of the American Psychological Association.

Library of Congress Cataloging-in-Publication Data

Beidel, Deborah C.
    Shy children, phobic adults : nature and treatment of social anxiety disorder / Deborah C. Beidel and Samuel M. Turner.— 2nd ed.
        p. cm.
    Includes bibliographical references and index.
    ISBN-13: 978-1-59147-452-4
    ISBN-10: 1-59147-452-3
    1. Social phobia. I. Turner, Samuel M., 1944–   . II. American Psychological Association. III. Title.
    [DNLM: 1. Phobic Disorders. WM   178 B422s 2007]

RC552.S62B45   2007
616.85′223—dc22   2006009554

British Library Cataloguing-in-Publication Data
A CIP record is available from the British Library.

Printed in the United States of America
Second Edition

To Sam

When describing our work, the words *I, my,* or *mine* were never part of your vocabulary. For you, it was always *we, us,* and *ours.* And so it will always be. Your courageous heart and generous spirit inspire me still.

Debbie

Contents

Preface

Clinical and research interest in the field of social anxiety disorder has increased dramatically since the publication of the first edition of this volume in 1998. This interest has translated into increased knowledge regarding the psychopathology, epidemiology and long-term impact, assessment strategies, and treatment outcome (both psychological and pharmacological) of the disorder. For example, in several areas of the first edition, we were able to state that data were "beginning to emerge." Now the data are firmly established, allowing us (and others) to draw more substantive conclusions. In fact, it is difficult to identify any aspect of social anxiety disorder for which there has not been a substantial increase in knowledge. Thus, we felt that the time was right for an update of this volume. In the following paragraphs, we highlight some of the revisions that are found in this second edition.

One of the first changes that a reader will notice is the change in the name of the disorder. As a result of the clear documentation of its extensive and pervasive distress, *social anxiety disorder* (rather than *social phobia*) has become the preferred term because *phobia* is still associated with a circumscribed pattern of distress, and this clearly is not descriptive of social anxiety disorder. In fact, over the past 8 years, clinicians and researchers have seen many changes in several aspects of its clinical presentation in both adults and children. For adults, we now know that social anxiety disorder is a chronic condition, much more so than depression or panic disorder, and that it results in significant impairment across all areas of functioning. An exciting new development is the emergence of neuroscience and sophisticated neuroassessment strategies. The use of magnetic resonance imaging, for example, is yielding new data regarding the role of neuroanatomical structure and function in social anxiety disorder. There is no doubt that this area will continue to produce substantive findings over the next decade. Among children and adolescents, there are now sufficient data to characterize clearly the presentation of social anxiety disorder in these age groups and, particularly, how the disorder manifests itself differently depending on developmental age. Similarly, there are now more substantive data available regarding the prevalence of social anxiety disorder across various cultural groups, although regrettably most samples are still limited to Caucasian populations in Europe and North America. It is hoped that data from other continents will follow soon.

Another significant change from the first edition is that there are now a variety of assessment instruments specifically developed to assess social anxiety disorder in adult, adolescent, and child populations. These new strategies include well-validated self-report instruments and clinician rating scales. In fact, the assessment chapter has been substantially revised to reflect the burgeoning research in this area. The same word, *burgeoning*, aptly describes the literature addressing pharmacological treatment. Although the first edition was published less than a decade ago, at that time there were no controlled trials examining SSRIs. Now SSRIs are the pharmacological treatment of choice for patients of all ages. Chapter 7 is the one that has undergone the most substantial revision in this second edition, and the difference is striking. Although there are still few studies comparing pharmacological and psychosocial interventions, clear evidence is now available concerning the efficacy of many medication classes. The chapters on psychosocial treatment in adults and children have also benefited from the results of expanded controlled treatment trials that are now available. Previously, debate existed regarding the merits of a strictly behavioral versus a cognitive–behavioral approach to the treatment of social anxiety disorder in adults. That debate is now largely resolved, and the cumulative data clearly indicate that the crucial therapeutic ingredient is exposure to the feared situation. Chapter 9, on psychosocial treatment in children and adolescents, has also undergone substantial revision, and unlike the state of the literature at the time of the first edition, a number of controlled trials now indicate the efficacy of behavioral treatments for this disorder.

Consistent with the changes in the empirical literature, this volume benefits from the inclusion of new case descriptions and clinical materials to assist clinicians in providing treatment to those suffering from this disorder, which in our opinion still remains the primary reason for conducting research. In summary, the wealth of new research data examining all aspects of social anxiety disorder make this second edition long overdue. We are pleased that it is finally here.

Acknowledgments

M any individuals kindly contributed their time and effort to the
development of this book. First and foremost, we thank our
patients and their families who contributed their time and taught us so
much about this disorder and how to treat it. Second, we thank Brennan
Young and Adam Collins for their technical assistance in the completion
of the manuscript and the anonymous reviewers who so carefully and
thoughtfully made suggestions that improved the volume. Finally, we
thank Susan Reynolds, Susan Herman, and Tiffany Klaff in the Books
Department at the American Psychological Association for their consistent support, encouragement, and suggestions.

Shy Children,
Phobic Adults

Introduction

"I didn't know anyone else felt like me. You mean that there really is a name for this? Other people have it? And somebody knows how to treat it?"

—An adult patient with social anxiety disorder
during an initial interview at our clinic

The experience of social anxiety and fear is a universal aspect of the human condition. For most individuals, episodes of anxiety are mild and transitory, but for others, the fear is more severe, pervasive, and enduring. The recognition and discussion of severe social fear dates back to at least the time of Hippocrates, but in the United States social anxiety disorder was not an officially recognized diagnosis until the publication of the third edition of the *Diagnostic and Statistical Manual of Mental Disorders* (*DSM–III*; American Psychiatric Association [APA], 1980). Underrecognition of maladaptive social anxiety is apparent in the above comment from one of our patients. Although increasingly well known, this condition was historically considered merely a developmental phase of childhood. Among adults, there sometimes was the perception that everyone gets anxious when giving a speech. Thus, until 25 years ago, prevailing views among professionals and laypersons alike minimized the significance of social anxiety disorder or attributed it to a simple case of shyness. Perhaps this is why many individuals with social anxiety disorder did not seek treatment and why they tended not to reveal the extent of their distress. In 1985, Liebowitz, Gorman, Fyer, and Klein referred to social anxiety disorder as the *neglected anxiety disorder*, and indeed, this was an apt description at that time. Although there is considerable overlap with the construct of shyness, and the exact relationship between these two conditions has not yet been determined, when current diagnostic criteria are applied, social anxiety disorder differs considerably from shyness with respect to epidemiology, course, severity of symptoms, and clinical correlates.

SOCIAL ANXIETY DISORDER (SOCIAL PHOBIA) AS A CLINICAL SYNDROME

Even after the recognition of social anxiety disorder as a diagnosable disorder in the *DSM–III*, acceptance as a significant clinical syndrome was slow. Initially described as a relatively circumscribed disorder, researchers had to overcome skepticism regarding its real significance as a clinical syndrome by clinicians and by those reviewing grant applications for the National Institute of Mental Health. Over the past 25 years, a considerable body of research has emerged demonstrating that social anxiety disorder is a highly prevalent and serious disorder in the general population. As a testament to the recognition of the disorder's pervasive and serious nature, *social anxiety disorder*, rather than *social phobia*, is now the preferred diagnostic term and the one that we use throughout this volume.

On the basis of available epidemiological data, social anxiety disorder is the most common anxiety disorder in the U.S. population. Research into phenomenology and clinical features reveals that people with social anxiety disorder experience significant emotional distress, social isolation, and occupational maladjustment. In fact, severity of functional impairment has emerged as much more significant than it was previously considered to be. Individuals with social anxiety disorder suffer from depression, suicidal ideation, generalized anxiety disorder, avoidant personality disorder, and obsessive–compulsive personality disorder. When the revised version of the *DSM–III* (*DSM–III–R*; APA, 1987) was published, the description had changed as a result of research findings. In this revision, two patterns of social anxiety disorder were acknowledged, one characterized by a relatively circumscribed pattern of fear and avoidance and one characterized by a pervasive pattern of social timidity. This description of social anxiety disorder was maintained in the fourth edition of the *DSM* (*DSM–IV*; APA, 1994).

From its introduction, social anxiety disorder was considered to be an early-onset anxiety disorder, appearing most often in midadolescence (most other major anxiety disorders had been considered adult-onset conditions at the time). However, reports of earlier onset from patients and research with younger adolescents and children revealed that social anxiety disorder was quite prevalent in childhood, existing in children as young as age 8 (Beidel & Turner, 1988). Social anxiety disorder has been estimated to occur in about 1% to 2% of children (McGee et al., 1990), but specific childhood descriptions were included in *DSM–IV* for the first time. Because descriptors of social anxiety have been removed from the diagnostic criteria of other childhood conditions and are now attributable to social anxiety disorder, the prevalence of the condition in children no doubt is considerably higher, perhaps as high as 3% to 5% in the general population (Shaffer et al., 1996). Features of social anxiety disorder in childhood are remarkably similar to those in adults, when appropriate developmental stages are considered. Thus, it is clear that some individuals with this disorder manifest the condition in early childhood and adolescence and remain affected through adulthood.

Although its etiology remains uncertain, the disorder's early onset and familial pattern have raised the question of genetic or biological causation. Similarly, shyness and social anxiety have been studied for their relationship to the early-appearing temperamental style known as behavioral inhibition. Examination of the literature, however, reveals numerous other ways in which social anxiety disorder might develop, and it is hypothesized in this volume that there are multiple pathways to the development of the disorder.

THE TREATMENT OF SOCIAL ANXIETY

The results of treatment studies conducted over the past 2 decades demonstrate that adult social anxiety disorder is a highly treatable condition. In addition, the literature has progressed substantially to the point that recommendations regarding both pharmacological and psychological treatment can be made. Although the research base is much smaller, a number of studies have indicated that childhood and adolescent social anxiety disorder can be effectively treated with psychological strategies similar to those used to treat adults, but the status of drug treatment is less certain. We discuss the current pharmacological and psychological treatments, outlining their implementation and, in the case of drug treatments, explicating guidelines promulgated by pharmacotherapists for the safe use of medication in children.

Empirical research on the syndrome of social anxiety disorder and its treatment has grown rapidly since its inclusion in the diagnostic system. Furthermore, since the time of the publication of the first edition of this volume, the body of research data has continued to expand. Because of this, it is a particularly appropriate time for a second edition that can integrate these new findings into the existing literature. This book is designed to discuss the syndrome of social anxiety disorder across the ages—its various clinical presentations, demographic characteristics, theories of etiology, and empirically supported treatment strategies. In some cases, we have incorporated the discussion of child, adolescent, and adult presentations into one chapter; in others, separate chapters for adults or children and adolescents seemed more appropriate. We endeavor to enrich the discussion by integrating our clinical experience with adults and children with the findings from empirical studies and by presenting case material from our clinical and research practice to illustrate important points regarding the syndrome as well as its assessment and treatment.

THIS EDITION

Much of the material in this revision was not even in existence when the first edition of this book was published. Thus, readers will find that each chapter has undergone substantial revisions to include this expanded amount of data. The first section of the book focuses on the psychopathology of social anxiety disorder. Chapters 1 and 2 address the clinical syndrome and differential diagnosis in adults and children, respectively. In this edition, emergent data allow us to address more fully the severely chronic nature of this disorder as well as its extensive impact on academic, occupational, social, and emotional function in adults, adolescents, and children. The differences between the first and second editions are particularly striking when examining the clinical syndrome of social anxiety disorder in children and adolescents. At the time of the first edition, there were no controlled studies of the psychopathology of social anxiety disorder in children and adolescents—only clinical descriptions. Now such descriptions are based on rigorously diagnosed patients and compared with control samples, allowing much firmer conclusions to be drawn. These two revised chapters are followed by a chapter on epidemiology (chap. 3), which now includes data from a number of studies outside of the United States, thereby showcasing the universal nature of this disorder. In chapter 4, we review etiological and developmental factors, where there are now substantive new data regarding our understanding of temperamental factors such as behavioral inhibition and social anxiety disorder. We know now that there is some relationship between these two variables, although behavioral inhibition is neither necessary nor sufficient for the development of social anxiety disorder.

We then turn to issues of measurement across the various ages (chap. 5), including assessment for the purposes of diagnosis, treatment planning, and determining treatment outcome. One of the most significant changes in this revised chapter is the plethora of measures that are now available, measures that are specific to the assessment of social anxiety disorder. Furthermore, new neurological assessment strategies such as functional magnetic resonance imaging hold significant promise for understanding the potential role of neuroscience in social anxiety disorder. Chapter 6 addresses overall clinical management, including patient management, and, in the case of child and adolescent patients, addresses child management. Chapter 7 is also extensively revised in this edition. There are many new controlled trials examining pharmacological interventions for adults, adolescents, and children with social anxiety disorder, thereby providing clinicians with an extensive overview of currently available treatment outcome literature. Finally, chapters 8 and 9 review behavioral and cognitive–behavioral treatments for adults, children, and adolescents, including how these strategies are implemented. The number of controlled, clinical trials has also increased dramatically, particularly those studies with children and adolescents, and in this revised edition, we are able to make specific treatment recommendations.

This book was written for clinicians, researchers, and students. We endeavor to present an integrated discussion of the nature of social anxiety disorder in children and adults as well as a discussion of how the nature of the syndrome affects the manner in which treatment is conducted. Each chapter includes a review of the relevant literature. As often occurs in psychology, different specialty areas develop parallel lines of research but often with little communication across specialties. Thus, clinical, developmental, experimental, and social psychologists all have made contributions to the literature on social fears. In only a few cases have the contributions from one field been recognized and used by another. Therefore, we attempt to integrate the relevant literature to present a more comprehensive presentation of the disorder.

In addition to integrating the diverse psychological literature on the nature of social anxiety and fear and to discussing etiological variables, a primary aim of ours was to make this book practical. Therefore, readers will find case vignettes, clinical examples from our own practice, actual assessment instruments, examples of other clinical material, and case examples of how we assess and treat child and adult social anxiety disorder. In addition, the chapters on treatment implementation describe the parameters associated with how to make these interventions work and common problems associated with implementation. We believe this practical focus will be useful for clinicians who treat patients with social anxiety disorder. Likewise, researchers should find this clinical material useful for enhancing their understanding of the problems faced by patients and the clinicians who treat them. Finally, for students, the clinical presentation should provide a richer understanding of the patients and the challenges those who treat them face in understanding and treating this condition. It is our hope that the contents of this volume will serve to educate the clinician about the clinical characteristics of social anxiety disorder, provide assistance for the implementation of successful treatment, provide the researcher with helpful insight into the nature of the disorder, stimulate thought about areas of controversy, and point out many of the areas in which we are in need of additional inquiry. As for the student, we hope the contents of this book will stimulate interest in this disorder, provide the foundation for understanding the nature of the condition, and give guidance in how its treatment should be approached.

1

Clinical Presentation of Social Anxiety Disorder in Adults

Elaine was a 40-year-old advertising executive. She was well educated, enjoyed a high income, and lived in a fashionable neighborhood. Elaine came to our clinic because of a conversation with the owner of her company. He told her that he had decided to retire and wanted to turn over the business to Elaine. Although tremendously excited by the opportunity to own her own business, she was upset because for many years she had avoided securing clients and other social aspects of her upper management position, constantly arranging her schedule to work in the background. As a result, she minimized her distress in social situations by avoiding almost all social contacts while still performing her duties exceptionally well. The prospect of assuming the leadership of the company frightened Elaine so much that she was seriously considering resigning. According to Elaine, the tasks associated with ownership were almost all social in nature, and the thought of assuming the role evoked considerable anxiety. The distress associated with her dilemma increased her general anxiety such that she suffered from constant tension and muscle aches and pains, and she complained of difficulty sleeping, crying episodes, and anergia.

This scenario is not atypical for those who experience social anxiety disorder. Although able to maintain employment, those with the disorder often find limited occupational choices, roles dictated or constrained by social fears, and personal lives characterized by extensive social avoidance. Frequently, individuals seek treatment when they can no longer maintain their avoidant lifestyle; when they become dissatisfied with the inability to reach their goals; when a significant life event forces a change in their occupational, personal, familial, or social responsibilities; or when a significant other can no longer accept this severely restricted lifestyle. Oftentimes, as was the case with Elaine, those with social anxiety disorder are considered reserved or shy, but others rarely understand the extent of their social inhibition or their personal distress. Patients with social anxiety disorder frequently experience dysphoric mood and sometimes frank depression, and, as was the case with Elaine, high levels of general anxiety and other somatic symptoms are common. This chapter discusses the symptoms, detrimental effects, comorbidity, and differential diagnosis of social anxiety disorder in adults.

DIAGNOSIS

Recognition of social anxiety disorder dates back to the writings of Hippocrates (Marks, 1985). Although Marks and Gelder (1966) and Marks (1970) described the syndrome as it is currently conceptualized, the formal diagnosis of social anxiety disorder did not enter the United States psychiatric nomenclature until the publication of the third edition of the *Diagnostic and Statistical Manual of Mental Disorders* (*DSM–III*; American Psychiatric Association [APA], 1980). The criteria established were essentially those outlined by Marks and Gelder (1966) and Marks (1970). Despite some minor revisions during the 1980s and 1990s, the clinical description has remained generally unchanged. In fact, the most significant change has been the wording of criteria to allow for two subtypes known as the generalized and specific (nongeneralized). The essence of social anxiety disorder is extreme social inhibition and timidity. The more specific description found in the fourth edition of the *Diagnostic and Statistical Manual of Mental Disorders (DSM–IV*; APA, 1994) is discussed in the following sections.

The *DSM–IV* characterized social anxiety disorder as "a marked and persistent fear of one or more social or performance situations in which the person is exposed to unfamiliar people or possible scrutiny by others" (APA, 1994, p. 416). Those with social anxiety disorder may fear virtually any situation that includes the possibility of observation or scrutiny by others. Common socially distressful situations include formal speaking, interacting with others, attending social events, maintaining social dialogue, and eating or writing in front of others. Less common but nonetheless distressful situations reported by those with social anxiety disorder include being observed while typing or using photocopying equipment, using public restrooms, or merely saying one's name at a public meeting. Leisure activities also may be distressful. Some adults describe anxiety and avoidance when playing golf, dancing, or walking down the aisle at church, again because of the fear of observation and evaluation by others. However, the disorder is not limited to situations in which one's performance is under specific scrutiny. Rather, it often involves anxiety and dread whenever any type of social interaction is anticipated. Thus, individuals with social anxiety disorder frequently do not interact with others at work and do not attend social events such as parties or meetings where social exchange would be expected. In addition, a relatively rare but often particularly debilitating form of social anxiety disorder is fear of using public restrooms (see the section on paruresis in this chapter). In these cases, the fear is not concern about cleanliness or contamination by germs but rather is related to concerns about social evaluation and the process of bodily elimination.

A second characteristic of social anxiety disorder is that "exposure to the feared social situation almost invariably provokes anxiety, which may take the form of a situationally bound or situationally predisposed panic attack" (APA, 1994, p. 417). Although most clinicians were aware of it earlier, *DSM–IV* criteria officially recognized that individuals with any type of anxiety disorder could have panic attacks. In fact, those with social anxiety disorder often experience panic attacks when in a social encounter or even when anticipating a social event. The physical symptoms of these attacks are the same as those of panic disorder and can be severe. In addition, the pattern of the physiological response when in a distressful social situation is one of the features that differentiate those with social anxiety disorder from individuals who have "normal" speech anxiety (Turner, Beidel, & Larkin, 1986). Specifically, when those who do not meet criteria for an anxiety disorder (i.e., nonphobic control participants) begin a speech, their blood pressure and heart rate increase. After approximately 3 to 5 minutes, physiological responses return to normal baseline levels. The physiological response of those with social anxiety disorder differs from that of nonphobic control participants. Blood pressure and pulse rates also increase at the start but remain elevated until the speech is completed. Thus, those with social anxiety disorder do not experience the decrement in physiological arousal characteristic of those without the disorder. This difference in physiological response to social settings and encounters also has been found in "shy" rhesus monkeys and behaviorally inhibited children (Turner & Beidel, 1989), suggesting the presence of common reactivity across these conditions.

Finally, in regard to social anxiety disorder, the *DSM–IV* stated, "The person recognizes that the fear is excessive and unreasonable" (APA, 1994, p. 417). Those with social anxiety disorder often present for treatment by saying, "I know it is crazy to feel this way, but I cannot help it." That is, those with the disorder recognize that often there is no reasonable basis for their fears, but this knowledge does little to alleviate their anxiety. This criterion helps to distinguish social anxiety disorder from other conditions such as paranoid personality disorder. Patients with paranoid personality disorder, although experiencing considerable social distress, often believe that others are thinking critically about them or may actually be planning to embarrass, humiliate, or harm them (see the section in this chapter on differential diagnosis). Developmental considerations also are important when considering this diagnostic criterion, however. Young children often cannot acknowledge the irrational basis of their fears. Thus, lack of recognition of the unreasonableness of the fear is more common in children and adolescents (see chap. 2, this volume).

Many with social anxiety disorder live in constant fear that they will embarrass themselves, appear foolish, or appear less intelligent than others. The most common difficult situation is public speaking (Holt, Heimberg, & Hope, 1992; M. B. Stein, Walker, & Forde, 1994; Turner, Beidel, Dancu, & Keys, 1986). As noted, other commonly reported fears include eating or drinking in public, writing in public, attending informal social settings such as parties, and a variety of other social performance situations. The significant distress frequently leads to avoidance behavior (Turner, Beidel, & Larkin, 1986). Avoidance may be overt and sometimes dramatic (as in Elaine's case) or it may be subtle. As an example of the latter,

> Tina related how she avoided drinking in public. Unable to pick up a glass when in the presence of others because of her fear of trembling, she would always order a very large glass of iced tea. Because of the size of the glass, she felt that it was appropriate to slide the glass toward her (rather than pick it up) and, using a straw, bend over to sip from it.

This example illustrates the extreme strategies that patients may use to manage or hide their distress. It also illustrates how subtle avoidance behaviors may be. Table 1.1 lists common fears and avoidance behaviors seen in adults with social anxiety disorder.

As illustrated in Table 1.1, although difficulty making public speeches is a problem for a large majority of those with social anxiety disorder, the disorder typically is not restricted to formal public speaking fears. Most people with social anxiety disorder, particularly the generalized

Table 1.1
Situations Commonly Feared by Adults With Social Anxiety Disorder

Situation	Distress (%)	Avoidance (%)
Formal speaking	97	89
Informal speaking and meetings	79	75
Eating and drinking in public	25	33
Writing in public	13	10
Initiating and maintaining conversations	77	84
Parties	80	79
Using public restrooms	18	25
Dating	54	53

Note. Patients were diagnosed with the *Diagnostic and Statistical Manual of Mental Disorders* (4th ed.; American Psychiatric Association, 1994) criteria for social anxiety disorder.

subtype (see discussion of subtypes later in this chapter), are unable to form and maintain satisfying interpersonal relationships, and they have a chronic restricted range of social activities (Turner & Beidel, 1989). Even chance activities such as meeting a new neighbor over the back fence can cause considerable distress. When interviewing an individual with social anxiety disorder, it is important to remember that the situations that provoke distress may be extensive and variable. Similarly, not all patients with social anxiety disorder experience an identical pattern of physical symptoms or negative cognitions that characterize their distress. For example, when faced with a social encounter, one patient might experience the full set of typical somatic symptoms (e.g., blushing, rapid heart rate, shaking, and trembling), whereas another might only experience general tension and stuttering.

It is important to note that although the condition is defined by anxiety and fear associated with specific situations, the fear is not defined strictly by the physical parameters of those situations. Individuals who have anxiety in public speaking situations, for example, may only experience distress under certain circumstances. One patient treated in our clinic only had difficulty if the audience included individuals he considered to be authorities in his field. His high performance anxiety was fueled by his concerns about his abilities. This is an important point with respect to treatment and is addressed further in chapter 8 when we discuss the selection of *core fears* for exposure treatment. Components of the fear will be as unique as each individual who seeks treatment. Furthermore, in any discussion of social anxiety disorder, it is important from the outset to distinguish this clinical disorder from behavior that is usually labeled shyness, as we do in the next section.

SOCIAL ANXIETY DISORDER AND SHYNESS

The term *shy* is used by professionals and laypersons alike to describe people who are socially reticent. Shy persons often are not considered to have an emotional disorder but rather are considered to be temperamentally reserved. Although socially reticent, less gregarious, and less socially inclined than others, many shy individuals can socially engage when necessary at the interactional as well as specific performance levels. Data have begun to emerge addressing the relationship of shyness and social anxiety disorder. One hypothesis is that shyness might be on a continuum such that those at the upper extreme meet criteria for social anxiety disorder, and those at the lower extreme do not. Alternatively, the two conditions, although sharing similar features, could be completely independent. Finally, the term *shy* could be merely a generic label describing a host of conditions characterized by social reticence.

Some of the initial conceptualizations regarding the relationship between shyness and social anxiety disorder were based on data addressing adult outcomes of American (Caspi, Elder, & Bem, 1988) and Swedish (Kerr, Lambert, & Bem, 1996) children identified as shy. Among boys in both groups, those who were shy at ages 8 to 10 years married later and became fathers later than boys who were not shy. Shy American boys also endorsed more occupational impairment in adulthood, but this was not found in their Swedish counterparts. Among girls, marriage and motherhood did not differentiate either the American or Swedish shy sample from their non-shy peers. Both groups of shy girls had lower levels of academic achievement than non-shy girls, however. This was particularly striking in the Swedish sample, in which the rate of college attendance for the non-shy girls was 44% compared with 0% for the shy girls. Thus, shyness appeared to result in some long-term impairments similar to those found in samples of socially anxious patients, fueling speculation of an overlap between these conditions.

In an early overall review of the empirical literature on shyness and social anxiety disorder (Turner, Beidel, & Townsley, 1990), six dimensions of functioning were examined: somatic features, cognitive characteristics, behavioral responses, daily functioning, clinical course, and onset characteristics. The review indicated that both shy and socially anxious samples had similar somatic symptoms and cognitions in distressing settings. They differed, however, on social and occupational functioning, onset characteristics, course of the disorder, and overt behaviors. On each dimension, those with social anxiety disorder were more severe than those who were labeled shy. There were epidemiological differences as well. Whereas up to 40% of college students reported feelings of shyness, about 13% of adults met criteria for a lifetime diagnosis of social anxiety disorder in the National Comorbidity Study, an epidemiological sample (Kessler et al., 1994; see chap. 3, this volume).

Two studies using similar strategies also addressed the overlap of shyness and social anxiety disorder among adults (Chavira, Stein, & Malcarne, 2002; Heiser, Turner, & Beidel, 2003), and these data indicate that there is some relation, but it is far from conclusive. Among the 10% of individuals who endorsed the most extreme level of shyness, 36% met criteria for generalized social anxiety disorder; among those with "average" levels of shyness, only 4% met criteria for social anxiety disorder (Chavira et al., 2002). Thus, higher levels of shyness are associated with an increasing frequency of social anxiety disorder, although even among the most shy, only slightly more than one third meet diagnostic criteria. Similarly, Heiser et al. (2003) reported that 18% of individuals who were designated as shy met criteria for social anxiety disorder compared with only 3% of those who described themselves as non-shy. There was a moderate and positive correlation between severity of shyness and the presence of social anxiety disorder, but the data do not support the conclusion that social anxiety disorder is merely severe shyness. The most parsimonious explanation is that the two syndromes are not identical but do overlap on some core characteristics (Turner et al., 1990). Thus, these terms, or the representative participant samples, cannot be used interchangeably. The question of whether these two conditions share common etiological factors or are otherwise related remains to be elucidated.

DETRIMENTAL EFFECTS

Originally dismissed as a minor problem affecting only public speaking situations, we now know that social anxiety disorder is the third most common psychiatric disorder in the general population (after major depression and alcohol abuse; Keller, 2003). Some available data indicate that those with social anxiety disorder report increased suicidal ideation and suicide attempts (Keller, 2003; Liebowitz, Gorman, Fyer, Campeas, et al., 1985), although a meta-analysis of the Food and Drug Administration (FDA) database reported only one completed suicide and no suicide attempts among 917 participants in an FDA clinical trial of paroxetine versus placebo (Khan, Leventhal, Khan, & Brown, 2002). It is interesting to note that the patient who completed suicide was receiving paroxetine (see chap. 7). Social anxiety disorder is associated with increased use of alcohol, anxiolytics, and other drugs, often to meet daily demands of living and working (Amies, Gelder, & Shaw, 1983; Liebowitz, Gorman, Fyer, Campeas, et al., 1985; Schneier, Johnson, Hornig, Liebowitz, & Weissman, 1992; Turner, Beidel, Borden, Stanley, & Jacob, 1991; Turner, Beidel, Dancu, et al., 1986). Furthermore, it is now evident that social anxiety disorder is a severe and chronic condition that may affect performance in various spheres of functioning (Keller, 2003; Kessler, 2003), including reduced opportunities for employment, marriage, and educational achievement.

Those with social anxiety disorder experience significant emotional distress, and we now know that the disorder is much more serious than previously considered. When engaged in or anticipating social encounters, those affected experience increased somatic arousal (Amies et al., 1983; Turner, Beidel, Dancu, et al., 1986). In fact, social anxiety disorder is characterized by a particular constellation of physical symptoms mediated by the beta-adrenergic system, including heart palpitations, trembling, sweating, and blushing (Gorman & Gorman, 1987). In the 1980s, this characteristic physiological response generated substantial interest in the use of beta-blockers as a treatment for this disorder (see chap. 7, this volume).

Social anxiety disorder is unremitting, although symptom severity may wax and wane depending on particular life circumstances. Those with the specific (nongeneralized) subtype are usually least affected, whereas those with the generalized subtype and comorbid avoidant personality disorder (APD) are most affected (Kessler, 2003). Characteristic of its chronic nature, an episode of social anxiety disorder lasts an average of 18 years compared with 6 years for panic disorder and 1 year for major depression (Keller, 2003). Factors affecting chronicity include the presence of alcohol abuse or dependence (Keller, 2003); lower level of educational attainment or earlier age of onset (Davidson et al., 1993); and, in women, comorbid agoraphobia or a history of suicide attempts (Keller, 2003). Additionally, data from long-term investigations (Alnæs & Torgersen, 1999; Keller, 2003) have indicated that 6 to 8 years after the initial assessment, 44% to 64% of those with social anxiety disorder still meet diagnostic criteria compared with 24% to 28% of those with panic disorder. Even among those few who do recover, 29% experience a relapse (Keller, 2003).

With respect to social functioning, common features include inability to work, incomplete educational attainment, lack of career advancement, and severe social restriction (Kessler, 2003; Lecrubier et al., 2000; Liebowitz, Gorman, Fyer, Campeas, et al., 1985; Turner, Beidel, Dancu, et al., 1986), and data indicate that the presence of social anxiety disorder affects the decision to attend college (Kessler, 2003). Among a treatment-seeking sample (Turner, Beidel, Borden, et al., 1991), 91% reported that their social fears resulted in academic impairment, including lower grades because of lack of class participation (i.e., they could not speak in class and thus demonstrate their knowledge of the material). Some avoided classes thought to require oral participation or presentations, whereas others decided not to attend graduate or professional school or based the decision regarding their college major on their social fears. For example,

> Nick described enrolling and dropping out of three different colleges until he found one that did not require a speech class for graduation. Jean waited until the last term to take a required speech class then dropped the class and had to return for an extra semester to finish. When she again was unable to complete the course, she sought treatment.

Similar to the extensive academic impairment, 96% of one clinical sample (Turner, Beidel, Dancu, et al., 1986) reported occupational impediments. In most instances, this consisted of refusing promotions (as Elaine, quoted at the beginning of the chapter, was considering) or deliberately selecting careers that require minimal social contact. In severe cases, our patients have described hiding in office lavatories or behind filing cabinets to avoid speaking to coworkers or joining them for lunch in the cafeteria. Other researchers have reported that those with social anxiety disorder have higher rates of unemployment than a comparative group of patients with panic disorder, although those with the latter disorder report more disruptions in employment (Simon et al., 2002). Those with social anxiety disorder also have reported lost work productivity (Lecrubier et al., 2000; Van Ameringen, Mancini, & Streiner, 1994; Zhang, Ross, & Davidson, 2004), and compared with those with no disorder have been more likely to be unemployed (24%

vs. 4%; Zhang et al., 2004), to be financially dependent on others, and to rely more heavily on public assistance (Schneier, Johnson, et al., 1992). Even those with specific (nongeneralized) subtype had rates of financial dependency (welfare or disability payments) that were significantly higher than control participants with no disorder (22.3% vs. 10.6%; Schneier, Johnson, et al., 1992).

Impairment in social functioning is common among those with social anxiety disorder (Kessler, 2003; Lecrubier et al., 2000) even when comorbid conditions are not present (Simon et al., 2002); in one sample (Turner, Beidel, & Larkin, 1986), 80% felt that the disorder impaired their social relationships. Many patients felt stymied in their attempts to join clubs or organizations in which they had an interest because of the need to introduce themselves to others or participate in social activities affiliated with the organization. Some who managed to do so then faced additional difficulties because they would be nominated for leadership positions that they could not assume. With respect to heterosocial relationships, 44% of a community sample of those with social anxiety disorder were married, compared with 65% of those with no psychiatric disorder (Lepine & Pelissolo, 2000). Among an unmarried clinical sample ($N = 29$; Turner, Beidel, & Larkin, 1986), 79% felt that their heterosocial interactions were restricted by their fears, leaving them unable to date or establish meaningful intimate relationships. Even among those with social anxiety disorder who are married, marital conflict regarding socialization and social activities is common. Patients report that spouses are often unhappy with the patients' preference to stay home and watch television rather than socialize with other couples or simply go out. Similarly, some parents report fearing that their social impairment may affect their children's opportunities for socialization as well, thus leading children into the same cycle of social distress and isolation (see chap. 4, this volume).

Further complicating matters, alcohol use has been linked to social anxiety disorder. Alcohol and other substances, such as anxiolytics, sometimes are used in a deliberate attempt to minimize distress. Among one clinical sample (Turner, Beidel, Dancu, et al., 1986), 46% used alcohol to feel more sociable at a party. In addition, 50% intentionally used alcohol prior to social encounters such as parties or meetings to get themselves there, and 13% used anxiolytics specifically for this purpose. A review of the self-medication hypothesis (Carrigan & Randall, 2003) confirms these clinical data. Individuals with social anxiety disorder use alcohol in an attempt to reduce anxiety in social settings; however, the notion that alcohol actually reduces anxiety is not well supported.

Other research has also addressed the relationship between alcoholism and social anxiety disorder. Rates of social anxiety disorder among alcoholic inpatient populations range from 8% to 56% (Bowen, Cipywnyk, D'Arcy, & Keegan, 1984; Chambless, Cherney, Caputo, & Rheinstein, 1987; Mullaney & Trippett, 1979; Smail, Stockwell, Canter, & Hodgson, 1984; Stravynski, Lamontagne, & Lavallee, 1986), rates that are equal to or higher than the rates of social anxiety disorder in the general population (Heckelman & Schneier, 1995). Conversely, 16% of a sample of patients with social anxiety disorder abused alcohol (Schneier, Martin, Liebowitz, Gorman, & Fyer, 1989), and rates of alcohol abuse appear to be higher among those with social anxiety disorder than among those with other anxiety disorders (Kushner, Sher, & Beitman, 1990).

High rates of comorbidity among those with either a primary diagnosis of social anxiety disorder or alcoholism and reports that alcohol is often used to diminish social distress fuel speculation of an etiological link between these disorders. A number of our patients have traced their alcohol use back to their adolescent years, after the onset of their social anxiety disorder, and empirical data now substantiate these clinical observations. For the majority of cases in which alcohol abuse is part of the clinical presentation, abuse onset followed the onset of social anxiety disorder (Kushner et al., 1990; Schuckit et al., 1997), and among patients on an alcohol inpatient unit, alcohol was a form of self-medication for social distress (Kushner et al., 1990). Despite all of these clinical observations, the exact nature of the relationship between social anxiety disorder and substance abuse remains unclear (e.g., Carrigan & Randall, 2003). What is clear is that social anxiety disorder results in significant impairment in many areas of life functioning and can result in outcomes as severe as limited occupational achievement, restricted social interactions, suicidal ideation, and alcohol and drug abuse.

SOCIAL ANXIETY DISORDER SUBTYPES

Current diagnostic criteria allow for the designation of two social anxiety disorder subtypes: generalized and specific (the latter is sometimes also known as nongeneralized or circumscribed). Generalized social anxiety disorder is characterized by anxiety in, and frequent avoidance of, many social situations. This often includes performance situations as well as common social interactions. For example,

> Walter came to our clinic initially because he had difficulty giving formal presentations that were part of his job as head of computer operations at his company. However, during the diagnostic interview, Walter revealed that he also was anxious when in a private meeting with a superior or when chatting with coworkers in the cafeteria. He noted that his wife had complained that he always made excuses whenever she suggested that they go out to dinner or to a movie with another couple.

Approximately 70% of patients seeking treatment for social anxiety disorder meet the generalized criteria (Turner, Beidel, & Cooley, 1994), whereas the specific subtype may occur more frequently among community samples (Wittchen, Stein, & Kessler, 1999).

Specific social anxiety disorder is characterized by a more circumscribed pattern of fear, frequently in just one situation such as public speaking, and specific social anxiety disorder may be circumscribed but still severe. Another situation also characteristic of specific social anxiety disorder is illustrated by

Gail, who did not have any difficulty speaking before groups. She was, however, a member of a competitive dance troupe. She experienced performance anxiety when her group was in a competition (that is, when the audience was very knowledgeable about dance). In fact, on one occasion her group was heavily favored to win the competition, but Gail "froze" and they did not even place in the top 10.

Although the exact diagnostic distinction for the subtypes is ambiguous and various research clinics have defined the subtypes in slightly different ways, the subtype distinction can be made reliably (Heimberg, Hope, Dodge, & Becker, 1990; Turner, Beidel, & Townsley, 1992). Various comparative studies examining subtype characteristics have reported similar findings (Herbert, Hope, & Bellack, 1992; Holt et al., 1992; Turner et al., 1992). The generalized subtype, by far the most common type seen in clinics (approximately 70%; Scholing & Emmelkamp, 1993b; Turner, Beidel, & Jacob, 1994), is associated with more severe anxiety, depression, social inhibition, fear of negative evaluation, avoidance, fearfulness, and self-consciousness (Bruch, 1989; Heimberg et al., 1990; Herbert et al., 1992; Holt et al., 1992; Turner et al., 1992). Furthermore, those with generalized social anxiety disorder appear to be less educated, less likely to be employed, and more likely to have an additional Axis I or II diagnosis (Herbert et al., 1992; Turner, Beidel, Borden, et al., 1991; Wittchen et al., 1999). Thus, it is clear that the generalized subtype differs from the specific subtype on a number of demographic and clinical variables and presents a more severe and challenging clinical presentation.

The primary distinction between the subtypes appears to be the pervasiveness of fear and degree of symptom severity. However, subtypes may differ on other dimensions as well. For example, individuals with generalized social anxiety disorder have an earlier age of onset ($M = 10.9$ years) than the specific subtype ($M = 22.6$ years; Holt et al., 1992). Early-onset social anxiety disorder in particular is associated with a pattern of increased severity and chronicity during adulthood (Davidson, 1993). Examining developmental background, those with generalized social anxiety disorder reported more severe shyness symptoms and a family social style characterized by social isolation (Bruch & Heimberg, 1994). In a study from our clinic (Stemberger, Turner, Beidel, & Calhoun, 1995), a number of subtype differences, including greater neuroticism, more frequent history of childhood shyness, and higher introversion were more common among the generalized subtype compared with the specific subtype and with control participants with no disorders. Together, these findings suggest that the generalized subtype has characteristics, some of which may be biologically influenced, that lead to an earlier onset and a more severe clinical picture. When these findings are combined with others, they suggest that the subtypes are qualitatively different.

In perhaps one of the few areas where the generalized subtype is less severely affected, those with the specific subtype manifest greater autonomic reactivity in social performance tasks (Heimberg, Hope, et al., 1990; Hofmann, Newman, Ehlers, & Roth, 1995), further suggesting that the two subtypes might be qualitatively different. One explanation (Stemberger et al., 1995) is that specific social anxiety disorder might represent a true conditioned emotional reaction with the typical associated autonomic features. The generalized subtype might, however, be the result of a more insidious onset resulting from a long history of social inadequacy. Another possibility is that generalized social anxiety disorder is related to the Axis II dimension of APD. In other words, the specific subtype is a "true" phobia, whereas the generalized subtype has some phobic features but might be a variant of personality disorder and in particular APD. Some researchers (e.g., McNeil, Ries, & Turk, 1995) have conceptualized subtype differences by differentiating the terms *anxiety* and *fear*. In this context, fear responding is described as physiologically robust (highly reactive) and closely tied to a specific situation. Anxiety responding is considered to be more diffuse and less consistent with measures of psychopathology (e.g., physiological reactivity). If one applies these labels to the physiological responses of the specific and generalized subtypes, then one might speculate that generalized social anxiety disorder may be more characteristic of an anxiety response, whereas specific social anxiety disorder is more characteristic of a fear response. As we have noted, available data indicate that the generalized subtype is more severe and more common and that it may have a different developmental course. In addition, physiological response to anxiety-producing situations may differentiate the subtypes. Further research in this area is necessary to confirm initial findings.

Despite differences in symptom presentation, to date no study of behavioral or cognitive–behavioral treatments has deliberately set out to examine the effects of treatment for the two subtypes. In fact, most of the recent treatment trials (whether pharmacological or psychological) have focused solely on those with the generalized subtype. Yet our preliminary studies (discussed in detail in chap. 8 of this volume) suggest that current treatments are less efficacious for the generalized subtype, the most commonly occurring pattern seen in clinics. For example, in 1994, we published a major outcome study comparing exposure (*flooding*), atenolol, and pill placebo groups (Turner, Beidel, & Jacob, 1994). A retrospective analysis of treatment outcomes for the specific and generalized subtype, although not a part of the final published report, revealed that the generalized group had significantly more severe symptoms at pretreatment across virtually all dimensions of functioning. In addition, although both groups improved significantly over treatment, the posttreatment scores for the generalized subtype were still higher than the specific subtype scores at pretreatment, indicating that the generalized group, despite statistically significant improvement, still had significant impairment (see Table 1.2).

SOCIAL ANXIETY DISORDER AND SOCIAL SKILLS

As noted earlier in the chapter, the generalized subtype is more severe and complex than the specific, with a higher frequency of comorbidity

Table 1.2

Pre- and Posttreatment Scores for People With Specific and Generalized Social Anxiety Disorders Treated With Flooding

Instrument	Subtype	
	Specific	Generalized
Self-Report		
SPAI Difference score		
Pre	72.9	110.8
Post	48.1	94.3
SAD		
Pre	7.7	20.6
Post	3.3	18.2
FNE		
Pre	13.0	25.1
Post	13.4	22.1
FQ—Social anxiety disorder		
Pre	10.6	21.4
Post	3.0	15.3
Behavioral assessment		
Speech length (min)		
Pre	6.2	4.7
Post	8.8	7.9
SISST—Positive		
Pre	41.8	26.8
Post	52.8	35.3
SISST—Negative		
Pre	41.6	51.9
Post	25.0	32.1

Table continues

Table 1.2 *(Continued)*		
Pre- and Posttreatment Scores for People With Specific and Generalized Social Anxiety Disorders Treated With Flooding		
	Subtype	
Instrument	Specific	Generalized
Independent evaluator ratings		
HAM-A		
Pre	18.0	24.0
Post	6.0	17.0
CGI—Severity		
Pre	3.9	4.6
Post	2.0	3.3

Note. From "Social phobia: A comparison of behavior therapy and atenolol," by S. M. Turner, D. C. Beidel, and R. G. Jacob, 1994, *Journal of Consulting and Clinical Psychology, 62,* pp. 350–358. Copyright 1994 by the American Psychological Association. SPAI = Social Phobia and Anxiety Inventory; SAD = Social Avoidance and Distress Scale; FNE = Fear of Negative Evaluation Scale; FQ = Fear Questionnaire; SISST = Social Interaction Self-Statement Test; HAM-A = Hamilton Anxiety Scale; CGI—Severity = Clinical Global Improvement Scale, Severity subscale; min = minutes.

with other Axis I and II conditions. Another area of differentiation may be the presence of social skills deficits. Although data from extant studies are mixed, it appears that those with the generalized subtype are deficient in social skills (i.e., they lack many of the skills necessary to engage in effective interpersonal discourse). In an early discussion of social anxiety disorder, Marks (1985) distinguished between what he termed "pure social phobics" and individuals he thought to have APD. According to Marks, pure social phobics do not evidence skill deficiencies, whereas those with APD do. Recent reports of subtype differences lend some empirical support for Marks's contention. Before presenting those data, however, a discussion of the diagnostic classification difficulties of social anxiety disorder and the related condition of APD should prove helpful. Because the boundary between generalized social anxiety disorder and

APD is unclear (cf. Heimberg, Holt, Schneier, Spitzer, & Liebowitz, 1993; Turner, Beidel, & Townsley, 1992), and because there is overlap in diagnostic criteria, many of the patients whom Marks believed had APD no doubt also met criteria for generalized social anxiety disorder. The current diagnostic nomenclature allows APD and social anxiety disorder to be diagnosed concurrently. Empirical studies have confirmed that the generalized subtype is highly comorbid for APD (Herbert et al., 1992; Turner, Beidel, & Townsley, 1992) and that APD is present in the generalized subtype significantly more often than in the specific. Thus, Marks's pure social phobics likely were the specific subtype, and his APD group probably was mixed and comorbid for generalized social anxiety disorder. If Marks's distinction is correct, this would support the contention that skills deficits and general social deficiency are part of the clinical picture of generalized social anxiety disorder. Currently, we have a study underway examining the presence of social skills in those with specific social anxiety disorder, generalized social anxiety disorder, and no psychiatric disorder.

In addition to the usual skill deficiencies in areas such as maintaining conversations, initiating conversations, and perceiving social cues, our clinical experience is that those with the generalized subtype tend to have a number of specific deficiencies that are perhaps unique to social anxiety disorder. One such deficit is an inability to listen in social settings because of an overactive cognitive system. That is, when in a social encounter, those with social anxiety disorder are so worried about the perception of their behavior by others that they spend their energy trying to formulate a "perfect" response rather than attending to the details of the conversation. Thus, when it is their turn to speak, they often do not know what to say or whether their "perfect" response is appropriate because they have not followed the conversation. This hypothesis is supported by new neuropsychiatric data indicating that when giving a speech, those with social anxiety disorder experience arousal in subcortical brain areas, whereas those with no disorder experience arousal in cortical areas, suggesting that different areas of the brain are active in different subjects during the task (Tillfors, Furmark, Marteinsdottir, et al., 2001; for more on this issue, see chap. 4, this volume).

Other social skills deficits that may be particular to the syndrome include difficulty conceiving of places where normal social discourse can occur and the inability to take action in planning social activities. Given the data indicating that generalized social anxiety disorder has a long insidious onset and course (Holt, Heimberg, & Hope, 1992) and an earlier age of onset, one can speculate that social skills deficits result from the long history of limited socialization experiences and, in particular, the lack of recurring socialization experiences. Several intervention strategies (Turner, Beidel, & Cooley-Quille, 1995; Wlazlo, Schroeder-Hartwig, Hand, Kaiser, & Munchau, 1990) have been designed to address these general and specific social skills deficiencies (see chap. 8, this volume).

Patient performance during in vivo social interaction tests has supported the idea that those with the generalized subtype of social anxiety disorder are deficient in social skills. These deficiencies are evident in both molar and molecular behaviors. For example, as part of our standard assessment battery for social anxiety disorder, patients participate in two unstructured in vivo social interactions: one with a confederate of the same sex and one with a confederate of the opposite sex. Interactions are rated with standard 5-point Likert rating scales for social skills (facial gaze, speech length, vocal tone, and overall skill; cf. Turner, Beidel, Dancu, et al., 1986). On the basis of an analysis of 53 patients with generalized anxiety disorder and 23 patients with specific social anxiety disorder, comparisons between the groups indicated that for each variable, those with the specific subtype appeared more skilled, although the difference only reached statistical significance on one variable (speech length, $p < .01$) and approached significance on another (overall skill, $p < .06$). Currently, our ongoing investigation includes an expanded and extensive investigation of social skills, including the variables discussed earlier. Because this new study includes a normal control comparative group as well as both those with the specific and generalized subtypes, we soon will be able to provide substantive data on this important issue.

In that same report (Turner, Beidel, Dancu, et al., 1986), patients with APD diagnosed according to *DSM–III* criteria were significantly different from those with *DSM–III* social phobia (without APD) on a host of social skills measures. The earlier diagnostic criteria did not allow for subtyping, but many patients in the former group probably met criteria for generalized social anxiety disorder. In contrast, there do not appear to be differences in social skills between those with generalized subtype and those with APD (Herbert et al., 1992), probably because overlap of the generalized subtype and APD is so extensive. Differences in social skills are more likely found when the latter two groups are compared with a group with the specific subtype or a group with no disorder. As previously indicated, there are at least two primary reasons why reports regarding social skills deficits in individuals with social anxiety disorder have been mixed: Patients have not been divided along the specific–generalized dimension in all cases, and the measurement strategies that have been used were not developed specifically for deficits commonly found in social anxiety disorder. Our ongoing investigation will address this issue.

A final indication of the presence of social skills deficits in patients with social anxiety disorder is that social skills training has been used successfully in the treatment of this disorder (see chaps. 8 and 9, this volume). These outcome data further bolster the small amount of descriptive psychopathological data and clinical observation that inadequate social skills are part of the clinical presentation of this syndrome. Because social anxiety disorder is a relatively early-onset anxiety disorder, one can speculate that social anxiety and resulting avoidance of social situations might prevent the development of normal prosocial behavior. Consistent with this hypothesis, childhood shyness and social isolation may lead to a withdrawn behavior style, restricted peer interaction, and impairment in social skills and interpersonal relationships (Rubin,

LeMare, & Lollis, 1990; see chap. 4, this volume, for an extended discussion).

PARURESIS

Sometimes known as "shy bladder syndrome," *paruresis* is the fear of being unable to urinate in public bathrooms. Some individuals experience this condition in isolation, although mental health professionals view it as one of the situations in which those with social anxiety disorder might experience distress or avoidance. On the basis of an Internet survey of 63 members of the International Paruresis Association, the most common emotional disorder among this group was social anxiety disorder, endorsed by 29% of the sample (Vythilingum, Stein, & Soifer, 2002). Those with paruresis most commonly endorsed physical symptoms of trembling, sweating, shortness of breath, blushing, and nausea, representing activation of the beta-adrenergic system and symptoms characteristic of those diagnosed with social anxiety disorder (Gorman & Gorman, 1987). Furthermore, like social anxiety disorder, this condition has a significant effect on social and occupational functioning (Vythilingum et al., 2002). The sample size in this study precludes drawing sweeping conclusions, but as noted by the authors, some data suggest that paruresis, like public speaking fear, may represent a specific performance anxiety (i.e., a form of specific social phobia) that may or may not be associated with a broader pattern of social distress.

COMORBIDITY AND DIFFERENTIAL DIAGNOSIS

One of the most frustrating interactions for those with social anxiety disorder is confiding to others about their distress when giving a speech or attending social events. Most laypersons are likely to respond by saying, "That's not unusual. Everyone gets nervous when they give a speech," or "Everyone gets nervous from time to time." Just as it is difficult for laypersons to differentiate social anxiety disorder from normal public speaking fears, it often is difficult for patients and clinicians to differentiate social anxiety from social anxiety disorder. That is, individuals with many Axis I or II disorders may experience social distress and social withdrawal. In those cases, however, the reasons for their distress are different from those that characterize social anxiety disorder. Differential diagnosis is necessary to establish a proper treatment plan. In other instances, patients with social anxiety disorder may have secondary comorbid conditions. In the sections that follow, we detail other conditions that are often found to coexist with social anxiety disorder. In addition, we review other disorders for which social anxiety might be part of the clinical presentation and discuss how to make the diagnostic distinctions.

Comorbidity and Differential Diagnosis With Other Axis I Disorders

Among adults, social anxiety disorder has a high rate (70%–80%) of comorbidity with other Axis I disorders (Keller, 2003; Turner, Beidel, Borden, et al., 1991). Other anxiety disorders are the most common comorbid conditions. Among one treatment-seeking sample, 33% met criteria for generalized anxiety disorder (Turner, Beidel, Borden, et al., 1991). In addition, 11% also met criteria for specific phobia, whereas 6% met criteria for dysthymic disorder, 3% for panic disorder, 3% for major depressive disorder, and 1% for obsessive–compulsive disorder (OCD). It is interesting to note that the most common comorbid Axis I disorders found in adults with social anxiety disorder (generalized anxiety disorder and specific phobia) also are the most common disorders found in children and adolescents with social anxiety disorder (see chap. 2, this volume). Depression is also a common comorbid disorder, with rates as high as 56% in one epidemiological sample (Keller, 2003). Although other researchers also have reported a substantial number of coexisting conditions in those with a primary diagnosis of social anxiety disorder, specific comorbid rates often differ somewhat by the particular site and sample characteristics and are secondary to different referral patterns and screening practices at various clinics. Nevertheless, it is fair to conclude that a substantial number of patients with social anxiety disorder have clinical presentations complicated by the presence of one or more additional disorders.

Panic Disorder

Because anxiety disorders are now recognized by clinicians and the lay public, differential diagnosis among the various anxiety diagnostic categories has become much easier. Nevertheless, the diagnostic distinction between panic disorder with agoraphobia and social anxiety disorder still may be difficult because patients with panic disorder often avoid social settings (Heckelman & Schneier, 1995). For example,

> Tony came to the clinic and described fear and anxiety when in social situations or when in a shopping mall but also reports panic attacks in both of these settings. Does Tony have social anxiety disorder, panic disorder, or both?

In such instances, we always have found Marks's distinction (1970) to be useful in guiding diagnostic decisions: Those with panic disorder fear the crowd, whereas those with social anxiety disorder fear the individuals who make up the crowd. Furthermore, for a diagnosis of social anxiety disorder to be appropriate, social avoidance must not be caused by fear of panic symptoms. Careful questioning disclosed that Tony's feelings of anxiety occurred even when the mall was virtually deserted and that what he feared was meeting an acquaintance and then having to engage in small talk. Panic attacks did not occur unless Tony recognized (or appeared to recognize) a familiar face. This clinical presentation would rule out a diagnosis of panic disorder as the primary condition.

Differential diagnosis of panic disorder and social anxiety disorder can also be made on the basis of several empirically established group differences. Panic attacks in those with social anxiety disorder are believed to be situationally bound, whereas they often are considered spontaneous or uncued in those with panic disorder (APA, 1994). Although the idea that panic attacks are ever uncued is debatable (Craske, 1991), individuals with panic disorder do experience panic attacks in nonsocial settings. One of the earliest studies to compare physical symptomatology found that blushing and muscle twitching were more common among individuals with social anxiety disorder, whereas changes in respiration, dizziness, palpitations, headaches, blurred vision, and ringing in the ears were more common in patients with panic disorder (Amies et al., 1983). In fact, blushing, trembling, heart palpitations, and sweating were the physical symptoms most commonly characteristic of social anxiety disorder (Gorman & Gorman, 1987). Less commonly experienced among those with social anxiety disorder are symptoms of respiratory distress (difficulty breathing, shortness of breath, chest pain). Finally, compared with panic disorder, social anxiety disorder had an earlier age of onset (mid-teens as opposed to the mid-20s or mid-30s) and the gender ratio was more likely to be equivalent or only slightly higher for women, whereas the gender ratio was more likely to be predominantly female for panic disorder with agoraphobia (Keller, 2003; Mannuzza, Fyer, Liebowitz, & Klein, 1990).

An important issue is that panic disorder patients frequently develop social fears subsequent to the onset of panic. The question is whether a second diagnosis of social anxiety disorder is appropriate. Most of the secondary social anxiety disorder symptoms seen in patients with panic disorder appear to be related to negative evaluation resulting from panic. In our view, although functionally the behavior appears to be the same as for other patients with social anxiety disorder, the diagnosis is not made. Although there are no data available to address this issue, we suspect that once panic is controlled, there will be no need to address social anxiety disorder separately. In other words, the social fears are secondary to panic attacks.

Other Anxiety Disorders

Social anxiety disorder can be distinguished from generalized anxiety disorder because the latter diagnosis includes unreasonable worries about a broad range of events (personal finances, family members' health, minor matters), whereas worries in social anxiety disorder are restricted to fears of evaluation in social settings. However, a number of patients are truly comorbid for these disorders (Brawman-Mintzer et al., 1993). Patients with OCD often are apprehensive in social encounters because they fear others will detect their ritualistic behaviors or that others might contaminate them. However, this diagnostic distinction is fairly easy to make because those with social anxiety disorder ordinarily do not have frank obsessions and compulsions. Conversely, those with OCD do not fear that they will do or say something that will be humiliating or embarrassing (except for blurting out obscenities).

Depression

Because of the impact that this disorder exerts on life functioning, it would not be surprising to find symptoms of depression or even major depressive disorder among those with social anxiety disorder. As noted earlier, in one sample, 56% of those with primary social anxiety disorder also had a comorbid depressive disorder (Keller, 2003). In 75% of those cases in which comorbidity existed, social anxiety disorder preceded the onset of major depression by at least 1 year, again emphasizing the extensive impact of this disorder on all aspects of social functioning.

Sometimes when we advertise available treatment programs for individuals with social avoidance, some who seek treatment actually meet criteria for major depression and not social anxiety disorder. Those with depression often exhibit social withdrawal and avoidance (Dilsaver, Qamar, & Del Medico, 1992), but social withdrawal in most of these cases is caused by depressed mood, anhedonia, and lack of interest in social activities. In many cases, these problems are eliminated when depression is treated. Furthermore, individuals with depression usually describe premorbid histories that are dissimilar to social anxiety disorder (i.e., these individuals typically have "normal" socialization patterns prior to the development of their depressive state). In such cases, an additional diagnosis of social anxiety disorder is not warranted.

In addition to diagnostic accuracy, there is another reason for the need to attend to comorbid Axis I disorders. Those with social anxiety disorder and comorbid mood disorders often report greater severity of social anxiety than those with social anxiety disorder alone (Erwin, Heimberg, Juster, & Mindlin, 2002). This same study found that those with a comorbid mood disorder also had an earlier age of onset of social anxiety disorder and lower levels of global functioning than those with social anxiety disorder alone or those with social anxiety disorder and a comorbid anxiety disorder. As noted previously, the addition of a comorbid condition increases the likelihood of suicidal ideation and suicidal attempts and also affects treatment-seeking behavior (Schneier, Johnson, et al., 1992). Compared with control participants with no disorder, even those with uncomplicated social anxiety disorder had more thoughts about death but not higher rates of suicidal ideation or suicide attempts. Thus, clinicians need to be aware of the presence of these disorders and the clinical complications they might present.

Medical Conditions Sometimes Associated With Social Anxiety Disorder

When the fear of negative evaluation results from medical conditions such as stuttering or benign essential tremors, current diagnostic practices suggest that a diagnosis of social anxiety disorder is not warranted. However, this distinction is controversial, because it is possible that those with these conditions may experience social distress in excess of what is considered "normal." For example, when compared with a normative sample, those who stuttered had higher scores on measures of social anxiety and fear of negative evaluation (Mahr & Torosian, 1999), although their scores were significantly lower than a group of individuals diagnosed with social anxiety disorder. Among those with essential tremor (Schneier, Barnes, Albert, & Louis, 2001), 22% had a lifetime diagnosis of social anxiety disorder, a percentage that was not significantly different from a normal control group (16%). Social anxiety disorder preceded the onset of the tremor in slightly more than half of the cases. When social anxiety disorder was primary, respondents indicated that their social distress was independent of their tremor diagnosis. When social anxiety disorder developed after the tremor's onset, patients reported that their social fears were a result of the tremor. Objective measures indicated that tremors were more severe among those with a secondary diagnosis of social anxiety disorder compared with those who had a primary diagnosis or no social anxiety disorder diagnosis.

The results of these investigations indicate that there is no clear one-to-one relationship between these medical conditions and social anxiety disorder. Similar to the general population, a percentage of individuals with these medical conditions (as well as many others) may also meet criteria for social anxiety disorder. Additionally, even among those with a particular medical condition, social anxiety disorder may be completely unrelated to the medical disorder in some instances, whereas in others it is related to it. Thus, there is the need for careful assessment, particularly with respect to the age of onset of the various diagnoses.

Comorbidity and Differential Diagnosis With Axis II Disorders

Among one sample of patients with primary social anxiety disorder, 44% had a comorbid Axis II condition (Keller, 2003). With respect to differential diagnosis, there are no clinical studies that have compared the psychopathology of social anxiety disorder with Axis II conditions except for the comparisons with APD (discussed subsequently). Both APD and obsessive–compulsive personality disorder (OCPD) are common comorbid conditions with social anxiety disorder. Although the presence of these two personality disorders may make the process of treatment more difficult, they usually do not preclude treating patients with social anxiety disorder using the standard interventions. However, additional treatment directed specifically at the personality disorder might be needed after social anxiety disorder is treated successfully.

As we noted in the introduction to the discussion of Axis I disorders, not every complaint of anxiety in social situations indicates the presence of social anxiety disorder. For example, anxiety in social settings that arises secondary to mistrust of the motives of others would not be conceptualized as social anxiety disorder. Thus, the presence of Axis II disorders such as paranoid personality disorder precludes a separate diagnosis of social anxiety disorder, and interventions commonly used for social anxiety disorder are not appropriate for those with paranoid personality disorder. This rule of thumb can be applied to several other Axis II disorders as well. Some guidelines that have proved useful in our clinical setting are offered in the following sections.

Avoidant Personality Disorder

Avoidant Personality Disorder is probably the most common comorbid Axis II condition among people with social anxiety disorder (Turner, Beidel, Borden, et al., 1991). In one sample, 22% of those with a primary diagnosis of social anxiety disorder met criteria for APD. Another 53% exhibited features of APD even though they did not meet full diagnostic criteria. Others have found similar rates of comorbidity (Herbert et al., 1992; Holt et al., 1992; Schneier, Spitzer, Gibbon, Fyer, & Liebowitz, 1991), which is not surprising given the extensive diagnostic overlap (e.g., avoidance of occupational activities that require interpersonal contact, preoccupation with being criticized or rejected by others, and inhibition in new interpersonal situations because of feelings of inadequacy; APA, 1994).

Several researchers have compared the clinical presentation of social anxiety disorder with and without comorbid APD (Herbert et al., 1992; Holt et al., 1992; Turner, Beidel, & Townsley, 1992). Overall, these studies revealed that those with comorbid APD were more severe on a host of self-report and clinician-rated instruments assessing social anxiety disorder symptomatology as well as general measures of anxiety, depression, and social functioning. As summarized (Turner, Beidel, & Townsley, 1992), the similarity in diagnostic criteria for social anxiety disorder and APD suggests that those with the generalized subtype may differ primarily on the basis of the severity of their social fears and degree of social impairment. We now discuss how the additional diagnosis of APD may affect the treatment outcome for social anxiety disorder.

It has been our observation that patients with APD do not respond well to intensive imaginal treatment, in vivo exposure treatments, or both. Psychologically, they do not tolerate the intensive arousal well, and there appears to be an increase in general anxiety and depression after the treatment session. Also the dropout rate and the need for nonprotocol treatments for this group appear to be greater. In analyzing the effectiveness of flooding treatment with this group, outcome is probably less positive. We have found a graduated rather than an intensive approach to exposure therapy to be somewhat helpful but not entirely satisfactory, leading us to the use of alternative interventions such as social skills training.

Patients with social anxiety disorder who also have APD tend to have greater deficiencies in interpersonal skill and greater general inhibition, are less prepared vocationally, and are frequently less educated. They often have poor work histories and a lifelong pattern of reclusiveness and failure to develop social networks (see the section on social anxiety disorder and social skills in this chapter). Empirical studies of social skills deficits in those with social anxiety disorder have produced mixed results (there have been few studies in this area). The generalized–specific dichotomy has not been explored, although we currently are engaged in such an investigation. As a result, the type of deficits manifested by those with social anxiety disorder may not be detected by standard paradigms for assessing social skills. Thus, despite the lack of clarity from research studies, it is our clinical impression that a skills training strategy is essential for patients with social anxiety disorder with APD (see chap. 8, this volume).

Obsessive–Compulsive Personality Disorder

A second common comorbid Axis II disorder is OCPD (Turner, Beidel, & Townsley, 1992). Approximately 13.0% of those with primary social anxiety disorder meet criteria for OCPD. In addition, another 48.5%

had subsyndromal features of this disorder. Although not sharing many diagnostic criteria with social anxiety disorder, those with the comorbid OCPD condition are perfectionistic; devoted to work (perhaps to avoid social interactions); overconscientious; scrupulous; inflexible about matters of morality, ethics, or values; and rigid or stubborn. Those with this set of behavioral characteristics are known to have interpersonal difficulties. Similarly, individuals with social anxiety disorder frequently are overly concerned about their outward behavior, believing that it must be perfect or others will think negatively of them. Such behavior has similarities with the perfectionistic beliefs of those with OCPD. It is not clear whether OCPD or features of OCPD are a predispositional or correlational component of social anxiety disorder. It is notable, however, that children with social anxiety disorder frequently have rigid behavioral styles as well (Beidel, 1991; see chap. 2, this volume).

One of the most important findings from our ongoing research program is the presence of significant obsessive features in many patients with social anxiety disorder. The features range in severity from relatively moderate to actually meeting diagnostic criteria (e.g., Turner, Beidel, Borden, et al., 1991). In our view, it is unlikely that these features are pathonogmonic by themselves, but they likely combine with other vulnerability factors (i.e., high general anxiety and traumatic conditioning) to produce the disorder. It has been our experience that patients with social anxiety disorder who have significant obsessional attributes present a considerable challenge for treatment. They may be less able to use imagery, which makes imaginal exposure more difficult to implement (see chap. 8, this volume). Even more problematic for the exposure strategies is that these patients frequently use projection and rationalization to explain their deficiencies. Thus, if an exposure session consists of being placed in a situation in which negative expectations are realized, the patient will blame someone else or rationalize that the situation is unnatural and thus unimportant. Although we have not attempted their use with these patients, our clinical experience suggests that the defensive strategies adopted by patients with OCPD probably would make the implementation of cognitive strategies difficult at best.

We also have made a number of other observations, with respect to psychopathology as well as treatment, about the patient with OCPD who also has social anxiety disorder. The problem is whether social distress is a true comorbid condition or whether patients with OCPD have social anxiety because of their personality attributes. We will illustrate why this distinction is important. Although those with OCPD fear negative evaluation, they do not attribute the failure of a social interaction to their own behavior. Rather, they tend to attribute the problem to other individuals or to physical aspects of the social setting (e.g., the room was too hot). Those with social anxiety disorder always blame themselves, even when it is not warranted. We think this is a significant issue if using some type of exposure treatment, primarily because in cases in which the patient externalizes the source of the distress, exposure to the situation tends not to elicit arousal.

As noted previously, APD and OCPD represent the most common comorbid Axis II disorders in individuals with social anxiety disorder (Turner, Beidel, & Townsley, 1992), and the presence of either Axis I or II comorbid disorders results in a more severe syndrome than social anxiety disorder alone (Turner, Beidel, Wolff, Spaulding, & Jacob, 1996; Turner, Beidel, & Townsley, 1992). Other personality disorders that appeared less frequently in a sample of patients with primary social anxiety disorder included histrionic (4.0%), antisocial (3.0%), dependent (1.5%), paranoid (1.5%), narcissistic (1.5%), and borderline (1.5%), and it is to some of these disorders that we now turn our attention.

Paranoid Personality Disorder

Those with paranoid personality disorder frequently seek treatment because of interpersonal distress, but the basis of their social distress is different from those with social anxiety disorder. Those with paranoid personality disorder have difficulty developing trust because of a distorted perception about the motives of others. It is crucial that these patients be identified, because in our experience, they respond poorly to behavioral interventions for social anxiety disorder. For example, in one case that we treated with intensive exposure, a full-blown paranoid state was instigated that required a considerable period of time to dissipate. The problem was that the patient did not appear paranoid even following a thorough assessment that had included a clinical interview, a semistructured personality disorder inventory, and a battery of psychological assessments including the Minnesota Multiphasic Personality Inventory. We have seen a number of these patients over the past 20 years, and although we have not developed a foolproof way to identify all of those with significant paranoid features, there are several anomalies that appear in their clinical history. First, in a number of cases, the frank onset of social anxiety disorder appears to be later than is typical, usually well after young adulthood. Second, when placed in a behavioral performance task requiring an impromptu speech, these patients report feeling humiliated. Individuals with social anxiety disorder easily understand the purpose of this task; they see it as distressing but nevertheless an important part of gauging their distress and thus of treatment planning efforts. In summary, the number of patients with social anxiety disorder comorbid for paranoid personality disorder is about 1.0% to 1.5%, but the problem is significant when it does occur. Clinicians should be vigilant regarding this possibility in those presenting with apparent social anxiety disorder.

Schizoid Personality Disorder

Although not among the personality disorders commonly found in those with social anxiety disorder, there is a critical clinical distinction between social anxiety disorder and schizoid personality disorder. Those with the latter diagnosis arrive at the clinic because someone other than the patient is not pleased with his or her level of social interaction. The differentiating factor is that those with social anxiety disorder desire to interact with others, whereas those with schizoid personality disorder prefer their own company to the necessity of social discourse. They are not necessarily anxious when in these settings; they simply prefer not to engage in social activities.

CONCLUSION

Elaine's case, described at the beginning of this chapter, illustrates how her social distress affected her personal and professional functioning. Existing data indicate that social anxiety disorder is a significant psychiatric disorder that affects a substantial percentage of the adult population. Over the past 20 years, data have accumulated to demonstrate that this disorder results in considerable emotional distress, social inhibition, and occupational and social maladjustment. The boundary between social anxiety disorder and shyness is still not fully understood, but it is clear that at least some of those individuals referred to as "shy" meet diagnostic criteria for social anxiety disorder. The exact nature of the relationship, however, awaits further study.

Using the current diagnostic criteria, there are two patterns of social anxiety disorder. The first, referred to as the *specific* or *nongeneralized* type, is characterized by social fear and avoidance of social performance situations as exemplified by fear of public speaking. Although its impact may be less pervasive, those with this subtype still experience considerable distress when faced with their fearful situation. Furthermore, even the specific subtype can significantly affect areas of functioning such as educational attainment or occupational choice. The second pattern, the generalized subtype, consists of pervasive social anxiety and fear associated with most social situations and activities. The generalized subtype is far more common in clinical settings and significantly more severe symptomatically. In addition, the generalized subtype is more often associated with concurrent Axis I and II conditions, and among this group significant depression and suicidal thoughts are more common. Also, considerable social skills deficits appear to characterize this subtype, and preliminary data suggest that treatment incorporating social skills training is needed for this group.

As noted earlier, social anxiety disorder, like other anxiety disorders, frequently is comorbid with other Axis I and II conditions. The relationship of social anxiety disorder to APD particularly is an issue because of the overlap in diagnostic criteria. Although not affecting the use of current treatment for social anxiety disorder, the presence of a comorbid condition can affect the management of patients and their degree of improvement. Therefore, other interventions will be needed to treat the comorbid condition, and the time required to treat the social anxiety disorder may be longer. In the next chapter, we discuss issues of the clinical presentation of social anxiety disorder in children and adolescents.

2

Clinical Presentation of Social Anxiety Disorder in Children and Adolescents

Lawrence was a 14-year-old who refused to attend school. His guidance counselor and school principal considered him a truancy problem because he had been seen on school grounds after school, watching football practice. Lawrence did try to attend school, however. Every morning, he got in the car and allowed his mother to drive him to school. When he arrived, however, he was overcome by fear and could not get out of the car. Because his mother could identify with his feelings (she experienced anxiety as a child), she brought him to the clinic for an evaluation.

Lawrence readily acknowledged his school refusal. He indicated that he was very interested in attending school and was worried that because he missed classes, he would not pass eighth grade. He explained that being around the other children made him nervous, noting that when he is with other teens, his heart races, he sweats, and he becomes nauseated. On several occasions, he had vomited in the school lavatory because of his distress. He described being increasingly afraid that the next time he would vomit in the classroom, which would be extremely embarrassing. His mother reported that he had a long history of social fearfulness and reluctance to interact with others. On the basis of the interview, a battery of self-report inventories, and behavioral monitoring, Lawrence was diagnosed with social anxiety disorder.

I n this chapter, we discuss the clinical syndrome of social anxiety disorder in children and adolescents. For the sake of brevity and unless otherwise noted, we use the terms *childhood social anxiety disorder* or *children with social anxiety disorder* to include both children and adolescents. We noted in chapter 1 that research on social anxiety disorder in adults is of relatively recent vintage. Even more recent is clinical and research interest in this syndrome in children. Lawrence's case illustrates how easily adults can misinterpret children's social fears, primarily because of a lack of understanding of the disorder. As a result, school administrators interpreted Lawrence's school refusal as a conduct problem, particularly because he was on the school grounds after school. In reality, Lawrence watched football practice from a distance. If others approached, he would leave. It is clear that his fearfulness centered on social engagement with others, which is the hallmark of social anxiety disorder.

DEVELOPMENTAL CONSIDERATIONS

The existence of social anxiety disorder in childhood is firmly established, but some questions still remain: How early in childhood does this syndrome appear? Are there precursors to social anxiety disorder that can be identified before a diagnosis can be made? Are there other factors that may be associated with social anxiety and avoidance in children other than social anxiety disorder?

No data are available on the presence of social anxiety disorder in infants, but developmental psychologists have long studied aspects of temperament that relate to socialization. *Sociability,* for example, is defined as the preference for affiliation and companionship rather than solitude (Buss & Plomin, 1984; Thomas & Chess, 1977). Another term, *shyness* (discussed in chap. 1, this volume), is defined as social withdrawal motivated by social-evaluative concerns, particularly in novel situations (Rubin & Asendorpf, 1993). The terms *sociability* and *shyness* are not opposite ends of the same continuum. Rather, the two constructs appear to represent distinct traits (Cheek & Buss, 1981). Social withdrawal, for example, need not be motivated by concern with negative evaluation. There are those individuals who simply prefer solitude to social interaction; social situations do not elicit distress. These individuals are considered to have low sociability but not to be shy. Therefore, social inhibition or reluctance to engage in social interactions does not automatically indicate that a child is shy or suffering from social anxiety disorder. Other factors, such as emotional distress or functional impairment that result from nonparticipation in social situations, must also be considered.

Developmental psychologists have also studied social isolation in young children, and its long-term detrimental effects have been documented clearly. In second graders, passive isolation (the type most commonly associated with social anxiety), low perceived social competence, or both significantly predicted depression and loneliness when these students reached the fifth grade (Rubin & Mills, 1988). Similarly, internalizing problems (anxiety, depression) in middle childhood were significantly predicted by earlier (second grade) childhood difficulties, including poor peer acceptance and social isolation (Hymel, Rubin, Rowden, & LeMare, 1990). Among young adolescents who recently had moved to a new school district, higher social anxiety predicted less social interaction and fewer friendships even many months later (Vernberg, Abwender, Ewell, & Beery, 1992). Other studies of children identified as shy, socially isolated, and withdrawn (children who are isolated and not approached by others) or as peer-neglected (children whom others ignore) indicate that the characteristics of these various groups overlap considerably with the diagnostic categories of social anxiety disorder and avoidant disorder of childhood. For example, children with an anxiety disorder are more likely than other children to be classified as peer-neglected (Strauss, Lahey, Frick, Frame, & Hynd, 1988). Conversely, peer-neglected children report the highest level of social anxiety among various sociometric groups (LaGreca, Dandes, Wick, Shaw, & Stone, 1988).

Despite interest in the constructs of sociability, shyness, and social inhibition by other psychologists, clinicians' interest in social anxiety disorder is more recent. One reason may be that children's fears were considered to be transitory in nature (Barrios & O'Dell, 1989), although Achenbach (1985) noted that this axiom did not necessarily apply to social fears. Long-term studies with adults confirm this early hypothesis that childhood social fears are chronic (Alnæs & Torgersen, 1999; Davidson, 1993; Keller, 2003). Some shy children do seem to outgrow their shyness, however. Retrospective reports indicate that about 50% of college students who were shy as children outgrew their fears during adolescence and early adulthood (Bruch, Giordano, & Pearl, 1986; see chaps. 1 and 4, this volume, for a more extended discussion on shyness and social anxiety disorder). Currently, however, there are no predictors that will identify children who will outgrow social fears and those who will not. In addition, as the data in this chapter illustrate, children with social fears suffer immediate as well as long-term consequences. Thus, attention in the form of research and clinical intervention is well founded.

DIAGNOSIS

Epidemiological data confirm that social anxiety disorder is one of the earliest onset psychological disorders (Kessler, 2003; Merikangas, Avene-voli, Acharyya, Zhang, & Angst, 2002). On the basis of child and adolescent samples, the average age of onset ranges from 11 to 13 years (DeWit, Ogborne, Offord, & MacDonald, 1999; Last, Perrin, Hersen, & Kazdin, 1992; Strauss & Last, 1993). Others (Beidel & Turner, 1988; Beidel,

Turner, & Morris, 1999; Spence, Donovan, & Brechman-Toussaint, 1999) have reported that children as young as age 8 can be diagnosed with the disorder. Among a pediatric primary care clinic sample who met criteria for social anxiety disorder, the average age of onset was 7.1 years (Chavira, Stein, Bailey, & Stein, 2004). Also, many adults with social anxiety disorder date the onset of their social fears to childhood, reporting that they have been socially anxious all their lives (Otto et al., 2001; Stemberger, Turner, Beidel, & Calhoun, 1995). In one sample of adults with social anxiety disorder, 80% reported that the onset occurred in childhood (Otto et al., 2001). When a comorbid anxiety disorder was present, the onset of social anxiety disorder occurred at a significantly younger age (10.8 years for onset of social anxiety disorder) than for those with social anxiety disorder but without a comorbid anxiety disorder (15.2 years). These data reinforce the notion that those with an earlier age of onset are likely to have the most chronic and severe course.

Prior to 1994, children with social-evaluative fears could be diagnosed with social anxiety disorder, overanxious disorder, or avoidant disorder of childhood. With the publication of the fourth edition of the *Diagnostic and Statistical Manual of Mental Disorders (DSM–IV;* American Psychiatric Association [APA], 1994), the elimination of avoidant disorder and the significant revision of overanxious disorder now ensures that all children with social fears will be consistently diagnosed with social anxiety disorder (Beidel & Morris, 1995). In turn, future epidemiological studies will determine more specifically the prevalence of this disorder in children. Because the clinical syndrome may manifest differently in young children when compared with adults, the current diagnostic criteria include specific descriptors to assist in the diagnosis. These descriptors are presented here.

As we noted in chapter 1, social anxiety disorder is "a marked and persistent fear of one or more social performances in which the person is exposed to unfamiliar people or to possible scrutiny by others" (APA, 1994, p. 416). The individual fears that he or she will act in a way (or show anxiety symptoms) that will be humiliating or embarrassing. "In children, there must be evidence for capacity for social relationships with familiar people and the anxiety must occur in peer settings, not just in interaction with adults" (APA, 1994, p. 416). This statement highlights two important issues related to the diagnosis of social anxiety disorder in children. First, the children must be capable of social interactions. This differentiates children with social anxiety disorder from those with pervasive developmental disorders such as autism, for example. In reality, determining the capacity for social interaction is a fairly easy distinction for most clinicians. Parents often describe children with social anxiety disorder as socially engaging with siblings, cousins, or close family friends. Outside this small family circle, however, the child is reclusive and socially isolative.

A second important qualifier with respect to the diagnosis of social anxiety disorder in children is that the anxiety must occur in peer settings, not just in interactions with adults. Obviously, because of the inherent differences between children and adults (age, experience, authority), many children are somewhat reticent when interacting with adults, particularly unfamiliar adults or those in authority (e.g., the school principal). For a child to be diagnosed with social anxiety disorder, the child must express or demonstrate fearfulness in peer settings. Again, assessing this is not difficult. For example, children with social anxiety disorder often stand at the perimeter of other children's social activities (e.g., during recess). They often are reluctant to speak in class and refuse to attend pleasant events such as parties. In all of these instances, the anxiety is occurring in peer settings.

> Michael was in the gifted and talented program at school and captain of the debate team. He was quite popular with his teachers but had no friends and refrained from any type of peer interaction. Because of his talent in school and debating, he had the opportunity to spend a day shadowing the U.S. ambassador to the United Nations. He had no difficulty talking to the ambassador, but the next

week, he was unable to attend a birthday party because of his fears of interacting with other children.

Although they are in the minority, some children with social anxiety disorder interact comfortably with adults but are still extremely anxious when asked to interact with peers.

The *DSM–IV* criteria also specify that "exposure to the feared social situation almost invariably provokes anxiety, which may take the form of a situationally bound or situationally predisposed panic attack." Although adolescents may report having panic attacks in social settings, such a response is uncommon for young children. Thus, the *DSM–IV* includes the descriptor that "in children, the anxiety may be expressed by crying, tantrums, freezing or withdrawal from the social situation" (APA, 1994, p. 417). In relatively rare cases, the anxiety may manifest as selective mutism, when the child refuses to speak in certain social situations (see the discussion on selective mutism later in this chapter). These various expressions of distress highlight a particularly important aspect of the disorder's clinical presentation, especially in reference to younger children. Perhaps because of their immature cognitive development, young children (younger than 10 years) often cannot describe many specific symptoms of distress (although they may complain of butterflies in the stomach or headaches). Parents, however, often report that the child has crying episodes, tantrum behaviors, freezing, or withdrawal. It is important to note that some children may be mistakenly diagnosed as oppositional. For these children, fears are so extensive that when it comes to social engagement, they refuse to do what their parents ask but are unable to explain why.

> Jackie refused her mother's directions to wear her "nice clothing" to school. In addition, she refused to wear jewelry or allow her mother to style her hair, preferring a straight part down the middle of her long hair, with no curls, barrettes, or other accessories. Although her mother did not understand why she chose to dress

this way, after analysis it seemed evident that a plain appearance decreased the likelihood of drawing attention to herself.

Thus, this oppositional behavior was motivated by the child's social fear. Similarly, Lawrence's truant behavior described in the beginning of this chapter was motivated by his social fear.

Another *DSM–IV* criterion is that the person recognizes that the fear is excessive and unreasonable. However, it also states, "Note: In children, this feature may be absent" (APA, 1994, p. 417).

> Maria, age 10, eloquently described feeling different from the other children and wondering why she felt sick when she was going to a birthday party, when the other children were so obviously without distress.

In our clinical practice, we have found that children as young as age 8 are able to discern that their fears are excessive, although, as they do with other types of fears, girls more readily report the presence of social fears than boys. To gauge whether children recognize the unreasonable nature of their fears, we often ask them if they think they are "more nervous" or "more shy" than other children in their class or in their neighborhood. Some children readily acknowledge that their social distress is greater than that of their peers; it is interesting that nonanxious children, too, can easily identify shy peers. The problem is that even if they think they are "more shy," not all children with social anxiety disorder readily acknowledge that their fear is in need of treatment.

This last point is most important. A common diagnostic rule of thumb for clinicians working with children is that when parents and children disagree on the presence of symptoms, the parental report is given more weight when symptomatology relates to externalizing disorders (e.g., conduct disorder). The child's report is given more weight, however, with reference to internalizing disorders (operating under the belief that parents may not be aware of their children's internal mood status). Although this clinical lore may be a good general axiom to follow, it sometimes is incorrect with respect to social anxiety disorder. A number of children who come to our clinic readily admit to shyness, but others, referred by parents or guidance counselors, do not. We have interviewed children who denied the presence of any anxiety, claiming that they had several friends and were not inhibited in school activities. Their parents, however, described socially reclusive children with few, if any, friends and a restricted range of social interactions. Because our clinic conducts behavioral assessments of children's social skills and social performance, we have used those data to help determine whether parental or child reports are more valid. Using a same-age peer, we ask the children to engage in several social encounters: responding to requests for help, giving compliments, receiving compliments, and being assertive. In addition, we ask the children to read aloud before a small group. In virtually every instance in which parent and child disagree, the skills and performance data are more consistent with the parent's report than with the child's self-report. That is, in the behavioral assessments, the children who denied social difficulties were unable to display behaviors that would suggest the ability to form friendships, sustain social inter-actions, or be effective in social performance tasks. Thus, we strongly advise that parental reports be given sufficient weight when determining the possible presence of social anxiety disorder in children.

PHENOMENOLOGY

The situations that are stressful for children and adolescents with social anxiety disorder are much the same as those that are stressful for adults. Furthermore, there are no differences in clinical phenomena based on race, ethnicity, or gender. The percentage of children and adolescents with social anxiety disorder who fear particular types of social situations is presented in Table 2.1. As depicted, children and adolescents endorse distress and avoidance across a range of situations, demonstrating the extensive and severe impact of this disorder. Furthermore, as illustrated,

Table 2.1

Percentage of Children and Adolescents With Social Anxiety Disorder Endorsing at Least Moderate Distress in Social Settings

Situation	Children[a]	Adolescents[b]
Reading aloud in front of a group	71	90
Music or athletic performances	61	87
Initiating or joining a conversation	59	87
Writing on the blackboard	51	76
Ordering food in a restaurant	50	70
Attending dances or activity nights	50	91
Taking tests	48	76
Parties	47	90
Answering a question in class	46	75
Working or playing with other children	45	75
Asking the teacher for help	44	87
Physical education class	37	65
Group or team meetings	36	75
Having picture taken	32	71
Using public bathrooms	24	75
Inviting a friend to get together	24	81
Walking in the hallway at school	16	76
Eating in the cafeteria or in front of others	23	68
Answering or talking on the telephone	13	75
Dating	NA	54

Note: Child data taken from "Psychopathology of Childhood Social Phobia," by D. C. Beidel, S. M. Turner, and T. M. Morris, 1999, *Journal of the American Academy of Child and Adolescent Psychiatry, 38,* p. 645. Copyright 1999 by Lippincott Williams & Wilkins. Adapted with permission. [a]$N = 50$. [b]$N = 63$.

adolescents with social anxiety disorder appear to be more severely impaired than younger children with the same disorder (Rao, Beidel, & Turner, 2006).

As noted in chapter 1, there remains controversy regarding the determination of social anxiety disorder subtypes. Among our child and adolescent samples, only 11% and 8%, respectively, endorsed fears only in the area of public performance (i.e., the specific subtype; Beidel et al., 1999; Beidel, Turner, Young, Ammerman, et al., in press). Other studies report a much lower rate of those with the generalized subtype, with rates ranging from 33% to 58% of the sample (Chavira et al., 2004; Hofmann et al., 1999; Wittchen, Stein, & Kessler, 1999). These samples do not consist of those seeking treatment, however, and thus, as with adult data, those who seek treatment may represent the most severely impaired. Parents described their children with the generalized subtype as having more severe social anxiety symptoms, an earlier age of onset (5.1 vs. 8.0 years), and significantly poorer social skills (Chavira et al., 2004). Thus, although limited, emerging evidence suggests that even among children, those with the generalized subtype are more impaired.

Daily diaries (self-monitoring) can be used to determine specific aspects of social behavior and initially were instrumental in documenting the presence and impact of social anxiety disorder in children (e.g., Beidel, Neal, & Lederer, 1991). Diaries require the child to complete a brief checklist after an event or at the end of the day, typically indicating the occurrence or frequency of specific events and the child's response (see chap. 5, this volume, for a discussion and examples of self-monitoring forms). Results of one study indicated that children diagnosed with social anxiety disorder encountered a socially distressful event about every other day, and the majority of the events occurred in the school setting (Beidel et al., 1991). This should not be surprising because children spend a large percentage of their time at school. Another investigation using a larger sample of 50 children with social anxiety disorder indicated that a broad range of events were distressing, including both performance and social interaction settings (Beidel et al., 1999; see Table 2.2). It is interesting that, with respect to their responses to socially distressing events, "doing what I was supposed to do" was most frequent, highlighting the fact that these children often "suffer in silence." Other responses, including a variety of avoidant strategies, were also reported. Finally, it is interesting that a subset of children reported the use of

Table 2.2
Daily Diary Data: Frequency of Distressful Events and Children's Responses

	% Events/responses endorsed
Event	
I had to perform in front of others	17
The teacher called on me to answer a question	15
A popular child at school spoke to me	13
I had to talk on the telephone	11
I had to eat in a public place	9
I had to use a public restroom	6
I had to work with a popular child at school	4
Other (write in events)	27
Response	
Did what I was supposed to do	37
Pretended I was sick	14
Cried	11
Waited to go to the bathroom until I got home	9
Told myself not to be nervous, it would be OK	6
Got a stomachache or headache	6
Pretended I didn't hear the person talking to me	4
Refused to do what I was asked	3
Did not go someplace so I would not have to perform	3
Hid my eyes so I was not called on	1
Other (write in responses)	9

Note. N = 50. From "Psychopathology of Childhood Social Phobia," by D. C. Beidel, S. M. Turner, and T. M. Morris, 1999, *Journal of the American Academy of Child and Adolescent Psychiatry, 38*, p. 645. Copyright 1999 by Lippincott Williams & Wilkins. Adapted with permission.

behaviors that might be considered coping responses, for example, "Told myself not to be nervous, it would be OK." In summary, although most children will readily report feeling anxious when reading aloud in front of a group, unstructured interactions with peers are also frequent and moderately to severely distressing situations. Because such encounters may not be readily identified on the basis of casual observation, clinicians need to assess carefully the presence of anxiety during informal social situations.

Other authors also have described physical, cognitive, and behavioral symptoms associated with childhood social anxiety disorder. The most common physical symptoms reported by children between the ages of 8 and 12 with social-evaluative fears (and which differentiated them from normal control children) included choking, flushes or chills, palpitations, fainting, shaking, feeling like dying, and headaches (Beidel, Christ, & Long, 1991). These are many of the same symptoms reported by adults with social anxiety disorder. Symptoms characteristic of panic attacks (dizziness, shortness of breath, numbness, or tingling) are less common in children with social anxiety disorder. Additionally, behavioral manifestations can include stuttering, poor eye contact, mumbling, nail biting, and a trembling voice (Albano, DiBartolo, Heimberg, & Barlow, 1995), and cognitive content may include thoughts of escape from the social situation, negative evaluation, failure, humiliation, embarrassment, and inadequacy and self-criticism.

Finally, the play activities of children with social anxiety disorder sometimes are unusual. Many children with social anxiety disorder develop unusual hobbies for their given age, including collecting Civil War facts, programming computers, or tracking weather reports (Albano et al., 1995), and the lack of more common interests may be because of limited opportunities for social interactions as a result of their social fears and avoidance. In addition, many of our children never participated in typical childhood activities such as bowling or roller-skating or rollerblading. Thus, because they are socially isolated, these children miss out on the opportunities to participate in traditional childhood activities.

The issue of the presence of negative cognitions in children and adolescents with social anxiety disorder is a controversial area. In some instances, there appears to have been wholesale adoption of adult models of this disorder with minimal to no attention to the issue of basic cognitive development (see Alfano, Beidel, & Turner, 2002, for a review of this area). In fact, when the actual presence of negative thoughts during social encounters is addressed directly, the results have been inconsistent (Beidel, 1991; Bögels & Zigterman, 2000; Spence et al., 1999; Treadwell & Kendall, 1996). Furthermore, the clinical relevance of the negative thoughts is unclear. In one investigation, children with social anxiety disorder were significantly more likely to report the presence of negative cognitions than the normal control group, although perusal of actual frequency indicated that the means were less than 1 thought different (4.3 vs. 3.6 thoughts; Spence et al., 1999), illustrating that if these thoughts are present, they do not occur at high frequency or at a much greater frequency than for those without a disorder.

In an investigation of the cognitive correlates of children and adolescents with social anxiety disorder, Alfano, Beidel, and Turner (2006) used a videotape recall procedure to examine several aspects of cognitive phenomena in both children and adolescents engaged in two social interactions (reading aloud and interacting with a same-age peer). This study revealed several important findings. First, both children and adolescents with social anxiety disorder had higher scores on the cognitive items on the Social Phobia and Anxiety Inventory for Children (SPAI–C; Beidel et al., 1995) than adolescents (but not children) with no psychological disorder. Furthermore, both children and adolescents with social anxiety disorder anticipated performing more poorly on a role-play task, and after completing the role-play task, both groups with social anxiety disorder believed that they had performed more poorly. Their negative expectations and negative ratings of performance were not "unrealistic," however; observers unaware of group status rated the children and adolescents with social anxiety disorder as significantly more anxious and less skilled when compared with the control group. Thus, others viewed those with social anxiety disorder as performing more poorly. Furthermore, some of the specific ratings included under these broad categories were only significantly different for adolescents with social anxiety disorder, again reinforcing the notion that basic developmental factors must be considered before merely assuming that the clinical presentation of this disorder is consistent across all developmental ages. These data suggest that despite the presence of the disorder in young children, the cognitive component of expectation is not present until adolescence, when cognitive maturity occurs.

In addition to expectations, this study (Alfano et al., 2006) also directly examined the presence of cognitions during social and performance interactions. It is important to note that there was a main effect for age—regardless of group, adolescents reported a significantly higher frequency of cognitions than children, and reinforcing the notion that metacognition (the ability to think about thinking) develops with age. Group differences were found only for the role-play task and indicated that those with social anxiety disorder were significantly more likely to report the presence of negative thoughts compared with those having no disorder. A close examination of the mean number of negative thoughts for each group indicated, however, that the mean for those with social anxiety disorder was 0.26 and 0.03 for the control group. In fact, an examination of the individual scores indicated that only 20% of the social anxiety disorder group reported the presence of any negative thoughts during the social interaction task, and among those who did, all were adolescents. This study highlights two important issues. First, although the results of the statistical analysis suggest that negative cognitions are characteristic of those with social anxiety disorder, an actual examination of the data indicated that only one in five adolescents (20%) reported the presence of negative thoughts during a social interaction. Second, thoughts were present only during the social interaction task, and not the read-aloud task. Therefore, on the basis of the methodology used in this investigation, the most parsimonious conclusion is that although negative thoughts are part of the clinical presentation of social anxiety disorder for a subset of adolescents, they do not necessarily characterize the majority of children and adolescents with this disorder. Furthermore, the issue is not necessarily whether these cognitions exist but whether they are etiological in nature and how their presence affects the course of treatment.

Clinical correlates of social anxiety disorder in youth include significantly higher levels of depression, higher trait anxiety, and a more rigid temperamental style compared with children without psychological disorders (Beidel, 1991; Beidel et al., 1999; Beidel, Turner, Young, Ammerman, et al., in press). Those with a rigid temperamental style become distressed when aspects of their normal routine are changed or interrupted. The behaviors characteristic of this rigid temperamental style are very similar to obsessive–compulsive personality disorder, which is a relatively common comorbid condition in adults with social anxiety disorder (Turner, Beidel, Borden, et al., 1991; also see chap. 1, this volume). Children and adolescents with social anxiety disorder also have lower scores on measures of extraversion and higher degrees of loneliness than children with no disorder (Beidel et al., 1999; Beidel, Turner, & Young, in press).

The primary coexisting disorders that are present in adults with social anxiety disorder (generalized anxiety disorder and specific phobias) also are present in children (Beidel & Turner, 1992b; Last, Strauss, & Francis, 1987). Table 2.3 presents the range of comorbidity for a sample of children and adolescents with social anxiety disorder (Beidel et al., 1999; Beidel, Turner, Young, Ammerman, et al., in press). As illustrated, the majority of children and adolescents seeking treatment for this disorder present with a comorbid disorder, primarily additional anxiety disorders. Among an epidemiological sample of German adolescents, 41% had a comorbid somatoform disorder, 29% had a depressive disorder, and 24% had a substance abuse disorder (Essau, Conradt, & Petermann, 1999). Among a pediatric primary care sample in the United States (Chavira et al., 2004), 39% had comorbid specific phobia, 29% had generalized anxiety disorder, 6% had major depressive disorder, 11% had separation anxiety disorder, and 28% had attention deficit hyperactivity disorder. Although less frequently, conduct and oppositional behavioral problems as well as substance abuse or dependence,

Table 2.3

Range and Percentage of Comorbid Diagnoses in Children and Adolescents With Social Anxiety Disorder

Comorbid diagnosis	Children (%)[a]	Adolescents (%)[b]
None	40	43
Generalized anxiety disorder	10	32
Attention-deficit/hyperactivity disorder	10	5
Specific phobia	10	6
Selective mutism	8	2
Separation anxiety disorder	6	2
Obsessive–compulsive disorder	6	2
Depression	6	7
Panic disorder	2	0
Adjustment disorder	2	2
Oppositional defiant disorder	0	2

Note: [a]$N = 50$. Child data taken from "Psychopathology of Childhood Social Phobia," by D. C. Beidel, S. M. Turner, and T. M. Morris, 1999, *Journal of the American Academy of Child and Adolescent Psychiatry, 38*, p. 647. Copyright 1999 by Lippincott Williams & Wilkins. Adapted with permission.

also occur among some samples of adolescents with social anxiety disorder (D. B. Clark, 1993, DeWit, MacDonald, & Offord, 1999; Essau et al., 1999). In many instances, different diagnostic strategies distinguish epidemiological, primary care and clinical (treatment-seeking) samples, perhaps accounting for some of the differences in the type of comorbid conditions reported.

DETRIMENTAL OUTCOMES

Empirical data on the detrimental outcomes of childhood social anxiety disorder now are established. School refusal behavior is one such negative outcome (Last et al., 1992) as are complaints of depression (Perrin & Last, 1993), loneliness (Beidel et al., 1999; Beidel, Turner,

Young, Ammerman, et al., in press) and among boys with social anxiety disorder, conduct problems, difficulty getting along with peers, and truancy (Clark, 1993). Peer acceptance and friendships also are affected by the presence of social anxiety disorder in children. Specifically, among elementary school children, childhood social anxiety is associated with low levels of peer acceptance, although the relation was mediated to some extent by the presence of social skills (Greco & Morris, 2005). Furthermore, for girls, a highly negative relationship with a best friend exacerbated the risk for negative peer outcomes. It is clear that social anxiety has a significant impact on the ability to achieve the developmental milestones of peer relationships.

On the basis of the Epidemiological Catchment Area survey data, Davidson (1993) noted that conduct problems and truancy were part of the childhood history of adults with social anxiety disorder and that the disorder's onset before age 11 was predictive of nonrecovery in adulthood. Furthermore, when distress reaches a certain level, children with severe social fears may refuse to engage in certain activities (Beidel et al., 1999; Beidel, Turner, Young, Ammerman, et al., in press), thus appearing oppositional, at least on an intermittent basis. It is clear then that social anxiety disorder can be related to a host of maladaptive child behaviors.

In addition to these short-term correlates, childhood social anxiety disorder has long-term detrimental effects as well. It is increasingly apparent that the course of the disorder is chronic, although there are episodic variations in symptom severity (Merikangas et al., 2002). Among epidemiological samples, early onset social anxiety disorder results in a more persistent and severe course (Kessler, 2003). When examining life transitions among an epidemiological sample, social anxiety disorder, when present in adolescence, significantly predicted the failure to attend college (Kessler, 2003). A 15-year follow-up of adolescents diagnosed with social anxiety disorder indicated that 57% reported occupational impairment and 44% reported social impairment (Merikangas et al., 2002). Furthermore, only 39% received any type of treatment during the 15-year follow-up period. Although some of these data are preliminary and the retrospective data reported by Davidson (1993) must be regarded cautiously, these consistent findings document the pervasive negative long-term outcome when childhood social anxiety disorder is unrecognized and untreated.

SOCIAL SKILLS

Since the first edition of this volume was published, substantial evidence has accumulated to suggest that social skills deficits are part of the clinical presentation of social anxiety disorder in children and adolescents (Beidel et al., 1999; Beidel, Turner, Young, Ammerman, et al., in press; Spence et al., 1999). When engaged in social interactions with a same-age peer or reading aloud before a small audience, children and adolescents with social anxiety disorder displayed significantly poorer social skills and significantly greater anxiety than age-matched peers with no psychiatric disorders (Beidel et al., 1999; Beidel, Turner, Young, Ammerman, et al., in press). Spence et al. (1999) also reported the presence of social skills deficits in this population, on the basis of parental and self-report data as well as behavioral observation.

One study reported that independent observers were unable to distinguish between high and low socially anxious groups when children engaged in an unstructured interaction with an adult, thereby concluding that cognitive distortion, rather than social skills deficits, is the primary factor in this population (Cartwright-Hatton, Tschernitz, & Gomersall, 2005). Because this study used an analogue population (children were designated as high or low socially anxious on the basis of their scores on a self-report measure), it is unclear whether any of the children would have received an actual diagnosis of social anxiety disorder. Second, the interaction was with an adult not another child, and as noted earlier, some children with social anxiety disorder are able to interact comfortably with adults but not with other children. Thus, these findings are contradictory to data using carefully diagnosed samples of children with social anxiety disorder and appropriate analogue situations. The database is still quite small, however, and further investigations are needed to clarify these discrepancies.

RELATED CONDITIONS

Selective Mutism

Behavioral inhibition, a temperamental style identified in about 10% to 20% of Caucasian toddlers, is characterized by fear of unfamiliar situations, people, objects, and events (Garcia-Coll, Kagan, & Reznick, 1984; see chap. 4, this volume). One of the most consistent behaviors in this group is the lack of spontaneous verbal communication with strangers (e.g., Reznick et al., 1986). In the clinical literature, the behavior known as *selective mutism* is characterized by refusal to speak in certain social situations. Children with selective mutism have the linguistic ability to converse with others and are vociferous in the immediate family environment and perhaps with a few close family friends. Yet in virtually every other situation, children with selective mutism will not verbally initiate or respond to communications. The behavior is uncommon (0.18%–0.76% of the general population; Bergman, Piacentini, & McCracken, 2002; Elizur & Perednik, 2003; Kopp & Gillberg, 1997) and more likely to occur in the preschool to early elementary school ages (Bergman et al., 2002). An extensive discussion of this behavior is beyond the scope of this chapter, and the interested reader is referred to several reviews of selective mutism (Beidel & Turner, 2005; Freeman, Garcia, Miller, Dow, & Leonard, 2004).

Although few studies have described the clinical presentation of selective mutism, data suggest that in some cases it may be a variant of, and perhaps an extreme form of, childhood social anxiety disorder. Early descriptions reported higher levels of trait anxiety, fearfulness, and shyness and noted that most children with selective mutism have at least one shy or socially reticent parent (J. B. Brown & Lloyd, 1975). Initial controlled investigations reported that 95% to 100% of children with selective mutism also met diagnostic criteria for social anxiety disorder (Black & Uhde, 1995; Dummit et al., 1997). Thus, it appears clear that these children experience significant social anxiety. Not all children with social anxiety disorder have selective mutism, however, and there is increasing interest in further defining the characteristics of this condition, particularly, in the presence of oppositional behaviors. This should not be surprising because, as we observed earlier, as a result of social distress, children with social anxiety disorder sometimes avoid situations or refuse to participate in social activities as a way to minimize their distress. We now discuss the data for the presence of oppositional behaviors and oppositional defiant disorder in children with selective mutism.

Aspects of the clinical presentation of selective mutism suggest that externalizing behavioral problems exist in at least some children with selective mutism, and a minority of children with selective mutism also meet criteria for oppositional defiant disorder (Black & Uhde, 1995; Dummit et al., 1997). Clinically, we have had children with selective mutism in our lobby area talk loudly to their parents and siblings as they played. When we appear for the session, they immediately assume a defiant posture (feet apart, arms folded across the chest, and eyes that issue the challenge, "I dare you to make me talk"). Such a stance is not characteristic of typical socially anxious children, whose oppositional behavior is more likely to consist of crying, hiding, or refusing to leave the parent. Furthermore, although not all children with selective mutism meet criteria for oppositional defiant disorder, we have observed many operant features that help to maintain the condition. In fact, we believe that to treat these children effectively, additional strategies to those typically used to treat social anxiety disorder are needed.

In an effort to understand more clearly why some children with social anxiety disorder do not speak in front of others whereas others are able to engage in at least limited conversation, several investigations have directly compared the clinical presentation of children comorbid for selective mutism and social anxiety disorder and children with social anxiety disorder alone (Manassis et al., 2003; Yeganeh, Beidel, & Turner, 2006; Yeganeh, Beidel, Turner, Pina, & Silverman, 2003). Across all three samples, children with social anxiety disorder alone and those with social anxiety disorder and selective mutism reported equivalent levels of social distress when asked to engage another child in a social interaction or read aloud in front of a small group (Yeganeh et al., 2003, 2006). Children with selective mutism and social anxiety disorder were judged as significantly more socially anxious and significantly less socially skilled on the basis of clinician ratings, diagnostic interview data, and independent observer ratings of the quality of the social interactions. It is unclear, however, whether these higher ratings were simply based on the fact that those with selective mutism did not speak during these interactions and clinicians interpreted this behavior as a sign of distress. Consistent with this interpretation, children with generalized social anxiety disorder, compared with children having the specific subtype, were rated by their parents as having more distress in social interactions, but children's self-report ratings did not differentiate the two groups (Chavira et al., 2004). With respect to the issue of oppositionality, the data are less clear. When children with selective mutism and social anxiety disorder are compared with children with social anxiety disorder alone, one study reported higher scores on the aggression and delinquency subscales of the Child Behavior Checklist (Yeganeh et al., 2003), and higher rates of comorbid oppositional defiant disorder were reported in children with selective mutism (compared with those with social anxiety disorder alone or normal control participants; Yeganeh et al., 2006). Yet in this same investigation, dimensional ratings of oppositionality failed to distinguish the groups, so this puzzling relationship remains unresolved.

Currently, the empirical data examining the relation between social anxiety disorder and selective mutism are limited. In many instances, selective mutism appears to be a characteristic of a proportion of children with social anxiety disorder, and as such, treatments developed for social anxiety disorder may also be useful for selective mutism. Recently, our clinic has successfully treated children with selective mutism and social anxiety disorder using a basic shaping strategy to increase verbalizations. Once the children respond consistently, they are included in our Social Effectiveness Therapy for Children program (SET–C; see chap. 9). It has been our clinical experience, however, that some children with selective mutism are in the autism spectrum, and in these cases, our SET–C intervention is not appropriate or efficacious. We propose that an alternative way to conceptualize selective mutism is similar to how we now understand school refusal—that is, it is a behavior, not a disorder unto itself. When conceptualized in that fashion, selective mutism may be seen as a behavior related to a variety of psychiatric disorders. One additional note: It is our clinical experience that oppositional problems in children with social anxiety disorder are sometimes the result of poor parenting skills (see chaps. 6 and 9, this volume) and that various reinforcement contingencies may serve to foster and maintain the behavior. Thus, thorough attention to all aspects of parent–child interactions is necessary, and in some cases, basic parent management training is an important component of the treatment of children with selective mutism.

Test Anxiety

Test anxiety is a condition commonly related to social anxiety disorder. Significant test anxiety appears to occur in approximately 40% of elementary school-age children (Beidel & Turner, 1988). Like social anxiety disorder, test anxiety is a fear of negative evaluation that has cognitive, somatic, and behavioral components. Children with test anxiety fear that they will perform poorly on tests just as children with social anxiety disorder fear that they will make a mistake when performing in front of others. Heart palpitations, sweating, and blushing are common among children with test anxiety, as they are in children with social anxiety disorder (Beidel et al., 1991). Finally, children with test anxiety will "play sick" to avoid going to school on a test day. Thus, school refusal (at least on an intermittent basis) also occurs in this population.

In addition to its similar clinical presentation, approximately 60% of children with test anxiety meet diagnostic criteria for social anxiety disorder or overanxious disorder (Beidel & Turner, 1988). Furthermore, this percentage is consistent for White and African American children (there is also consistent similarity in the clinical presentation across these two racial groups; see chap. 3). These data suggest that test anxiety may serve as an indicator for the presence of more pervasive social fears in at least half of children with test anxiety. Complaints of test anxiety in children should prompt clinicians to do a thorough evaluation for other anxiety problems, particularly social anxiety disorder.

DIFFERENTIAL DIAGNOSIS

Children with anxiety disorders rarely present with just one type of fear, and social anxiety disorder is no exception. Particularly when using the previous diagnostic schemas, comorbidity rates are high, with up to 87% of children with social anxiety disorder meeting diagnostic criteria for an additional diagnosis (Last et al., 1992). In many of these cases, the comorbid diagnosis was overanxious disorder or avoidant disorder of childhood. This pattern of comorbidity has changed somewhat with the revisions that accompanied the publication of the *DSM–IV* (APA, 1994) because overanxious disorder was revised significantly, and avoidant disorder of childhood was eliminated. As discussed in chapter 1, social anxiety may be found in disorders other than social anxiety disorder. In the following sections we discuss distinctions regarding differential diagnosis.

Panic Disorder

As noted in chapter 1, one of the most difficult diagnostic distinctions is differentiating social anxiety disorder from panic disorder. Because children are less likely to experience panic disorder, the clinician is faced with the challenge of making this distinction less often than with adults. Nevertheless, the guidelines offered in chapter 1 are still useful when identifying children and adolescents with panic disorder. To reiterate, those with panic disorder experience the constellation of symptoms that define a panic attack. Although those with social anxiety disorder fear that their physical symptoms may be observable to others, unlike those with panic disorder, they do not fear the symptoms themselves. In addition, their symptoms occur only in the presence or anticipation of social situations.

School Refusal

Although the term *school phobia* is no longer used, school refusal is a behavioral symptom of anxiety (as well as other disorders). There are four behavioral patterns that may be associated with school refusal: avoidance of objects or situations that provoke negative affect, escape from aversive social or evaluative situations, attention-getting behavior, and positive tangible reinforcement (Kearney & Silverman, 1990). In fact, school refusal may be associated with a variety of disorders. For some children, staying at home is more reinforcing than going to school. Among children with internalizing disorders, those with depression may simply lack the energy or interest to attend school. Children with anxiety disorders such as separation anxiety disorder, social anxiety disorder, obsessive–compulsive disorder (OCD), or specific phobias may also refuse to attend school. Children with specific phobias may fear a particular class, a particular teacher, or a particular activity (e.g., jumping on a trampoline), which may result in school refusal. Children with separation anxiety disorder (discussed later) refuse to attend school because of their fears of separation from or harm to a caretaker. Children with OCD may refuse to attend school because the school environment might contain a contaminant they fear.

For children with social anxiety disorder, reluctance or refusal to attend school stems from their fears of social interactions. School necessitates engagement in many social and performance activities that are distressing for those with social anxiety disorder. As we have mentioned before, these include answering questions in class, reading in front of the class, writing on the blackboard, eating in the cafeteria, talking to the principal, participating in physical education classes, and performing in front of others (e.g., being in a play or a recital). With few, if any, opportunities to avoid these activities, it is clear why children with severe social fears may be reluctant to attend school. Unlike children with conduct disorder or those who receive tangible reinforcement for non-attendance, children with social anxiety disorder want to attend school. Their refusal (avoidance) is fueled by their fear of the social aspects of the school setting. Lawrence's case, described in the introduction to this chapter, exemplifies this distinction.

Specific Phobia

Specific phobia involves fears of objects or situations that do not involve social encounters or panic attacks (e.g., dogs, heights, and needles). Comparing clinic-referred children with social anxiety disorder and those with specific (simple) phobia, those with social anxiety disorder were older and, on the basis of self-report instruments, were significantly more lonely, generally fearful, and depressed (Strauss & Last, 1993). Comorbid conditions such as avoidant disorder and overanxious disorder were more likely to be present in children with social anxiety disorder than simple phobia. As we noted earlier, the presence of these two comorbid conditions may have resulted from the vagaries of the older diagnostic systems. Because this overlap has, to a large extent, been eliminated, it is unclear whether the higher presence of comorbid disorders will continue to differentiate social anxiety disorder and specific phobia.

Separation Anxiety Disorder

An important distinction, and one that is not always easily accomplished, is differentiating social anxiety disorder from separation anxiety disorder, conceptualized as excessive concern about separation from a major attachment figure. Children with separation anxiety disorder fear that some harm will befall them, their parents, or someone else who serves a major caretaker role. Thus, whereas separation anxiety disorder involves distress over being separated from a significant other, social anxiety disorder entails distress over approach or interaction with others (Beidel & Morris, 1995). In clinical practice, this distinction is often difficult to make, particularly in young children, because both groups can experience and display anxiety when in social settings. For example, the clinging behavior so often seen in anxious children could result from a desire to stay close to a caretaker or fear of approaching an unfamiliar social situation.

As noted earlier, school refusal behavior cannot differentiate these two disorders because both groups report feeling fearful in the school setting (Strauss & Last, 1993). Therefore, behavior in other settings may be clinically significant. For example, unlike children with separation anxiety disorder, children with social anxiety disorder do not exhibit inordinate distress when parents leave them at home or when they are away from their parents. Children with social anxiety disorder typically do not report nightmares or dreams of separation from parents. In contrast, children with separation anxiety disorder do not have significant fears when speaking, eating, or writing in front of others. Thus, it is clear that there are avenues by which to differentiate these two disorders. Relying on school refusal alone will not be sufficient, however. Furthermore, the problem is complicated by the fact that a child can have both conditions simultaneously, and each may have to be treated separately.

Generalized Anxiety Disorder
(Overanxious Disorder)

Previously, it was often difficult to differentiate children with social anxiety disorder from those with overanxious disorder because social-evaluative fears were part of both diagnoses. Using the *DSM–IV* diagnostic criteria (APA, 1994), children with generalized anxiety disorder (overanxious disorder in children) express significant worry about myriad concerns and have somatic symptoms such as feeling keyed up, on edge, or restless; being easily fatigued; having difficulty concentrating; feeling irritable; experiencing muscle tension; and experiencing sleep disturbance. Children with this disorder worry about a broad range of situations, not just social encounters, making this diagnostic distinction easier. However, 16% of our sample of children with social anxiety disorder (Beidel et al., 1999) and 32% of adolescents with social anxiety disorder (Beidel, Turner, Young, Ammerman, et al., in press) also had a concurrent *DSM–IV* diagnosis of generalized anxiety disorder (overanxious disorder in children), and the implications of this comorbidity for treatment are not yet clear.

Depression

Also important is the distinction between social anxiety disorder and depression. Rates of comorbid depression in child and adolescent samples range from 6% to 10% in those with primary social anxiety disorder (Beidel et al., 1999; Beidel, Turner, Young, Ammerman, et al., in press; Strauss & Last, 1993), but with respect to differential diagnosis, no empirical data are available to guide the decision-making process. Like those with social anxiety disorder, children with depression often refuse to attend social engagements and may even refuse to attend school, but the reason for the refusal is often markedly different. Children with depression often have a low energy level and have lost interest in participating in many activities (i.e., things are not fun anymore). In addition, on the basis of research with depressed adult women, dysphoric mood can inhibit social behavior, making social interactions less rewarding and therefore less likely to occur (Hersen, Bellack, Himmelhoch, & Thase, 1984). It appears that depressed children avoid or refuse to participate in social activities because of their anergia and anhedonia; reasons similar to those of depressed adults. In contrast, those with social anxiety disorder avoid social settings not because of a lack of energy and interest but because of their fears. It should be clear, then, that to arrive at a proper diagnosis, the motivating factor for the inhibited social behavior must be understood fully. Of course, both patterns of social avoidance may be present in those who have both disorders concurrently. In such instances, it would be necessary to treat the depression and anergia before beginning treatment (especially behavioral treatment) for children with social anxiety disorder.

Externalizing Disorders

Sometimes anxiety disorders co-occur with externalizing disorders. Among a sample of 91 children referred to an anxiety disorders clinic, 21% also had conduct disorder, oppositional defiant disorder, or attention-deficit/hyperactivity disorder (ADHD; Last, Hersen, Kazdin, Finkelstein, & Strauss, 1987). Other evidence for comorbidity comes from rates of anxiety disorders ranging from 23.5% to 11.0% among first- and second-degree relatives of children with ADHD (without a concurrent anxiety disorder). Although it would appear to be easy to differentiate social anxiety disorder from externalizing disorders such as ADHD or oppositional defiant disorder, such distinctions are not always so clear. Part of the difficulty is that children with ADHD often report substantial distress in social settings. In some cases, children with ADHD are afraid that their impulsive actions will result in embarrassment or in ridicule from others. For these children, their concerns are reality-based. That is, children with ADHD often actually act impulsively (e.g., blurting out answers, knocking things over) and draw scrutiny from others. Thus, their fears are not unrealistic, as is required for a diagnosis of social anxiety disorder. Children with ADHD do, intentionally or unintentionally, engage in behaviors that draw unwanted scrutiny and negative evaluation by others.

Other children with ADHD experience social anxiety for a different reason. Some children with ADHD can be bossy or intrusive; they interrupt others' conversations, are unable to wait their turn in line or during games, and often inappropriately "break in" during a group activity. Unlike children with social anxiety disorder, who often are neglected by peers, children with ADHD are actively rejected by peers.

Their behavior is so negative that others openly ostracize or ignore them. Because social encounters with others often lead to such negative consequences, it is likely that children in these situations would report social anxiety in the presence of others (particularly a peer group). Once again, however, this expression of anxiety is not social anxiety disorder because the social anxiety and fear of negative consequences is not unrealistic. Rather, social rejection is an unfortunate regular occurrence for some children with ADHD.

Sometimes anxious children can be misdiagnosed with ADHD. For example,

> Ricardo came to our clinic because his teacher felt that he was inattentive and hyperactive. He was fidgety in the classroom (glancing out the windows, squirming in his seat) and daydreaming. His teacher felt that he was performing below grade level on the basis of his classroom participation, although individual testing in the clinic indicated that he was functioning at grade level in all academic subjects. His parents denied any evidence of hyperactivity at home but did describe behaviors consistent with social anxiety. When in social settings (and only in social situations), his motor activity increased. He would shrink away from groups of children and was reluctant to engage even one other child in conversation. In addition, he would refuse to answer the telephone, even if his parents instructed him to do so. In the behavioral assessment, he had adequate social skills, but he did not use them in social settings, even when he was sought out by other children.

Several key indicators ruled out ADHD in Ricardo. First, there was no increased motor activity except when he was in social situations (i.e., motor hyperactivity appeared to be cued by the presence of others). This is inconsistent with ADHD. Furthermore, although disruptive behaviors consistent with ADHD often increase in unstructured encounters, Ricardo's behavior was cued by the social content of the situation, not the nature of its structure. Second, Ricardo was not necessarily inattentive in the school setting. Although his teacher thought that he was performing below grade level, his achievement scores indicated otherwise. To us, this suggested that his social anxiety disorder was inhibiting his ability to perform well in school (i.e., answering questions in class). Third, his social skills were adequate, although he did not use them (possibly because of inhibitory anxiety). Fourth, sometimes other children sought out Ricardo, even though he would consistently shrink away from social contact. That is, he did not actively seek to join other children, but he was not actively rejected by them. On the basis of this clinical presentation, Ricardo's behavior was more consistent with a diagnosis of social anxiety disorder than ADHD. Intervention using SET–C (see chap. 9, this volume) was effective in remediating his anxious behaviors and increasing his social interactions.

The discussion of comorbidity with oppositional defiant disorder has received little attention in the literature. Although some children may have both disorders (see Russo & Beidel, 1994), clinicians must be aware, as we have noted in several places throughout this chapter, that oppositional behavior and oppositional defiant disorder are not interchangeable terms. Oppositional behaviors, for example, may occur in the context of social fears. When such fears are remediated, tantrums and refusal behaviors should subside.

Personality Disorders

Adolescents with social anxiety disorder can present with features of Axis II personality disorders. In adults with social anxiety disorder (see chap. 1), the two most common personality disorders are avoidant personality disorder and obsessive–compulsive personality disorder. Parents of one adolescent with social anxiety disorder and school refusal behavior presenting at our clinic described behaviors such as preoccupation with details, perfectionism, overconscientiousness and scrupulousness, and rigidity and stubbornness (all characteristic of obsessive–compulsive personality disorder). In addition, the patient avoided occupational activities involving interpersonal contact, had only one friend, viewed himself as personally unappealing, and was unwilling to take risks (all characteristic of avoidant personality disorder). Although adolescents may not exhibit enough behaviors or enough consistency in these behaviors to meet diagnostic criteria, many of the core features were present in this adolescent. In addition, the presence of these personality disorders (and perhaps the personality features) may suggest the need for alterations in administration of the intervention (see chap. 8, this volume). Thus, careful attention to the presence of these characteristics is necessary.

CONCLUSION

The clinical presentation of social anxiety disorder in childhood and adolescence is both similar to and different from its presentation in adults. Excessive and unreasonable fears are acknowledged, but children, particularly children younger than age 12, frequently do not acknowledge that they have fewer friends or that they engage in social activities less often than their peers. Parent and teacher input are needed to help determine whether the child's social behavior is a significant problem. Other features of the syndrome in children may differ as well, owing to their developmental stage. Children may cry or throw temper tantrums when faced with fearful events or situations, whereas this is rarely seen in adults. Adults have more degrees of freedom regarding how they manage their anxiety and fears. Rather than refusing to work, they seek types of employment that minimize the need to engage in behaviors they fear, and they develop subtle avoidance strategies, such as those discussed in chapter 1 of this volume. Children and adolescents often do not have this flexibility. Instead, they may refuse to go to school (although we have known children who have begged their parents to be homeschooled). Other strategies include complaints of vague physical symptoms to avoid certain activities. In short, developmental parameters exert some influence on the manner in which the behavioral expression of the syndrome is manifested, but the motivating factors are the same.

Some studies indicated that the negative cognitions reported by adults with this disorder may be present in adolescents (Albano et al., 1995). In our clinical experience, such cognitions are not typically part of the clinical picture in children younger than age 12. They frequently cannot report specific ideation while engaged in an anxiety-arousing task. This may simply be because of their cognitive immaturity. Therefore, the clinician will have to use other variables, such as report of physical symptoms, behavioral avoidance, social behavior history, and parent and teacher reports, to make a diagnosis.

Many clinical features of childhood, adolescent, and adult social anxiety disorder are strikingly similar. For example, the types of social situations feared and avoided are virtually identical, although there are differences with respect to frequency across the groups. Likewise, the pattern of co-occurrence of Axis I and II conditions is similar; the percentage of those with childhood social anxiety disorder with comorbid specific phobia and the percentage with comorbid generalized anxiety disorder are virtually identical. Furthermore, it is interesting to point out that children with social anxiety disorder manifest many features of behavioral rigidity and obsessionality, features that are highly prevalent among adults with social anxiety disorder. This similarity strengthens the conclusion that the syndrome in children overlaps with the clinical picture in adults.

Despite the numerous similarities in the clinical syndrome, a number of conditions sometimes associated with childhood social anxiety disorder are not typically seen in adults. Sometimes children are labeled as having externalizing disorders when, like Lawrence and Ricardo, they actually have social anxiety disorder. Of course, social anxiety disorder may not be the motivating factor for externalizing problems in all cases (i.e., the disorders could coexist independently). Similarly, some children with behavior problems frequently have social difficulties because other children reject them, preferring not to interact with them. Furthermore, although some oppositional and school refusal behavior is motivated by social fears, this is not true in every case. Finally, socially phobic children are sometimes fidgety and may appear overactive, particularly to teachers. This could lead to a misdiagnosis of ADHD. A careful evaluation is required to determine the correct diagnosis. It is clear that a thorough understanding of the clinical picture of social anxiety disorder in children and adolescents is required to diagnose the syndrome properly. Furthermore, the possible role of social anxiety disorder in other externalizing and internalizing disorders needs to be considered when evaluating and treating these children.

3

Prevalence of Social
Anxiety Disorder

*I'm here because I saw the newspaper story. That woman sounded
just like me. I was so relieved to find out that others also
feel the same way. I thought I was alone.*

—An adult patient with social anxiety disorder during
an initial interview at our clinic

The ability of mental health professionals and the lay public to
recognize the symptoms of social anxiety disorder has improved
significantly since the 1980s. Nevertheless, a survey in 1999 found that
a significant number of psychiatrists (52%) and primary care physicians
(54%) in Europe and Canada felt that social anxiety disorder was not
a distinct diagnosis but a symptom of another disorder, whereas only
14% of primary care physicians and 16% of psychiatrists in the United
States failed to recognize the distinct nature of social anxiety disorder
(den Boer & Dunner, 1999). Most physicians claimed to be able to
recognize social anxiety disorder among their own patients, but follow-
up diagnostic interviews indicated that almost 25% of adults presenting

with other psychiatric diagnoses met diagnostic criteria for social anxiety disorder but were undiagnosed. As noted (den Boer & Dunner, 1999), it is often the existence of another disorder than prompts an individual with social anxiety disorder to seek treatment. In fact, those who seek treatment may not be the most severely affected. An Internet survey revealed that survey respondents reported more severe symptoms of social anxiety and social impairment than a treatment-seeking sample (Erwin, Turk, Heimberg, Fresco, & Hantula, 2004). Furthermore, only 36% of Internet responders ever sought treatment for social anxiety disorder, which exists across all ages, in both sexes, in various racial and ethnic groups, and cross-nationally. In this chapter we present the prevalence of social anxiety disorder in all its variations.

PREVALENCE ACROSS AGE GROUPS

The most current epidemiological data available for childhood social anxiety disorder are based on *Diagnostic and Statistical Manual of Mental Disorders* criteria (3rd ed., revised; *DSM–III–R*; American Psychiatric Association [APA], 1987), which have been identified as problematic for children and adolescents. Using those criteria, about 1% of the general U.S. child and adolescent population have social anxiety disorder (Kashani & Orvaschel, 1990). Consistently, about 0.9% of 11-year-olds in New Zealand met criteria for social anxiety disorder (J. C. Anderson, Williams, McGee, & Silva, 1987). When these children were reassessed 4 years later (at age 15), the prevalence rate was 1.1% (McGee et al., 1990). These rates most likely underestimate the true prevalence of the disorder because fear of public speaking was classified as a specific phobia and not a social anxiety disorder. Fears associated with social situations were reported by 21.4% of 8-year-olds, 45.7% of 12-year-olds, and 55.7% of 17-year-olds (Kashani & Orvaschel, 1990). Similarly, "worrying about what others think of me" was reported by 38.6% of 8-year-olds and 67.1% of 12- and 17-year-olds. Thus, consistent with the age-of-onset data derived from adult populations, it is clear that concerns about social evaluation increase as children age, and, by extrapolation, the incidence of frank social anxiety disorder probably does as well.

As noted, prevalence estimates of social anxiety disorder are only approximate because under *DSM–III–R* criteria, children with social fears could be given a diagnosis of social anxiety disorder, overanxious disorder, or avoidant disorder of childhood. If these prevalence rates are combined, the epidemiological estimates for social fears would increase to 9.6% (Kashani & Orvaschel, 1990), a rate strikingly similar to prevalence rates reported for adults on the basis of the adult epidemiological study (the National Comorbidity Study, or NCS, discussed later in this chapter). Using criteria from the fourth edition of the *DSM* (*DSM–IV*; APA, 1994), a German epidemiological sample of adolescents reported an overall prevalence of 1.6% (1.0% and 2.1% for male and female adolescents, respectively; Essau, Conradt, & Petermann, 1999).

In specialty anxiety clinics, 15% of children seeking treatment had a primary diagnosis of social anxiety disorder, and another 3% had a primary diagnosis of avoidant disorder of childhood (Last, Perrin, Hersen, & Kazdin, 1992). Albano and colleagues (Albano, DiBartolo, Heimberg, & Barlow, 1995) reported that 18% of children seeking treatment at an anxiety clinic had a diagnosis of social anxiety disorder. These two figures are remarkably consistent and indicate that almost one in five children presenting to specialty anxiety clinics have severe social fears.

To some degree, even the prevalence rates among adults are dependent on the decision-making rules invoked by the investigators. For example, in one telephone survey, 22.6% of adult respondents endorsed the presence of irrational social fears (Pollard & Henderson, 1988). When diagnostic criteria were strictly applied, however, the prevalence rate dropped to 2.0%. Surveying 500 Canadian adults (M. B. Stein, Walker, & Forde, 1994), 33.0% reported feeling much more nervous than other people in one of seven social situations. Yet when functional impairment or marked distress criterion was imposed, the prevalence rate dropped to 7.1%.

Among adults, the Epidemiological Catchment Area survey (ECA) provided one of the largest epidemiological samples for the study of psychopathology in the United States. On the basis of data from several sites and the use of a structured interview schedule, the lifetime prevalence rate for social anxiety disorder (using *Diagnostic and Statistical Manual of Mental Disorders, Third Edition* [*DSM–III*] criteria) was 2.4% (Schneier, Johnson, Hornig, Liebowitz, & Weissman, 1992). This figure is consistent with international studies of lifetime prevalence rates in which the same diagnostic interview instrument was used. Prevalence rates were 0.99% in Italy, 1.6% in Puerto Rico, 1.7% in Canada, and 3.0% in New Zealand. Rates appear to be much lower in Asian countries, ranging from 0.5% in South Korea to 0.6% in Taiwan (Chapman, Mannuzza, & Fyer, 1995). It is unclear why the rates are lower in East Asian countries, but these authors discussed several possibilities. First, inconsistencies in translation, cultural differences in willingness to admit the presence of fears, or issues of cultural relevance may have limited symptom acknowledgment (i.e., the specific situations assessed may have been more culturally relevant for American or English-speaking populations). Second, as the authors noted, the assessment did not address the existence of *taijin kyofu-sho* (discussed later in this chapter). This condition, perhaps a variant of social anxiety disorder, is common in several East Asian countries. Because it was not assessed, existing prevalence rates of social anxiety disorder in Asian countries may have underestimated the true rate of social fears and anxieties existing in that population.

Those who developed the diagnostic interview used in the ECA study noted that among its limitations was that it sampled only a restricted number of potentially fearful situations (Chapman et al., 1995). This may have occurred because at the time of its construction, social anxiety disorder was understudied, and the extent and severity of this condition was unknown. As a result, there is some suspicion that the 2.4% U.S. prevalence rate was an underestimate. In fact, a later study in the United States (the National Comorbidity Study [NCS], using *DSM–III–R* criteria) reported a 12.9% lifetime prevalence rate and a 6.8% 12-month prevalence rate (Kessler et al., 2005). The NCS differed from the earlier ECA survey in several respects. The NCS used a national probability sample, updated diagnostic criteria, and a different diagnostic instrument; thus, variations between the two studies might account for the differences. In fact, follow-up validity checks on the study and prevalence rates reported from countries other than the United States using either *DSM–III–R* or *DSM–IV* criteria (Furmark et al., 1999; Lecrubier et al., 2000; Lepine & Lellouch, 1995; M. B. Stein et al., 1994; Wacker, Mullejans, Klein, & Battegay, 1992) suggest that the higher figures are an accurate estimate. Furthermore, the lifetime prevalence of generalized anxiety disorder appears to have increased in recent years (Heimberg, Stein, Hiripi, & Kessler, 2000). Compared with an odds ratio of 1.0 for social phobia among participants born from 1936 through 1945, the odds ratio increased to 1.9 by the period of 1966 to 1975, and this increase was more pronounced among participants who were Caucasian, educated, and married. It is interesting to note that there was no increase in the rate of social phobia when it was restricted to those who endorsed only phobia related to public speaking (e.g., the specific subtype). On the basis of all these data, it seems clear that social anxiety disorder is a highly prevalent condition. In addition, on the basis of NCS data, it is the most common of the anxiety disorders and the third most common psychiatric disorder in the United States.

GENDER

Among children, girls are generally more likely to report the presence of fears than are boys. Using a sample of children recruited through a public school district, approximately 70% of those with a diagnosis of social anxiety disorder were girls (Beidel & Turner, 1992b). Among clinical populations, however, the gender distribution is more equal; 44% of one treatment-seeking sample of children were girls (Last et al., 1992). Among adults, the gender ratio from epidemiological populations was reported as 3:2 women to men in several studies (Kessler et al., 2005; Mannuzza, Fyer, Liebowitz, & Klein, 1990; Pollard & Henderson, 1988). As with children, the ratio of male to female adult patients seeking treatment is reported to be equal (e.g., Turner & Beidel, 1989).

RACIAL AND ETHNIC FACTORS

Earlier in this chapter, we noted the cross-cultural prevalence of adults with social anxiety disorder as assessed by one particular diagnostic interview. There are, however, relatively few data examining the prevalence of social anxiety disorder by various racial and ethnic groups. Among our sample of adults seeking treatment for social anxiety disorder, 52% were Caucasian, 25% African American, 11% Asian, 5% Latino/ Latina, and 2% other or biracial (Turner & Beidel, 2002). Among our clinic sample of children and adolescents, 64% were Caucasian, 20% African American, 7% Latino/Latina, 5% Asian, and 3.2% other or biracial (Rao et al., 2006). Strauss and Last (1993) reported that 86% of their sample was European American. The differences among samples, at least in part, likely reflect the racial makeup of the communities where these clinics are located. The differences also suggest that the prevalence of social anxiety disorder among these groups mimics the racial composition of the general population. Similarly, although no specific figures were given, social anxiety disorder was about equal among Caucasian and African American adults in the NCS study (Kessler et al., 2005). Among European American and Latino/Latina children seeking treatment at an anxiety clinic, social anxiety disorder was present in 15.2% of the Latino/Latina children and 9.8% of the European American children, a difference that was not statistically significant (Ginsburg & Silverman, 1996).

Although the primary symptomatic picture across racial and ethnic groups appears to be the same (Bassiony, 2005; Dinnel, Kleinknecht, & Tanaka-Matsumi, 2002; Gökalp et al., 2001; Merikangas & Angst, 1995), racial factors can play an important role in the maintenance and treatment of these conditions, particularly when the patient represents a minority group. In chapter 8, we illustrate how lack of careful attention to the presence of racial factors that were part of an African American woman's core fear did not allow for a complete understanding of the patient's disorder (Fink, Turner, & Beidel, 1996). Refining the case conceptualization to include attention to these cues made a substantial improvement in the efficacy of the intervention.

In addition to differences in clinical symptomatology, social skills often are dictated by cultural norms. For example, pause time in a conversation is longer among Native Americans than among European American dyads (Renfry, 1992). Similarly, downcast eyes are an appropriate sign of respect among Native Americans rather than an indication of unassertiveness. Furthermore, silence may be a form of communication. Clinicians must take such differences into account when assessing the presence of social anxiety in various ethnic and racial groups.

A study of Japanese children (Ihenaga et al., 1996) found that a substantial number had social fears. Fear of eye-to-eye contact was present in 40% to 50% of children between the ages of 10 and 17 (the specific percentage varied slightly by age and gender). Similarly, fear of flushing (blushing) was common among 20% to 40% of these children. In addition to the substantial prevalence, the phrasing of the terms used to describe these fears suggests that questions typically used in Western diagnostic interviews (e.g., "fear of speaking" or "fears of social interaction") may not detect the presence of relevant social fears in some ethnic groups. Thus, knowledge of the verbal expressions used by a particular culture is necessary for a valid assessment.

Perhaps best exemplifying the culture-specific nature of some forms of social anxiety disorder is *taijin kyofu-sho,* commonly found in East Asian countries. First reported in Japan, the syndrome is also common in Korea and possibly other Asian countries (Chapman et al., 1995). Taijin kyofu-sho is a fear of causing offense or embarrassment to others. As noted, these concerns, occurring most frequently in young men, appear to be unique to East Asians, and may reflect a cultural emphasis on politeness. An investigation examining symptoms of social anxiety disorder, taijin kyofu-sho, and independence–interdependence revealed that students from the United States and Japan had equivalent scores on a self-report measure of social anxiety disorder, whereas Japanese students scored higher on a measure of taijin kyofu-sho (Dinnel et al., 2002). The results indicated that social anxiety disorder symptoms appeared to be general across cultures, but taijin kyofu-sho was specific to the Japanese culture, thereby reinforcing the need to rephrase traditional assessments of social anxiety disorder to include an assessment of this important variant for patients from Asian cultures.

SOCIOECONOMIC STATUS

Schneier, Johnson, et al. (1992) was the first to report an inverse correlation between social anxiety disorder and several socioeconomic variables. Specifically, the highest rates of social anxiety disorder were found among those with the lowest socioeconomic status and the lowest level of education. As noted by Rapee (1995), there may be multiple reasons for these findings. First, individuals with social anxiety disorder sometimes select specific careers, decide whether to attend college, or decide which college to attend on the basis of their fears. Patients seeking treatment at our clinic often recount personal histories of social fears dictating decisions not to attend college (thereby limiting career options) or specifically selecting a career that minimizes interpersonal contact (thereby eliminating most managerial or administrative positions). Second, impairment in social and occupational functioning as a result of social anxiety disorder may result in job or promotion loss or in demotion. Similarly, because most administrative positions involve some level of interpersonal contact, individuals with limited social skills and substantial social fears may be passed over for promotion or may turn down promotional opportunities. One of our patients refused the vice presidency of a corporation (as well as a substantial pay raise) because of the severity of social fears. Lawyers with social anxiety disorder, for example, will work as law clerks rather than as practicing attorneys as a way to minimize their social distress. Using a community epidemiological sample, it may be that social anxiety disorder is more prevalent among lower socioeconomic groups. On the basis of those seeking treatment in our specialty clinic, however, individuals with social anxiety disorder exist across all socioeconomic strata.

CONCLUSION

It is clear that social anxiety disorder is a prevalent disorder among children, adolescents, and adults. On the basis of an epidemiological sample, the first onset of public speaking fear occurs during adolescence, and the risk for the onset of this specific subtype of social anxiety disorder becomes low after age 20 (Heimberg et al., 2000). In contrast, for generalized social anxiety disorder, onset rise begins before age 10 and continues to rise steeply through the mid-20s. After that time, the onset rise continues but at a lesser rate. Thus, these data provide further confirmation that generalized social anxiety disorder has an early age of onset. It appears, however, that it can occur across a broad age range, unlike public speaking fears that tend to have an onset during the teens and early 20s.

As noted at the beginning of this chapter, social anxiety disorder exists across both genders and within various racial and ethnic groups. Different cultural norms or forms of expression may affect the specific manner of clinical presentation. Therefore, clinicians must be aware of and sensitive to cultural nuances that could influence the determination of a diagnosis and the success of treatment outcome.

4

Etiology of Social
Anxiety Disorder

*I played big-time college football. I was used to getting out in front of 100,000
people every Saturday. I never got nervous about the crowds. I gave speeches at
football banquets and I did well. Then, one day, my note cards got mixed up. I
couldn't get them straight, and I couldn't find my place in the speech. The silence was deafening, and I was horribly embarrassed. Now I cannot even make
a presentation in front of the five-member school board, let alone a crowd.*

—An adult patient with social anxiety disorder

*I was always shy. I came from a big family and never needed to seek out
friends. My siblings were my friends. Now I see my daughter is just like I was.
Did I do something to cause this?*

—Parent of a child with social anxiety disorder

Professionals and laypersons alike typically think of the causes of
emotional disorders, including social anxiety disorder, in unidimensional terms, favoring either a biological or psychological explanation.

However, in all likelihood, most disorders are due to both biological and psychological factors. Over the past 15 years, there has been a resurgence in emphasis on biological models to explain most of the major psychiatric disorders, including the anxiety disorders. In this chapter, we review empirical research related to major biological and psychological explanations for social anxiety disorder. Specifically, we consider evidence for a genetic hypothesis, and we examine evidence related to direct conditioning, observational learning, and information transfer. Also, we devote some attention to the issue of predispositional factors and discuss what we believe to be an integrated perspective on the genesis of social anxiety disorder.

PSYCHOLOGICAL FACTORS

Direct Conditioning

Considerable behavioral literature attests to the fact that fear behavior is often the result of negative emotional or traumatic experiences (e.g., Watson & Rayner, 1920). Perhaps one of the more striking illustrations of the effects of trauma on human emotional behavior is revealed through studies of posttraumatic stress disorder (PTSD). In fact, although not yet fully exploited, paradigms centered on PTSD have the potential to provide unique insight into the development of fear in humans. During clinical interviews, many of those with social anxiety disorder report a past traumatic event that is associated with the onset of their disorder. Sometimes even when problems with socialization and performance existed before the specific event, patients attribute much to the traumatic episode in terms of responsibility for their current condition (i.e., the event exacerbated their fears). The opening case description illustrates the potency of traumatic events. Here are some additional recollections that patients with social anxiety disorder reported as being responsible for their social fears:

> Gretchen was in her seventh-grade English class and had to give a
> speech. The other students counted the number of times she said

"uh" during a class presentation and later made fun of her. Since that time, she has had debilitating performance anxiety. Monica had to sing a solo of "Rudolph the Red Nosed Reindeer" during the school Christmas concert. Instead of singing "Then one foggy Christmas Eve," she sang "Then one froggy Christmas Eve," and the audience laughed. Since then, she has been afraid that she would embarrass herself again in public.

A number of formal studies (discussed in this chapter) corroborate the importance of events such as those in these clinical vignettes.

In a survey designed to examine the acquisition of fear and anxiety, 58% of those with social anxiety disorder attributed its onset to the occurrence of a traumatic event (Öst, 1985). When the prevalence of traumatic conditioning experiences in patients with social anxiety disorder is compared with those of control participants with no disorders, 44% of those with social anxiety disorder recalled a conditioning experience that marked the onset or clear exacerbation of social fears (Stemberger, Turner, Beidel, & Calhoun, 1995). It is interesting to note that 20% of the participants also reported episodes meeting criteria for a traumatic conditioning experience, yet they did not develop social anxiety disorder. When examined by subtype, 56% of those with the specific subtype identified a traumatic conditioning experience, compared with 40% of those with the generalized subtype. When rates were compared across groups, however, only the rate for the specific subtype was significantly higher than for the normal control group. The data suggest that traumatic conditioning experiences may be more common in the etiology of the specific subtype of social anxiety disorder, a finding consistent with the "fear" versus "anxiety" subtype distinction that we proposed in chapter 1. However, a sizable portion of those in each group did not report experiencing a traumatic event, and a number of control participants experienced traumatic episodes but did not develop social anxiety disorder or any other anxiety disorder. It is unclear why some control participants who had experienced traumatic social events did not develop social anxiety disorder. One hypothesis is that some individuals are more prone to develop anxiety and fear than others. That is, when those with a heightened tendency to become anxious experience a traumatic event, perhaps as a function of their biological or psychological makeup, anxiety or social anxiety disorder results (see the section on genetic and biological etiology in this chapter).

Although this issue remains unclear, we do know that the process of conditioning is a complex phenomenon. For example, conditioning experiences do not occur in a vacuum but are associated with a multitude of contextual variables (Mineka & Zinbarg, 1995). Also, conditioning need not occur as a result of a single extremely traumatic event. In many cases, conditioning is cumulative (e.g., Mineka & Zinbarg, 1991, 1995). That is, rather than a single traumatic event, a series of smaller conditioning events may combine to produce a fear response at some point in time. For example, in the studies reported in the previous paragraph, some participants were unable to recall specific conditioning experiences. In such cases, small conditioning episodes may have accumulated over an extended period of time, resulting in a conditioned fear response through the process of cumulative conditioning. Also, cumulative conditioning could serve to "prime" an individual to develop a fear response. In this scenario, the results of cumulative conditioning place one in a high vulnerability state such that a traumatic event triggers the onset of a fear response.

Observational Learning

Although the potent effects of observational learning and the variables affecting such learning were eloquently demonstrated several decades ago by the work of Bandura and others (cf. Bandura, 1969), experiments by Mineka and her colleagues clearly demonstrate observational learning of fear responses in nonhuman primates. Mineka and Cook's important studies (Cook & Mineka, 1991; Mineka, 1987; Mineka & Cook, 1988) on the vicarious acquisition of snake fear in laboratory-bred rhesus monkeys provide some of the strongest evidence to date for vicarious (observational) learning of fear. Laboratory monkeys, who initially did not show any fear of snakes, observed wild-born monkeys behaving fearfully in the presence of snakes. After only 4 to 8 minutes of observation, the laboratory monkeys acquired a fear of snakes. It is interesting to note that the monkeys not only acquired the specific avoidance behavior but also behaved in a manner suggesting that they acquired also the emotional aspect of fear. To date, there have been no direct studies of observational learning as a mode of acquisition for social anxiety disorder, although retrospective reports indicate that 3% of those with social anxiety disorder identified vicarious learning as instrumental in the onset of their disorder (Öst & Hughdahl, 1981). Thus, the observation of another undergoing a traumatic social experience could lead to the emergence of social fear in the observer. Many individuals with social anxiety disorder have parents or other close relatives who have social anxiety disorder (see the sections on genetic and family studies in this chapter), and one could speculate that observational learning as well as genetics might contribute to the greater prevalence of social anxiety disorder among their relatives. In this chapter's section on predispositional factors, evidence for the role of parents in the onset of the disorder is discussed.

Information Transfer

The least studied form of learning with respect to the acquisition of fear in general, and social fears in particular, is information transfer. However, data from our clinic on verbal and nonverbal communication from parents to children suggest that fear may be acquired by this pathway. Parents with an anxiety disorder, parents with no disorder, and both groups of children interacted in a setting that included traditional playground equipment such as a jungle gym (Turner, Beidel, Roberson-Nay, & Tervo, 2003). During a 15-minute interval, their behaviors were observed by raters unaware of the parent's group status. When behaviors of anxious parents and control parents were compared, normal control parents were much more likely to join their children on the equipment, engaging in the play activity with the child. In contrast, parents with anxiety disorders remained physically distant, looking more apprehensive and reporting higher levels of peak distress as their children played on the equipment. Although not addressed directly in this investigation, it is possible that children observe and interpret these nonverbal anxious behaviors as warnings that these play behaviors are risky (Turner, Beidel, et al., 2003). It can also be reasoned, then, that this might lead to the development of fear, although in this case the fears were not of a social nature. Although it would not be ethical to conduct studies with humans to test this hypothesis fully, some less direct evidence supports the view that fears can be acquired in this fashion.

Specific data on the acquisition of social anxiety disorder fear through information transfer are sparse, but it appears that 3% of those with social anxiety disorder reported that they acquired their fear in this manner (Öst, 1985). Furthermore, although not a direct test of information transfer, Bruch, Heimberg, and their colleagues (Bruch & Heimberg, 1994; Bruch, Heimberg, Berger, & Collins, 1989) assessed the role of family sociability, concern about the opinions of others, isolation of the child, and emphasis on shame in generalized and nongeneralized (specific) subtypes of social anxiety disorder. Compared with control participants who had no disorders, patients with both types of social anxiety disorder reported significantly greater parental concern with the opinions of others and greater parental use of shame as a disciplinary procedure. Those with the generalized subtype, compared with those with the nongeneralized subtype and normal control participants, reported greater isolation and less family socializing. Despite some group differences, these data clearly do not allow one to determine how these factors might have been expressed in these families. Nevertheless, in light of the data on anxious parents and their children presented earlier (Turner, Beidel, et al., 2003), it is tempting to speculate that parents, either verbally or nonverbally, may model socially fearful and avoidant behavior by being socially timid and withdrawn. Similarly, parents' expressions of concern about the opinions of others or instructions that certain situations may be embarrassing, fear producing, or socially dangerous could also provide opportunities for learning to be afraid through information transfer.

GENETIC AND BIOLOGICAL FACTORS

Twin Studies

One of the strongest designs to examine genetic influence on etiology is through the study of twins. Although there are relatively few twin studies of social anxiety disorder, two studies provide some insight into possible genetic factors. Monozygotic (MZ), or identical, twins share identical genetic makeup, whereas dizygotic (DZ), or fraternal, twins share no more genetic similarity than regular siblings. Therefore, if social anxiety disorder more commonly occurs in MZ twins, compared with DZ twins, this higher rate of occurrence (i.e., concordance rate) would be evidence of a genetic contribution. Two studies did not find a higher concordance rate for social anxiety disorder among MZ twins compared with DZ twins (Skre, Onstad, Torgersen, Lygren, & Kringlen, 1993; Torgersen, 1983). In this latter investigation, concordance rates for social anxiety disorder were high for both MZ and DZ twins (50% and 57%, respectively). In both studies, however, the sample of twins for any particular disorder was small, and the results must be interpreted cautiously.

In contrast, using a large sample of twins, Kendler and colleagues (Kendler, Neale, Kessler, Heath, & Eaves, 1992) found a concordance rate for social anxiety disorder of 24.4% for MZ twins compared with 15% for DZ twins. The heritability estimate was approximately 30%, however, and statistical models determined that environmental factors were also important in determining the presence of social anxiety disorder. Thus, data from twin studies at this point are inconclusive, and to date no specific gene or genetic combination has been identified (Elizabeth, King, & Ollendick, 2004; Merikangas, Lieb, Wittchen, & Avenevoli, 2003). Data do suggest, however, that there likely is a genetic component in at least some cases.

Family Studies

Another method of studying the role of genetics is to examine the clustering of disorders within families. Overall, these studies support the notion that anxiety disorders run in families (e.g., Beidel & Turner, 1997; Noyes et al., 1986; Turner, Beidel, & Costello, 1987; Weissman, Leckman, Merikangas, Gammon, & Prusoff, 1984); individuals with anxiety disorders are more likely than nonpsychiatric control participants to have relatives with an anxiety disorder, although not necessarily the same disorder.

When restricted specifically to probands with social anxiety disorder, there were higher rates of social anxiety disorder among first-degree relatives (6.6%) than there were among first-degree relatives of patients with panic disorder (2.2%) or normal control participants (0.2%; Reich & Yates, 1988a). When first-degree relatives were interviewed directly (i.e., the family method was used), and the clinician was unaware of the patient's diagnosis (Fyer, Mannuzza, Chapman, Liebowitz, & Klein, 1993), 16% of relatives of patients with social anxiety disorder also met criteria for this disorder compared with 5% of relatives of participants with no psychiatric disorders, a difference that was statistically significant. When examined by subtype (Mannuzza et al., 1995), 16% of first-degree relatives of patients with the generalized subtype also met criteria for social anxiety disorder, a rate significantly higher than for the specific (nongeneralized) subtype (6%). Similarly, first-degree relatives of patients with generalized social anxiety disorder were 10 times more likely to have generalized social anxiety disorder than those with no disorder (M. B. Stein, Chartier, et al., 1998). In contrast, there was no between-group difference in the rates of specific social anxiety disorder among first-degree relatives. Compared with those with no disorder, relatives of probands with social anxiety disorder with or without avoidant personality disorder (APD) had a two- to threefold increase in risk for both social anxiety disorder and avoidant personality disorder (Tillfors, Furmark, Ekselius, & Fredrikson, 2001).

Finally, the Yale Family Study reported a significant association between social anxiety disorder in probands and their relatives (Merikangas et al., 2003) and a nonsignificant association between social anxiety disorder in probands and panic disorder in relatives, suggesting that factors leading to social anxiety disorder are different from those that lead to panic disorder.

Each study used all available first-degree relatives. Other investigators have examined rates of psychopathology in the offspring of parents with social anxiety disorder (Mancini, Van Ameringen, Szatmari, Fugere, & Boyle, 1996). Although this was an uncontrolled trial and raters were not blinded to parent diagnosis, the results indicated that 49% of the offspring had at least one anxiety disorder, most commonly overanxious disorder (30%), social anxiety disorder (23%), and separation anxiety disorder (19%). The rates were much lower in a controlled investigation, however, in which 9.6% of offspring of parents with social anxiety disorder also had the disorder, compared with a 2.1% prevalence rate among the offspring of parents with no psychiatric disorder (Lieb et al., 2000). This difference was statistically significant. Overall, however, the results of both twin and family studies support the contention that anxiety disorders, including social anxiety disorder, are familial and that genetics likely play a role in at least some cases.

Neuroendocrine System

Although much of the literature regarding the endocrine system is conflictual and, in part, may depend on the particular assessment paradigm, one review (Moutier & Stein, 2001) concluded that social anxiety disorder was not associated with basic abnormalities of the hypothalamic–pituitary–adrenal axis or the hypothalamic–pituitary–thyroid axis. When engaged in mental stressor tasks (mental arithmetic or memory tasks performed in front of an audience), however, patients with social anxiety disorder had a significantly greater change in cortisol response (delta max cortisol response) than those with no disorder (Condren, O'Neill, Ryan, Barrett, & Thakore, 2002). As indicated, one important issue may be the type of challenge that is used to determine reactivity. As noted subsequently, naturalistic challenges may be more appropriate than pharmacological challenges for social anxiety disorder (Argyropoulos, Bell, & Nutt, 2001), and this factor may be important in interpreting the findings from all of the biological investigations.

Neurotransmitter Functioning Via Pharmacologic or Naturalistic Challenges

In many instances, data on the reactivity of patients with social anxiety disorder to various pharmacological challenges come from studies in which those with social anxiety disorder serve as a psychiatric control group for studies of panic disorder. There is little evidence of reactivity in patients with social anxiety disorder when pharmacological challenges consist of lactate, CO_2, caffeine, adrenaline, cholecystokinin, and flunazenil (Bell, Malizia, & Nutt, 1999). In contrast, fenfluramine challenges suggest that those with social anxiety disorder may have hypersensitive postsynaptic 5-HT receptors (Tancer, 1993; Tancer et al., 1994–1995), and one study suggests that generalized social anxiety disorder may be associated with low dopamine system activity (Schneier et al., 2000). The data from these studies must be regarded as preliminary; in some instances, the reactivity may not be specific to patients with social anxiety disorder (e.g., low D_2 receptor binding potential in the striatum is also found in those with substance abuse; Schneier et al., 2000). Thus, further investigation is necessary.

In contrast, naturalistic challenges appear more relevant for an examination of neurobiological and psychophysiological reactivity in patients with social anxiety disorder (Argyropoulos et al., 2001). Early challenges used public speaking tasks (Heimberg, Hope, et al., 1990; Hofman, Newman, Ehlers, & Roth, 1995; Levin, Saoud, Strauman, & Gorman, 1993), and those with the specific subtype had significantly higher heart rate reactivity compared with control participants. Those with generalized social anxiety disorder did not differ from either group. This is one of the few areas in which those with the specific subtype have more severe symptomatology compared with their generalized counterparts (see chap. 1 for an examination of these differences). As we noted in chapter 1, the specific subtype might represent a "true" phobia, whereas the generalized subtype might be an example of a broader anxiety state or perhaps a variant of avoidant personality disorder.

Neuroimaging Studies

New strategies by which to study brain structure and function provide exciting possibilities for understanding the neurobiological basis of social anxiety disorder. A review concluded that there is not enough evidence to support the existence of structural abnormalities in social anxiety disorder (Argyropoulos et al., 2001). Nevertheless, studies using new technologies such as positron emission tomography (PET) scans and functional magnetic resonance imaging (fMRI) suggest that certain areas of the brain may become activated when those with social anxiety disorder are exposed to fear-relevant stimuli. For example, when exposed to a series of faces, neutral expressions elicited amygdala activation (suggestive of a fear response) in those with social anxiety disorder but not in normal control study participants (Birbaumer et al., 1998). Despite these group differences in reactivity, it is interesting that there were no group differences in patients' subjective ratings of anxiety. Similarly, when presented with novel (but not familiar faces), adults previously classified in their second year of life as behaviorally inhibited had significantly greater responses in both right and left amygdalar regions than their uninhibited counterparts (Schwartz, Wright, Shin, Kagan, & Rauch, 2003), and the effect remained even when two participants with social anxiety disorder were excluded. Greater left-sided amygdalar activation also occurred in those with generalized social anxiety disorder (compared with normal control study participants) when both groups viewed angry or contemptuous faces (M. B. Stein, Goldin, Sareen, Eyler-Zorrilla, & Brown, 2002). Using an even more naturalistic situation, PET scans revealed that normal control participants responded to a public speaking task with increased regional cerebral blood flow (rCBF) in cortical regions of the brain, whereas those with social anxiety disorder responded with increased rCBF in subcortical regions such as the amygdalar complex (Tillfors et al., 2001). M. B. Stein et al. (2002) appropriately cautioned, however, that both neuroanatomical and functional complexity do not allow for the simplistic conclusion that there is abnormal amygdalar functioning in those with social anxiety disorder. Furthermore, inasmuch as the studies to date have not included a psychiatric control group, it is possible that enhanced amygdala responding may exist in various disorders and not be specific to social anxiety disorder. In summary, these investigations suggest that increased amygdalar activation occurs in those with social anxiety disorder under challenge conditions, but more studies are needed to determine whether any of these responses are specific to social anxiety disorder or even to other anxiety disorders.

PREDISPOSITIONAL INFLUENCES AND MAINTAINING FACTORS

As illustrated by the findings just described, it is well established that anxiety disorders are familial, although it is unclear whether genetic or family environment variables exert primary influence or whether they interact in some fashion to produce social anxiety disorder. Many theorists long considered emotional disorders to result from a diathesis of biological and environmental factors (e.g., Akiskal, 1985). Social anxiety disorder might develop through observational learning, direct conditioning, or information transfer, and vulnerability factors may predispose those who develop the disorder through these mechanisms. Thus, just because the onset of social anxiety disorder may be attributed to one of the proposed psychological pathways, biological factors may still be involved. Furthermore, it is possible that different factors are responsible for the onset of the disorder in different individuals (i.e., there could be multiple pathways to the disorder). It is evident that the precise etiology of social anxiety disorder remains difficult to unravel. In the next section, we discuss additional factors, culled primarily from the developmental and social psychology literatures, which may predispose someone to the development of social anxiety disorder. In addition, these factors also may play a role in the maintenance of the disorder, once onset occurs. Because most of these studies were conducted on those who already have the disorder, or who have designations such as shy or socially isolated (rather than socially phobic), it is not possible to determine whether these factors actually are etiological in nature. Therefore, we use the terms *predispositional* and *maintenance* factors.

Family Environment Factors

We explored the idea that higher rates of social anxiety disorder in families of individuals with this disorder may represent a genetic contribution to the etiology of this disorder. In this section, we discuss other familial factors that may be influential. Within the developmental literature, there is strong evidence for the relation between parental behaviors and children's social competence (e.g., Ladd & Goiter, 1988; Parke & Bhavnagri, 1989; Radke-Yarrow & Zahn-Waxler, 1986). For example, there is much support for the relation between style of infant–parent attachment and the child's subsequent social relationships with peers (Putallaz & Heflin, 1990). Specifically, secure attachments are predictive of children who easily join social groups and establish healthy peer relationships. Other studies have found that maternal warmth and engagement are also positively related to children's prosocial engagement with other children (Attili, 1989; Hinde & Tamplin, 1983).

In addition to the influence of their own personality characteristics, other parental behaviors can affect a child's social behavior. Parents arrange many of the opportunities for social interaction among young children. In some cases (see the section on behavioral inhibition that follows), parents who recognize their child's social reticence deliberately arrange for social encounters in an effort to decrease social inhibition. If social inhibition runs in families (as it seems to), however, mothers who are shy or socially phobic may avoid exposing their socially inhibited children to social situations (to minimize the parent's own social distress), thereby increasing the likelihood of perpetuating a fear cycle (Daniels & Plomin, 1985). For example,

> Annie and her 11-year-old daughter Alicia were extremely shy. Annie reported that although she recognized Alicia's shyness and knew she should do something about it, she was unable to do so because of the extent of her own social fears. In fact, when Annie and Alicia came in for the interview, they were accompanied by another relative who answered most of the interviewer's questions because Annie was too distressed by the social nature of the interview to do so.

These parental behaviors can affect a child in at least three ways. First, parents may pass on an *anxious predisposition* (the genetic component). Second, parents may restrict or prevent the child's ability to engage in social situations, thereby possibly setting up a pattern of social isolation and social avoidance. Finally, parents may pass on their fears and anxieties to their children through modeling (observation learning) or information transfer.

Early studies highlighted the role of parental behavior in perpetuating children's social inhibition. For example, mothers of peer-neglected children were less likely to facilitate their child's entry into the group (Finnie & Russell, 1988). Fathers of peer-neglected boys engaged in less affectively rough-housing play (i.e., physical rough-and-tumble play) than fathers of popular or peer-rejected boys (MacDonald, 1987), and children reported a more restrictive family environment compared with nonphobic control children (Messer & Beidel, 1994).

Parental characteristics of overprotection and rejection are also associated with children, adolescents, and young adults with social anxiety disorder (Bögels, van Oosten, Muris, & Smulders, 2001; Caster, Inderbitzen, & Hope, 1999; Lieb et al., 2000). Among children in grades 7 through 11, high levels of social anxiety were associated with perceptions of parents as restricting children's social interactions; being more socially isolative; and having greater concern about others' opinions, the child's social anxiety, and poor performance (Caster et al., 1999). These self-report data are bolstered by two behavioral observation studies in which controlling behaviors of the father (Greco & Morris, 2002) and negative feedback by both parents (Hummel & Gross, 2001) were more common behaviors among parents of children with social anxiety disorder. Because the children already had an anxiety disorder, one cannot assume that the parental personality factors and restrictive family environment precipitated the disorder in these children. Nevertheless, the consistency of these data with the others reported earlier in the chapter (and to be discussed later) suggests that these influences may function to help maintain the disorder.

Dadds, Barrett, and their colleagues directly examined the role of parental influence in children with anxiety disorders. Although not solely limited to children with social anxiety disorder, those with this disorder (as well as those with overanxious disorder) were included in the sample. The results indicated that parents of anxious children often reinforce anxious avoidance and discourage courageous behavior (Dadds, Barrett, Rapee, & Ryan, 1996). In this paradigm, an ambiguous situation is presented (e.g., you see a group of children playing one of your favorite games) and children describe what they would do. After providing responses, the situation is presented again with the parents present, and the family discusses potential responses. Compared with parents of children without any disorder, parents of anxious children discouraged their children's attempts to behave courageously and instead reinforced avoidance strategies. Again, because these children already had an anxiety disorder, it is impossible to determine whether the parent behaviors preceded or followed the onset of the child's disorder. Surely parents would want to protect their anxious child from experiencing distress and anxiety, but protective behavior on the part of the parent can keep children from approaching situations that they fear, and exposure is the critical element in the treatment of the disorder (Turner, Cooley-Quille, & Beidel, 1995). If these parental behaviors preceded the child's disorder, they indeed may have been contributory. Even if they are the result of the child's disorder, however, they still may be problematic because they can function to help maintain the disorder or interfere with the child's treatment program (Dadds et al., 1996; Silverman & Kurtines, 1996; see chap. 6, this volume).

Peer Relationships and Loneliness

Developmental psychologists and developmental psychopathologists assess peer relationships through the use of sociometric ratings, whereby groups of children (usually classroom groups) nominate other children with whom they enjoy playing or having as friends. They also identify children with whom they do not like to play or would not want as friends. The procedure can be controversial. Some laypeople feel that the harm in labeling children as popular or not popular outweighs the importance of the research questions. Nevertheless, sociometric ratings can provide important data for understanding the relation of children's psychopathology to peer popularity. In general, as we noted in chapter 2, children without psychopathology are usually average or popular children. Those with externalizing disorders (conduct disorder, attention-deficit/hyperactivity disorder) are usually rejected by peers. Finally, children with internalizing disorders (e.g., anxiety disorders) usually are neglected. In other words, they are not actively liked or disliked but simply ignored. Young children who attempt to initiate social interaction and are neglected (or rejected) by peers may experience social failure, which exacerbates existing tendencies for social isolation (Asendorpf, 1990b).

Social anxiety is significantly higher in peer-neglected children than it is in popular children (e.g., LaGreca, Dandes, Wick, Shaw, & Stone, 1988). Conversely, children with an anxiety disorder were more likely to be peer-neglected than both psychiatric and nonpsychiatric control participants (Strauss, Lahey, Frick, Frame, & Hynd, 1988), and a 5-year longitudinal investigation (Morris, 2004) indicated a significant relation between peer-neglect status in grade 1 and self-report of anxiety in grade 5, corroborating retrospective reports of shy adults indicating that unpleasant experiences with peers may contribute to the development of shyness (Ishiyama, 1984). Although the retrospective nature of these data means that they must be interpreted cautiously, the reports are consistent with the findings from socially anxious children and suggest that negative early peer relationships are associated with social anxiety.

Cognitive Development

As noted in chapters 1 and 2, social anxiety disorder is characterized by the fear that one's behavior may result in humiliation or embarrassment. Embedded in this definition is the idea that children must be able to take on the perspective of another person; that is, for children to be socially fearful, they must be able to take the perspective of another person. There does appear to be a developmental trajectory for this ability (Darby & Schlenker, 1986). Children in second grade can recognize signs of worry, uneasiness, and lack of confidence in others and expect less socially competent children to fidget, act clumsy, avoid making eye contact or smiling, and to communicate less. By fourth grade, children can associate social anxiety with high motivation to make a positive impression, and this ability is even more enhanced by ninth grade. These data clearly indicate that an understanding of the experience of anxiety occurs at an early age and the ability to recognize these fears increases with development.

Temperament (Behavioral Inhibition)

One early-developing predisposition that appears most strongly linked to shyness and social unease, and ultimately social anxiety disorder, is the temperamental variable of behavioral inhibition (BI). Perhaps the most researched sample of children with this characteristic is the Harvard cohort studied by Kagan and his colleagues. According to these authors, BI is an early-appearing behavioral characteristic that is expressed as shyness, social withdrawal and avoidance, social uneasiness, and fear of unfamiliar situations, people, objects, and events (Garcia-Coll, Kagan, & Reznick, 1984). This behavioral style is found in 10% to 20% of Caucasian children. When placed in unfamiliar or novel settings, toddlers (14–31 months) with BI cry, fret, emit distressful vocalizations or display distressful facial expressions, withdraw socially, and show an absence of initiation or interaction with the experimenter. Also, when in these challenging situations, those with BI show a characteristic physiological response of higher heart rate and minimal heart rate variability (Garcia-Coll et al., 1984). At later ages, children with BI have larger pupillary dilation during testing periods and higher salivary cortisol levels in laboratory and home environments (Reznick et al., 1986). Finally, the correlation between epinephrine activity and BI was found to be modest but statistically significant, suggesting that higher epinephrine activity was more characteristic of children with BI (Kagan, Reznick, & Snidman, 1987). From these early-appearing behaviors, a subset of these children continued to manifest this pattern during childhood and preadolescence (e.g., Reznick et al., 1986).

Other researchers have also studied BI. Like social anxiety disorder, BI appears to be a cross-cultural phenomenon. Behaviors consistent with BI have been documented in Swedish (Bromberg, 1993) and German children (Asendorpf, 1990a, 1993). Precursors to BI (high-motor, high-crying activity found in 4-month-olds; Kagan et al., 1994), however, show some differences across cultures. American children are more motorically active than Irish infants, who are in turn more motorically active than Chinese infants. Although the relation of this initial reactivity to later expressions of BI is unclear, the data suggest that this initial temperamental reactivity may be more common in American, or perhaps among Caucasian, children than in other racial and ethnic groups. For a more extensive review of the construct of behavioral inhibition and its relation to anxiety, see Turner, Beidel, and Wolff (1996).

For the purposes of this chapter, three types of BI studies are relevant: family studies assessing the presence of BI in the children of anxious parents, family studies assessing anxiety in the parents of BI children, and studies assessing psychiatric disorders in children with BI. As with any research, these investigations are not without limitations. Because a close critique of all of these studies is beyond the scope of this chapter, the reader is referred to Turner, Beidel, and Wolff (1996) for the details.

Initial studies of the relation of BI to anxiety disorders revealed that rates of BI were 85% for children of parents with panic disorder (PD) only, 70% for children with PD and major depressive disorder (MDD), 50% for MDD only, and 15% for control participants (Rosenbaum et al., 1988). Parents of children with BI were more likely than parents of children without BI to have histories of two or more anxiety disorders, a childhood history of anxiety disorders, higher risk for a current anxiety disorder (specifically social anxiety disorder), and higher risk for the childhood disorders of avoidant disorder of childhood and overanxious disorder (Rosenbaum, Biederman, Hirshfeld, Bolduc, & Chaloff, 1991). Using a larger sample (Rosenbaum et al., 1992), the prevalence of social anxiety disorder in the parents of children with BI (10%) was higher than in the parents of children without BI (0%). Although the prevalence rates were small, these data suggest a relation between BI and social anxiety disorder and are similar to the rates of first-degree relatives of probands with social anxiety disorder (reviewed in the family studies section of this chapter). Thus, if social anxiety disorder runs in families, and does so because of genetic transmission, BI may be the manifestation of the biological substrate from which social anxiety disorder could develop.

In fact, social anxiety disorder (defined as the presence of social anxiety disorder or avoidant disorder) was significantly more likely among behaviorally inhibited young children (17%) than uninhibited children (5%; Biederman, Hirshfeld-Becker, & Rosenbaum, 2001). Furthermore, childhood BI was associated with generalized social anxiety (Schwartz, Snidman, & Kagan, 1999) or social anxiety disorder (Hayward, Killen, Kraemer, & Taylor, 1998). The relation between BI and adolescent social anxiety (Schwartz et al., 1999) was stronger in girls than boys. Furthermore, the relation between BI and social anxiety appeared to be specific because there was no association between BI and specific fears, separation anxiety, or performance anxiety.

Not all children remain behaviorally inhibited throughout childhood, and stability may be an important mediating variable in determining those children who will develop anxiety disorders and those who will not. Children who consistently received inhibited ratings throughout childhood (stable inhibited) were significantly more likely to have two or more anxiety disorders, and specifically more likely to have phobic disorders, than the nonstable comparison group or an uninhibited group (Hirshfeld et al., 1992). Also, parents of these stable inhibited children were more likely to have a childhood history of two or more anxiety disorders, and specifically avoidant disorder of childhood. Thus, like the data presented previously, BI may be a possible precursor to the development of anxiety disorders, including social anxiety disorder, but BI alone does not appear sufficient for development of the disorder and, as we discuss later, neither does it appear necessary (Turner, Beidel, & Wolff, 1996).

Shyness

As we noted in chapter 1, it is unclear how shyness and social anxiety disorder are related. Not all those who are shy meet criteria for social anxiety disorder (Chavira, Stein, & Malcarne, 2002; Heiser, Turner, & Beidel, 2003), although there is much overlap in these two conditions. Somatic responses of both groups were similar (heart palpitations, sweating, trembling, and blushing), as were the type of negative cognitions (fear of negative evaluation or of doing something humiliating or embarrassing; Turner, Beidel, & Townsley, 1990). The groups differed, however, with respect to occupational and social functioning, behavioral characteristics, age of onset, and course of disorder. Those with social anxiety disorder were more likely to be occupationally and socially impaired, more likely to avoid social encounters, and had an earlier age of onset and a more chronic course. About 40% of college students describe themselves as shy, although a much lower percentage of the general population meets diagnostic criteria for social anxiety disorder (approximately 8% point prevalence). In fact, although the constructs of shyness and social anxiety disorder overlapped, there were important differences as well (Turner et al., 1990). From an etiological perspective, rates of childhood shyness among adults with either the specific or generalized subtypes of social anxiety disorder or normal control study participants indicated that 76% of those with the generalized subtype reported a history of childhood shyness, compared with 56% with the specific subtype and 52% of the normal control participants (Stemberger et al., 1995). The rate for the generalized subtype was significantly higher than for the control participants, indicating that childhood shyness may be more characteristic of those with the generalized subtype.

A separate body of literature on childhood shyness exists in the developmental literature. For example, mothers of shy children were significantly more likely to have anxiety disorders in general, and social anxiety disorder in particular, than mothers of nonshy children (Cooper & Eke, 1999). Additionally, early-appearing shyness may have implications for later psychopathology. Shy and passively isolated second graders reported high levels of depression and loneliness when they were in fifth grade (Rubin & Mills, 1988). Similarly, lower perceptions of social competence, poor peer acceptance, and social isolation in second grade predicted anxiety and depression in fifth grade (Hymel, Rubin, Rowden, & LeMare, 1990). In a 15-year follow-up study, childhood shyness increased the odds of adolescent anxiety disorders two- to threefold, and children with anxiety disorders were more likely to be rated as shy (Schmidt & Schulkin, 1999, cited in M. B. Stein, Chavira, & Jang, 2001). It is important to note, however, that the majority of shy children did not develop anxiety disorders and that many adolescents with an anxiety disorder were not shy as children, again underscoring the point that although shyness may be a contributing factor in some cases, it is neither necessary nor sufficient for the development of social anxiety disorder.

In summary, although supporting a relation between shyness and social anxiety disorder, the data are far from definitive. Rather, they illustrate the limitations of attempting to extrapolate from developmental data to the clinical condition of social anxiety disorder. *Shy* is a term used to describe a pattern of reticence associated with social situations. As we have noted, there are many reasons for social reticence. Thus, although reports of extreme shyness should alert the clinician to assess carefully for the presence of psychopathology, it cannot be used as a de facto indicator of social anxiety disorder.

Early Attachment

A 20-year prospective study examined the relation between an anxious–resistant attachment style in infancy and the presence of anxiety disorders in childhood and adolescence (Warren, Huston, Egeland, & Sroufe, 1997). Among infants who were anxiously–resistantly attached, 28% had a lifetime history of anxiety disorders compared with 13% who had a different form of attachment behavior. This represents a twofold increase in the presence of anxiety disorders, which were primarily separation anxiety disorder, overanxious disorder, or social anxiety disorder. Although not indicating a specific relation between early attachment and social anxiety disorder, it does suggest that an anxious–resistant attachment style is a risk factor for the development of anxiety disorders, including social anxiety disorder.

Social Skill

From reviews of studies of socially anxious children and adults, shy children and adults, and children who are neglected by their peers, a picture of a child who is not only socially reticent but also appears to lack the necessary social behaviors for engaging in effective interpersonal discourse emerges. How do these social skill deficits develop? Children who fit any of these descriptors seem ideal candidates for maladjustment in social functioning. Those who are shy or socially anxious tend to avoid social interactions and do not have the typical developmental learning experiences as their nonshy and non-socially anxious peers. At least for those who have social anxiety disorder, the presence of high social anxiety likely interferes even when these children attempt to engage in social interaction. Because social anxiety disorder is an early-onset disorder, a lifelong history of avoidance and social reticence develops. Social learning theorists view impairment in social functioning as the result of a lack of effective social skills, performance inhibition caused by anxiety, or a combination of both factors (Arkowitz, 1981). In the case of children with social anxiety disorder, their learning history could put them in a situation in which both of these factors apply, and the presence of both factors could lead to further withdrawal behavior, restricted peer interaction, and then further impairment in social skills and interpersonal relationships (cf. Rubin, LeMare, & Lollis, 1990; Vernberg, Abwender, Ewell, & Beery, 1992). The majority of behavioral programs designed to remediate social withdrawal have assumed that socially isolated children lack social skills. In most cases, social skills training (SST) has proved effective in increasing social interactions in children with mild to moderate levels of social withdrawal (e.g., Finch & Hops, 1982; Jupp & Griffiths, 1990; Ladd, 1981; Paine et al., 1982; Schneider & Byrne, 1987; Sheridan, Kratochwill, & Elliott, 1990; Whitehill, Hersen, & Bellack, 1980; see also chap. 9, this volume), although it is unclear whether the skills training or the exposure to group social interactions in which the skills training occurs is the active therapeutic ingredient. Nevertheless, although providing indirect confirmation, these data on skills training support the contention that skill deficiencies are an important part of the clinical picture. Similarly, among adults, it remains unresolved whether patients with social anxiety disorder are deficient in the skills necessary to engage in successful interpersonal discourse. As we noted in chapter 1, few studies have directly addressed the question of skills deficits in those with social anxiety disorder, and the results from those that have are mixed. Our study, currently under-way, should help to resolve this issue. Yet when both child and adult studies are considered, the evidence is strong that social skills deficiencies are an important part of the clinical picture for at least some individuals with this disorder.

COGNITIVE PROCESSES

Some researchers have hypothesized that those with social anxiety disor-der have a number of distorted beliefs including the following: negative social events lead to negative evaluation by others, the negative evaluation of others are true judgments of the individual's personal characteristics, and singular negative events can have long-term consequences (e.g., Wilson & Rapee, 2005). Since the publication of the first edition of this volume, there has been an increase in studies aimed at understanding cognitive processes that may be associated with social anxiety disorder. In some instances, researchers have attempted to draw etiological infer-ences on the basis of their results. Because the studies use individuals who already have the disorder, however, it is not clear that these cognitive processes preceded or even contributed to the disorder's onset. Thus, although in some instances these cognitive processes may be part of the clinical presentation, the reader is cautioned against drawing etiological conclusions at this time.

Overall, the focus of these studies has been to examine more closely the cognitive processes that may contribute to cognitive biases reported by those with social anxiety disorder. A number of studies have addressed the relation between attentional processes and social anxiety disorder. An extensive review of the literature is beyond the scope of the chapter, and the interested reviewer is referred to an excellent review by Bögels and Mansell (2004), the conclusions of which are briefly reviewed here. As these authors noted, there are data to suggest the existence of brief vigilance and prolonged avoidance of social threats among those with high social anxiety or diagnosed social anxiety disorder when paradigms high in ecological validity are used. There are, however, many contextual factors and experimental paradigms that mediate these responses. For example, those with social anxiety disorder showed enhanced vigilance to angry faces (relative to happy and neutral faces) when the presentation interval was 500 milliseconds, but the differences disappeared when the interval was lengthened to 1,250 milliseconds (Mogg, Philippot, & Bradley, 2004). Similarly, there is some evidence for the concept of heightened self-focused attention in those with social anxiety disorder, although its causal role has not been addressed (Bögels & Mansell, 2004), and the studies examining self-focused attention have methodological limitations. This review also notes that many of the deficits observed in those with social anxiety disorder are found in those with other psychological disorders as well, including depression, other anxiety disorders, alcoholism, and schizophrenia (e.g., Rinck & Becker, 2005), suggesting that these factors are characteristic of those with an emotional disorder rather than social anxiety disorder in particular (see also Coles & Heimberg, 2002; Heinrichs & Hofmann, 2001). Similarly, whereas those with social anxiety disorder alone demonstrated more negative biases regarding the interpretation of social events (compared with normal control participants), the biases were even more extreme when those with social anxiety disorder and comorbid depression were included in the analysis (Wilson & Rapee, 2005), again suggesting that the findings may be an outcome of the presence of psychopathology in general rather than social anxiety disorder in particular.

A host of studies have examined whether memory biases exist among those with social anxiety disorder. In an excellent review of this area (Coles & Heimberg, 2005), it appears that the specific assessment strategy has a significant effect on outcome (similar to the outcome of the pharmacological challenge literature). Whereas there is little support for explicit memory biases when patients with social anxiety disorder are presented with linguistic stimuli, two studies (Coles & Heimberg, 2005; Lundh & Öst, 1996) found that those with social anxiety disorder are more likely to remember previously viewed critical faces (compared with accepting faces), yet they are no more or less accurate at correctly identifying accepting or critical faces. Among children with social anxiety disorder, the data are more conflictual, with one study reporting less accurate identification of facial expressions among children with social anxiety disorder (Simonian, Beidel, Turner, Berkes, & Long, 2001) and a second reporting that such differences did not exist (Melfsen & Florin, 2002).

To summarize, the role of cognitive processes in social anxiety disorder remains unclear. Even among those who consider distorted cognitive processes to be an etiological factor, the origin of the biased perceptual processes is yet to be explained. Some have suggested that early experiences are what initially lead to cognitive biases (D. M. Clark & McManus, 2002), thereby suggesting the proper conceptualization of these processes is as a maintenance factor rather than an etiological one.

CONCLUSION

In this chapter, we discussed the various theories of how social anxiety disorder develops. Not surprisingly, there is no one unified theory, but rather data exist to support a number of different hypotheses. On the basis of the available data, we conclude that there are multiple pathways to the development of social anxiety disorder. This is not a new concept, and others have speculated that various disorders have multiple pathways, but in the case of social anxiety disorder, sufficient data exist to propose some specific hypotheses.

One possible pathway is through genetic transmission. On the basis of extant data, there is support for the position that social anxiety disorder runs in families, and this typically is interpreted as the direct genetic transmission of the disorder to the offspring. Not all individuals with social anxiety disorder have a parent or other relative who also has the disorder, however. The available evidence from the best family study to date indicates that 16% of the relatives of patients with social phobia meet diagnostic criteria for social anxiety disorder (Fyer et al., 1993). Additionally, even the concordance rate for MZ twins is only about 24% versus 15% for DZ twins. Thus, it seems clear that the majority of social anxiety disorder cases cannot be explained by genes alone. Furthermore, the results of the large Kendler et al. (1992) study revealed that nongenetic factors accounted for a significant portion of the variance, although the nature of these nongenetic factors was not discussed. Because genetic researchers have long recognized that the presence of a gene does not indicate that a disorder will develop, but rather that some type of gene × environment interaction seems to be necessary (e.g., Scarr, 1969). Therefore, as noted, it is unlikely that those with social anxiety disorder acquire their conditions solely through genetic transmission. A more reasonable hypothesis is that one acquires vulnerability through genetic inheritance and that for the disorder to develop, other factors are necessary. Others have reached similar conclusions suggesting that social anxiety disorder results from an interaction between individual vulnerability factors such as temperament, stress reactivity, learning experiences, and environmental factors (Merikangas et al., 2003). [1]

With respect to psychological theories of social anxiety disorder, we outlined three mechanisms for which there is some empirical evidence: direct conditioning, observational learning, and information transfer. It appears that direct conditioning or traumatic conditioning is the most important of these by far. Traumatic conditioning is followed in importance by observational learning and then by information transfer. Each psychological mechanism may be a viable avenue for the development of social anxiety disorder, at least in some cases. If we assume that the available data are correct, as many as 71% of those with social anxiety disorder report experiences consistent with direct conditioning or observational learning (Öst, 1987). It must be pointed out, however, that just because someone has experienced what might be considered a traumatic episode (either through direct conditioning or indirectly through observation) or has been exposed to information transfer mechanisms, the development of social anxiety disorder is not inevitable. In one study (Stemberger et al., 1995), 20% of individuals without psychiatric disorders reported histories of traumatic conditioning, and many of us can recall embarrassing social faux pas that do not result in the development of social anxiety disorder. Just as genetic transmission alone probably cannot account for the development of social anxiety disorder, conditioning, observational learning, or information transfer cannot fully explain etiology either. As might be expected, then, the precise causal factor for social anxiety disorder is difficult to pinpoint, even though we appear to have various pieces of the puzzle.

Another plausible explanation (pathway) for the etiology of social anxiety disorder is that it results from some combination of the factors discussed here. For example, those who are genetically predisposed might be more susceptible to traumatic conditioning, observational learning, or information transfer. In other words, these modes of acquisitions may be more potent in individuals with certain predispositions. To date, there are no studies to test directly the hypothesis that those who are considered more vulnerable (because of genetic inheritance) are more susceptible to direct conditioning, observational learning, or information transfer. A few data do suggest, however, that the offspring of a group of parents with various anxiety disorders are more responsive to different types of stimuli than the offspring of parents without anxiety disorders (Turner, Beidel, & Epstein, 1991; Turner, Beidel, & Roberson-Nay, 2005).

Additional factors also may predispose one to the onset of social anxiety disorder or function to help maintain the disorder after its emergence. As noted, family environment variables, including parental personality factors and behaviors and parenting skill, may combine with a biological predisposition or specific traumatic events to contribute to the onset of anxiety disorders and, in this case, to social anxiety disorder. To illustrate the powerful impact of family interaction style, Barrett, Dadds, Rapee, and Ryan (1996) demonstrated how protective parental behaviors may serve to maintain avoidance behaviors in anxious children. Also, findings with behaviorally inhibited children show that even if they initially were inhibited temperamentally, they became less so when their parents deliberately engaged them in social interactions with others. These findings suggest that parental behavior plays a significant role in the manifestation of social fears despite one's genetic makeup.

Behaviors such as social reticence, behavioral inhibition, shyness, or social isolation clearly are related to poor peer relationships and loneliness, although to date conclusions are limited by the correlational nature of the data. Nevertheless, it is likely that a vicious cycle develops. For example, children who are socially isolated have limited opportunities for interaction and thus do not acquire the social skills necessary to develop friendships. As a result, they feel lonely and isolated, which further limits their interactions with peers and further retards their skill development. As Davidson (1993) and others noted, it is those with the earliest onset of social anxiety disorder who probably have the most chronic course.

To reiterate, there is no definitive answer for how social anxiety disorder develops, yet the current clinical, social, and developmental literature all address what appear to be relevant factors likely associated with onset and maintenance. We think that in most cases, a combination of factors is present, including a biological vulnerability to become anxious. Some cases can develop through direct as well as indirect conditioning. Even here biological vulnerability could be important, however. The past decade provided further evidence toward building an etiological model, and as we noted in the first edition, we envision that the next decade will lead to further clarification of how these many factors interact to contribute to development of social anxiety disorder.

5

Assessment of Social Anxiety Disorder

My life is perfect except for this fear of giving speeches.

—Introductory statement from a patient who was determined after assessment
to have the generalized form of social anxiety disorder

The proper assessment of social anxiety disorder, as with any disorder, involves a careful and multifaceted inquiry into the presenting problem as well as the individual's overall emotional and social functioning. In this chapter, we discuss the assessment of social anxiety disorder in children and adults, review various assessment methods and procedures, discuss issues particularly relevant to the diagnosis of social anxiety disorder, and provide a number of practical suggestions for facilitating the assessment process. Finally, we highlight the methods used to explicate those specific variables that are critical to the conceptualization and treatment of social anxiety disorder in each individual (i.e., the core fear; see chaps. 8 and 9, this volume). We begin by discussing the initial interview.

THE INITIAL INTERVIEW

Several factors should be considered when interviewing someone with social anxiety disorder, whether the individual is a child, adolescent, or adult. Individuals with social anxiety disorder experience substantial anxiety during social interactions and, throughout their lives, often attempt to hide their distress. Therefore, although motivated to enter treatment, discussing their fears with a stranger can be distressful. One of the clinician's initial tasks is to create an atmosphere in which individuals with social anxiety disorder feel calm and secure discussing their fears and anxieties.

People with social anxiety disorder may be secretive about their distress for a variety of reasons. Sometimes they may be embarrassed about their inability to control what they, as well as others, believe they should be able to control. Many patients report that when they have tried to discuss their anxieties with others, they have been told, "Well, everyone feels that way when they make a speech," or "Don't worry, you'll get over it." Of course, neither of these statements is quite true. Although most people do experience some anxiety in social performance situations, as we noted in chapter 1, everyone does not have an identical physiological response during public speaking presentations (Beidel, Turner, & Dancu, 1985). Although people with and without social anxiety disorder respond with elevated blood pressure and pulse rate when starting a speech, those without the disorder quickly adjust to the situation, and their blood pressure and pulse rate return to baseline levels. This indicates that they become relatively comfortable in the setting. However, blood pressure and pulse rate of those with social anxiety disorder remain elevated throughout the task. Thus, individuals with social phobia never physiologically adjust to the setting.

The therapist's ability to communicate understanding has a particularly important effect for people with social anxiety disorder. For so many years, researchers neglected this disorder, and little information was available in the popular media about the condition or its treatment. Those with social anxiety disorder have been described as "suffering in silence." Even in the early 1990s, a number of patients who sought treatment in our clinic remarked that they "feel 50% better just knowing it [social anxiety disorder] has a name and somebody knows how to treat it." Of course, this good feeling is only temporary and in itself is not an intervention. Nevertheless, it illustrates the relief that those with social anxiety disorder experience when they finally talk to someone who understands that everyone does not feel the way they do when engaging in social interactions.

Initially, some with social anxiety disorder (primarily adults) present as only having a public speaking problem. Only about 30% of adults with social anxiety disorder who seek treatment have the specific subtype, however, and even then, it rarely involves just one particular situation. Rather, there is often distress in several related settings, although the patient may be unaware of the significance of these additional situations. It has also been our observation that some patients are committed to the idea that their problem is centered on one specific situation, usually speech anxiety or some other specific performance situation. In some cases, patients have had the disorder for so long that they have constructed their environment to provide maximum protection from threatening situations. This extensive avoidance pattern becomes their lifestyle, and they are no longer aware of the motivating factors. In other cases, personality features (e.g., obsessive–compulsive personality disorder, see chap. 1, this volume) may play a role. Those with social anxiety disorder are often perfectionistic and rigid in their thinking styles. In a number of cases, this appears to be related to the need to see the condition as a unidimensional problem. Typically, when this scenario is applicable, other factors reveal themselves as treatment progresses.

We have referred to this lack of awareness of the severely restricted lifestyle as the *social phobia cocoon* (Turner, Beidel, & Cooley, 1994). Given the disorder's chronic nature and relatively early onset, patients often exist within a limited social environment and in some cases are often unaware of the extensive behavioral avoidance that functions to minimize their distress (i.e., because they are not engaging in social encounters, they are not anxious). Conversely, if they were to engage in these interactions, they would become extremely anxious. The cocoon not only alleviates distress but also limits any opportunities for social interactions. Therefore, although individuals initially may present as merely having speech phobia, careful assessment often reveals a more extensive pattern of fear and avoidance.

There is another issue to consider during the initial interview with children and adolescents. As we have noted, children rarely seek treatment on their own volition. Thus, the task of forming a positive relationship is more difficult because the child often does not want to participate in treatment, even when the impairing consequences of the fears are clear. One exception may be children whose fears result in school refusal. Sometimes children are motivated for treatment so they can return to school, but others remain reluctant, preferring homebound instruction. In any case, when treating children and adolescents the clinician is faced with a formidable task. Therapeutic relationships must be forged not only with the child but also with the primary caregiver (usually a parent).

One approach that seems to be successful in breaking the ice with patients of any age is to begin by explaining the parameters of the initial meeting. By speaking first, the therapist allows the patient a few moments to adjust to the office setting and perhaps to become slightly more comfortable before discussing his or her social distress. Once we have explained the purpose and structure of the initial interview, we allow the patient (or parent) to begin wherever he or she wants by saying something such as, "What brought you in today?" Greist and colleagues (Greist, Kobak, Jefferson, Katzelnick, & Chene, 1995) recommend a similar approach, suggesting opening questions such as, "What is the nature of your difficulty? What problems are you having? How can I help?" Details of the situation can be addressed once the big picture is established. These details should include all of the salient aspects of the disorder, including negative cognitions, overt behaviors, physiological responses, range of social situations affected, and any coping strategies currently used to deal with the distress.

The importance of a general diagnostic interview cannot be over-emphasized. As we noted in chapters 1 and 2, like other anxiety disorders, social anxiety disorder has a high prevalence of co-occurring conditions (other anxiety as well as nonanxiety disorders). The presence of these other conditions could affect how treatment is conceptualized and implemented. In addition, other disorders may mimic social anxiety disorder. Thus, a clear differential diagnosis and knowledge of the presence of co-occurring conditions is critical for the treatment planning process. Because the assessment of psychopathology is so crucial to patient diagnosis, management, and treatment planning, we recommend using a general semistructured interview schedule in addition to the typical open clinical interview. Use of such an instrument ensures a thorough diagnostic evaluation. We now discuss the nature of structured and semistructured interviews and a number of specific instruments and procedures for conducting a semistructured interview.

STRUCTURED AND SEMISTRUCTURED DIAGNOSTIC INTERVIEWS

Semistructured interview schedules guide the clinician through the diagnostic decision-making process yet allow for the exercise of clinical judgment. It is important that clinicians understand that these interview schedules do not determine an individual's diagnosis. Rather, by following the interview schedule, clinicians will be certain that they have asked all of the questions necessary to determine the proper diagnosis. Unlike structured interviews in which a computer algorithm method sometimes assigns a diagnosis, semistructured interview schedules leave diagnostic decision making in the hands of the clinician. Therefore, these schedules require some training to be administered properly, and they also require extensive knowledge of psychopathological states. The clinician's level of experience determines the extensiveness of the training required to administer the interview properly. Semistructured interview schedules cannot be used effectively by lay interviewers.

Because semistructured interview schedules require 1.5 to 2.5 hours to complete, we recommend conducting this interview in a second session (following the initial interview). Several semistructured interview schedules are available, each having advantages and disadvantages. In addition, some of these interview schedules have a version for administration to children and adolescents (and their parents). We now describe available instruments that are relevant for the assessment of social anxiety disorder.

The Structured Clinical Interview for *DSM–IV* Axis I Disorders— Research Version (SCID–I; First, Spitzer, Gibbon, & Williams, 2002) and the Structured Clinical Interview for *DSM–IV* Axis II (SCID–II; First, Gibbon, Spizter, Williams, & Benjamin, 1997) are the latest versions of these well-established semistructured interviews. Together they assess the entire range of Axis I and II psychopathology and are presented in a modular format. These modules allow the clinician to assess certain aspects of psychopathology selectively. We discourage selecting only specific modules for the interview, however, because social distress can result from many disorders (see chap. 1, this volume). Deleting certain modules (perhaps with the exception of the psychosis module) may result in the neglect of information significant for case formulation and treatment planning. An advantage of the SCID and SCID–II is that they use a branching logic structure (Greist et al., 1995), thus allowing the clinician to skip-out of sections when it is clear that the patient is not endorsing psychopathology consistent with the diagnosis. The SCID's developers correctly noted that because the interview requires clinical judgment, diagnostic reliability is a function of the particular circumstances of the interview, but kappa coefficients for various diagnostic categories range between .70 and 1.00 (First et al., 2002). The SCID–I and SCID–II are thorough, and administrative time decreases as proficiency and level of clinical expertise increases.

More recently, many pharmacological trials have used the Mini-International Neuropsychiatric Interview (M.I.N.I.; Sheehan et al., 1998) to determine patient diagnosis. The M.I.N.I. is a short structured diagnostic interview that is geared to both *DSM–IV* and *International Classification of Diseases* (10th ed.; *ICD–10*) psychiatric disorders. Developed as a result of a perceived need for a short but accurate diagnostic interview, the M.I.N.I. assesses 17 Axis I disorders, suicidality, and antisocial personality disorder using a few questions that appear to address the core features of each disorder. Most of the diagnoses are made with reference to current (rather than lifetime) clinical status. The brief administration time of the M.I.N.I. (15 minutes) is a distinct advantage. To achieve this reduced time, questions regarding disability, illness, and drug rule-outs were eliminated from the interview process. A comparison of current social anxiety disorder diagnoses made by the M.I.N.I. and the SCID–I yields a kappa coefficient of .51, however (Sheehan et al., 1998), indicating only moderate validity. What is also of concern is that in that investigation, the M.I.N.I. resulted in 44 false-positive cases (individuals diagnosed with the disorder using the M.I.N.I. who were not given the diagnosis using the SCID–I). It is interesting to note that in this same sample, there were only 38 true cases of social anxiety disorder identified and the positive predictive value was .46, one of the lowest positive predictive values for this instrument (and may be an artifact of the lack of questions regarding illness and disability). Recall from chapter 3 that rates of significant social fears ranged from 22.6% to 33.0% (Pollard & Henderson, 1988; M. B. Stein, Walker, & Forde, 1994), but rates of social anxiety disorder dropped to 2.0% to 7.1% when impairment criteria were applied. Thus, subject selection based solely on the M.I.N.I. is of some concern because it would suggest that clinical trials may be including subsyndromal cases, which may, in turn, affect response rates. The M.I.N.I. may be a good screening device for primary care settings, although we believe a more thorough diagnostic interview would be necessary to establish with confidence the presence of the disorder. There is a version for children and adolescents, the M.I.N.I.–Kid, currently in development.

Developed as a semistructured interview specifically for the diagnosis of anxiety disorders, the Anxiety Disorders Interview Schedule for *DSM–IV* (ADIS–IV; DiNardo, Brown, & Barlow, 1995) allows for the diagnosis of all anxiety disorders and selected affective and other disorders. The ADIS–IV has added use for the clinician's assessment of anxiety disorders. In addition to the diagnostic criteria and impairment severity rating, the ADIS–IV assesses clinical history; cognitive, physiological, and behavioral components; situational parameters that may affect symptomatic expression; ratings of fear intensity; and avoidance of anxiety-producing situations. In addition, the Hamilton Rating Scale for Anxiety (Hamilton, 1959) and the Hamilton Rating Scale for Depression (Hamilton, 1960) are included, thus allowing for clinician ratings of general anxiety and depression. The social anxiety disorder section assesses fear intensity and avoidance across 13 settings, thereby allowing the clinician basic data on the extent of the individual's social fears. This is an excellent interview schedule for the anxiety disorders and is particularly helpful for treatment planning, particularly for planning behavioral interventions. The limited coverage of other disorders may require the need for additional assessment to have a full diagnostic picture, however.

The child version of the ADIS–IV, the ADIS–IV C/P (C/P indicates child and parent versions; Silverman & Albano, 1995), assesses all *DSM–IV* anxiety disorders as well as affective disorders, externalizing disorders (conduct disorder is only assessed on the parent version), and the presence of substance abuse. The structure of the ADIS–IV C/P is more "child-friendly" than other available semistructured interview schedules. It begins with questions about the child's functioning in the school setting. This is an area that most children are accustomed to discussing with adults, and thus it allows the child time to adjust to the interview format before embarking on a more detailed discussion of fears and clinical status. Additionally, the ADIS–IV–C and ADIS–IV–P ask specific questions about the child's friendships and socialization patterns, areas that are particularly appropriate for the assessment of childhood social anxiety disorder.

When administering a semistructured interview, the clinician should remember that the interview situation is artificial for children (and perhaps even adolescents). Thus, they often do not respond well to structured or semistructured interview formats. Sometimes they will not answer the interviewer's questions or will answer every question by saying "no." Particularly if they notice that by saying no the interviewer skips several pages, they may come to realize that continuing to say no will quickly end their ordeal. Clinicians can counteract this tendency in several ways. First, prior establishment of good rapport will enlist cooperation. Second, an interview schedule such as the ADIS–IV C/P begins with a conversation about school and friends. Thus, rather than initially discussing specific fears or problems, topics with which children are much more comfortable are discussed first. Third, we find it easier to interview the parents first, usually because they are the ones who initiated the clinic contact. After discussing the situation with the parent, the interview with the child is more productive. Finally, asking the child whether he or she would like a break during the interview may assist in keeping the child's cooperation.

When interviewing a patient of any age, we must emphasize the need for training to administer these diagnostic interviews. Most are accompanied by manuals that provide many of the necessary guidelines. In addition, many of these interviews have instructions regarding when the therapist ceases administration of one line of questioning and how to proceed next. In some cases, however, these instructions are not easily discernible and can be overlooked during the course of an interview.

To become proficient, we recommend that the clinician practice administering the interview on several occasions before conducting patient interviews.

Particularly for novice clinicians, there is the temptation to treat the diagnostic interview as a self-report instrument, wherein the clinician asks a question and just records the patient's answer verbatim. As noted earlier, the purpose of semistructured interview schedules is to guide the clinician through the diagnostic process. Many of these schedules require the clinician to rate the behavior as mild, moderate, or severe. Although it is tempting to ask the patient to provide symptom ratings along this dimension, it is really the clinician's judgment (on the basis of experience) that is relevant for the rating and the final diagnostic decision.

Using these interview schedules with children requires conducting separate interviews with parent and child, although we often find that children younger than age 10 are sometimes more comfortable and forthcoming when they are interviewed in the presence of their parents. Most interviews developed for use with children actually consist of two parallel schedules, one for children and one for parents. For most, the major difference is a change in pronoun; that is, for the child version a question is phrased, "Do you get nervous when . . . ," whereas for the parent version the question is phrased, "Does your child get nervous when . . . ." In a few cases, certain disorders, such as conduct disorder, are only found in the parent's schedule (Silverman & Albano, 1995). We have found the use of separate interview forms for parents and children somewhat cumbersome. When using separate schedules, notes that we might have written on the schedule itself in response to what a child said are not readily available when interviewing the parent (using a separate form). Our solution is to use one schedule (usually the parent schedule) and score both the parent and child responses using two colors of ink, such as red and black. In this way, notes conducted during the first part of the interview are readily available when conducting the second half. With respect to the change in pronouns, we do not find it difficult to remember to say "you" when interviewing a child or "your child" when interviewing a parent.

CLINICIAN RATING SCALES

Several clinician rating scales are designed to rate various dimensions of social anxiety disorder. The first was the Liebowitz Social Anxiety Scale (LSAS; Liebowitz, 1987), which consists of 24 situations, including 13 performance situations and 11 social interaction situations. Each item is rated on two 4-point scales; the first assesses severity of fear and the second assesses severity of avoidance. The LSAS has good internal consistency (.92–.96; Tharwani & Davidson, 2001) and is highly correlated with self-report measures of social anxiety disorder (Tharwani & Davidson, 2001). There is established criterion validity (E. J. Brown, Heimberg, & Juster, 1995; Holt, Heimberg, Hope, & Liebowitz, 1992), and the LSAS is sensitive to treatment outcome (e.g., Davidson et al., 1993; Liebowitz et al., 1992). The scale is fairly easy to administer and score and has become a standard outcome measure in most pharmacological treatment trials both for determining the severity criterion necessary for admission to the protocol and for determining the degree of treatment outcome. A child version, the Liebowitz Social Anxiety Scale for Children and Adolescents (LSAS–CA; Masia, Hofmann, Klein, & Liebowitz, 1999) also contains 24 items and has two subscales (social interactions and performance situations). Items are rated on a 0- to 4-point scale and provide anxiety and avoidance scores for both social and performance situations. Psychometric data (Storch, Masia, Pincus, Klein, & Liebowitz, 2001) include good reliability, convergent and discriminative validity, and treatment sensitivity (Masia, Klein, Storch, & Corda, 2001).

Another rating scale (11 items), appropriately named the Brief Social Phobia Rating Scale (BSPRS; Davidson, Potts, et al., 1991), allows for separate ratings of fear and avoidance (on a 5-point scale) in seven situations. In addition, there is a 4-item physiological scale that allows for assessment of the four most common physical symptoms (blushing, palpitations, trembling, and sweating). The BSPRS is scored after completion of a clinical interview. This rating scale has good test–retest reliability ($r = .99$) and interrater reliability ($r = .99$; Davidson, Potts, et al., 1991). It also has good concurrent validity as measured by correlations with the LSAS ($r = .76$) and the Social Phobia and Anxiety Inventory (SPAI; Turner, Beidel, Dancu, & Stanley, 1989; $r = .86$). Finally, the scale is sensitive to treatment effects (Davidson et al., 1993) and has been adapted for computer administration (Tharwani & Davidson, 2001).

A more specialized clinician rating scale is the Kutcher Generalized Social Anxiety Disorder Scale for Adolescents (K–GSADS–A; Brooks & Kutcher, 2004). Developed to be consistent with *DSM–IV* criteria, the K–GSADS–A consists of three components. Section A consists of 18 common social situations, each rated on a 4-point scale for anxiety and avoidance. Section B acknowledges the idiosyncratic nature of the disorder and allows adolescents to list and rate their three most problematic situations, allowing detection of anxiety in social settings not covered in section A. Section C allows for ratings of affective and somatic symptoms, again rated on a 4-point scale. In the initial psychometric study, internal consistency was good except for the somatic subscale. Convergent and discriminant validity was obtained with other measures of social anxiety and depression, and in one investigation, the scale appears sensitive to treatment response (Brooks & Kutcher, 2004). This scale is new, and thus more psychometric data should be forthcoming.

Rating scales can be useful as a quick quantification of the extent of an individual's fear and avoidance. Like semistructured interviews, however, they are designed to be administered by qualified clinicians who have some experience with the disorder. Although Greist et al. (1995) noted that the LSAS has been used as a self-report instrument and that the BSPRS might also be used in this way, we believe that this would be a misuse of these scales because they were not developed for that purpose. Furthermore, no psychometric properties exist to support their use in this fashion. These scales are an important assessment tool when used correctly—that is, when the clinician makes ratings either during or after the completion of a clinical interview.

SELF-REPORT INVENTORIES FOR ADULTS

In their review of self-report inventories for the assessment of social anxiety disorder, McNeil, Ries, and Turk (1995) noted that there were a number of instruments available to assess social anxiety. Many were developed before the publication of social anxiety disorder as a separate diagnosis in the *DSM* nomenclature, however, and although these instruments may assess anxiety in social settings, as we noted in chapter 1, this does not automatically indicate they are appropriate to assess social anxiety disorder. Fortunately, the situation has changed since the time of that review, and a number of validated scales specifically designed for social anxiety disorder exist, which we review in this section.

The Social Phobia Scale (SPS) and the Social Interaction Anxiety Scale (SIAS) were developed by Mattick and Clarke (1989; as cited in McNeil, Reis, Taylor, et al., 1995) to assess two dimensions of social anxiety disorder: social performance and social interaction. The SPS and the SIAS each contain 20 items rated on a 5-point Likert scale. Although the initial data remain unpublished (McNeil, Reis, Taylor, et al., 1995), Heimberg and his colleagues (Heimberg, Mueller, Holt, Hope, & Liebowitz, 1992) reported that the scales have good test–retest reliability ($r > .90$ for intervals up to 13 weeks). The SPS and the SIAS are correlated significantly with other measures of social anxiety (Mattick & Clarke, 1989). The SIAS is capable of differentiating patients with social anxiety disorder from those with other anxiety disorders (Rapee, Brown, Antony, & Barlow, 1992), except for patients with panic disorder and agoraphobia (E. J. Brown et al., 1997). In addition, the SIAS can, to some extent, differentiate the generalized from the specific subtype (Heimberg et al., 1992). The scales are sensitive to the effects of cognitive–behavioral treatment (Tharwani & Davidson, 2001), and a Spanish-speaking version is available (Olivares, Garcia-Lopez, & Hidalgo, 2001). One troubling aspect of the SPS and SIAS is that they are supposed to measure different aspects of social anxiety disorder, but in actuality they are highly correlated ($r = .72$; E. J. Brown et al., 1997), suggesting that (a) the scales do not address different components of the clinical presentation of social anxiety disorder or (b) these two dimensions of social anxiety disorder are not as independent as suggested by these scales. Perhaps an answer to this issue is forthcoming.

On the basis of the clinician-rated BSPRS (Davidson, Potts, et al., 1991), the Social Phobia Inventory (SPIN; Connor et al., 2000) consists of 17 items assessing fear, avoidance, and physiological symptoms of social anxiety disorder. Each item is rated on a 5-point scale. The SPIN had good internal consistency (ranging from .82 to .94), test–retest reliability ($r = .78$ to .89), and convergent and divergent validity. The scale is sensitive to changes in symptoms over time and changes in treatment status (Connor et al., 2000; Tharwani & Davidson, 2001). There is an abbreviated version, the mini-SPIN (Connor, Kobak, Churchill, Katzelnick, & Davidson, 2001), which consists of three items that best discriminated those with social anxiety disorder from normal control study participants (i.e., "Fear of embarrassment causes me to avoid doing things or speaking to people"; "I avoid activities where I am the center of attention"; "Being embarrassed or looking stupid are among my worst fears"). Using a cut score of 6 or higher, the mini-SPIN achieved sensitivity of 88.7% and specificity of 90.0% and 90.0% accuracy in diagnosing the presence or absence of generalized social anxiety disorder in a managed care population (Connor et al., 2001).

Another self-report instrument for the assessment of social anxiety disorder in adults is the Social Phobia and Anxiety Inventory (SPAI; Turner, Beidel, et al., 1989). The SPAI was developed to address specifically various components of social anxiety disorder, including overt behaviors, cognitions, and physiological response. The Social Phobia subscale has 32 items that are rated using a 7-point Likert scale format. The SPAI allows for separate ratings of anxiety on the basis of audience characteristics (e.g., opposite gender, authority figures). In addition, there is a 13-item Agoraphobia subscale that assists in differentiating those with social anxiety disorder from those with panic disorder and agoraphobia (see chap. 1, this volume). Scores on the Agoraphobia subscale are subtracted from the Social Anxiety subscale, resulting in a difference score, which has been validated as a "purer" measure of social anxiety disorder (Turner, Stanley, Beidel, & Bond, 1989).

Primarily on the basis of the pattern of correlations between the SPAI Social Phobia subscale, the difference score, and scores on various instruments used to determine the SPAI's concurrent validity, Herbert, Bellack, and Hope (1991) suggested that the social phobia subscale was a slightly better measure of social anxiety disorder symptoms. Although at first glance such an interpretation might have merit, there are several factors that militate against accepting such a conclusion (Beidel & Turner, 1992a). First, the conclusion that the correlations between the Social Phobia subscale and various measures are larger than the correlations between the difference score and the various measures (Herbert et al., 1991) was not reached on the basis of a statistical test. Some of the correlation coefficients were larger by a mere point or two, making it highly unlikely that they were either statistically or clinically significant. Second, the SPAI was developed as a specific measure of social anxiety disorder, and the original discriminant function analysis indicated that only the difference score could differentiate patients with social anxiety disorder from those with agoraphobia. This is an important distinction for diagnosis and treatment planning, particularly given the inability of other self-report instruments (e.g., the SIAS) to differentiate these two groups (E. J. Brown et al., 1997). Third, the concern that the subtraction of the Agoraphobia subscale from the Social Phobia subscale (to derive the difference score) would artificially deflate the scores of those who are comorbid for both social anxiety disorder and panic disorder is not based on any empirical data. Therefore, we strongly feel that the original scoring and decision-making procedures, which were empirically derived over the course of a 4-year period, should be retained. In short, the SPAI difference score is that which should be used to assist in diagnosis and treatment outcome evaluation.

The psychometric properties of the SPAI have been studied extensively, and the inventory has been translated into at least 10 languages (e.g., Olivares, Garcia-Lopez, Hidalgo, et al., 2002). The SPAI has good test–retest reliability and concurrent, external, and discriminative validity (Beidel, Borden, Turner, & Jacob, 1989; Beidel, Turner, Stanley, & Dancu, 1989; Turner, Beidel, et al., 1989; Turner, Stanley, et al., 1989). It successfully discriminates patients with social anxiety disorder from those with other anxiety disorders and from control study participants without any disorders. Furthermore, the SPAI has the ability to reflect clinically significant change as a result of treatment (Beidel, Turner, & Cooley, 1993). Finally, although developed as an adult instrument, the SPAI has been validated for use with an adolescent population (Clark et al., 1994; Olivares, Garcia-Lopez, Hidalgo, et al., 2002). A brief version of the scale (the SPAI–23) is in final development (Roberson-Nay, Beidel, Turner, & Strong, 2006).

A new measure that specifically assesses thoughts and beliefs commonly found among adults with social anxiety disorder is the Social Thoughts and Beliefs Scale (STABS; Turner, Johnson, Beidel, Heiser, & Lydiard, 2003). Empirically derived, the STABS consists of 21 items and has two factors: Social Comparison (beliefs that others are more socially competent and capable) and Social Ineptness (beliefs that one will act awkwardly in social situations or appear anxious in front of others). Initial psychometric properties of the STABS reveal that the scale has adequate test–retest reliability and internal consistency. It is important to note that both the STABS total score and the factor scores significantly differentiated those with social anxiety disorder from individuals with other anxiety disorders or those with no disorder. Although its psychometric data are not as extensive as the SPAI, the STABS appears to be a valid tool for the specific assessment of the thoughts and beliefs associated with social anxiety disorder.

SELF-REPORT INVENTORIES FOR CHILDREN

Two instruments have been developed specifically to assess social anxiety and social anxiety disorder in children. The first was the Social Anxiety Scale for Children—Revised (SASC–R; LaGreca & Stone, 1993). The scale consists of 22 items that comprise three factors: fear of negative evaluation, social avoidance and distress in new situations, and social avoidance and distress in general. There is a companion version for adolescents, the Social Anxiety Scale—Adolescent Version (SAS–A). Both the SASC–R and the SAS–A have good internal consistency and test–retest reliability (Storch, Masia-Warner, Dent, Roberti, & Fisher, 2004) and correlate moderately with general anxiety, social competence, self-worth, and conduct (deportment). With respect to validity, the sensitivity of the SAS–A was reported to be 43.6% and its specificity to be 82.7% (Inderbitzen-Nolan, Davies, & McKeon, 2004). A Spanish-speaking version is available (Olivares, Garcia-Lopez, Hidalgo, et al., 2002).

The Social Phobia and Anxiety Inventory for Children (SPAI–C; Beidel, Turner, & Morris, 1995) is a 26-item empirically derived inventory that assesses distress in a variety of social settings and includes separate items measuring cognitive, somatic, and behavioral components of the disorder using a 3-point Likert scale. It has high internal consistency and good to excellent test–retest reliability over short- (2-week) and long-term (10-month) intervals. It is moderately correlated with general anxiety, fear of criticism, and parental ratings of internalizing behaviors and social competence (Beidel et al., 1995; Inderbitzen-Nolan et al., 2004; Morris, Hirshfeld-Becker, Henin, & Storch, 2004; Morris & Masia, 1998; Storch et al., 2004). Additionally, the scale correlates with children's daily social behaviors (as measured by a daily diary) and differentiates children with social anxiety disorder from control study participants, from those with externalizing disorders (primarily attention-deficit disorder; Beidel, Turner, & Fink, 1996), and from children with other types of anxiety disorders (Beidel, Turner, Hamlin, & Morris, 1998). A score of 18 on the SPAI–C appears to be a good indicator of the need to conduct a diagnostic interview for the presence of social anxiety disorder. The scale is most useful for children between the ages of 8 and 14. Below that age, the parent SPAI–C alone may be most useful. Over age 14, the adult SPAI is recommended. Like its adult counterpart, the SPAI–C has been translated into approximately 10 languages (e.g., Gauer, Picon, Vasconcellos, Turner, & Beidel, 2005). A parent version of the SPAI–C is currently under development.

We have some recommendations concerning the use of self-report inventories, culled from the available literature and our own clinical experience. Self-report inventories are useful to assist in the quantification of symptoms, and several (including the SPAI and the SPAI–C) provide scores that have been empirically validated as an indicator of the possible presence of social anxiety disorder. Nevertheless, these inventories cannot take the place of a clinical interview for diagnostic purposes, and we do not recommend that they be the sole means by which to determine a diagnosis. However, they can be used to survey the range of experiences and, in the case of the SPAI and SPAI–C, to allow for an assessment across interpersonal partners. An important advantage for the administration of any self-report instrument is that it can trigger recall of additional aspects of the disorder in the patient. This is particularly helpful in final diagnostic decision making and crucial for appropriate treatment planning.

SELF-MONITORING PROCEDURES

Self-monitoring (daily diary) can play an important role in the assessment of social anxiety disorder, both before and during treatment. Self-monitoring forms can be developed to assess various dimensions of the clinical presentation. Commonly assessed aspects include entry into or avoidance of social encounters, ratings of distress and cognitions associated with events, associated somatic responses, and behavioral responses to distressing events. This information can be used (a) to assist in the diagnosis (e.g., does the patient actually experience as much or as little distress on a daily basis as described during the diagnostic interview?); (b) to generate appropriate behavioral practice situations (e.g., exposure to the feared situations); (c) to determine fear-producing situations or avoidance patterns (e.g., are there particular people, places, or events that elicit fear?); and (d) to determine treatment outcome (e.g., are ratings lower at posttreatment than they were at pretreatment?). Therapists can request that patients record information as the events occur (event basis) or provide a summary at the end of the day (daily basis). No empirical data attest to the advantages of an event-based versus a daily-based monitoring system; however, it is our clinical impression that the closer the recording occurs to the actual event, the more valid the record will be. This would argue for an event-based record.

What probably is more important than when the recording occurs, however, is the amount of material that the patient is expected to record. Again, although few empirical data are available, it is our impression that patient compliance is inversely correlated with the length of the self-monitoring forms. Forms that require 5 minutes or less to complete are most likely to be completed consistently and conscientiously. Figure 5.1 illustrates a self-monitoring form successfully used by adults with social anxiety disorder. For some patients, expanding the monitoring to include a description of the actual thoughts or events that elicited the distress may be helpful. For others, simple frequency counts are all that is necessary.

As an example of how self-monitoring can be useful in the treatment-planning process, consider the statement that we used to open this chapter ("My life is perfect except for this fear of giving speeches"). The clinical interview and the self-report measures hinted at the presence of a more pervasive condition, but the patient could not (or would not) identify any additional distressful situations. However, he was asked to

Date: _____   Place: _____

Check which occured

_____ Occurrence of a Distressful Thought

_____ Occurrence of a Distressful Event

_____ Avoidance of a Distressful Event

Rate how anxious you were when the above occurred:

1	2	3	4	5	6	7
Not at All Anxious			Moderately Anxious			Extremely Anxious

Figure 5.1

Self-monitoring form used with adults.

complete the self-monitoring form depicted in Figure 5.1 for a 2-week period. The self-report data indicated that the patient experienced at least moderate distress anytime that he had to speak to three or more people, even if it was an informal conversation in the hallway at work. Therefore, self-monitoring revealed a more pervasive pattern of distress than that expressed by the patient at the initial interview.

Self-monitoring is less commonly used with children and adolescents, but it is nonetheless valuable. Because adolescents and children usually do not come into treatment entirely voluntarily, they may be less motivated to participate in self-monitoring strategies. In addition, written forms such as that depicted in Figure 5.1 may be unappealing to young children, limiting their cooperation. In a study of the feasibility of daily diary procedures, children as young as age 8 were able to use a daily diary to monitor distressing activities for a 2-week period of time (Beidel, Neal, & Lederer, 1991) Younger children (ages 8–10), however, were more likely to complete the monitoring if the diary was presented in a picture, rather than a written, format. There was no difference in rate of compliance for children age 10 or older, although some of the older children did confide to us that they found the pictures "childish." Nevertheless, this study demonstrated that children (even as young as age 8) can use self-monitoring procedures effectively if the child's stage of development is taken into consideration. Figures 5.2 and 5.3 illustrate two self-monitoring forms used successfully with children. Forms developed for adults tend to be more appropriate for use with adolescents.

When using self-monitoring procedures, we have found that issues of compliance are most important. Completing these forms is something that most individuals do not expect to be part of their treatment plan. This method can nonetheless provide important adjunct data to that collected using other assessment methods. Unlike self-report instruments that collect the same information for every patient, self-monitoring forms can be modified to address the unique aspects of the patient's fears. Thus, they provide a highly personalized assessment that may more clearly reflect the patient's clinical status both before and after treatment compared with any standardized measure. Therefore, a careful explanation will help ensure the patient's cooperation. We explain the necessity of self-monitoring data to patients and inform them that for therapy to continue in an orderly fashion, they need to complete the monitoring sheets as directed. To reinforce their importance, the forms are checked promptly at the beginning of each session. Of course, it is up to the therapist to make the forms easy to complete. In addition, we have found that asking for the forms at the beginning of every session and graphing the data for the patient's inspection at various points in therapy also increases compliance.

The situation is more challenging with children. Telling them that therapy may not continue if they do not complete the forms may be just what they want to hear and could actually encourage noncompliance. In addition, clinicians must be cautious about using parents to ensure

Daily Diary

Date _____ Morning _____ Afternoon _____ Evening _____

Where were you? School - Which class _____ Home _____ Outside _____

Cafeteria _____ With Friends _____ Other - Where? _____

What happened?

_____ A popular kid spoke to me
_____ The teacher called on me to answer a question
_____ I had to work with a popular kid in class
_____ I had to talk to someone on the telephone
_____ I had to perform in front of others (sing, dance, play a sport or instrument)
_____ I had to eat in a public place
_____ I had to use a public restroom
_____ Other- What? _____

What did you do?

_____ Pretended I didn't hear the person talking to me
_____ Hid my eyes so I was not called on
_____ Pretended I was sick, so I would not have to go
_____ Told myself not to be nervous, it would be okay
_____ Refused to do what was asked
_____ Did not go to the place (baseball game, school, recital) so I would not have to do it
_____ Waited to go to the bathroom until I got home
_____ Got a stomachache or headache
_____ Cried
_____ Did what I was supposed to do
_____ Other - What? _____

PUT AN X UNDER THE PICTURE THAT SHOWS HOW NERVOUS YOU WERE WHEN THIS HAPPENED

****
Today I did not feel nervous

Figure 5.2

Self-monitoring form used with children.

Daily Record

Date _____

Circle the number that describes how nervous you were today

1	2	3	4	5
Not nervous at all		Medium nervous		Very nervous

Today I worried about:

_____ Something bad happening to my family

    What was the thought? _____

    How many times did you have it? _____

_____ Something bad happening to me

    What was the thought? _____

    How many times did you have it? _____

_____ Doing something to embarrass myself

    What was the thought? _____

    How many times did you have it? _____

_____ Other _____

    What was the thought? _____

    How many times did you have it? _____

Figure 5.3

Self-monitoring form used with children.

children's compliance, thereby potentially setting up a power struggle between the child and parents regarding the completion of the monitoring forms. However, the offer of a small reward (by either the parent or the therapist) for the completion of the forms may be effective. These rewards may take the form, for example, of a later bedtime, a special snack food, stickers from the therapist, and so forth. The receipt of a small token emphasizes the importance of the forms and acknowledges the child's effort in completing them. Adults usually are asked to complete monitoring forms throughout treatment. It is unlikely that children will be able to accomplish such a task and to do so validly. Therefore, it is recommended that with children, self-monitoring be completed on an intermittent basis, perhaps 1 week of every month.

BEHAVIORAL ASSESSMENT TESTS

Behavioral Assessment Tests (BATs) represent a useful strategy to determine the extent of an individual's fear. BATs have a long history in the assessment of other anxiety disorders, but only more recently they have been used in the assessment of social anxiety disorder. As we noted in chapter 2, children who verbally denied any difficulties making friends were unable to demonstrate friendship-making skills in a behavioral test. In addition, BATs can differentiate treatment responders from nonresponders even when other outcome measures do not. For example, in a study of atenolol and flooding treatment for adults with social anxiety disorder, there were no differences between the two active interventions when assessed by self-report or clinician ratings (Turner, Beidel, & Jacob, 1994). When asked to give an impromptu speech, however, those treated with flooding were significantly more likely to complete the task than were those treated with atenolol. Without this assessment, inaccurate conclusions regarding the efficacy of these interventions may have been drawn. Similarly, as noted earlier in this chapter, BATs can be useful in helping to define the presence and nature of social fears. For social anxiety disorder, behavioral assessments may consist of several types. Some address the presence of social skills by using role-play tests and engage the patient in a simulated social interaction with a confederate. Others have focused more on the ability to perform certain activities in front of others, such as giving a speech.

Initially, BATs for social anxiety disorder were primarily role-play tests of social skills. In this paradigm, the patient is asked to imagine a social encounter with another individual. A trained confederate plays the role of the interpersonal partner. The patient's behavior is either audiotaped or videotaped and is scored for various indicators of skill or anxiety (e.g., eye contact, appropriate verbal content). The results of social skill assessments for social anxiety disorder are mixed. Early studies suggested that those with social anxiety disorder diagnosed according to the third edition of the *Diagnostic and Statistical Manual of Mental Disorders* (*DSM–III*) had significantly better social skills than those with *DSM–III* avoidant personality disorder (Turner, Beidel, Dancu, & Keys, 1986). Changes in the diagnostic criteria since that time have clouded these results, however. To date, no study has definitively established the existence of social skill deficits in adults with social anxiety disorder compared with control participants with no disorders or skill differences between those with the specific and generalized subtypes, although some data suggest that differences might exist (Turner, Beidel, Cooley, Woody, & Messer, 1994), and we have such a study currently underway. However, results from assessments of social skills in children with social anxiety disorder do reveal significant differences compared with a peer group with no disorders (Beidel et al., 1999; Spence, Donovan, & Brechman-Toussaint, 1999). One problem may be that the variables currently used to assess social skills are based on deficits noted in conditions other than social anxiety disorder. It may be that a set of measures developed specifically to address the behaviors of patients with social anxiety disorder would identify deficits heretofore undetected. Our ongoing investigation is using an expanded paradigm.

More recently, BATs have focused on the patient's behavior in a performance situation, primarily an impromptu speech task. Although individual patients present with a unique fear pattern, virtually all patients endorse at least moderate anxiety during a speech. Thus, the impromptu speech is an all-purpose task that can be used for all patients with this disorder (Beidel, Turner, Jacob, & Cooley, 1989). In one paradigm, patients are asked to give a speech in front of a small live audience. They are given several topics and are asked to speak for 10 minutes. They may end the task prematurely (i.e., escape) if they become too distressed. The length of time that the patient is able to speak is the primary dependent variable (Beidel, Turner, Jacob, et al., 1989). Other variations include using a camera instead of a live audience, varying the length of time the patient is required to speak, and rating social skill during the speech. Some researchers have used individualized assessment tasks rather than one standard task (Heimberg, Hope, Dodge, & Becker, 1990). Each approach has advantages and disadvantages, and there are no data to suggest the superiority of one approach over another.

As with any assessment tool, there are issues to consider when using a BAT. The behavioral assessments described in this section require the use of analogue situations and confederates to play the role of the interpersonal partner. Nevertheless, information obtained from BATs can be important in determining diagnosis and treatment outcome, making the effort worthwhile (e.g., Turner, Beidel, & Jacob, 1994; see chaps. 7 and 8, this volume). Thus, BATs can provide substantial information about the actual patient behavior when in a social setting, although they are not easily adapted for use by most clinicians. Even if the assessment cannot be standardized as it is in most outcome studies, asking the patient to interact briefly with the therapist in a role-play situation or asking the patient to make a short impromptu speech that is videotaped (even without an audience) can provide important clinical information about a patient's skill and comfort in these types of settings. The tests can also be adapted to many types of situations to allow therapists to test various hypotheses. Thus, the importance of this form of assessment cannot be discounted. Familiarity with BATs will allow the clinician to better evaluate the treatment literature and make a decision regarding the effectiveness of intervention options and provide a valuable tool in treatment planning and outcome determination for any individual patient.

PSYCHOPHYSIOLOGICAL ASSESSMENT

The study of the somatic component of social anxiety disorder has indicated that those with this disorder have many of the same physiological responses as do those with other anxiety disorders, but the disorder is often characterized by a specific set of symptoms that appear to be mediated by the beta-adrenergic system. Activation of this system results in heart palpitations, trembling, shaking, sweating, and blushing. During BATs, physiological measures are often included as part of the assessment protocol. The autonomic nervous system, particularly heart rate and blood pressure, has been the most commonly studied (Heimberg, Dodge, et al., 1990; Turner, Beidel, & Larkin, 1986). Other variables that have been assessed include electrodermal activity (Lader, 1967) and respiration rate (Rapee et al., 1992). All of these variables differentiate individuals with social anxiety disorder from control participants and from individuals with the specific and generalized subtypes (Heimberg, Dodge, et al., 1990; Heimberg, Hope, et al., 1990; Hofmann, Newman, Ehlers, & Roth, 1995). To summarize the outcome of these studies, those with social anxiety disorder show increased physiological response in anxiety-producing situations. Increased physiological response is important not only for its theoretical relevance but also because these responses can serve as an important indicator of arousal during imaginal and in vivo exposure sessions. Most clinicians will not have the luxury of conducting psychophysiological assessments of patients with social anxiety disorder, thus we do not elaborate further on this method of assessment.

CONCLUSION

In discussing the assessment of social anxiety disorder, we have emphasized the necessity of conducting a thorough clinical evaluation of individuals presenting with a complaint of social anxiety. Table 5.1 provides
our recommendation for conducting an assessment of social anxiety
disorder. The general clinical interview is important for determining the
patient's overall clinical status as well as determining that the presenting
complaint satisfies the criteria for social anxiety disorder. We noted, in
particular, the need to differentiate social anxiety disorder from other
similar conditions (see chaps. 1 and 2, this volume). To assist in the
diagnostic process, the clinical interview and the use of self-report and
clinician rating scales and semistructured interviews were highlighted.
The core of any assessment in the clinical setting is an open interview,
for it is here that patients get the opportunity to describe the condition
in their own words. Similarly, the therapist has the latitude to search

Table 5.1
Recommended Assessment Strategy for the Assessment
of Social Anxiety Disorder

Session	Assessment strategy
Initial session	Conduct clinical interview.
	Provide self-monitoring forms and instruction.
Second session	Administer structured clinical interview.
	Complete clinician rating scales.
	Administer self-report instruments.
	Check on validity of self-monitoring and instruct patient to continue for another week.
Third session	Review self-monitoring data.
	Discuss results of evaluation with patient and present treatment plan.
	Begin treatment.

and discover areas of importance that could be critical to the diagnosis and subsequent treatment.

To supplement the general clinical interview, we recommended the use of semistructured interview schedules and discussed the advantages and disadvantages of a number of instruments available for this purpose. These interview schedules ensure that a broad range of questions is posed so that relevant information needed for a wide range of diagnoses are revealed. The use of these instruments reduces the likelihood that an improper diagnosis will be made or that co-occurring conditions will be missed. In addition, self-report inventories and clinical rating scales can be used to assess the magnitude of the disturbance and, in the case of the SPAI, to help ascertain the pervasiveness of the disorder and identify critical variables for treatment planning.

An important assessment component in social anxiety disorder is the use of self-monitoring strategies. We pointed out the ways in which this strategy can aid in the diagnostic process and assist in elucidating the parameters associated with social anxiety. We also discussed how self-monitoring strategies might be used to gauge treatment progress and outcome.

The use of overt analogue behavioral assessment was also discussed. Behavioral tasks can be constructed to meet virtually any purpose, but in the case of social anxiety disorder, they have primarily been used to assess anxiety during performance situations and to measure social skills. For example, behavioral tasks have proved useful in helping to determine whether patient fears are limited to performance situations or whether the difficulty extends to casual social interactions as well. In treatment outcome studies, this type of task frequently provides a stringent test of the overall efficacy of a given treatment and serves as an overt indicator of what the patient can or cannot do.

Finally, assessment of psychophysiological response can prove helpful in clinical decision making, particularly within the context of BATs. Highly reactive autonomic responses reassure the clinician that proper fear cues were selected. Conversely, decreased autonomic responsiveness when confronted with these cues helps to confirm that treatment progress has been made. Fancy equipment is not necessary to conduct this type of assessment. Simple heart rate or pulse readings can be used. Together these strategies represent a comprehensive approach to the assessment of social anxiety disorder by assisting in the establishment of the diagnosis, delineating associated conditions, elucidating the relevant parameters associated with the disorder, and providing evidence of treatment progress and outcome

6

Managing Patients With Social Anxiety Disorder (and Their Parents)

Dr. Turner: Mr. Brown called to cancel his appointment for today.
He said he is uncertain whether he will be able to do the homework
assignments as discussed in his last session.

—A telephone message from a patient

Dr. Beidel: Mrs. Smith called. She won't be bringing Bobby (her 8-year-old son)
in for his session. She says he doesn't want to come, and
she cannot make him get into the car.

—A telephone message regarding a patient's appointment

The problems described in the following two examples do not concern technical aspects of treatment implementation. Rather, they can best be described as patient management issues because they illustrate patient or parent difficulties that have the potential to derail the treatment process. How these problems are managed can determine whether a patient remains in treatment and whether the outcome will be positive.

Patient management is as important as any other factor in the overall care of those with social anxiety disorder, and the therapist should do as much as possible to prevent problems from occurring and to address the problems directly when they do occur. In this chapter, we elaborate on patient management issues, pointing out particular difficulties associated with the management of children.

EDUCATION

Adult Educational Sessions

One important factor that can significantly affect the occurrence of management problems during treatment is whether time is taken to educate the patient. By education we mean a formal session during which the patient (including the patient's family when appropriate) is informed about the nature of the disorder (including any co-occurring disorders). Thus, we always spend a session educating the patient about the phenomenology, epidemiology, clinical correlates, and course of the disorder. This is a detailed discussion, and time is taken to answer questions from the patient and family members. In addition to information about the nature of the disorder, available treatment options are explored in detail, including their advantages and disadvantages. A synthesis of the treatment outcome literature is provided because we feel that if the patients understand that they will be receiving a treatment known to produce positive results, their willingness to engage in behaviors typically avoided increases. Finally, the nature and requirements for the treatment are spelled out clearly, and patients are informed of their responsibilities in the treatment process (e.g., maintaining self-monitoring data, attending regular sessions, completing homework assignments as directed). The patient agrees to a treatment plan in which the therapist explains what treatment involves and what will be required of the patient (see Exhibit 6.1 for an example of a successful education session).

Exhibit 6.1

Patient Management

Patient Educational Session Content

1. The educational session begins with a presentation of what is known about the disorder (in this case, social anxiety disorder). Included in this discussion are the disorder's etiology, its clinical presentation, and related demographics. The material presented to the patient is similar to that found throughout these chapters but without some of the more advanced statistical concepts. We also discuss potential developmental pathways and variations in the clinical presentation.

2. After presenting information about the clinical aspects of the disorder, the most current data on treatment outcome are presented. Pharmacological and psychological interventions are discussed. This is an empirically based presentation, and the advantages and disadvantages of each intervention are discussed. The presentation is continuously updated so that the information remains current.

3. An overview of the treatment package used in our clinic, including outcome data, is presented. This includes the rationale for why we developed (or why a clinician selected) the treatment program, the purpose of each individual treatment component, and the effectiveness of the intervention. We try to set positive but realistic expectations for treatment outcome. We emphasize that we cannot guarantee treatment efficacy for any particular patient. In the case of behavioral treatments, it would be important to emphasize the active nature of the intervention and the patient's need to be an active partner in the treatment process. Similarly, pharmacological interventions require a commitment on the part of the patient to take the medication as prescribed by the physician.

Exhibit continues

Exhibit 6.1 *(Continued)*

Patient Management

4. The details of the treatment program, including specific procedures and time commitment, are presented. We present the individual treatment components and the methods used for each component. In addition, a substantial amount of time is spent discussing the time commitment involved in treatment: the length of the sessions, the number of sessions per week, the average treatment duration, and the necessity of completing homework assignments. In the case of pharmacological treatments, a description of the dosage schedule, potential side effects, drug interaction effects, and the expected positive effects (and when they can be expected to occur) are discussed.

5. Finally, it is important to assess the motivation of the patient (and significant others) for participating in the presented intervention. Patients who express uncertainty about their ability to commit to the treatment or who try to bargain for a reduced number of sessions or for a more limited intervention should be encouraged to take some time to consider whether they want to participate in the intervention. In each case, the clinician must decide what is reasonable while maintaining the integrity of the treatment. If the patient cannot commit to what is viewed as minimally acceptable, referral should be considered.

Parent and Child Educational Session

Educational sessions are also conducted for children with social anxiety disorder and their parents (see Exhibit 6.2). The presentation is geared toward the child's understanding but covers all of the areas included in the adult presentation. The presentation is organized in terms of questions that parents and children might ask.

This educational process does not prevent difficulties from arising during the course of treatment, but it significantly reduces their occurrence and decreases the possibility of incongruent treatment expectancies

---

Exhibit 6.2

Educational Outline for Children and Parents

1. How many children have social anxiety disorder?
2. What kinds of situations make boys and girls feel shy?
3. What happens to my body when I feel shy?
4. What do I think about when I feel shy?
5. What do I do when I feel shy?
6. Why do I feel shy, and how did I get this way?
7. Can I get better?
8. How do I get better?

---

on the part of therapist and patient. Successful treatment of social anxiety disorder involves more than mere application of a specific intervention strategy. It includes managing all aspects of the patient's clinical state. Furthermore, management of children's clinical status must be expanded to include potential management of parents' clinical status. Finally, comprehensive treatment of the child may involve consideration of the parent's child management skills.

PATIENT MANAGEMENT

In some cases, managing the patient is just a matter of setting reasonable expectations regarding therapy and expected treatment outcome. Complicated clinical conditions, however, often require an active and ongoing clinical management program. Some of the problems encountered in treating patients with social anxiety disorder are discussed in this section.

Setting Appropriate Treatment Expectations

Treatment expectations will vary with respect to the type of intervention. For example, patients receiving pharmacological treatments will have a different therapeutic regimen than those receiving psychological treatment, although in some cases both interventions are used concurrently.

In the case of children, parents may not initially understand that they may be called on to play an active role in treatment.

Sometimes, a patient enters treatment at a time of crisis. For example, an adult has an impending major presentation, meeting, or social event in the next week, or a child refuses to go to school. Some adults feel that their heterosocial relationships may be in imminent danger because of their reluctance to accompany a partner to social events. Children often are brought to the clinic because the school is threatening immediate expulsion, there is a truancy hearing because of school refusal, or a selectively mute child is in danger of being forced to repeat a grade because the school is uncertain of reading ability. Unless the patient is going to receive a short-acting beta-blocker or benzodiazepine (see chap. 7, this volume), therapeutic effects will not be immediate enough to provide quick relief. To handle the immediate crisis, temporary interventions may be necessary before implementation of the full behavioral treatment program.

Some patients attribute their social fears to a lack of self-esteem. That is, they believe that if they just had more confidence in themselves (i.e., higher self-esteem), then they would not feel so distressed and anxious in social encounters. Certainly, some patients with social anxiety disorder have low self-esteem, and some interventions specifically focus on improving this aspect of personality. Other approaches to treatment (e.g., those based on behavioral and cognitive–behavioral theory) address this problem more indirectly, however, and assume that patients gain confidence and self-esteem through the behaviors in which they engage. Successful and rewarding experiences in social interactions change perceptions of oneself and one's abilities (e.g., Turner, Beidel, & Jacob, 1994). Therefore, behavioral interventions focus on changing behavior, and improvement in self-esteem naturally results when the change from maladaptive social behavior to more functional social behavior occurs. We explain to patients that the way they feel about themselves probably is a function of their life experiences, which in this case have not been very positive. Therefore, the task is to focus on improving skills and developing the abilities and confidence to interact with others in a manner that will be productive and positive. Once they begin to have success in their interactions, patient concerns that their poor self-esteem is not being addressed tend to subside.

Most of the cognitive–behavioral or behavioral treatments and many of the pharmacological treatments for social anxiety disorder include some form of exposure to the feared setting or situation. In the case of behavioral or cognitive–behavioral treatment, exposure is the key ingredient, and assignments may be quite structured. In the case of pharmacological treatment, exposure instructions may be less specific, encouraging the patient to try out new behaviors to see whether the medicine is effective. Therapists may have to deal with patient reluctance to enter anxiety-producing settings and resulting noncompliance with exposure instructions. We now discuss several ways to address this issue.

To begin, the therapist needs to be certain that the patient understands the rationale for the homework assignments. Asking the patient to repeat the rationale may reveal misunderstandings that may affect compliance. It may also reveal the patient's motivation to participate in treatment. The therapist needs to be certain that the assignment is not too difficult for the patient. Devising initial assignments so that they are successful will build patient confidence. For example, an individual who has trouble interacting with others even on an informal basis may be given a first assignment to enter a crowded store (e.g., at a mall) but not be required to speak to anyone. When the patient becomes comfortable completing this assignment, more advanced assignments can be given.

For patients with a severe form of the disorder, the clinician may need to accompany the patient on the first few exposure assignments. We have found that patients' anticipatory anxiety often is more severe than the distress they experience once they are engaged in the task. Patients often remark to us afterward that worrying about doing the assignment was more distressful than actually completing it. Therefore, accompanying patients on the first assignment and allowing them to see that their distress is not as severe as they imagined may increase compliance with future tasks. If it is impossible to accompany a patient, a significant other may be engaged for this assignment.

Although in vivo exposure exercises can be planned, the behaviors of other individuals in most social interactions cannot be scripted. Interactions with the general public often will not go as planned (and sometimes not as desired). Clinicians must plan for these contingencies when conducting in vivo exposure sessions (i.e., have an alternate plan ready for use). In planning the exposure session, careful consideration should include the likelihood that the assignment can be completed successfully. Also, there is a need to arrange specific opportunities for engagement in various types of social encounters, thus allowing patients to interact with a broad range of individuals, groups, and situations. This is necessary because one significant feature of social anxiety disorder is that patients often fear uncertainty. Even after they have had success with one person or one situation, new persons or situations still generate apprehension. One of the treatment goals is to ensure that those with social anxiety disorder learn to accept some uncertainty regarding the actions of others when in social encounters. This necessitates experiences with multiple persons and situations.

Other Associated Clinical and Personality Issues

Additional Axis II Disorders

Social anxiety disorder involves the fear of doing something that is humiliating or embarrassing. It is our clinical impression, supported by a small amount of empirical data, that those with social anxiety disorder often have a tendency to see the world in a rigid and perfectionistic fashion; either they do things perfectly or they have failed miserably. Such behavior is also characteristic of those with obsessive–compulsive personality disorder (OCPD), which is characterized by a pervasive pattern of orderliness, perfectionism, and mental and interpersonal control at the expense of flexibility, openness, and efficiency (American

Psychiatric Association, 1994, p. 672). As we noted in chapter 1, 13.2% of those with social anxiety disorder in one sample also met criteria for OCPD, and another 48.5% had a subclinical form of the disorder (Turner, Beidel, Borden, Stanley, & Jacob, 1991). Among children, those with social anxiety disorder score higher on temperamental scales assessing rigidity and inflexibility (Beidel, Turner, & Morris, 1999), behavioral characteristics that are similar to those found in adults with OCPD. Because these behaviors exist in individuals who already have a disorder, it is unclear what role they might play in etiology. It is clear, however, that this behavior can have an impact on the process of treatment.

Our clinical experience indicates that the presence of OCPD can affect patient management considerably. First, clinicians should be particularly attuned to issues of control. Second, those with this syndrome might present more difficulties with imaginal exposure because of the perfectionistic manner by which they approach the material, often attending to minute details rather than the overall scenes. For example,

> Mark told us he was having difficulty imagining a scene because he could not decide whether the woman he was imagining should be wearing earrings.

Verbalization of the scene is one method used to get around these perfectionistic tendencies. Third, those with OCPD have greater difficulty interpersonally, and it is particularly difficult to get them to engage in novel social interactions. Finally, even when frank OCPD is not present, if subclinical features exist, they may affect the therapeutic process. Therefore, careful clinical assessment is required to prepare an adequate treatment plan and to structure sessions appropriately.

Among adults with social anxiety disorder, about 22% also meet criteria for avoidant personality disorder (APD; Turner, Beidel, Borden, et al., 1991). In our sample discussed earlier, another 53% had behavioral traits characteristic of this disorder, although they did not meet full diagnostic criteria (Turner, Beidel, Borden, et al., 1991). Even those with subclinical features of APD are extremely sensitive to criticism, particularly when they are under a great deal of stress. Patients with APD or characteristics of this disorder often exhibit a "paranoid-like" quality to their thinking, again usually when they are under duress. Such distressful situations might include interventions (pharmacological or psychological) that require the patient to try out the medicine or their newly developed social skills. For example,

> As a homework assignment, Frank was asked to go to the bank and greet a teller who in the past had always been friendly. However, on this occasion, the teller was polite, but cold and distant. Frank immediately interpreted the teller's behavior as persecutory toward him and berated us for forcing him to "embarrass himself in public."

Obviously, there were many other reasons the teller might have behaved as she did on that particular occasion. In such cases, a cognitive strategy, such as generating alternative explanations, might be helpful, although currently no empirical data on such a strategy for those with APD are available.

Clinicians must be prepared to deal with the unusual interpretations of a patient with comorbid APD, particularly if treatment involves exposing the patient to fearful situations. There are several actions that the clinician can consider to address this situation. First, careful explanations of the role of exposure in the treatment of social anxiety disorder (as is done in our education session) may help the patient understand its purpose. Most adult patients intuitively understand that to reduce their anxiety, they ultimately must face their fears. Children, particularly younger children, are less likely to understand this necessity, and age might dictate how much effort is expended toward helping the patient understand the rationale. Similarly, the intensity of the patient's fear and clinical sensitivity in general might be such that a high-intensity strategy should be avoided. This is a decision that must be made by the clinician. Second, a clear statement to the patient (and, if necessary, the parents) that the purpose of exposure to socially feared situations is not to humiliate but to assist in overcoming fears may be effective in setting appropriate expectations. Third, if explanations are ineffective and paranoid-like interpretations regarding social interactions or the therapist's motives continue, changing strategies to use a low-intensity (rather than a high-intensity) exposure paradigm (see chap. 8, this volume) may avoid this problem. Finally, as noted in our program, Social Effectiveness Therapy, individual sessions are particularly useful to establish a trusting relationship (Turner, Beidel, Cooley, Woody, & Messer, 1994). Each patient will need to be evaluated to determine the most appropriate method of exposure.

One particularly critical disorder to discriminate is paranoid personality disorder. Although this condition has been detected in only a small number of patients (e.g., Turner, Beidel, Borden, et al., 1991), we have seen such patients in our clinic who seek treatment because of difficulty in social interactions. Although typically recognizable, in a minority of cases the condition can be difficult to detect. In our experience, paranoid patients do not respond well to behavioral treatments for social anxiety disorder, and, in fact, exposure often results in increased anxiety and exacerbation of paranoid thinking. In other words, the patient's condition worsens. These patients typically view exposure sessions as humiliating. Careful diagnostic practice is necessary to detect the presence of these features. One clue that might alert the clinician is the atypically late onset (i.e., after young adulthood) of social distress. Social anxiety disorder is an early onset disorder, and it is among those who claim a later onset that we have found some patients with paranoid personality disorder (threshold or subthreshold) as well as some who have significant paranoid features.

Additional Axis I Diagnoses

In addition to the presence of Axis II disorders, comorbid Axis I conditions also require attention and clinical management. Patients with comorbid Axis I disorders appear to improve as a result of treatment designed for social anxiety disorder (E. J. Brown, Heimberg, & Juster,

1995; Hofmann, Newman, Becker, Taylor, & Roth, 1995; Mersch, Jansen, & Arntz, 1995; Turner, Beidel, Cooley, et al., 1994; Turner, Beidel, Wolff, Spaulding, & Jacob, 1996; see chap. 8, this volume, for a review). For example, although patients with or without comorbid disorders made equivalent improvements over the course of treatment, there is a trend for patients without a comorbid diagnosis to have a higher end-state functioning status at posttreatment than those with comorbid disorders (e.g., Mersch, Jansen, & Arntz, 1995; Turner, Beidel, Wolff, et al., 1996). This means that their status was more similar to that of those with no disorder than to those with a comorbid condition. At posttreatment, those with comorbid disorders had higher scores on several measures of general anxiety and ratings of clinical severity. Similarly, an examination of depression, personality disorders, and treatment outcome expectancy variables as predictors of treatment outcome revealed that a higher level of pretreatment depression was associated with less reduction in anxious apprehension, social interaction anxiety, and skill (Chambless, Tran, & Glass, 1997). When taken together, these findings indicate that the posttreatment clinical status of patients with a comorbid condition was worse than that of those who did not have a comorbid condition, despite equivalent decreases in social anxiety. In summary, these data indicate that those with comorbid Axis I conditions may be successfully treated, although the extent of improvement may be less than that expected to occur in patients without comorbid conditions.

In a minority of cases, such as when panic disorder is intimately intertwined with social anxiety disorder, treatment for social anxiety disorder may result in considerable improvement of panic symptoms. Yet here, too, additional treatment directed at panic disorder likely will be needed to achieve an optimal outcome. Individual patient needs must be determined on a case-by-case basis. Data on treatment effects for children with social anxiety disorder and comorbid conditions are limited, although the presence of depression among adolescent girls may be associated with relapse (Hayward et al., 2000; see chap. 9, this volume).

In summary, the presence of Axis I comorbid conditions does not preclude the usual treatment for social anxiety disorder. However, such treatment likely will not significantly affect an existing comorbid condition, such as generalized anxiety disorder or panic disorder. Our experience is that these conditions will require an additional specific intervention. For those with comorbid severe depression and for whom suicidal behavior is an issue, immediate treatment with antidepressants or other treatments specifically directed toward depressive symptomatology might be necessary. Even in those cases in which depression is severe but the patient is not necessarily suicidal, symptoms such as sleeplessness, lethargy, and loss of interest in activities may prevent full engagement in exposure and social skill training activities, thereby limiting their effectiveness. In these cases, patients need to be treated for depression before beginning behavioral treatment for social anxiety disorder.

Patient Educational Session

As noted earlier, it is our position that one of the most important aspects of clinical management is patient familiarity with the disorder and its prognosis. If a patient understands what to expect from the disorder and the intervention, full participation in the treatment process is more likely. Patient and parent expectations can sometimes be unrealistic. Some expect that psychological treatment follows the medical tradition; that is, a patient sees the doctor once, receives a prescription, and usually does not return for an additional visit for some time. Patients need to understand that psychological treatments, even short-term treatments, do not operate according to a traditional medical model. Also, lay perceptions of psychological treatments are still shaped largely by the media, which depict psychological treatment as a verbal enterprise in which the goal is to uncover hidden motives deep in the patient's psyche that are responsible for the patient's difficulties. Although verbal therapies may help develop insight into one's functioning, current empirically supported therapies do not rely on insight as the primary mechanism of therapeutic change. Similarly, most pharmacological treatments require a series of visits during which medication is titrated to a therapeutic dose and side effects are monitored. Thus, the educational process should address this issue specifically to ensure that the patient understands the treatment process.

PARENT MANAGEMENT

As noted throughout this volume, clinicians face a special challenge when treating children with social anxiety disorder. They must forge a therapeutic relationship not only with the patient but also with the patient's parents or primary caregiver. Throughout this chapter, the term *parent* is used to refer to either the child's parent or primary caregiver. When considering issues of general clinical management, there are two primary aspects of parental behavior that merit consideration: parental psychopathology and child management skills. Each is discussed in this section.

Parental Psychopathology

As discussed in chapter 4 of this volume, studies indicate that rates of anxiety disorders are higher in families of an individual with an identified anxiety disorder. Because the presence of anxiety disorders in parents may play a role in the etiology or maintenance of anxiety disorders in children (see chap. 4, this volume), a closer understanding of psychopathology in the parents of anxious children is necessary. Among children with anxiety disorders, 40% to 42% had parents who had a current or lifetime anxiety disorder diagnosis (Last, Hersen, Kazdin, Finkelstein, & Strauss, 1991; Last & Strauss, 1990). Other familial relationships were discussed at length in chapter 4 of this volume, and the reader is referred there for a more extensive discussion of this issue.

Knowledge of the presence of anxiety disorders in the parent is important when treating a child with social anxiety disorder for several reasons. First, parents with the disorder may be reluctant to have their child enter treatment. For example,

> Jessica was diagnosed with social anxiety disorder as was her father. He had never been in formal therapy but managed his disorder by avoiding activities that precipitated his anxiety. The father's response to his daughter's evaluation was that she did not need behavior therapy but could be homeschooled to eliminate her distress. Further education of the father (particularly an examination of the outcome data for childhood social anxiety disorder) convinced him to allow Jessica to undergo a trial of behavior therapy.

In other instances, even if the anxious parent agrees that treatment is needed, the parent's own fears may limit his or her ability to assist with necessary homework assignments. For example, socially phobic parents may be unable to arrange for their children to play or interact with other children (i.e., expose the child to a social encounter) if parents themselves are so anxious that they are reluctant to speak to other parents or arrange an activity. Parents with severe agoraphobia may not be able to drive their children to another child's house for the children to play together. Also parents who refused school themselves might be more sympathetic to their child's distress to the degree that they are reluctant to reintroduce the child to school. In such cases, the parents' own fears may have to be managed before effective treatment can be implemented.

Other Parental Behaviors That May Affect Treatment Outcome

In addition to anxiety, other factors that merit consideration when treating anxious children are the parental expectations and attitudes. Kendall's (1994) study of cognitive–behavioral therapy for anxious (but not necessarily socially phobic) children indicated that parents' participation in therapy was variable across the child participants. Degree of parental involvement (on the basis of therapist ratings) was modestly related to treatment outcome, however. Thus, parental participation in treatment may enhance outcome, and although not consistent for every child, our experience is that when a behavior problem is an issue, it is a critical one. Additionally, parent behaviors outside the therapeutic setting may also affect outcome. As we noted in chapter 4 in this volume, Barrett and Dadds and their colleagues (Barrett, Dadds, Rapee, & Ryan, 1996; Dadds, Barrett, Rapee, & Ryan, 1996) analyzed the verbal communications between anxious children and their parents and found that family processes more often serve to enhance rather than eliminate avoidant responses in anxious children. Furthermore, it is possible that family interaction patterns may play a major role in the development and treatment of such disorders (Dadds et al., 1996). Thus, family interaction may serve to reinforce maladaptive behavioral patterns and may need to be altered for treatment to be successful.

Silverman (e.g., Silverman & Kurtines, 1996) described problematic parental behavior similar to Barrett and Dadd's findings. She termed these behaviors the "Protection Trap," the tendency of parents to protect their children, even during therapy, from exposure to objects or situations that create anxiety or distress. In such cases, parents' misdirected efforts at protection from discomfort serve to foster the maintenance of the maladaptive behaviors. When present to a significant degree, this problem must be controlled before progress can be expected. The Protection Trap is not unique to psychological interventions. Psychiatrists usually provide encouragement to try out medication as part of the treatment program. In summary, even though exposure can be accomplished in several ways (see chaps. 8 and 9, this volume) and need not be delivered in a high intensity fashion, parents may be reluctant to get the child upset or allow the therapist to put the child in a situation that may cause emotional distress. Additionally, patients and parents sometimes have unreasonable expectations about what therapy (particularly behavior therapy and drug therapy) will entail. They sometimes envision unusual (and sometimes cruel) exposure situations coupled with uncontrollable distress reactions or terrible side effects from medication. Therapists must be certain to dispel these notions.

A final consideration when treating children is that although some parents may allow their child to participate in exposure sessions conducted by the therapist, they may be unwilling to assist the child with homework sessions because they do not want the child to become distressed or do not feel they have the time to assist the child with the session. Homework is an integral part of exposure and social skills interventions, thus both of these parental behaviors can negatively affect treatment outcome.

Clinicians must address these disruptive parental behaviors. Because exposure to the feared situations is the core of all the empirically supported psychosocial treatments for social anxiety disorder and is also frequently used with drug therapy, therapists must be assured that parents understand its importance for successful treatment outcome. For example, parents might observe an exposure session conducted by the therapist to view firsthand the child's distress. Our experience is that when parents understand what happens during an exposure session, they are more likely to allow their child's participation and to assist their child in completing homework assignments.

Child Management Skills

As noted, parents may (either purposefully or accidentally) encourage avoidant behaviors in their anxious children. Some parents, however, are lacking in even more basic parenting behaviors, such as reinforcement skills. Parents will not reward courageous behavior and discourage avoidance until they understand and can implement differential reinforcement schedules. When such skills are lacking, child management training (e.g., Hembree-Kigin & McNeil, 1995) should be an integral part of the treatment program. Our experience is that child management training works best when conducted before treatment for social anxiety disorder.

Exhibit 6.3

**Assessment of Potential Parental Influences on
Child Treatment Outcome**

1. Assess the potential presence of parental psychopathology.
2. Assess parental child management skills.
3. Assess parental understanding of the child's disorder and the parameters of the proposed intervention.
4. Assess the parent's motivation for the child's participation in the treatment program.

ASSESSMENT OF PARENTAL INFLUENCE ON TREATMENT OUTCOME

We recommend a four-step assessment plan to determine parental influence on treatment outcome for children with social anxiety disorder (see Exhibit 6.3). This plan includes the assessment of parental pathology as well as parenting skills. Because the child is the identified patient, however, clinicians are cautioned that conducting full diagnostic interviews with the parent at the initial assessment is inappropriate. We think it is appropriate, however, to inquire about others in the family, including the parents, who may suffer from anxiety disorders now or who may have suffered from them in the past. This line of questioning could yield information regarding familial factors that may be important in understanding and treating the child's disorder.

RECOMMENDATIONS FOR GENERAL CLINICAL MANAGEMENT OF PARENTS

In Exhibit 6.4, we offer suggestions for the clinical management of parents when children and adolescents are involved in treatment for social anxiety disorder. One of the clinician's first decisions is whether the parent's anxiety is severe enough to affect the child's treatment. In

---

Exhibit 6.4

Clinical Management for Parents of Anxious Children

1. Advise impaired parent to seek treatment.
2. If assessment reveals poor child management skills, provide specific skills training. This may take the form of bibliotherapy or direct intervention.
3. Provide an explanation and allow for discussion of the "Protection Trap."
4. Include the parents in the educational session about the nature of the disorder (see outline for parent and child educational session noted in Exhibit 6.2).

---

such cases, it might be necessary to refer the parent for treatment. In severe cases, the child's treatment might even need to be deferred until the parent's disorder has been controlled.

In addition, the clinician will need to consider whether part of the child's difficulty results from poor parenting skills and whether formal intervention is needed. In many instances, a simple discussion coupled with one of the many available parent training manuals may be all that is required. In other cases, a more formal and prolonged training program may be necessary. It is critical that parents understand reinforcement principles and are able to apply them correctly because rewarding the child for completion of various tasks is an important treatment component. Clinicians need to be assured that parents understand the basic concepts and use them appropriately.

Furthermore, the behaviors of all parents must be examined to make certain that they are not reinforcing behavioral avoidance. The clinician should assess the willingness of parents to help the child complete homework assignments when necessary. This can usually be accomplished as part of the diagnostic interview. If the parent demonstrates protective behaviors that will interfere with treatment, they should be addressed during the initial treatment phase. Parents should be advised that treatment is not likely to be effective until this issued is resolved.

CONCLUSION

This chapter was devoted to a discussion of the many issues that have the potential to militate against successful treatment outcome for children and adults with social anxiety disorder. We have dubbed one set of potential problems as patient management issues. Grouped under this rubric are all of the nondiagnostic- and nonsyndrome-specific issues that can interfere with effective treatment. In addition, we delineated a number of examples of patient management problems with children and adults.

The most effective approach to prevent management problems is to provide education about the nature of the disorder, available treatment options, the specific treatment plan that will be implemented, and the responsibilities of both patient and therapist. If patient management issues still arise, they must be addressed in a straightforward fashion, or treatment might be stalled or even derailed.

There are two sets of issues with respect to Axis I and II disorders and patient management. One potential problematic area that could affect the process of treatment as well as treatment outcome is the existence of Axis II disorders (most commonly APD and OCPD) concurrent with social anxiety disorder. Although the available evidence indicates that the presence of these conditions does not preclude the use of behavioral treatments for social anxiety disorder, when present, overall improvement rate may be attenuated (Feske, Perry, Chambless, Renneberg, & Goldstein, 1996). It is unclear at this juncture what strategy should be used to enhance outcome. Although a longer treatment period would likely be beneficial, specific interventions aimed at the personality dysfunction will probably be necessary to obtain optimal results. The situation essentially is the same when Axis I conditions are present. Current treatments are effective for social anxiety disorder, but other strategies will likely be necessary for the co-occurring condition.

Finally, in the case of Axis II conditions, which in most cases will be OCPD and APD, the manner in which treatment is conducted can be affected. For example, imaginal exposure may be more difficult with patients who have OCPD. Also, because of their rigidity, it may be more difficult to gain patient cooperation for the range of exposure situations needed to adequately address their fears. For those with APD, a more gradual approach to exposure rather than an intensive one may be needed.

Patient management with children is even more problematic for a number of reasons. Children typically do not seek treatment voluntarily and may not wish to cooperate. It has been our experience that there are several ways to increase cooperation and interest in these children. First, establishing a contract with adolescents for a certain number of sessions, during which improvement can be evaluated and a decision made about whether to continue or not, is effective. Second, the provision of small reinforcers (stickers, fast-food coupons) will increase compliance, particularly among younger children. Third, additional reinforcers, provided by the parents, can also increase compliance for youngsters of any age. For example, one of our parents would buy her child an ice cream cone immediately after the session as a reward for compliance and hard work during the session.

Parenting skill and parent–child interaction are other patient management issues with child patients. We do not wish to imply that the parent–child relationship and parenting skill are always problems because we see many families for whom they are not. When either is an issue, however, it must be recognized and handled in an appropriate manner. In some cases, parent training in child management might be required before treatment can be carried out effectively. Patient and parent management issues are an integral part of successful treatment for patients with social anxiety disorder. Ignoring or downplaying their importance may result in attenuated outcomes, discouraged patients, and frustrated clinicians.

7

Pharmacological Treatment of Social Anxiety Disorder

I've noticed that my heart does not beat fast since I started on the medication.
Because my heart is not beating fast, I don't worry so much about the blushing.
In general, I am less worried about the physical symptoms and whether or not
others might perceive them. But I have not felt the urge to go out and make
new friends.

—Elaine (from chap. 1, this volume) after 4 weeks on atenolol

O ne of the most significant changes since the publication of the first
edition of this volume is the substantial increase in the treatment
outcome literature for social anxiety disorder. Medication trials for adults
have increased exponentially, allowing for a clearer picture of the role
of pharmacological agents. Treatment trials for children with social
anxiety disorder are also beginning to emerge. Empirical data are now
available for various classes of pharmacological agents, primarily selective
serotonin reuptake inhibitors (SSRIs), but also tricyclic antidepressants
(TCAs), monoamine oxidase inhibitors (MAOIs), beta-blockers, high-
potency benzodiazepines, the atypical anxiolytic azapirone (Buspar), and

anticonvulsants (for a discussion of these agents, their neurochemical action, and their clinical usage, see Davidson, 2003; Liebowitz & Marshall, 1995). In this chapter, we review the empirical literature related to social anxiety disorder, including data on predictors of treatment response, relapse rates, and the role of pretreatment attrition. In addition to the empirical review, we present information pertinent to clinicians working with adults and children who may be taking these medications.

EMPIRICAL STUDIES OF PHARMACOLOGICAL INTERVENTIONS

Tricyclic Antidepressants

Until the advent of the SSRIs, TCAs were the most widely used drugs to treat depression and anxiety. TCAs modulate neurotransmitter activity by influencing the metabolism or reuptake of the neurotransmitters acetylcholine, norepinephrine, and serotonin (Viesselman, Yaylayan, Weller, & Weller, 1993), although there is variability in the degree to which the different TCAs affect each neurotransmitter. Research examining the efficacy of TCAs in the treatment of social anxiety disorder in adults is limited, but the results are overwhelmingly negative. In an open trial of imipramine, only 22% responded positively (Simpson et al., 1998). A controlled trial specifically treating patients with social anxiety disorder reported no difference between those treated with imipramine or placebo (Zitrin, Klein, Woerner, & Ross, 1983). Given their lack of efficacy, potent side-effect potential (Simpson et al., 1998), and poor safety profile for children and adolescents (e.g., Velosa & Riddle, 2000), TCAs are not useful for the treatment of social anxiety disorder.

Selective Serotonin Reuptake Inhibitors

It is now clear that SSRIs are the pharmacological treatment of choice for adults with social anxiety disorder. Rather than simultaneously affecting the metabolism or reuptake of several neurotransmitters, the mechanism of action for the SSRIs is to block selectively (more or less, depending on the specific compound) the reuptake of the transmitter serotonin at the neural synapse. SSRIs are much less likely to produce cardiotoxicity than TCAs, there is no necessity for restrictive diets (as is the case for the MAOIs, discussed later), and they are much less likely to produce side effects such as weight gain, dry mouth, and sedation (Velosa & Riddle, 2000). Over the past several years, numerous open label and controlled trials have examined the applicability of SSRIs to the treatment of social anxiety disorder. In examining this literature, there are three caveats that we note. First, unless otherwise specified, responder status is defined as a rating of *improved* or *much improved* on the Clinical Global Impressions—Improvement Scale (Guy, 1976). Second, the Liebowitz Social Anxiety Scale is the primary clinician rating scale used in the majority of these trials to assess severity of fear and avoidance (LSAS; Liebowitz, 1987). Third, all of the adult samples are composed exclusively or almost exclusively of those with the generalized subtypes, and thus, relevance to those with the specific subtype remains unclear.

Fluoxetine

Among the SSRIs, some of the initial investigations examined the use of fluoxetine. Across several open trials (Black, Uhde, & Tancer, 1992; Schneier, Chin, Hollander, & Liebowitz, 1992; Van Ameringen, Mancini, & Streiner, 1993), 67% to 77% of adult patients were judged as treatment responders. In the only randomized controlled trial (Kobak, Greist, Jefferson, & Katzelnick, 2002), responder rates for patients treated with fluoxetine and those treated with placebo were not significantly different (40% vs. 30%, respectively). Furthermore, LSAS symptom change scores for fluoxetine (22.6 points) were less than for some of the other SSRIs reviewed in this section, and placebo outcome was higher (23.4 points) than that reported for other investigations.

Initial interest in fluoxetine for children with social anxiety disorder followed early publications reporting some efficacy for children with selective mutism (Black & Uhde, 1992; Golwyn & Weinstock, 1990). In a retrospective chart review, 81% of anxious children (including some with social anxiety disorder) treated with fluoxetine were judged as moderately or markedly improved (Birmaher et al., 1994). Fluoxetine was judged as equally efficacious regardless of the primary anxiety disorder. In an open prospective trial (Fairbanks et al., 1997), 80% of children with social anxiety disorder were judged as clinically improved, although 62.5% still met diagnostic criteria at posttreatment, indicating continuing impairment. In contrast to the promising findings from open trials, the results of a randomized, placebo-controlled trial (Black & Uhde, 1994) revealed that selectively mute children treated with fluoxetine were improved on the basis of parental, but not clinician or teacher, ratings and most children remained symptomatic at the end of treatment. Finally, in a randomized controlled trial examining fluoxetine for children with various anxiety disorders (Birmaher, Axelson, & Monk, 2003), 76% of children and adolescents with social anxiety disorder were rated as much or very much improved compared with 21% for placebo; 45.5% of those treated with fluoxetine achieved a positive functional outcome (a more stringent outcome criterion) as did 10% of the placebo group.

Fluvoxamine

Two randomized, placebo-controlled, 12-week trials (den Boer, van Vliet, & Westenberg, 1994; M. B. Stein, Fyer, Davidson, Pollack, & Wiita, 1999) indicated that adults with social anxiety disorder treated with fluvoxamine were significantly more improved compared with placebo; in the latter investigation, responder rates were 43% for fluvoxamine and 23% for placebo. Longer treatment trials appear to result in even more improvement; an additional 12 weeks of fluvoxamine treatment (24 weeks total) resulted in further improvement on general anxiety and specific social anxiety disorder symptoms as rated by treating clinicians (den Boer et al., 1994). Similarly, in an extension phase of a multicenter, randomized, placebo-controlled trial (D. J. Stein, Westenberg, Yang, Li, & Barbato, 2003), those who were at least minimally improved at the end of the 12-week acute phase and continued into a 12-week extension phase showed further improvement with fluvoxamine, although the rate was less than during the acute phase.

Efficacy data on the use of fluvoxamine for children and adolescents with social anxiety disorder can be found in studies examining outcomes for children with a variety of anxiety disorders (Research Units for Pediatric Psychopharmacology [RUPP] Anxiety Study Group, 2002). Among children with a primary or secondary diagnosis of social anxiety disorder, 76% of those treated with fluvoxamine were judged to be treatment responders compared with 29% of those receiving placebo, and improvement was maintained at 6-month follow-up. These data are promising, although limitations include the fact that the number of children with a primary diagnosis of social anxiety disorder was small, and it is unclear how the presence of a second anxiety disorder may have affected treatment outcome. Furthermore, treating clinicians, not independent evaluators, rated both clinical outcome and adverse events. Any reports of side effects by patients may have broken the blind in some cases and affected the clinician's determination of treatment outcome.

Sertraline

Two studies (one with adults and one with children and adolescents) have examined the efficacy of sertraline for social anxiety disorder. Among adults, 12 weeks of treatment resulted in a responder rate of 55.6% for those treated with sertraline compared with 29% of the placebo group (Liebowitz et al., 2003). Changes on the LSAS also supported the drug's superiority to placebo. Among children, an open trial of sertraline resulted in a 36% treatment responder rate (Compton, Grant, & Chrisman, 2001), and an additional 29% were considered partial responders. Scores on the Social Phobia and Anxiety Inventory for Children were below the cut-off score indicative of social anxiety disorder. It is interesting to note that children were admitted to this protocol if they were judged to have failed to benefit from a four-session trial of cognitive–behavioral therapy; yet after sertraline treatment, children attributed their improvement to the combination of the two interventions. In fact, if sertraline functions to decrease general levels of arousal, it is possible that after its administration, children were able to implement previously acquired behavioral skills. Such a hypothesis requires empirical testing, however. Although the results of this trial are limited by the lack of a control group, they indicate that sertraline (or the combination of sertraline and brief cognitive–behavioral treatment) may be effective for children and adolescents with social anxiety disorder.

Paroxetine

Among all of the available SSRIs, paroxetine has the most efficacy data and was the first SSRI to receive a U.S. Food and Drug Administration (FDA) indication for social anxiety disorder. Results from three randomized, placebo-controlled double-blind, multicenter trials indicated that among adult patients treated for 11 or 12 weeks, paroxetine responder rates ranged from 55% to 71% compared with 17% to 48% for placebo (Baldwin, Bobes, Stein, Schwarwächter, & Faure, 1999; D. J. Stein et al., 1999; M. B. Stein, Liebowitz, et al., 1998). Decreases on the LSAS also showed similar group differences that favored paroxetine. In a randomized, double-blind, 12-week maintenance trial, the superiority of paroxetine compared with placebo continued (D. J. Stein, Versiani, Hair, & Kumar, 2002). Significantly fewer patients who remained on paroxetine relapsed (14%) versus those who crossed over to placebo (39%). Furthermore, those who crossed over to placebo relapsed sooner than those who continued paroxetine, and at the end of the maintenance phase, a significantly greater number of paroxetine-treated patients were judged to be responders (78%) compared with placebo (51%). Clinician ratings and self-report data also favored the paroxetine group.

In an effort to determine variables that might predict treatment outcome for paroxetine, the analysis of data from several randomized controlled trials did not elucidate any demographic, physiologic, and clinical variables predictive of treatment response (D. J. Stein, M. B.

Stein, Pitts, Kumar, & Hunter, 2002) with the exception of treatment duration. Specifically, among paroxetine-treated patients, 28% of non-responders at Week 8 were responders at Week 12, suggesting that 12-week trials may be necessary to achieve optimum treatment response. Whether this same treatment trial length is necessary for the other SSRIs is unclear.

Data on the efficacy of paroxetine for children and adolescents are fewer, and in the only multicenter, randomized, double-blind, placebo-controlled investigation (Wagner et al., 2004), 77.6% of those treated with paroxetine and 38.4% of those treated with placebo were judged as treatment responders at the end of the 16-week trial; treatment effects were evident as early as Week 4. Significant group differences were also evident on the Liebowitz Social Anxiety Scale for Children and Adolescents (LSAS–CA). There were no developmental differences in outcome on the basis of age; paroxetine was equally effective for children and adolescents. At posttreatment, however, only 34.6% of those treated with paroxetine and 8% of those treated with placebo met remission criteria, emphasizing the need for additional or alternative treatments. Finally, paroxetine was the first of the SSRIs to be associated with increased suicidal ideation among adolescents with depression, leading eventually to the FDA black box warning regarding the use of these medications with children and adolescents (see the summary to this section later in the chapter).

Citalopram

One of the most selective of the SSRIs is citalopram. Fewer data are available for this medication than for some other SSRIs, but the outcome appears similar. Specifically, in a 12-week open trial (Bouwer & Stein, 1998), 86% of patients with the generalized subtype were considered to be treatment responders. In a controlled comparison of citalopram and moclobemide (a reversible MAOI, discussed subsequently), treatment responder rates were identical (75% for citalopram and 74.3% for moclobemide; Atmaca, Kuloglu, Tezcan, & Unal, 2002).

Escitalopram, an isomer of citalopram, is generally considered to be more selective and better tolerated. In a randomized, double-blind, placebo-controlled trial (Lader, Stender, Bürger, & Nil, 2004), three escitalopram doses were compared with paroxetine and placebo. Responder rates for escitalopram were 79% (5 mg), 76% (10 mg), and 88% (20 mg), compared with 80% for paroxetine and 66% for placebo; rates for all three doses of escitalopram were significantly different from the placebo rate, and the rate for the 20-mg dose exceeded that for paroxetine. Improvement for all active medication groups was evident at Week 12. Results were identical when the LSAS was used as the outcome variable. A 66% placebo response rate is of some concern, however, and merits further consideration. For example, although the patients appeared to be severely impaired, the manner in which pretreatment diagnosis was determined was not clear. We raised concerns in chapter 5 about the need to include functional impairment criteria when assigning a diagnosis of social anxiety disorder. It is possible that a number of subsyndromal cases may have been included in this sample, resulting in the inordinately high placebo response rate.

In one of the few pharmacological trials specifically addressing comorbidity (Schneier et al., 2003), the efficacy of citalopram for patients with primary social anxiety disorder (generalized subtype) and comorbid major depression was examined. This was an open trial, and, consistent with other investigations, the treatment responder rate for social anxiety disorder was 66.7%. Citalopram was also efficacious for comorbid major depression, resulting in a treatment responder rate of 76.2%. The authors noted that depression symptoms responded more rapidly than social anxiety symptoms. That observation, coupled with the lower responder rate for social anxiety disorder, led to the conclusion that a 12-week trial may be insufficient to assess the full treatment response of social anxiety disorder when a comorbid condition is present.

To summarize, the extant treatment outcome literature supports the efficacy of SSRIs for reducing symptoms in adults with social anxiety disorder. Too few randomized controlled trials with sufficient samples of children with primary social anxiety disorder exist to allow firm conclusions to be drawn at this time, however. Currently, these medications are in widespread use for both adults and children, and although some improvement results, significant symptomatology remains for many with this disorder. An advantage is their relatively more benign side-effect profile and the ease with which patients can be withdrawn safely from them. Nevertheless, negative side effects have been reported, and withdrawal should always occur under the care of a qualified physician. One potential drawback is that, compared with some other classes of medication, it typically takes several weeks before the drug reaches a therapeutic level, meaning that there is a considerable wait before improvement can be expected. A recent challenge for the SSRIs is that the FDA issued a black box warning regarding the increased potential for suicidal ideation among children and adolescents with depression who are treated with these medications. Although there are no data to suggest that these higher rates exist among children or adolescents with anxiety disorders, the black box warning has dampened enthusiasm, at least among parents, for the use of SSRIs in pediatric populations (see the later section on pretreatment attrition).

Combination Reuptake Inhibitors

Venlafaxine

The mechanism of action for venlafaxine is different from that of the SSRIs because it inhibits reuptake of both serotonin and norepinephrine. Basic pharmacological data indicate that when administered an acute dose of a selective norepinephrine reuptake inhibition, healthy adults had an increase in social communication and attention to an interpersonal partner and a decrease in hand-fidgeting (Tse & Bond, 2002). Along with the established treatment outcome literature suggesting that noradrenergic and serotonin reuptake inhibitors were efficacious for both anxiety and depression (Rickels, Mangano, & Khan, 2004), there seemed to be sufficient rationale to examine the efficacy of a dual serotonergic–

norepinephrine reuptake inhibitor for social anxiety disorder. In an open trial with 12 adult patients who were nonresponders to SSRIs, 50% of whom also met criteria for avoidant personality disorder, 92% of patients exhibited moderate to marked improvement on fear symptoms, and 83% exhibited moderate to marked improvement on avoidant symptoms (Altamura, Pioli, Vitto, & Mannu, 1999). Follow-up double-blind, placebo-controlled, randomized 12-week trials confirmed the efficacy of venlafaxine extended-release (venlafaxine ER) compared with placebo (Allgulander et al., 2004; Liebowitz, Gelenberg, & Munjack, 2005; Rickels et al., 2004). Treatment responder rates were significantly higher for those treated with venlafaxine ER (50%–69%) than placebo (34%–36%), and LSAS scores were significantly lower for those treated with venlafaxine ER. Similar outcome was reported when a 6-month randomized design was used (M. B. Stein, Pollack, Bystritsky, Kelsey, & Mangano, 2005). Response rates were 58% for venlafaxine ER and 33% for placebo; actual remission rates were lower (31% for venlafaxine ER and 16% for placebo) but again demonstrated efficacy of the drug compared with placebo. Two investigations (Allgulander et al., 2004; Liebowitz et al., 2005) also compared venlafaxine ER with paroxetine. In both studies, there were no differences in responder rates for paroxetine (63%–66%) and venlafaxine ER (59%–69%), although, again, actual remission rates for each active medication were lower (38% for venlafaxine ER and 29% for paroxetine; Allgulander et al., 2004). Venlafaxine ER produced an earlier treatment response (compared with paroxetine), although changes in synaptic response is considered merely a first step in the process of synaptic re-adaptation, which may take longer than 12 weeks (Liebowitz et al., 2005). In summary, although venlafaxine ER may be efficacious for adults with social anxiety disorder (no data on children or adolescents are currently available), two studies that examined pharmacological action (Liebowitz et al., 2005; M. B. Stein et al., 2005) suggest that norepinephrine reuptake blockage does not contribute to its therapeutic effect. Furthermore, Liebowitz et al. (2005) noted that dosage reductions because of adverse events (e.g., nausea, insomnia, yawning) were more common among patients treated with venlafaxine ER than paroxetine and that some clinicians are reluctant to use this drug as a first-line agent because of the possibility of causing agitation or increasing anxious symptomatology.

Monoamine Oxidase Inhibitors

The class of drugs known as MAOIs actually consist of two types. The labels *nonreversible* (nonselective) and *reversible* (selective) MAOIs refer to whether the drug binds irreversibly to the monoamine oxidase enzyme and whether the compound is selective for both the A and B enzymatic forms (Potts & Davidson, 1995). Because the effects of the selective form can be reversed much more rapidly, dietary restrictions necessitated by the older, nonreversible type are not necessary. Although there are some data for the reversible types (brofaramine and moclobemide), these compounds are not marketed in the United States and are not discussed here. In this section, we address the literature for the nonreversible type.

Following an early study indicating that the MAOI phenelzine ameliorated associated social anxiety symptoms in adults with depression (Liebowitz et al., 1984), an open trial of phenelzine in 11 adults with social anxiety disorder (Liebowitz, Gorman, Fyer, Campeas, et al., 1985) indicated that 64% were rated as markedly improved and the other 36% as improved. Subsequently, a randomized, placebo-controlled trial (Liebowitz et al., 1992) compared phenelzine with placebo and the beta-blocker atenolol (see the subsequent section on beta-blockers). After 8 weeks of treatment, 64% of those treated with phenelzine were judged to be improved, as were 30% of those treated with atenolol and 23% of those who received placebo. Improvement was greater on clinician rating scales than on patient self-report measures (Potts & Davidson, 1995). During the discontinuation phase, 33% of the phenelzine responders relapsed, as did 33% of the atenolol responders. None of those who remained on phenelzine relapsed, whereas 50% of those who remained on atenolol did. The number of patients who participated in the discontinuation phase was small, however, and thus, these data must be interpreted cautiously. An important contribution of this study (Liebowitz et al., 1992) was the attempt to analyze outcome by subtypes. Among those with the generalized subtype, the improvement rate was 68% for phenelzine, 28% for atenolol, and 21% for placebo. Thus, atenolol was no more efficacious than placebo, and both atenolol and placebo were substantially less efficacious than phenelzine. Among the specific subtype, response rates were 50% for phenelzine, 40% for atenolol, and 29% for placebo, but the number of specific subtype subjects was small. Overall, data indicated the superiority of phenelzine for the generalized subtype.

In one final comparative trial, a double-blind evaluation of phenelzine, moclobemide (a reversible MAOI), and placebo revealed that after 8 and 16 weeks of treatment, both phenelzine and moclobemide were superior to placebo (Versiani et al., 1992). There were no differences between the two active treatments; improvement rates were 91% for phenelzine, 82% for moclobemide, and 43% for placebo.

To date, other than one case description of a child with selective mutism (Golwyn & Weinstock, 1990), we know of no reports of the use of MAOIs with children who have an anxiety disorder. In summary, phenelzine has demonstrated efficacy for improvement in social anxiety disorder symptoms among adults with this disorder. Some patients relapse once the drug is discontinued, and the effects of the medication can be toxic. Also, a significant deterrent to the use of the MAOIs is the need for a strict dietary regimen; 8% of those on long-term MAOI therapy develop hypertensive reactions, even when they follow the dietary restrictions (Davidson, 2003). On the basis of these concerns as well as the success of the SSRIs and their more benign side-effect profile, MAOIs are no longer considered first-line agents for social anxiety disorder and are used infrequently.

Beta-Blockers

Interest in beta-blockers as a possible treatment for social anxiety disorder stems in part from early studies indicating their ability to reduce anxiety in individuals with public speaking and musical performance fears (e.g., Gossard, Dennis, & DeBusk, 1984; Neftel et al., 1982). Overall, these drugs decreased subjective distress and ameliorated physical symptoms of anxiety. Because social anxiety disorder is characterized by physiological reactivity of the beta-adrenergic system (see chap. 1, this volume), it seemed reasonable to hypothesize that drugs blocking this system might eliminate the physiological response of patients with this disorder.

Despite this promising empirical database and the strong theoretical underpinnings, the efficacy of beta-blockers in the treatment of social anxiety disorder has not been impressive (e.g., Falloon, Lloyd, & Harpin, 1981; Gorman, Liebowitz, Fyer, Campeas, & Klein, 1985; S. M. Turner, Beidel, & Jacob, 1994; see the subsequent section on combination and comparative trials). This is particularly the case for the generalized subtype of social anxiety disorder for which atenolol has not proved to be superior to placebo. Also, we were unable to find any reports in the literature describing the use of beta-blockers with children. Thus, except in unusual circumstances, beta-blockers do not appear to be the drug of choice in treating social anxiety disorder, except perhaps for those with very specific social fears (Davidson, 2003).

High-Potency Benzodiazepines

Alprazolam is commonly used with chronic anxiety states, but its efficacy for social anxiety disorder is minimal. Two open trials in adults with social anxiety disorder (Lydiard, Larraia, Howell, & Ballenger, 1988; Reich & Yates, 1988b) and one trial with children with avoidant disorder (Simeon & Ferguson, 1987) were promising, but subsequent controlled trials did not support the initial positive results for either group (Gelernter et al., 1991; Simeon et al., 1992).

Several open trials of clonazepam (Davidson, Ford, Smith, & Potts, 1991; Ontiveros & Fontaine, 1990; Reiter, Pollack, Rosenbaum, & Cohen, 1990) reported substantial improvement for most adult patients on clinician ratings of symptoms and social anxiety disorder severity. When compared with a no-treatment control group (Munjack, Baltazar, Bohn, Cabe, & Appleton, 1990), 60% of those treated with clonazepam were judged to be much or very much improved compared with 20% of the no-treatment group. In the largest placebo-controlled trial (10 weeks; Davidson et al., 1993), those treated with clonazepam benefited early (at Week 1) and improved on various clinician-rated and self-report instruments. Overall, at the end of the trial, 78% of patients treated with clonazepam were judged responders compared with only 20% of patients treated with placebo. During withdrawal, rates of relapse were higher for clonazepam than for placebo. A study of clonazepam incorporated magnetic resonance spectroscopy to assess pre- and posttreatment changes. After 8 weeks, clonazepam did not alter initial low levels of N-acetyl aspartate or any other metabolite (Tupler et al., 1997). According to Davidson (2003), because metabolic changes did not occur as a result of treatment (whereas subjective feelings of distress were markedly changed), altered neuronal functioning may indicate a role for trait features of social anxiety disorder.

Currently, then, the results of controlled trials in adult populations are negative for alprazolam but positive for clonazepam. Major advantages of these drugs include their quick action and relatively benign side-effect profile, but there are a number of major drawbacks as well. They have significant sedative effects, which often limits dosing options. Impaired psychomotor performance is a common complicating factor. Furthermore, there are very real medical dangers when individuals taking these medications also ingest alcohol. Clinically, a particular problem for these drugs is their substantial relapse rate. In addition, dependence on these drugs can develop, and withdrawal can be difficult, particularly for alprazolam, resulting in the necessity for a strict withdrawal regimen. Because of the potential for abuse and dependence and withdrawal difficulties, and because, in our view, there are better choices, these drugs probably are not well suited as a first-line treatment for social anxiety disorder or even chronic anxiety states, despite their widespread use.

Anticonvulsants

It may not initially be clear why drugs developed to treat epilepsy would be useful for the treatment of social anxiety disorder, but outcome data for an epilepsy trial suggested secondary effects such as improved mood, decreased anxiety, and increased social well-being (Jefferson, 2001). In a randomized, placebo-controlled trial of gabapentin for adults with social anxiety disorder (Pande et al., 1999), the responder rate for gabapentin was significantly superior to placebo (38% vs. 17%, respectively). Similarly, in a 10-week double-blind, placebo-controlled trial of pregabalin (an analogue of the GABA [gamma-aminobutyric acid] neurotransmitter), 600 mg of pregabalin resulted in significantly more responders (43%) than 150 mg or placebo (21% vs. 22%, respectively). This is one of the few trials in which outcome using the LSAS did not mimic other responder criteria. Although LSAS scores did decrease significantly from pretreatment at the 600-mg dosage, few patients benefited from pregabalin when LSAS criteria were used (28% vs. 14% vs. 13%, respectively). Finally, an open trial of topiramate (another anticonvulsant) indicated that 75% were rated as responders after 16 weeks (Van Ameringen, Mancini, Pipe, Oakman, & Bennett, 2004). This was a small sample (only 12 patients completed treatment), however, and controlled trials are necessary before drawing any conclusions. At this time, none of these drugs have FDA indications for their use in the treatment of social anxiety disorder, and there have been no controlled trials of anticonvulsants for children with the disorder.

Comparative and Combination Trials

There now are a number of trials comparing medication and behavioral or cognitive–behavioral treatments. Using composite indexes of improvement and end-state functioning to evaluate the efficacy of flooding (exposure), atenolol, and placebo (Turner, Beidel, & Jacob, 1994), 89% of patients treated with flooding were moderately or significantly improved compared with rates for patients treated with atenolol and placebo (47% and 44%, respectively). Using end-state functioning status (which compares posttreatment outcome of patients with social anxiety disorder with that of nonsocially phobic patients), 75% of those treated with flooding achieved moderate or high end-state status, compared with 44% of the atenolol patients and 59% of the placebo patients. Thus, two independent research groups (Liebowitz et al., 1992; Turner, Beidel, & Jacob, 1994) using different measurement strategies have failed to confirm the superiority of atenolol to a placebo control group.

In a comparative trial of phenelzine, placebo, cognitive–behavioral group treatment (CBGT), and educational support (ES; Heimberg et al., 1998; see chap. 8, this volume, for a description of the components of CBGT), phenelzine produced a more rapid response than CBGT at 6 weeks, but this effect disappeared at 12 weeks. At posttreatment, responder rates were 75% for CBGT, 77% for phenelzine, 41% for placebo, and 35% for ES. Phenelzine was superior to CBGT on some of the outcome measures. After an untreated follow-up period, however, only 17% of those treated with CBGT relapsed compared with 50% of those treated with phenelzine (Liebowitz et al., 1999).

In another comparative trial (Gelernter et al., 1991) patients were randomized to phenelzine, alprazolam, placebo, or CBGT; all patients treated with medications also received exposure instructions. After 12 weeks, there were no group differences on self-report or clinician-rating scales. Basing responder criterion on a score in the "normal" range on a self-report measure of fear, 69% of those treated with phenelzine were responders, as were 38% of those treated with alprazolam, 24% of those treated with CBGT, and 20% of those who received placebo. These findings, particularly with regard to the outcome for CBGT, stand in stark contrast to the CBGT–phenelzine comparison cited earlier. It is beyond the scope of this chapter to discuss why these differences might have occurred, although variations in CBGT administration or a different measurement strategy are among obvious possibilities.

In a comparative trial of clonazepam and CBGT (Otto et al., 2000), both groups improved significantly on self-report and clinician-rated measures. Remission rates (defined as scores of less than 2 on the Clinical Global Impressions—Severity of Illness subscale), however, were 20% for the clonazepam group and 25% for CBGT. This study is limited by the small sample size (only 35 patients completed one of the two treatments) and the lack of a placebo control condition. A large, randomized, placebo-controlled trial compared fluoxetine, comprehensive cognitive behavioral therapy (CCBT), placebo, and the combinations of CCBT plus fluoxetine and CCBT plus placebo for adults with social anxiety disorder (Davidson et al., 2004). CCBT consists of in vivo exposure, cognitive restructuring, and social skills training conducted in a group setting. After 14 weeks of treatment, 64% of those treated with fluoxetine, 65% of those treated with CCBT, 60% of those treated with the combination of CCBT and placebo, 67% of those treated with CCBT and fluoxetine, and 41% of those treated with placebo were rated as significantly improved (i.e., responders). The overall chi-square test failed to attain the .05 level of significance, indicating no overall difference in response rates across groups. Single pairwise comparisons were nevertheless conducted and suggested that for the completer sample, fluoxetine, CCBT, and CCBT plus fluoxetine were significantly superior to placebo. The lack of a significant effect for the overall chi-square tempers conclusions regarding the efficacy of these interventions, and it is clear that the combination treatment was not significantly superior to either treatment alone.

In another comparative trial (D. M. Clark et al., 2003), adult patients were randomized to cognitive therapy, fluoxetine plus self-exposure, or placebo plus self-exposure. At both midtreatment and posttreatment, cognitive therapy was significantly superior to fluoxetine plus self-exposure and placebo plus self-exposure, whereas the latter two conditions did not differ from each other. It should be noted that cognitive therapy made extensive use of behavioral experiences in which patients specified their feared outcomes for various situations and then tested them during planned exposure sessions using in-session role-play as well as in-session and homework-based in vivo assignments. Therefore, this intervention is more typical of cognitive–behavioral treatments than solely cognitive therapy. Furthermore, the cognitive therapy was conducted by highly trained therapists, whereas the self-exposure that was part of the medication groups was conducted by those with minimal formal training in exposure treatment (although they were supervised by the senior author). Thus, it is unclear whether the two medication conditions would have been more efficacious if the self-exposure had been implemented by experienced therapists. Twelve-month follow-up data indicated that cognitive therapy remained superior to both medication conditions, and, again, analysis of pretreatment demographic and clinical variables failed to identify any predictors of treatment outcome.

Summary of Empirical Literature on the Pharmacological Treatment of Social Anxiety Disorder

Since the publication of the first edition, there has been an exponential increase in controlled trials of various pharmacological agents, and now the preponderance of evidence supports the efficacy of the SSRIs as the first-line treatment for social anxiety disorder for adults (e.g., van der Linden, Stein, & van Balkom, 2000). Fewer data are available for children, but those that exist suggest some efficacy for the SSRIs as well. Their more benign side-effect profile is a positive feature. Nevertheless, as noted earlier in the chapter, FDA black box warnings regarding the increased suicidal ideation in depressed children and adolescents has dampened enthusiasm for the use of these medications (at least among parents). Furthermore, a comparative analysis of paroxetine response for children versus adolescents with depression indicates that adolescents (age 15 years or older) had a more positive response rate than did those younger than age 15 (Carpenter, Lipschitz, Fong, Krulewicz, & Davies, 2005). In fact, there was no difference in response rate to paroxetine and placebo in the younger group. Adverse effects were more common in the younger children, although serious emotional liability (which may include suicidal ideation) was more common in the older group. In contrast, in the only study that assessed the efficacy of paroxetine for children and adolescents with social anxiety disorder, outcome was similar for both groups (Wagner et al., 2004). However, the cautionary tone of the Carpenter et al. (2005) study suggests a need to consider patient age when examining treatment efficacy.

Benzodiazepines and the nonreversible MAOI phenelzine remain alternative viable options for adults. Dietary restrictions for the MAOIs, the potential for psychological and physical dependence for the benzodiazepines, and the side-effect profile for both medications may preclude their administration for some patients, however. These dietary restrictions are particularly problematic for children and adolescents, who may not understand (or be willing to accept) the limitations (e.g., no pizza). In contrast to the positive effects for SSRIs and phenelzine, beta-blockers have not met initial positive expectations, although some investigators believe that they still may play a role in a select group of those patients with the specific subtype (e.g., Elaine). The exact characteristics of this subgroup have yet to be established, however. Finally, anticonvulsants represent a new class of medications, and initial trials demonstrate efficacy compared with placebo, although responder rates are lower than for the other classes of medications reviewed in this chapter.

One limitation of the current pharmacological treatments is that relapse rates for medications are substantial, although somewhat variable depending on the specific compound. This suggests that the effects last only as long as the individual continues to take the drug. As noted, it is unclear whether alternative methods of discontinuation, longer treatment periods, or both, would enhance maintenance for the pharmacological interventions (Turner, Beidel, Wolff, Spaulding, & Jacob, 1996). As noted earlier, doubling the treatment time from 12 to 24 weeks enhances outcome but only moderately. With respect to children, the data are so limited that it is difficult to offer any guidelines.

ISSUES RELATED TO MEDICATION USE IN SOCIAL ANXIETY DISORDER

There are numerous issues regarding treatment of social anxiety disorder with pharmacotherapy (e.g., Kutcher, Reiter, & Gardner, 1995; Liebowitz & Marshall, 1995). Factors to consider include education and the presentation of the rationale for the medication, assurance of adequate dosage, evaluation of side effects, evaluation of clinical response, medication withdrawal, attrition, and treatment nonresponders. Each factor is discussed in turn in the following sections.

Education and Presentation of the Rationale

In chapter 6, we presented a general outline for patient education and approaches to treatment. Liebowitz and Marshall (1995) offered three points for discussion when presenting a pharmacological treatment option: citing the treatment literature; proposing that if anxiety drives the phobic avoidance, then ameliorating the anxiety may eliminate interpersonal difficulties and perhaps phobic avoidance; and discussing the effects of medication on the key symptom of hypersensitivity to criticism or rejection. The first two points are useful when proposing psychological treatments as well. A recommended pharmacological educational strategy for children and adolescents includes (a) education about expected outcome with and without treatment, (b) a balanced discussion of the various treatment options available (including risks and benefits), and (c) a discussion of the potential role of medication in treating the disorder and the expected treatment length (Kutcher et al., 1995).

Attrition

Pretreatment Attrition and Parental Preference

As noted, the well-publicized FDA black box warning has raised concern about the use of SSRIs, and medication in general, for the treatment of childhood disorders, and perhaps for the treatment of childhood anxiety disorders in particular. Surveying parental opinions concerning treatment options for children with anxiety disorders (Chavira, Stein, Bailey, & Stein, 2003), parents endorsed favorable attitudes toward psychological intervention and somewhat neutral beliefs about medication. Caucasian parents, compared with non-Caucasian parents, were more accepting of both medication and counseling and saw counseling as more feasible.

Over the past 4 years, we have conducted a randomized, double-blind, placebo-controlled comparative trial of behavior therapy, fluoxetine, and placebo for the treatment of children and adolescents with social anxiety disorder (Beidel, Turner, Sallee, & Ammerman, 2000). Informally, we noted that a substantial percentage of parents who called to inquire about the treatment program declined participation once they heard about the medication condition. We decided to assess formally the reasons for parental decisions to decline participation. Understanding these decisions is necessary because pretreatment attrition, defined as the systematic self-exclusion of potential participants during the pretreatment phase of a protocol, can result in a significant threat to the validity of randomized clinical trials (Hansen, Collins, Malotte, Johnson, & Fielding, 1985). The results of our investigation (Young et al., in press) indicate that 45% of the 273 parents who refused to participate in the study did so because they did not want their child to take medication. This percentage was higher than for any other cited reason (including those who did not give a reason but just declined to participate). We then conducted a more formal analysis of the reasons parents seeking behavioral treatment for their children might choose to participate or not participate in a research program "examining behavioral and pharmacological treatments for children with social anxiety disorder." Among the respondents, 64% said that they would decline to participate in a study that included medication; 29% said that they would complete the pretreatment assessment and drop out if they were assigned to the medication group. The most common reason given for the refusal was risk of side effects (28%) followed by developing drug dependency (21%), the combination of these two reasons (19%), and inability of the child to discontinue the medication after the completion of the treatment trial

(6%). Other reasons were less commonly cited. Again, non-Caucasian parents had a greater dislike for the idea of being in a research study, for the possibility of receiving placebo, and for the idea of potential drug dependency. The results indicate that despite the best efforts of investigators, pretreatment attrition is a significant threat to the external validity of research trials and may be particularly skewed toward pediatric pharmacological trials. Among adult samples, between 12% and 35% of those eligible for a comparative trial (Davidson et al., 2004; Huppert, Franklin, Foa, & Davidson, 2003) declined participation because of the possibility they would be required to take medication. Although there likely is little that can be done about the issue of medication refusal, appropriate reporting of treatment trial outcomes should require the reporting of pretreatment attrition rates.

Treatment Attrition Rates

Among the clinical trials discussed throughout this chapter, attrition rates ranged from a low of 16% to a high of 34%. In many instances, higher attrition rates were found in the group receiving active medication and were caused by adverse effects. Although intent to treat analyses control statistically for dropouts, it is important to remember that a significant percentage of clinical trial participants do not complete randomized clinical trials.

Assurance of Adequate Dosage

Obviously, medication is ineffective if it is not taken at a therapeutic level, as directed, or for a sufficient length of time. Particularly for children and adolescents, much data regarding pharmacological treatment is based on open clinical trials or adult treatment outcomes, and therapeutic dosage ranges for all medications have not been established.

Evaluation of Side Effects

All medications can produce adverse effects in addition to their therapeutic effects. It is important to remember that many side effects are temporary (i.e., they subside as the patient continues to take the medication). Therefore, in addition to monitoring the occurrence of side effects, their severity and impact on patient daily functioning should be considered before determining the need for dosage reduction or complete discontinuation of a medication. Finally, issues of race and ethnicity need to be considered when determining drug efficacy and side effects. African Americans, Hispanics, and Asian Americans treated with antidepressants (a) achieve positive effects from lower dosages than what is needed for European Americans and (b) have more side effects from the TCAs than do European Americans (e.g., Turner, Cooley-Quille, & Beidel, 1995). To date, studies have not assessed the presence or severity of side effects separately for various racial and ethnic groups.

Dietary Restrictions With MAOIs

As noted, perhaps the greatest drawback of nonreversible MAOIs such as phenelzine is the need to follow a diet low in tyramine. Failure to do so can result in a hypertensive reaction that requires immediate treatment and could prove fatal. Dietary restrictions include avoiding most forms of cheese, alcohol (particularly red wine), aged meats, chocolate, cocoa, tomato sauce, ketchup, chili sauce, eggplant, yogurt, oranges, bananas, pineapples, raisins, and many other foods, as well as some medications. Again, as noted by Davidson (2003), the availability of the SSRIs means that MAOIs are no longer a front-line treatment for social anxiety disorder.

Evaluation of Clinical Response

In the first edition, we cited Liebowitz and Marshall's (1995) five criteria to determine treatment efficacy: decreased social anxiety, decreased anticipatory anxiety, decreased social avoidance, change in coexisting conditions, and decrease in functional impairment. Since that time, most pharmacological investigations for adults with social anxiety disorder use two primary outcome measures: the Clinical Global Impressions Scale—Improvement (CGI–I; Guy, 1976) and the LSAS (Liebowitz,

1987). The CGI–I is a one-item scale by which the clinician makes an overall judgment of improvement in symptomatology. The LSAS is a more extensive rating scale that specifically assesses various aspects of symptomatology. Both scales address the five criteria listed earlier and both are now standard measures of treatment outcome in pharmacological trials for adults. To date, there are too few pharmacological investigations with children and adolescents for similar conclusions regarding efficacy to be drawn.

As readers of this chapter may have noticed, one concern with the outcomes reported for pharmacological treatment trials (and for some psychosocial treatment trials as well; see chaps. 8 and 9, this volume) is the large placebo response rate ranging from 23% to 66% for the adult pharmacological trials reviewed here and 38% in two trials with children and adolescents. Even if the response rate for social anxiety disorder is significantly higher, there is some need for concern when almost one in four children with social anxiety disorder responds to placebo. A review of 15 adult pharmacological trials indicated that the placebo effect is moderately large (average effect size of 0.46); is highest in large, multicenter trials; and is independent of study duration (Oosterbaan, van Balkom, Spinhoven, & van Dyck, 2001). In fact, the larger the trial, the higher the placebo response rate even though medication response rate did not change with the size of the trial. Furthermore, this review noted that there was no validation for a placebo run-in phase because it did not decrease the percentage of placebo responders in those studies in which a 1-week run-in was used. As noted (Oosterbaan et al., 2001), to cope with the high placebo response rate, medication trials have been forced to include larger numbers of patients to achieve a statistically significant treatment effect, but the power needed to obtain a statistically significant effect sometimes results in differences so minute as to be clinically meaningless.

Another important consideration is the ongoing distinction between improved and remitted. The majority of randomized controlled trials have indicated that patients are statistically improved as a result of active medication, but many investigations also report that posttreatment scores on the LSAS are still above 50, a score often used as the minimum necessary for admission to a treatment protocol. In other words, even at posttreatment, a number of improved patients were still experiencing symptomatology significant enough to allow admission into the same treatment protocol. Among children, 62.5% of those in one study still met diagnostic criteria at posttreatment (Birmaher et al., 1994). Liebowitz et al. (2003) proposed that social anxiety disorder may need to be reconceptualized as a chronic illness, like obsessive–compulsive disorder, with a reasonable treatment goal of management of the disorder rather than remission. We should note that concerns about placebo response rates and responders versus remitters apply to psychosocial treatment trials as well (see chaps. 8 and 9, this volume). In the case of those treated with medication, augmentation of treatment response may be dependent on longer term therapy or adjunctive therapies (Liebotwitz et al., 2003).

Medication Discontinuation

If improvement occurs, the next questions to arise are (a) how long must the patient continue to take the medication, (b) when can it be discontinued, and (c) can it be discontinued safely? Published relapse rates for adult trials are high (Gelernter et al., 1991; Liebowitz et al., 1999; Potts & Davidson, 1995). A complicating factor with benzodiazepine withdrawal is that symptoms include anxiety, concentration difficulties, and memory disturbances. Because these behaviors are also characteristic of anxiety states, the clinician must determine whether such behaviors represent medication withdrawal or return of previous symptomatology. One method for determining this may be to track symptomatology over time. That is, withdrawal symptoms may dissipate, whereas a return of previous symptomatology will likely remain. It is clear, then, that the withdrawal of medication, and particularly benzodiazepines, must be carried out with considerable care. At this time, there are no clinical trials examining discontinuation of medication in children with social anxiety disorder.

Practically, all medications need to be tapered under the supervision of a qualified physician. Although some medications can be withdrawn easily, others, such as paroxetine and the benzodiazepines, require special care. Abrupt discontinuation can be dangerous for the patient. In addition to the actual withdrawal schedules, patients need to be educated about the possible side effects during the discontinuation phase and the need to work closely with their physician.

CONCLUSION

In this chapter, we reviewed the empirical outcome literature for the pharmacological treatment of social anxiety disorder. For adults, the established literature is much more substantial that what was available at the time of the first edition, although there are still few data available for children and adolescents. Both SSRIs and MAOIs have the highest published rates of improvement, but the more benign side effect profile favors the SSRIs as the first-line agent. MAOIs and benzodiazepines are viable second-line agents for adults, and there are emerging data that anticonvulsant agents also may have some effect, although to date, response rates are lower than for the other available agents. Other than SSRIs, no recommendations can be made for children and adolescents.

Although there is evidence that drug therapies can be helpful to reduce symptoms, one problem is that the positive treatment effects tend to dissipate rapidly once the medication is discontinued. This seems to be true, with some differences in rate, for all of the medications discussed here. Because the question has not been researched fully at this time, it is unclear whether the patient must remain on medication forever or whether there are critical phases during which the medication can be successfully withdrawn.

Side effects are another issue to consider when using medication for treating social anxiety disorder. Although the high-potency benzodiazepines have shown some degree of efficacy (particularly clonazepam) and are well tolerated by patients, the significant potential side effects suggest they should be used carefully, if at all. In our opinion, these compounds probably are not good initial choices for the treatment of social anxiety disorder or any chronic maladaptive anxiety state. Among the most problematic difficulties include the potential for dependence and significant withdrawal symptoms. The SSRIs enjoy a relatively benign profile compared with other antidepressants and do not have the same drawbacks as the other drugs in current use. This appears to be the case particularly for children, although the FDA black box warning raises some concern about the use of these medications in children and adolescents.

One question frequently posed is whether there is a synergistic effect from combining behavioral and drug treatment. This is another area in which there has been an increase in the literature since the publication of the first edition of this volume. The data that do exist suggest that there is nothing to be gained from combining the two treatments, at least in the case of adults. We noted that in our clinical experience, there are those instances in which the combination appears to facilitate a positive treatment outcome for a given patient. In particular, we noted this to be the case when severe depression or very high anxiety was present. This needs to be explored further through empirical studies, and, if confirmed, the exact features of those who benefit from such a strategy need to be delineated.

8

Behavioral and Cognitive–Behavioral Treatment of Social Anxiety Disorder in Adults

Dear Drs. Turner and Beidel:

Enclosed please find a copy of my wedding announcement. As you may remember, one of my final homework assignments was to invite a female coworker to lunch. Well, I completed that task successfully. In fact, I began dating the person I invited to lunch, and last month we married. Thank you for all of your help.

Sincerely, John Doe

We received this letter from a patient who participated in our behavioral treatment program for social anxiety disorder. Most outcomes are not quite this dramatic but are no less gratifying. As we noted in chapter 1 of this volume, although described as early as 1966 by Marks and Gelder, social anxiety disorder was introduced into the American psychiatric nomenclature in 1980 (American Psychiatric Association, 1980). Yet just 2.5 decades since its recognition, there is a substantive literature evaluating the efficacy of various behavioral and cognitive–behavioral treatments. In fact, the literature is sufficiently established to allow some rather firm conclusions about current treatment strategies and their short- and long-term effects. The behavioral and cognitive–behavioral treatments have been administered alone or as combinations using individual, group, or combination individual and group formats. The primary interventions include exposure, social skill training (SST), and various methods of cognitive restructuring. We limit our discussion to those studies involving the use of patients with a diagnosis of social anxiety disorder and to treatments that were examined empirically. For the sake of conceptual clarity, we have divided our review into two sections: those studies using traditional behavioral interventions (e.g., exposure, SST) and those involving the addition of a cognitive component and the newer cognitive therapies. First, we examine some new data pertaining to the recognition of social anxiety disorder and factors affecting the decision to seek treatment. We then review the empirical evidence for behavioral and cognitive–behavioral treatments for social anxiety disorder, describe the major treatment strategies currently in use, discuss the manner in which treatment strategies are implemented, and explore variables that might affect outcome.

THE DECISION TO SEEK TREATMENT

Available data indicate that only a small percentage of those with social anxiety disorder ever seek treatment. Among one epidemiological sample, only 23% of the generalized subtype and 13% of the specific subtype had ever sought treatment (Kessler, 2003). Thus, even though efficacious treatments are available, few of those with the disorder appear to take advantage of them. One reason may be that many consider social anxiety disorder to be a social problem, not an emotional disorder. Only 5% of those with social anxiety disorder believed that they might have an emotional problem, even though more than 33% of those with the generalized subtype experienced significant role impairment (Kessler, 2003). It is interesting to note that in that study, no other mental disorder had a rate for which the perceived need for treatment, after adjustment for level of impairment, was so low. Three major barriers to treatment have been identified (Olfson et al., 2000): uncertainty about where to go for help, financial barriers affecting the ability to pay for treatment, and fear of what others might think of them if they sought help. Over the past several years, it is gratifying that there has been increased discussion of social anxiety disorder, and this may increase the awareness rate. Whether that translates into an increase in the decision to seek treatment is not yet known.

REVIEW OF EMPIRICAL LITERATURE

Traditional Behavioral Treatment

An interesting publication by Fairbrother (2002) noted that in 1901, a French psychiatrist, Paul Hartenberg, described the symptoms of social anxiety disorder in a manner almost identical to its current conceptualization. Furthermore, his approach to its treatment was behavioral; specifically, Hartenberg advocated graduated exposure (for both adults and children). In the first edition of this volume, we also noted that exposure was the key ingredient for the successful treatment of this disorder. More recently, several substantive reviews further confirm our earlier conclusion (Fairbrother, 2002; Rodebaugh, Holaway, & Heimberg, 2004; Zaider & Heimberg, 2003), and it is to this core component that we now turn our attention.

Exposure involves confrontation with the feared object or situation and can be conducted in many forms. When conducted in a graduated fashion, a hierarchical approach to confronting the fear is used. Alternatively, an intensive approach focuses on the patient's most severe fear (see the implementation section of this chapter). Furthermore, the exposure sessions may be therapist-accompanied or merely therapist-directed. In the latter instance, the therapist and patient develop the exposure assignment together, and then the patient completes it before the next session. In the case of social anxiety disorder, self-exposure (therapist-directed) may be less effective than therapist-accompanied exposure (Al-Kubaisy et al., 1992). Certainly, our clinical experience supports the contention that most people with social anxiety disorder need therapist assistance to complete exposure sessions successfully, at least initially.

In a study examining classic behavioral treatments, patients with social anxiety disorder (some with concurrent avoidant personality disorder [APD]) were treated with a form of SST known as *personal effectiveness training* (Liberman, King, DeRisi, & McCann, 1975), group exposure, or individual exposure (Wlazlo, Schroeder-Hartwig, Hand, Kaiser, & Munchau, 1990). All patients improved significantly from pre- to posttreatment, but there were no between-group differences. Gains were maintained for up to 2.5 years. Although providing strong empirical support for exposure and SST, interpretation of the outcome of this investigation is complicated by several factors (see Turner, Cooley-Quille, & Beidel, 1995, for a more extensive discussion of this study).

In a study examining the efficacy of an intensive (rather than a graduated) exposure paradigm, patients with social anxiety disorder were randomized to flooding (imaginal and in vivo), the beta-blocker atenolol plus clinical support, or pill placebo plus clinical support (Turner, Beidel, & Jacob, 1994). Approximately 39% of the sample had a comorbid Axis I disorder (primarily generalized anxiety disorder or dysthymia), and 35% had a comorbid Axis II disorder (primarily APD or obsessive–compulsive personality disorder [OCPD]). After 3 months of treatment, flooding consistently was superior to atenolol and placebo, whereas atenolol rarely was superior to placebo. Treatment gains were maintained at 6-month follow-up. On a composite index of improvement, 89% of flooding patients were moderately or significantly improved, as were 27% of atenolol patients and 44% of placebo patients. Using an end-state functioning index based on a normal control sample, 75% of flooding patients were judged to have moderate or high end-state functioning, as were 44% of atenolol patients and 58% of the placebo group. The latter two groups were not significantly different. Using the Social Phobia and Anxiety Inventory (SPAI; Turner, Beidel,

Dancu, & Stanley, 1989) difference score, the effect size was 0.94 for flooding, 0.40 for atenolol, and 0.01 for placebo. For the Clinical Global Improvement rating, the effect size was 1.77 for flooding, 1.33 for atenolol, and 0.75 for placebo. On speech length, the effect size was 1.04 for flooding, 0.34 for atenolol, and 0.43 for placebo. These results provide compelling evidence for the efficacy of flooding in treating social anxiety disorder. This study is noteworthy because it was the first to use a flooding paradigm for social anxiety disorder and because it used a normative-based end-state functioning index.

SST is another behavioral intervention with a long history of positive treatment outcome for those with anxiety in social settings (e.g., Al-Kubaisy et al., 1992). Although there is some controversy regarding the extent of social skills deficits in those with social anxiety disorder, the weight of the empirical evidence clearly indicates that those with social anxiety disorder, particularly the generalized subtype, exhibit poor social skills when in social encounters (see chap. 1, this volume, for a detailed discussion of this issue). Thus, SST would appear to be a viable treatment strategy. Among adults with generalized social anxiety disorder (van Dam-Baggen & Kraaimaat, 2000a), SST decreased social anxiety, general psychopathology, and fearfulness, even among those who did not present with significant skills impairment at pretreatment (i.e., those who self-reported a high frequency of social interactions). These outcome data emphasize one of the current controversies regarding SST; that is, is group SST effective because it teaches new social behaviors, or does the group setting function as an exposure session that decreases social arousal? Currently, it is not possible to answer this question, although most likely both of these factors play a role.

The results of these studies, all of which included large samples of patients with clearly diagnosed social anxiety disorder, indicate that standard behavioral treatment consisting of exposure, SST, or both lead to significant improvement of social anxiety disorder symptoms. Furthermore, treatment gains are maintained for at least 6 months, with a small amount of data indicating maintenance for as long as 2.5 years. In the next section, we describe studies in which a cognitive component was included in the intervention.

Cognitive–Behavioral Treatment

Initially, cognitive–behavioral therapy (CBT) was based on the notion that negative cognitions presenting as part of a clinical syndrome were (a) etiological factors for the development of the disorder and (b) in need of specific intervention for there to be a positive treatment outcome. Although there were those who always challenged this view (e.g., Beidel & Turner, 1986; Hughes, 2002), it is gratifying that proponents of CBT now recognize that cognitions are not unique, etiologically responsible for the onset of a disorder, or necessarily in need of direct intervention, at least for treatment of social anxiety disorder. Specifically, CBT is now viewed as a generic label for myriad interventions held together by the acknowledgment that exposure (the behavioral ingredient described earlier) is the key ingredient of most CBT treatments (Rodebaugh et al., 2004).

The first and most widely used CBT intervention for social anxiety disorder was introduced by Heimberg and his colleagues. Cognitive–behavioral group therapy (CBGT) consists of cognitive restructuring, in-session exposure, self-guided in vivo exposure homework, and cognitive restructuring homework. When compared with a placebo condition called educational support (consisting of didactic lecture–demonstration–discussion regarding the nature of social anxiety disorder; Heimberg, Dodge, et al., 1990), both groups showed significant pre- to posttreatment within-group change, with no group differences on most variables. At 6-month follow-up, however, the CBGT group was significantly more improved than the ES group on most measures. It is clear that CBGT produced improvement in this socially phobic group, but substantive group differences emerged only at the 6-month follow-up. Improvement continued in the CBGT group even after treatment had been terminated. Failure to find differences between CBGT and control participants at posttreatment might have been because of the fact that the control group contained a number of active treatment components (albeit nonspecific). Other studies also support the efficacy of CBGT for those with social anxiety disorder (Chambless, Tran, & Glass, 1997; Herbert, Rheingold, Gaudiano, & Myers, 2004; Hope, Herbert, & White, 1995; Woody & Adessky, 2002). Furthermore, as reviewed in chapter 7 of this volume, a comparative trial of CBGT and phenelzine resulted in equal improvement at posttreatment (Heimberg et al., 1998), although follow-up data supported the superiority of CBGT compared with phenelzine (Liebowitz et al., 1999). Patients' scores on a quality-of-life measure indicate that CBGT leads to improvement in life satisfaction, although it should be noted that at posttreatment, their scores were not comparable to a normal control sample (Eng, Coles, Heimberg, & Safren, 2001). Furthermore, as with pharmacological treatment and behavioral interventions that use only one treatment modality, CBGT appears to be far more effective for the specific subtype, resulting in responder rates of 67% to 79% versus 18% to 44% with the generalized subtype (E. J. Brown, Heimberg, & Juster, 1995; Hope, Heimberg, & Bruch 1995). On the basis of these studies, CBGT appears to be an efficacious intervention, but similar to other psychosocial or pharmacological treatments, it does not appear to return the patient to a "normal" state of functioning. We now discuss studies in which behavioral and cognitive–behavioral treatments have been compared.

Behavioral and Cognitive–Behavioral Comparisons

A number of studies have compared various behavioral and cognitive–behavioral strategies to find the optimal treatment combination. Although the optimal combination remains elusive, these trials are instructive in determining factors that seem to be efficacious for this disorder. For example, exposure plus anxiety management (consisting of relaxation, distraction, and rational restructuring; EXP/AM) was compared with exposure combined with an attention-placebo treatment called *associative therapy* (history taking and allowing thoughts and memories to come freely to mind; EXP/AT), and a wait-list control group (Butler,

Cullington, Munby, Amies, & Gelder, 1984). In vivo hierarchical exposure sessions occurred between therapy sessions, whereas EXP/AM or EXP/AT were conducted within session. At posttreatment, both exposure groups were significantly improved compared with the control group, and there were no between-group differences. At 6-month follow-up, both exposure groups maintained their treatment gains, and on about half the measures, between-group differences favored the EXP/AM group. However, because exposure was not therapist-accompanied, there is a question whether this critical component was delivered in an optimal fashion.

Similarly, augmenting exposure with the addition of two cognitive strategies, rational emotive therapy (RET; patients analyze their feelings in terms of activating events, beliefs about the events, and the emotional or behavioral consequences of the events) and self-instructional training (SIT; practice preparing, confronting, coping, and reinforcing self-statements during imaginal presentation of problematic social situation), was not superior to exposure alone (Emmelkamp, Mersch, Vissia, & van der Helm, 1985). All groups improved from pre- to posttreatment across various domains, with few differences among treatments, suggesting little advantage to adding RET or SIT to exposure. The study is a prime example of the failure to obtain consistent findings across various measurement categories. Also, many of the findings reported reflected within-group improvements as opposed to between-group differences, indicating that all of the treatments were efficacious and that differences among them were minor. Again, it is noteworthy that these behaviorally treated patients (regardless of specific strategy used) continued to improve once the active treatment had been terminated.

A series of studies have either contrasted SST with CBT or examined the additive effects of CBT with SST. One of the first used a quasi-experimental design to compare SST with and without cognitive restructuring in patients with social anxiety disorder comorbid for APD (Stravynski, Marks, & Yule, 1982). SST consisted of instructions, modeling, role rehearsal, feedback, self-monitoring, and homework. CBT consisted of analyzing activating events, irrational beliefs, emotional consequences, disputing beliefs, and planning for new actions. Overall, there were no between-group differences at posttreatment or at 6-month follow-up, leading the authors to conclude that SST was effective for social anxiety disorder but that cognitive restructuring did not further enhance its effects. In contrast, a controlled comparison of CBGT and CBGT plus SST indicated that across all variables, adding SST resulted in significantly enhanced outcome compared with CBGT alone (Herbert et al., 2005). All patients in this investigation met criteria for generalized social anxiety disorder, and responder rates were 38% for CBGT versus 79% for the combination of CBGT and SST. The latter rate is similar to that reported by Turner, Beidel, and Jacob (1994; discussed subsequently), further supporting the need for SST in those with the generalized subtype.

Because patients differ in the extent to which they experience somatic and cognitive symptoms of social anxiety disorder, some have suggested that a more efficacious outcome might be achieved if the mode of intervention was matched to the patient's *reactor style* (cognitive or behavioral). For example, those who endorsed numerous negative cognitions might respond better to a cognitive intervention. In a test of this hypothesis (Mersch, Emmelkamp, Bögels, & van der Helm, 1989), patients were classified as cognitive or behavioral reactors and treated with group SST plus homework or group RET. Again, there were significant within-group changes but no between-group differences. Thus, the two treatments appeared about equally efficacious, and these results remained consistent at follow-up (Mersch, Emmelkamp, & Lips, 1991). A comparison of group SST or cognitive group therapy (van Dam-Baggen & Kraaimaat, 2000b) for patients with generalized social anxiety disorder used a quasi-experimental design. Both interventions decreased social and general anxiety, decreased severity of psychopathology, and increased social skills and self-control. Only SST, however, resulted in a significantly greater reduction in social anxiety and a significantly greater increase in social skill and produced posttreatment scores that matched a normative reference group.

Similarly, an integrated treatment consisting of RET, SST, and exposure in vivo resulted in outcome no better than exposure in vivo alone (Mersch, 1995), although both groups were significantly superior to the wait-list control and patients in both groups maintained their treatment gains at follow-up. Scholing and Emmelkamp (1993a, 1993b) failed to find significant differences between exposure only and cognitive therapy either at posttreatment or at 3-month follow-up. In addition, no differences emerged between individual or group treatment formats. In one instance, the combined condition was inferior to exposure alone. Using a complicated design, patients were randomized to in vivo exposure alone, cognitive therapy followed by in vivo exposure, or an integrated cognitive–behavioral treatment in which both procedures were integrated at the start. Half of the patients in each condition were treated in a group format and half in an individual format. Those treated with in vivo exposure using a group format fared best followed by the in vivo exposure alone and then by the integrated treatment (Scholing & Emmelkamp, 1996), an outcome consistent with a "dismantling" study examining the efficacious ingredients of CBGT (Hope, Heimberg, et al., 1995); exposure-only treatment produced superior results to the CBGT combination treatment.

Mattick and his colleagues (Mattick & Peters, 1988; Mattick, Peters, & Clarke, 1989) published some of the only controlled trials that used a cognitive intervention without some element of exposure. In fact, in their investigations, the cognitive restructuring group was discouraged from entering phobic situations. The 1989 study was conducted first (although it was published subsequent to the 1988 study) and compared three active treatments: graduated exposure (in vivo and homework assignments), cognitive restructuring (a combination of systematic rational restructuring and RET), and a combination of graduated exposure and cognitive restructuring. At posttreatment, all three treatment groups were significantly improved compared with the wait-list control group. Overall, the treatments were equally efficacious, although at follow-up, the combined group was judged to be superior to both the exposure group and the cognitive restructuring alone group. One limitation of this study is that the cell frequencies were small, raising questions about available power for the statistical analysis.

In the second study (Mattick & Peters, 1988), patients were randomly assigned to one of two treatments: graduated exposure with or without cognitive restructuring (as just described). The results indicated that the combined group was superior to exposure on a behavioral test and on a target phobia avoidance rating. There were no significant group differences on self-report measures. Of exposure patients, 48% still reported definite avoidance at the 3-month follow-up, whereas only 14% of the combined group did so, a difference that was significant. Of the combined group, 52% completed 100% of BAT items, whereas only 17% of exposure patients did so (a difference that was also significant). In addition, the combined group was superior to exposure alone on composite measures of improvement and end-state functioning. Contrary to other studies, the overall results here favor the combined group. These results nonetheless need to be interpreted cautiously because of a host of data-analytic questions, which are beyond the scope of this chapter (see Turner, Cooley-Quille, et al., 1995).

Given that the preponderance of empirical data suggests cognitive interventions do not affect short-term outcome more efficaciously than exposure alone, a number of investigations have examined whether CBT addresses specific cognitive variables more efficaciously and whether within-group cognitive changes predict longer term treatment outcome. One descriptive study examined patients' distorted beliefs that negative social events (a) would result in negative evaluation by others, (b) were associated with negative self-characteristics according to personal evaluations, and (c) would lead to negative consequences associated with interpersonal relationships and career outlook (Wilson & Rapee, 2005). CBT led to significant changes on all three variables and correlated with improvement in self-rated social anxiety symptoms. There was, however, no significant correlation between these cognitive variables and clinician ratings of symptom severity at posttreatment. Most important, only changes in the belief that negative social events were an indication of undesirable personal characteristics were associated with treatment outcome at 3-month follow-up. Furthermore, because this study did not include an exposure-only condition, it is not possible to determine whether these cognitive changes would have occurred with the use of exposure alone.

Can cognitive changes occur as a result of "pure" behavioral treatment? The answer appears to be yes. Exposure and didactic training in communication skills and speech-making skills (Newman, Hofmann, Trabert, Roth, & Taylor, 1994) and imaginal or in vivo flooding (Turner, Beidel, & Jacob, 1994) produce changes in cognitions even when they are not directly targeted by the intervention. Thus, consistent with similar comparisons (Mattick et al., 1989; Mersch et al., 1989), it is clear that when exposure is part of the treatment, the pattern of change obtained includes a reduction in maladaptive cognitions.

Can cognitive changes predict treatment outcome? A randomized controlled trial (Hofmann, 2004) of CBGT versus in vivo group exposure treatment (EGT) produces only partial support for this hypothesis. This well-conducted, controlled trial had one significant limitation: The EGT protocol focused primarily on public speaking anxiety. The content of the exposure sessions in the CBGT group was not clearly specified but may have included interpersonal as well as public speaking situations, which would result in a more comprehensive treatment strategy. With this limitation in mind, the results indicated that both active treatments were significantly superior to a wait-list control group on self-report and behavioral assessment measures. At 6-month follow-up, the CBGT group had a significantly lower score on a self-report measure of social phobia than the EGT group. Correlations of social phobia symptoms at 6-month follow-up and cognitive estimates of negative social cost were not significantly different for the two treatment groups. A further examination of treatment efficacy specifically examined the hypothesis that changes in negative self-focused thoughts would be associated with changes in social anxiety (Hofmann, Moscovitch, Kim, & Taylor, 2004). Compared with the wait-list group, negative thoughts decreased significantly for both active treatment groups. Although the correlation between change on self-report of social anxiety and negative self-thoughts attained statistical significance for the CBGT group but not for the EGT group, the difference between the two correlation coefficients was not significantly different, leading to the conclusion that changes in negative cognitions are associated with changes in the overall symptom presentation of those with this disorder, but again, cognitive changes are not unique to interventions that directly attempt to change cognitions.

Cognitive theories of social anxiety disorder emphasize the role of maladaptive beliefs and thought processes in the etiology and maintenance of social anxiety disorder (see Wilson & Rapee, 2005). Numerous studies document the presence of negative cognitions in those with social anxiety disorder, but one cannot infer etiology on the basis of these designs. An information-processing model that acknowledges the importance of behavioral and learning factors (D. M. Clark & McManus, 2002) proposes that as a result of early experiences, those with social anxiety disorder develop a series of problematic assumptions when they encounter a social situation. They then appraise the situation as dangerous, and this generates anxiety. Patients shift attention away from the social situation and become highly self-focused, using anxious feelings and distortions of how they perceive themselves to then make inferences about how they are perceived by others. They then engage in cognitive and behavioral strategies to prevent the occurrence of feared negative consequences.

It is important to note that although cognitive models postulate a number of biases, not all of these have been established in patients with social anxiety disorder (D. M. Clark & McManus, 2002). Furthermore, in some instances, the supporting data are based on analogue studies. A positive feature of this model is that many of its aspects are testable, and it is hoped that well-designed and adequately controlled studies will be forthcoming. Other criticisms of the basic tenets of this model have been explicated by Hughes (2002), and the interested reader is referred to that source for a more complete discussion.

On the basis of their model, D. M. Clark and Wells developed an intervention that aims to reverse what they see as the crucial maintenance factors in social anxiety disorder (see D. M. Clark, 2001). Specifically, their intervention emphasizes reversing self-focused attention, negative self-processing, and safety (avoidance) behaviors to "reconfigure social phobics' processing strategies in a way that will maximize opportunities for disconfirming negative beliefs by direct observation of the social situation rather than oneself" (D. M. Clark, 2001, p. 419). This reconfiguration process occurs through role-play sessions, which are used to assist patients in dropping their safety behaviors (i.e., preventing avoidance behaviors during the exposure session) and disconfirming their negative beliefs. The program makes extensive use of video and audio feedback to assist in the disconfirmation process. The model is based on exposure, although the goal is not habituation per se but cognitive change. According to the developers, exposure is used to test the patient's predictions about the danger in a particular social situation. Yet consistent with other interventions, exposure is still the vehicle by which other behaviors change. As noted in chapter 7, this version of cognitive therapy (a combination of cognitive therapy and exposure) was superior to fluoxetine plus self-exposure and placebo plus self-exposure, although several concerns regarding the implementation of exposure were noted (see chap. 7, this volume, for a more extensive discussion).

Substantive Reviews and Meta-Analytic Studies

In addition to individual studies, substantive reviews (Edelman & Chambless, 1995; Turner, Cooley-Quille, et al., 1995) and meta-analytic studies (Chambless & Hope, 1996; Federoff & Taylor, 2001; Feske & Chambless, 1995; Gould, Buckminster, Pollack, Otto, & Yap, 1997; Taylor, 1996) lead to the conclusion that there is little significant difference among available treatment variations, and when there is, the weight of the evidence supports the superiority of exposure. Thus, the findings from recent meta-analytic studies support our earlier conclusion (Beidel & Turner, 1998) and those of others (Rodebaugh et al., 2004; Zaider & Heimberg, 2003) that the addition of cognitive strategies to exposure-based treatments does not improve treatment efficacy and that the core ingredient for positive treatment outcome is exposure.

As we noted in the first edition of this volume, it appears that it is time for researchers to shift their attention from minuscule treatment variations to other issues of treatment outcome if we are to improve our intervention efforts, which still are not effective for all patients with the disorder. Chief among the candidates for study are issues of procedural variations. That is, the evidence is abundantly clear that exposure is the critical ingredient. Procedural factors such as length and frequency of treatment sessions or exposure to critical elements of the fear (core fear) may provide the keys to further enhance treatment outcome. Similarly, focus on patient characteristics and associated pathology likely will further define the boundaries of current treatments and provide insight into treatment refinements necessary to address these complications.

Social Anxiety Disorder Subtype and Treatment Outcome

Despite the substantial data indicating that the subtypes differ on severity, prevalence, associated psychopathology, and developmental factors, few studies have examined the issues of differential treatment outcome. Data that do exist support the general conclusion that patients with social anxiety disorder improved equally with flooding (Turner, Beidel, & Jacob, 1994) or CBGT (E. J. Brown et al., 1995) regardless of subtype, but the specific subtype was significantly less impaired than the generalized at posttreatment. For example, although both groups improved significantly after intensive exposure treatment, a comparison on end-state status indicated that all (100%) of those with the specific subtype treated

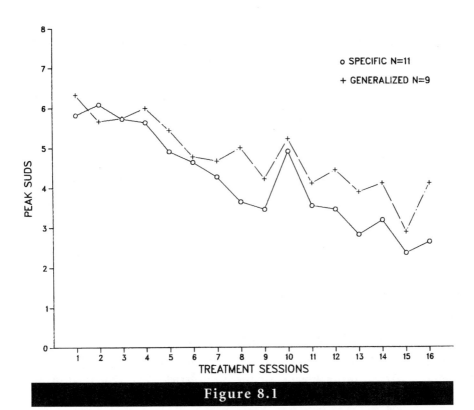

Figure 8.1

SUDS = Subjective Units of Distress Scale. From "Reduction of Fear in Social Phobics: An Examination of Extinction Patterns," by S. M. Turner, D. C. Beidel, P. J. Long, and J. Greenhouse, 1992, *Behavior Therapy, 23*, pp. 389–403. Copyright 1992 by the Association for Behavioral and Cognitive Therapies. Reprinted with permission.

with exposure achieved high or moderate end-state status, compared with only 33% of those with the generalized subtype *(p < .001;* Turner, Beidel, & Jacob, 1994).

In addition, treatment process data (i.e., the habituation patterns of specific and generalized subtypes) revealed several important findings (Turner, Beidel, Long, & Greenhouse, 1992). First, reactivity within the flooding session was the same for both subtypes; both groups experienced equivalent subjective distress during the session as measured by the Subjective Units of Distress Scale (SUDS; see Figure 8.1). Second, the pattern of between-session habituation was identical for both groups (Figure 8.1), suggesting that both groups have the same clinical response to flooding. Outcome for the generalized subtype was suboptimal. Therefore, we examined the clinical data more closely to elucidate rate-limiting factors in the generalized subtype. The results indicated that the generalized subtype had a more severe and complex symptomatic pattern, with a higher frequency of comorbidity with other Axis I and II conditions. Also, although data from extant studies are mixed, it appears that the generalized subtype is characterized by deficient social skills (see discussion in chap. 1, this volume). In view of the skill deficits, we devised a treatment program incorporating exposure and SST, which is designed to improve outcome for the generalized subtype beyond what is achieved with exposure alone. This treatment program is called Social Effectiveness Therapy (SET; Turner, Beidel, & Cooley, 1994).

The initial efficacy of SET was examined in 13 patients diagnosed with the generalized subtype according to *Diagnostic and Statistical Manual of Mental Disorders* (3rd ed., revised; American Psychiatric Association, 1987) criteria (Turner, Beidel, Cooley, Woody, & Messer, 1994). Of the 13 patients, 9 had an Axis II disorder (4 had both OCPD and APD). SET resulted in significant pre- to posttreatment improvement on most of the outcome variables. On the Social Phobia Endstate Functioning Index (SPEFI), 84% achieved at least a moderate improvement rating at posttreatment. This compares with 33% of the generalized subtype in the Turner, Beidel, and Jacob (1994) study. Therefore, this treatment strategy appeared to result in improved outcome in the generalized subtype.

SET is designed not only to reduce social anxiety but also to improve interpersonal skill and social functioning. As part of the process to determine treatment outcome, patients participated in two role-play encounters designed to depict traditional social interactions. On the basis of the judgment of an independent rater, there was significant improvement from pre- to posttreatment on ratings of social effectiveness and anxiety. Given the severity of the sample (including the presence of OCPD and APD) and the relatively short duration of treatment, these results are indeed impressive. Furthermore, treatment gains were maintained over a 2-year follow-up period (Turner, Cooley-Quille, et al., 1995). Currently, we are engaged in a large comparative trial examining SET and exposure alone for the treatment of patients with generalized social anxiety disorder, allowing us to assess the specific contribution of SST in a large sample.

Other Variables Associated With Treatment Outcome

Although the results of extant studies are impressive, little effort has been directed toward elucidating important clinical features that might predict treatment efficacy. In addition to the issue of subtypes, other obvious factors include degree of symptom severity and concurrent Axis I and II conditions. Similarly, little attention has been directed toward examining the characteristics of those who refuse treatment and those who drop out of treatment. In an initial investigation of these patients, we (Turner, Beidel, Wolff, Spaulding, & Jacob, 1996) reported that 15.5% of those eligible for our treatment outcome study refused to enter. No demographic (gender, age, marital status, educational attainment) or clinical factors (age of onset, comorbid diagnosis, social anxiety disorder subtype, self-report, independent evaluator ratings, or behavioral assessment data) appeared to be associated with treatment outcome. It is interesting to note, however, that those who refused treatment were rated as slightly less severely impaired than those who accepted treatment on a rating of social anxiety disorder severity. With respect to those who drop out of treatment, the rate for our study was 12.7%, lower than the 23.4% reported by others (Juster, Heimberg, & Engelberg, 1995) but similar to the average of 14% gleaned from other published studies.[1] Overall, then, it appears that the dropout rate for behavioral treatment

---

[1] Butler et al. (1984); Emmelkamp et al. (1985); Falloon, Lloyd, & Harpin (1981); Fava, Grandi, & Canestrari (1989); Hope, Heimberg, et al. (1995); Jerremalm, Jansson, & Öst (1986); Lucock & Salkovskis (1988); Mattick & Peters (1988); Mersch (1995); Mersch et al. (1991); Newman et al. (1994); Scholing & Emmelkamp (1993a, 1993b); S. M. Turner, Beidel, Cooley, Woody, & Messer (1994); S. M. Turner, Beidel, & Jacob (1994); Wlazlo et al. (1990).

studies of social anxiety disorder is low and less than that of pharmacological trials. In our investigation, there were no significant differences between patients who dropped out and those who completed treatment on demographic variables or clinical features (percentage of patients with a comorbid diagnosis, distribution of social anxiety disorder subtype, and rating of severity) or on self-report, independent evaluator, or behavioral assessment (Turner, Beidel, Wolff, Spaulding, et al., 1996).

As we noted in chapter 7, pretreatment attrition can be a significant problem for treating anxiety disorders and particularly for clinical trials; it is problematic for psychosocial as well as pharmacological trials. In one study, only 15% of those who made an initial inquiry to an adult anxiety treatment clinic actually started treatment (Coles, Turk, Jindra, & Heimberg, 2004). Three critical attrition points were identified: 19% did not schedule an appointment after an initial telephone interview; 48% of those who scheduled an initial interview did not attend (i.e., no show); and 52% of those who were eligible for services after the initial interview did not initiate treatment.

As noted, even after treatment is initiated, a second challenge facing researchers and clinicians is determining patient characteristics that might affect optimal treatment outcome. The presence of an Axis I or II condition does not affect the patient's ability to benefit from a flooding program (Turner, Beidel, Wolff, Spaulding, et al., 1996) on the basis of initial reactivity or habituation rate. When judgments pertaining to treatment outcome were based on the presence of a comorbid condition, however, there were significant differences on a number of measures. In each case, those with a comorbid condition were less improved. Thus, although both groups improved significantly, end-state functioning differed at posttreatment. Other empirical investigations as well as general reviews of the extant literature draw similar conclusions (Erwin, Heimberg, Juster, & Mindlin, 2002; Rodebaugh et al., 2004; Zaider & Heimberg, 2003). Overall, rates of improvement appear to be similar, but those with comorbid disorders remain more impaired at posttreatment. The exception may be when the comorbid disorder is depression. At least two studies (Chambless et al., 1997; Erwin et al., 2002) suggest that typical treatment outcome is attenuated when social anxiety disorder presents with comorbid depression as opposed to other comorbid anxiety disorders.

Similar to the findings for comorbidity, process and outcome differences on the basis of subtypes were illuminating (Turner et al., 1992). Across subtypes, imaginal flooding produces equivalent increases in subjective distress and equivalent habituation rates across sessions. When controlling for pretreatment differences, posttreatment scores for the two subtypes were not different, with the exception of the SPAI difference score and the Fear Questionnaire Social Phobia subscale (both of which reflected the more severe clinical picture of the generalized subtype). In summary, data from these investigations and reviews of the extant literature (Rodebaugh et al., 2004; Zaider & Heimberg, 2003) support the conclusion that both social anxiety subtypes experience equal benefit from behavioral and cognitive–behavioral treatments.

Nevertheless, actual posttreatment scores indicated substantial group differences in the clinical status of these patients even after intensive behavioral programs (Turner, Beidel, & Jacob, 1994; Turner, Beidel, Wolff, Spaulding, et al., 1996). Across all categories of outcome data (self-report, behavioral, and independent evaluator ratings), patients with the generalized subtype had a significantly more severe clinical picture, despite having made equivalent clinical gains. Similarly, the statistically significant difference in subtype percentages achieving high end-state status indicated that those with the generalized subtype were not functioning at the same level as their specific counterparts. Thus, although flooding produced equivalent amounts of change within both subtypes over treatment, it was not enough for most of the patients with the generalized subtype to achieve high end-state functioning level (i.e., a level similar to but not the same as control participants who had no disorder).

In summary, when comorbid conditions are present, patients still respond positively to behavioral (flooding) treatment, but their general clinical status at posttreatment is poorer than for patients without comorbid conditions. Similarly, patients with either the specific or generalized subtype improve equally, but overall functioning status of those with the generalized subtype is poorer than for their specific subtype counterparts. Our initial investigation adding SST to exposure appears to allow the generalized subtype to achieve posttreatment status similar to those with the specific subtype treated with exposure alone (Turner, Beidel, Cooley, Woody, et al., 1994). Currently, we are conducting a clinical trial to determine whether SET enhances treatment outcome when compared with exposure alone.

Summary of Outcome Findings

On the basis of the results of controlled outcome studies, substantive reviews, and meta-analytic studies, it is safe to conclude that behavioral and cognitive–behavioral treatments are efficacious for social anxiety disorder. A variety of interventions (various methods of exposure, SST, SET, and CBT) have some degree of efficacy after relatively short courses of treatment. Overall, it is clear that these interventions are superior to placebo and that treatment variations (i.e., cognitive–behavioral vs. behavioral) are minor when each embodies some form of exposure. It is clear that exposure is an essential component in virtually all of the available behavioral or cognitive–behavioral treatments (one condition in the Mattick et al. [1989] and one in the Scholing and Emmelkamp [1996] study did not contain exposure). Nevertheless, there remains no clear consensus about which form of exposure is best. In addition, SST alone results in significant improvement in some patients with social anxiety disorder as well and, when combined with exposure, appears to be particularly efficacious for treatment of the generalized subtype. Overall, there is little evidence that the addition of cognitive strategies either enhances or detracts from the efficacy of behavioral treatment (exposure or SST). Given the current findings, it appears that any of the strategies is a reasonable choice for clinicians as long as they include an effectively administered exposure component. Furthermore, the treatments are short term, usually lasting about 3 months.

An important and reasonably consistent finding is that not only are treatment gains maintained but additional improvement often occurs during follow-up in the absence of continued treatment. It appears that patients learned skills during treatment that facilitate additional improvement over time, all the more impressive given the relatively brief treatment periods. Despite these encouraging findings, there is some indication that many patients are in need of additional treatment following these treatment regimens. This information comes from several sources. First, there is some indication that booster sessions were needed during follow-up in some cases (e.g., Butler et al., 1984; Mattick & Peters, 1988; Mattick et al., 1989; Mersch et al., 1989, 1991). Second, the patients in one investigation who relapsed (Mersch et al., 1991) were described as being deficient in social skills, again suggesting the need for a multifaceted intervention. Third, it was our impression from the patients treated in our study (Turner, Beidel, & Jacob, 1994) that additional treatment would have been helpful in a number of cases, even though that treatment period was longer than in many other investigations. Thus, it is clear that we need to determine further the improvement-limiting factors. Is it related to characteristics of patients, to the treatments, or both? Finally, our clinical experience is that some patients can benefit from longer treatment periods, and many can benefit from such self-improvement groups as Toastmasters. For now, clinicians will have to make decisions about who might benefit from longer programs or extra interventions on an individual basis.

TREATMENT IMPLEMENTATION

Whether intentionally, unintentionally, or because a positive, trusting relationship has yet to develop fully, patients with social anxiety disorder sometimes initially minimize their fears in terms of intensity, pervasiveness, or both. For example, some patients initially enter treatment endorsing fear only in public speaking situations. Yet as we discussed in chapter 5, a detailed assessment often reveals a much more pervasive fear pattern. In many instances, their virtual "cocoon" is so comfortable that patients do not recognize their extensive social isolation. In other cases, there seems to be intense investment in seeing their disorder as circumscribed. Numerous issues of clinical management are presented in chapter 6, and the reader is referred there for this critical information. To reiterate briefly, the clinician needs to be aware of the role of various clinical issues in the intervention process. In the remainder of this chapter, we provide an overview of how the major behavioral and cognitive–behavioral treatments are implemented and examine several important clinical parameters. Because exposure is the most critical element, we begin our discussion here.

Exposure

Exposure involves the patient confronting the feared situation or stimulus. It is the key ingredient in the reduction of anxiety and fear in social anxiety disorder and virtually all anxiety disorders. Exposure per se is not a treatment because various methods are based on different behavioral models. Exposure is a generic term used to describe a group of treatments that are based on different theoretical models of fear reduction. Habituation is the most frequently invoked mechanism of fear reduction to account for change produced by exposure strategies, although there are cognitive interpretations of the process as well. We limit our discussion to the nature of exposure treatment, methods of exposure typically used in social anxiety disorder treatment, and procedural variables associated with treatment implementation.

When exposure treatment is used, the expectation is that over time the patient will habituate (i.e., cease to become emotionally aroused) to stimuli that previously elicited an emotional reaction. Habituation usually is determined by changes in physiological measures such as pulse

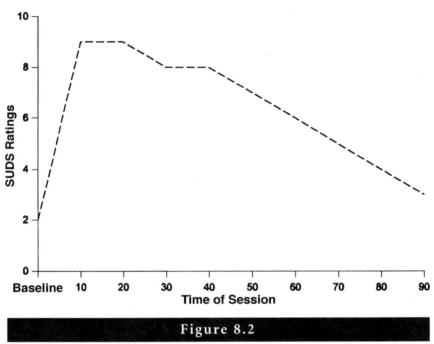

Within-Session Habituation

Figure 8.2

SUDS = Subjective Units of Distress Scale.

rate or blood pressure or, alternatively, subjective feelings of distress such as self-ratings on a rating scale (see chap. 5, this volume). At times, both types of indices are used. As we have stated throughout this volume, emotional distress is elicited when a patient with social anxiety disorder is placed in a social performance situation in which arousal (physical, subjective, or both) tends to be elicited. If the individual remains in the distressing situation for a sufficient period of time, arousal will decrease (see Figure 8.2). This decrement is usually referred to as *within-session habituation* (because it occurs during the course of an exposure session). Repeated contact between an individual and the feared stimulus over a number of days hastens the habituation process, and, with sufficient pairings, the stimulus loses its ability to elicit the fear response. When

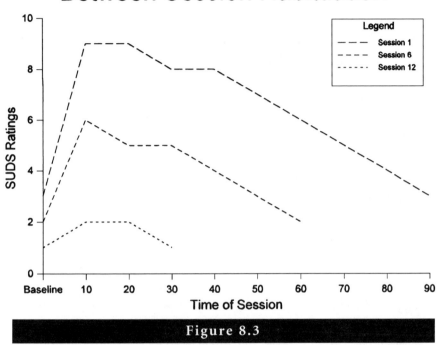

Between-Session Habituation

Figure 8.3

SUDS = Subjective Units of Distress Scale.

this happens, only minimal arousal occurs upon exposure to the feared situation, and between-session habituation has occurred (see Figure 8.3). Some patients report that they have tried this intervention on their own and it was unsuccessful. The difference is that when patients attempt this type of exposure alone, the distress they experience is so severe that they cannot continue to maintain contact with the feared stimulus (i.e., long enough for habituation to occur). Rather, they escape or avoid anxiety-producing situations. Escape or avoidance before habituation can function to increase or sustain the intensity of the fear response (Mowrer, 1947). In contrast, by maintaining contact through exposure treatment, within-session and between-session habituation occurs, and thus the fear response dissipates.

Imaginal Exposure

Imaginal exposure involves presenting the patient with feared situations or stimuli using the process of imagery. This requires construction of imaginal scenes, and the stimulus cues making up the scene are critical to its success. In constructing imaginal scenes for social anxiety disorder treatment, it is important that the scene captures what we refer to as the *core fear*. By core fear, we mean those critical features that serve to instigate and maintain the anxiety and fear. Although patients with social anxiety disorder are described as fearing others' scrutiny and negative evaluation, the problem is more complicated than this implies, and the specific parameters associated with the fear will differ considerably for individual patients. For example,

> Mr. A sought treatment for public speaking fears in our clinic. This fear had been present since about midadolescence following an experience in which he performed poorly while making a presentation in class. Since that time, he experienced a host of somatic symptoms whenever he attempted to speak before an audience, including blushing, rapid heart beat, shaking, and stuttering. Because he was afraid that others would see these reactions, his anxiety always increased whenever he perceived the onset of these symptoms, setting off a vicious cycle of spiraling fear.

Analysis of this case revealed that his primary concern was that others would see his physiological response and wonder how anyone could be that anxious. In essence, Mr. A feared that he would be evaluated in a less than positive light. His core fear was that others would see and evaluate this reaction negatively. In this case, the composition of the audience did not matter. Thus, Mr. A's scene would need to include content in which others clearly recognized these exaggerated physical symptoms and made a negative evaluation about him (i.e., the patient must experience the negative consequence during exposure).

> However, consider the case of Mr. X, the head of computer operations for a Fortune 500 company who also reported a severe public

speaking phobia. Mr. X did not have a degree in computer science but became head of the department because of his leadership and organizational skills. Mr. X could give presentations (with some difficulty) if the audience did not contain computer experts. The size of the audience was of little relevance; rather, the critical feature was the audience composition. In this case, Mr. X harbored considerable doubts about his abilities to head a computer department. He was concerned that his peers would detect his inadequacies, discover how uninformed he really was, and decide that he was not capable of heading the department.

In this case, the core fear was the patient's doubts about his own abilities and his peers' evaluation of his intellect and work performance. Thus, a scene incorporating his core fear would include all of the presumed weaknesses being revealed in front of his peers and their subsequent negative evaluations of his abilities.

From these case scenarios, it is clear that although both patients had speaking fears, and indeed they feared negative evaluation, the parameters associated with the fear were quite different. Efficacious exposure for these two cases would require the incorporation of somewhat different cues. It has been our experience that the core fear concept is difficult to grasp by the novice therapist and those not trained in behavior therapy. Also, failure to understand this concept, in our opinion, frequently is related to failure to obtain positive results with exposure treatment.

Another important element in scene construction is the inclusion of all relevant variables (Lang, 1968). This means that the scene must allow the patient to experience those unique physiological and cognitive symptom patterns associated with their fear. To be effective, an imaginal scene must capture the essence of each patient's fear and the associated parameters. Failure to do so could result in incomplete habituation, which in turn results in return of fear (Craske & Rachman, 1987). An example of an imaginal exposure scene used in treatment is presented in Exhibit 8.1. As background clinical information,

---

Exhibit 8.1

**Sample Imaginal Flooding Scene for an Adult
With Social Anxiety Disorder**

You are arguing a case before a judge and jury. This is an important case, and the senior partners from your firm are here in attendance. The case has received substantial attention from the media, and many reporters are in attendance as well. You are worried about the impression that you will make and whether these people will see you as incompetent and unfit to be an attorney. What if you make a fool of yourself? Your heart is beating rapidly, your palms are sweating, and you feel flushed. You begin to stumble over your words. You can see several members of the jury are yawning. The judge and prosecuting attorney are wondering how you ever passed the bar exam, let alone graduated from such a prestigious law school. The senior partners are shaking their heads in dismay about the mistake they made in hiring you. The reporters are smirking at your incompetence, and you cannot even make a simple argument in your area of expertise.

Mike was a 28-year-old graduate of a prestigious law school. He could not practice as a trial attorney, however, because of his extreme fear when arguing before a judge and jury. When doing so, he experienced heart palpitations, profuse sweating, and blushing. He feared that he would mispronounce words or be unable to speak and that others would criticize his performance. The core of his fear was that he was really an imposter (i.e., not qualified to fill this role) and that others would detect that he was not intelligent enough or competent enough to be a trial attorney at a major law firm.

To reiterate, Mike's core fear was that everyone, but particularly other attorneys whom he respected, would discover his perceived incompetence. Thus, it was not simply performing in a courtroom that was the primary concern but the negative judgments of peers and authority figures and the subsequent catastrophic consequence (i.e., these individuals would discover his incompetence). Therefore, this material was included in the imaginal exposure treatment. In addition, physiological cues were included because they represented an important element of the fear complex (i.e., the patient feared that his physical symptoms would be apparent to others). Furthermore, these symptoms, through associative conditioning, had acquired the ability to elicit fear in their own right.

Implementing Imaginal Exposure

Exposure procedures require that the patient stay in contact with the stimulus long enough for habituation to occur. In the case of imaginal exposure, this means that the patient is required to imagine the scene on a prolonged basis. If the session is terminated prematurely, sensitization may occur, and there may be an increase, instead of a decrease, in anxiety. On the basis of the available literature, flooding sessions should last for 90 minutes at a minimum. Preferably, the session should conclude when the patient's distress level is reduced by 50% of the within-session reactivity over baseline (usually judged by using the patient's self-rating of anxiety). Figure 8.4 illustrates a typical response during an early flooding session. Ending the session at 60 minutes would have been counterproductive and could have increased sensitization to the stimulus. Ending the session at 90 minutes would be acceptable because reduction in subjective units of distress, or SUDS, level was reached; however, extending the sessions to 110 minutes would be preferable (SUDS level returned to baseline). Therefore, at 90 or 110 minutes, within-session habituation was achieved (by two different definitions). Across sessions, the time required for habituation typically decreases, therefore session length decreases as well. Session length tends to be longer early in treatment and shorter as treatment progresses.

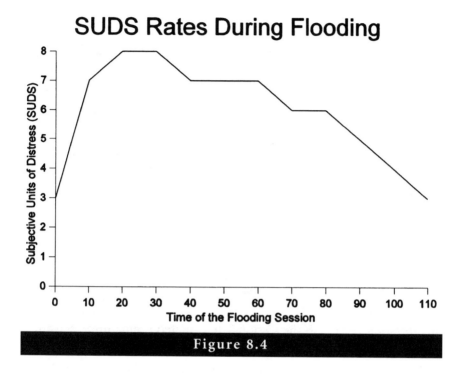

SUDS Rates During Flooding

(y-axis: Subjective Units of Distress (SUDS), 0–8; x-axis: Time of the Flooding Session, 0–110)

Figure 8.4

Setting

Imaginal exposure should be carried out in a quiet room with low lighting. Such a setting is ideal because the intrusion of noise can be distracting and interfere with the patient's ability to concentrate on the imagery. We conduct this treatment in a sound-attenuated room. In the absence of such space, one might choose an internally situated room far away from the possibility of outside noise. In any event, the quietest possible setting should be sought for imaginal exposure sessions.

Spacing of Sessions

Generally, the literature on exposure treatment, although not specifically for social anxiety disorder, suggests that sessions occurring within close time proximity (massed sessions) are preferable to those that are spaced farther apart. In our SET treatment program, we use once-per-week sessions for individual flooding and once-per-week SST sessions (for a total of two sessions per week). Most patients, in our experience, find it difficult to attend treatment sessions more than twice per week. One alternative is to use several days of massed treatment (e.g., 10 days), as we do with obsessive–compulsive disorder. Treatment is then reduced in intensity on the basis of the patient's clinical status. Typically, although treatment time is extensive during the early stages, overall positive response is achieved more quickly and total treatment time does not differ in the end. This highly intensive strategy is also useful when there is a need to obtain quick relief (e.g., when the patient comes for treatment because of an imminent task that must be completed).

Emergence of New Material During Exposure (Imaginal or In Vivo)

Participation in exposure sessions often prompts the revelation of new material that is part of the core fear. In many cases, the patient did not recognize this material before the intervention. Such material may consist of additional situations, individuals, or activities that create social distress. Emergence of new material occurs frequently during early exposure sessions. When it does, the new material should be incorporated into the subsequent sessions.

Anxiety Level

The goal of flooding is to make certain that contact with the fear-producing stimuli takes place. The patient's role is to participate fully in the session by imagining the scene (or to participate maximally in the exposure task in vivo; see the section on in vivo exposure later in the chapter). Thus, although some degree of anxiety is expected, it is not the patient's responsibility to generate distress. It is crucial that patients understand their role in the exposure session. Otherwise, the patient's focus will likely be on increasing and maintaining a high level of arousal, rather than on focusing on the fear cues.

Attention and Distraction

Patients often want to know whether they should do anything during the exposure sessions, such as trying to relax or using coping statements to assist in fear reduction. Distraction during exposure sessions interferes with habituation in patients with obsessive–compulsive disorder (e.g., Grayson, Foa, & Steketee, 1986), and this probably is the case for social anxiety disorder as well. Therefore, no method of distraction is recommended.

Relaxation After the Exposure Session

A short debriefing session conducted after the exposure intervention should allow the clinician to determine whether the patient is suffering from any residual distress. Clinicians treating patients with posttraumatic stress disorder often provide relaxation instructions to patients to decrease their anxiety after the exposure session. Relaxation is inconsistent with the habituation model, however, that underlies intensive exposure treatment. Exposure (whatever its mode of presentation) continues until a significant reduction in anxiety is achieved. Therefore, the patient should not be significantly distressed at the end of the therapy session, and there should be no need for relaxation training. If the patient does not show a decrease in emotional distress over time, the session might be too short, the core fear may not be incorporated into the scene, or the diagnosis might be inaccurate or incomplete.

Problems in Implementing Imaginal Exposure

The issue of the inability to use imagery is discussed in the section titled "Selecting Imaginal or In Vivo Exposure." Another potential problem in using imaginal exposure is that some patients engage in cognitive maneuvers to avoid the image. This should not be surprising because patients have spent much of their lives attempting to avoid the stimuli that they now are asked to confront, and the thought of doing so elicits at least some anxiety and fear. To avoid the feared stimuli, they may

	Table 8.1
	Sample Role-Play Scenes for Social Skills Training
Social skill	Role-play scene
Initiating a conversation	You are in the company cafeteria and there are no empty tables, so you have to sit at a table at which there is one other person. You walk over to the table and say:
Heterosocial interactions	You are on jury duty. You introduce yourself to the person sitting next to you, who tells you that he or she works in an office nearby. You, however, rarely get to this part of town. At the lunch break, this person turns to you and says, "I know a great place for lunch. The food is good and reasonably priced. Would you like to join me?" You respond:
Assertiveness	You have been planning a weekend getaway for several weeks. Your boss tells you that you will have to work on Saturday. You will lose your deposit if you cancel the trip. Your boss says, "I'm leaving now. You will have to work tomorrow to finish this. It is due on Monday." You respond:

imagine themselves coping well with the situation, imagining that other people cannot perceive their distress, or imagining that the performance is going well rather than poorly. They may also attempt to alter the scene to focus on certain elements that are less anxiety producing. For example, if the patient imagining the scene in Table 8.1 used coping behaviors, he might imagine performing flawlessly before the jury and enjoying the presentation rather than falling apart. Although coping responses can serve to reduce anxiety temporarily, they interfere with the habituation process (Craske, Rapee, & Barlow, 1992). During exposure, and particularly during flooding, there should be an initial increase in distress, followed by a decline over time (habituation). If there are no signs of arousal or distress during the exposure session, the patient should be asked to describe the scene aloud exactly as imagined. If coping behaviors are being used (e.g., the patient imagines doing very well), this strategy often reveals their presence. Asking for a description also provides a check to ensure that the person is able to imagine the scene. If coping behaviors are used, patients should be redirected to devote full attention to the material exactly as presented. If the scene is constructed correctly, anxiety should be elicited as a result of the presentation of the core fear.

As noted earlier, identification of the core fear is crucial for the success of the intervention. The scene itself is really just a vehicle to convey the important fear cues. For example, those with public speaking anxiety may not fear speaking before just any group. Rather, the critical elements often relate to specific aspects of the situation, such as the size and composition of the audience, the type of material to be presented, and specific aspects of the client's behavior. The core fear also includes the meaning of these situations, particularly what patients fear may happen in the situation (e.g., something that will be embarrassing or humiliating) and that others will think badly of them as a result. Therefore, a person with a public speaking fear may be fearful about making a mistake and may fear that others will attribute this fear to the patient's lack of intelligence (incompetence). Other patients fear that individuals will conclude that they are undeserving of a position they hold. Still other patients fear that individuals will judge them to be of a lower social status than the audience. The core fear is unique for each individual, and thus a unique scene must be constructed for each patient.

An often asked question is whether the therapist should present one scene or several. Even if the patient reports feeling anxious in different situations (e.g., speaking in public, eating in public, engaging in everyday conversations, and being assertive), the core fear usually cuts across all of these situations. If the clinician has done a proper behavioral analysis and identified the core fear cues, there typically is no need to construct multiple imaginal scenes. Conversely, scenes can be administered in hierarchical fashion, and the clinician might choose this approach when there is concern about patient oversensitivity (see the discussion of patients with APD later in the chapter).

In Vivo Exposure

Exposure conducted in vivo means that the individual is exposed to the feared situation or stimuli in real life. In vivo exposure can be carried out in an intensive fashion, or it can be implemented gradually (i.e., through a hierarchy). In vivo exposure is conducted in the same manner as imaginal exposure, and the issue of identifying and addressing the core fears are paramount here as well. In addition, all of the other issues discussed in relation to imaginal exposure pertain to in vivo exposure. The unique challenge in using in vivo exposure is to be able to create the real-life stimuli necessary for the treatment. In settings in which trainees and other colleagues are available, the problem is lessened to some degree but not eliminated totally. This is because some of the feared consequences simply cannot be replicated in vivo. Thus, the requirements for constructing in vivo exposure opportunities present the therapist with a considerable challenge. As experience accumulates, clinicians will increasingly be able to draw on that expertise to generate exposure opportunities. One alternative to creating analogue exposure opportunities is to have patients carry out their own exposure without therapist assistance. This might be possible in some cases, assuming that the patient and therapist understand the specific nature of the individual's fear. As we have indicated throughout this volume, however, we have found that self-exposure sessions for patients with social anxiety disorder are very difficult to accomplish (Al-Kubaisy et al., 1992), at least initially. It has been our clinical experience that in most instances the patient's fear prevents the ability to stay in the situation for an extended period of time. After all, if that were possible, the patient might not have sought therapy in the first place. If the therapist is not able to accompany the patient during the in vivo exposure, an alternative strategy is to use imaginal exposure initially and then follow up with in vivo once the fear has been moderately reduced. Also, in some cases, significant others might be used as surrogate therapists.

Selecting Imaginal or In Vivo Exposure

There is no specific rule regarding the selection of imaginal or in vivo exposure for patients with social anxiety disorder, and both have been used successfully. The overall goal is to capture and expose the patient adequately to the entire fear complex (i.e., those parameters that contribute to the fear response). In our experience, some amount of imaginal exposure is desirable for most patients with social anxiety disorder but particularly for those with the generalized subtype. In some cases, the intervention may require a combination of both imaginal and in vivo procedures. In these cases, the treatment begins with imaginal sessions, and, following success through imagery, the same material is covered as much as possible in vivo. Practical considerations as well as clinical parameters sometimes dictate which approach is used.

One practical consideration is whether a patient can use imagery. Although most patients can do so successfully, occasionally difficulty with the ability to imagine the material presents a problem. In those instances, imagery training often helps. Imagery training involves having patients imagine situations that are familiar to them and are not associated with social anxiety. For example, patients may be asked to imagine a number 5, then make it a blue number 5, then rotate it 180 degrees, and so on. Other training may include having the patient describe, in detail, his or her living room, kitchen, car, and so on. For those who cannot benefit from this training, in vivo exposure will be necessary. As we have mentioned before, it has been our clinical experience that many who have difficulty with imaginal procedures are those with concomitant OCPD or significant OCPD symptoms. Because of their rigid patterns of thought and behavior, these individuals often have great difficulty imagining a particular scene. They are often so concerned with scene details and spend such an inordinate amount of time making sure they have all the details "correct" that they are unable to imagine the entire scene and participate fully in the procedure. For example, one patient who was successfully treated with in vivo exposure in our clinic initially had difficulty focusing on the imaginal scene because he could not decide whether the table at which he was supposed to imagine sitting was square or round. Ambivalence over this detail prevented him from focusing on the most relevant aspects of the imaginal scene (i.e., the specific fear cues). This is but one example, and this problem can manifest in many ways. Other examples include preoccupation with ensuring that the exact image is imagined or resistance to the notion that an imagery strategy can be useful. Any of these factors can interfere with effective imaginal exposure. Therefore, if these tendencies cannot be overcome through instruction or imagery training, an in vivo strategy may be necessary.

Another issue that might dictate the use of a particular strategy is whether the feared situations can be accessed in real life and whether the appropriate people necessary to replicate the feared situation, or situations, are available. For example, some patients are primarily concerned about interactions with authority figures. In other instances, in vivo exposure may require the use of students, hospital volunteers, or other clinic personnel to serve as audience members for speeches or social interactions. In some cases when it is not possible to have such individuals available at the clinic for an in vivo strategy, patients might be able to carry out the exposure sessions alone or with the assistance of a significant other or friend. For other patients, these alternatives may not be feasible, and then an imaginal procedure might be the better choice.

It is clear that constructing in vivo exposure situations requires creativity on the part of the therapist. Some patients may be able to generate appropriate assignments quickly. Others require suggestions or firm direction from the clinician. Likewise, some patients may be able to carry out in vivo exposure sessions successfully on their own (i.e., set up presentations at work to practice speaking in front of a group). For others, the clinician may have to accompany the patient to the site of the exposure assignment, at least until the patient is comfortable carrying out the procedure alone. Simulated interactions (role-plays) in the clinician's office may allow for the replication of some situations not available in natural settings. Finally, for those core fears that are not readily available in the course of typical social interactions, some exposure sessions may be replicated in the clinician's office. If such is not possible (as might be the case for many clinicians engaged in private practice settings), an imaginal strategy may be the only alternative. Since the first edition of this book virtual reality therapy has been introduced as an alternative method of exposure for primary public speaking fears (P. Anderson, Rothbaum, & Hodges, 2003). The preliminary findings were positive, although controlled trials are necessary. It is important to note that the authors conceptualize the use of virtual reality therapy as a tool for exposure therapy within a comprehensive treatment for social anxiety disorder, not as an intervention unto itself.

Use of Homework

Some type of homework assignment typically is used with exposure treatment regardless of the particular strategy chosen. Thus, when imaginal exposure is used, it is typical to give the patient small in vivo assignments to carry out in the natural environment. Although these are not necessarily given in a strict hierarchical fashion, an effort is made to choose those tasks that have a high likelihood of being completed successfully. Homework is just as important when the therapist is conducting in vivo exposure and the exposure sessions are carried out in the office under therapist direction. Homework is important in aiding the transfer effects from the clinic to the natural environment and can also provide important information on the effects of treatment.

Social Skills Training

As noted earlier, there is some evidence that patients with social anxiety disorder, particularly the generalized subtype, manifest social skills deficiencies. Furthermore, treatment outcome studies using SST individually

Exhibit 8.2
Content Areas for Social Skills Training

Initiating conversations
Maintaining conversations
Attending and remembering information
Establishing friendships
Maintaining friendships
Heterosocial interactions
Assertiveness skills (general)
Assertiveness skills (authority figures)
Constructing the body of a speech
Effectively beginning a speech
Effectively ending a speech
Informal presentations

(Stravynski et al., 1982), as well as in combination with other strategies (Turner, Beidel, Cooley, Woody, et al., 1994), result in favorable outcome. We now turn to a discussion of how to implement SST.

The goal of SST is for patients to acquire those skills necessary for successful social discourse. In addition, as we discussed earlier in this chapter, those with social anxiety disorder manifest some specific skill deficiencies that also need to be addressed. Furthermore, our SST component includes attention to the skill and art of making speeches because patients with social anxiety disorder show substantial deficits in their ability to compose effective presentations. Content areas used in our SST program are presented in Exhibit 8.2; also see the section on SET in this chapter.

Social skills training programs normally make use of basic teaching strategies and include instruction, modeling, behavior rehearsal, corrective feedback, and positive reinforcement. Although these skills can be taught individually, we feel that SST is optimal in a group setting. The training sequence is identical regardless of the format selected.

Instruction provides the context for learning the task. When providing instruction, the therapist specifies all of the verbal and nonverbal parameters necessary to perform the behavior correctly.

Modeling then provides an opportunity to see the behavior performed correctly. The therapist first explains what should be observed and then demonstrates the skill. After completing the demonstration, the therapist reiterates the important aspects of the behavior or asks the patient to do so.

Behavior rehearsal (using role-play exercises) is the most crucial component of SST because it provides the opportunity to practice the skill in a controlled environment. As a general guideline, group members should have at least two practice opportunities per instructional component (this can be modified as time permits to address the needs of individual group members). The therapist addresses problems in performance through further instruction, modeling, and rehearsal. Group treatment sessions are an optimal forum for practicing the scenes with a range of interpersonal partners (e.g., male, female, older, younger), thereby further increasing opportunities for rehearsal and generalization of skills. The response of the role-play partner can be held constant or systematically varied to illustrate specific points.

Corrective feedback is used to guide behavior in the desired direction and should be given constructively. Further modeling may be necessary to ensure that patients discriminate between desirable and less desirable performances. Feedback is given by the therapist and elicited from other participants, particularly the role-play partner. After corrective feedback, the patient practices the skill again.

Positive reinforcement is important for acquiring the new skill as well as for facilitating the training process. Some patients are anxious in any type of performance setting. Thus, even the activities that are part of the group and that are designed ultimately to reduce anxiety may be anxiety producing. Thus, SST is likely to produce some anxiety in the patients, particularly during the initial sessions. Therefore, providing positive reinforcement encourages patients to continue participation in the training group.

Implementing Social Skills Training

The clinician must first decide which social skills are in need of improvement. Consideration must be given to nonverbal skills such as eye contact, body posture, and vocal tone, in addition to verbal content skills such as greetings or assertiveness. Nonverbal skills are usually taught in conjunction with verbal content. For example, patients are encouraged to make eye contact when they are greeting someone. The following is an example of how these procedures are used to teach patients how to introduce themselves to a stranger.

Instruction. First, the therapist provides didactic information about introductions to a stranger. This includes descriptions of settings in which such introductions are appropriate (and perhaps even required), discussion regarding the proper timing of such introductions, and examples of how introductions might be accomplished. The didactic presentation should be brief (no longer than 3 minutes) and provide the background for the skill's acquisition.

Modeling. Next, the therapist models the skill to be acquired. In this case, the therapist would set the appropriate scene and then actually introduce himself or herself to a stranger. One of the group members plays the second role. The therapist acts out the introduction, using all appropriate social skills. After the introduction is completed, the therapist reiterates the crucial information. For example,

> The setting was the cafeteria in the building where I work. I knew this individual worked in an office on the same floor, but we had never met. This person smiled at me and did not seem preoccupied, so I felt that he was interested in a small conversation. I said, "Hello, we seem to work on the same floor, but we haven't been introduced.

My name is Mary Jones." Then he told me his name. Then I said, "It's nice to meet you. I guess we will be seeing a lot of each other."

Behavior Rehearsal. Behavior rehearsal allows each group member to practice the skill. Initially, if there is enough time, the therapist should first practice with each patient. This ensures that the response of the interpersonal partner is consistent. In addition, it allows the focus of attention to remain on the patient practicing the skill. Following one or two brief trials for each person with the therapist, group members should continue the rehearsals with each other. In this way, each group member practices with different interpersonal partners (this provides the opportunity for interaction with different people and increases the likelihood of generalization). Instructions similar to the following should be used:

> Now it is your turn to rehearse the skill. Remember to make a small comment to start the conversation and then introduce yourself. This is practice, so feel free to use your imagination to fill in the details of the situation. For example, you could give yourself a different occupation if you like.

After rehearsal, corrective feedback and positive reinforcement is provided. Each group member gets as much rehearsal as needed. All patients should have several opportunities to practice the skill and also should have the opportunity to play the role of the interpersonal partner.

Constructive Feedback. Feedback should be directed not only at the specific content being taught but also at any other aspect of social performance that limits its effectiveness. Therefore, poor eye contact, inaudible voice volume, or inappropriate additional verbal content should be noted and corrected.

Positive Reinforcement. Patients should be reinforced whenever they rehearse a skill. Positive reinforcement should focus on those aspects completed correctly and any improvements that need to be made. At the very least, the therapist should reinforce the patient for attempting the interaction.

Once a specific skill is acquired, the therapist proceeds to the next skill and repeats the training sequence. Skills training is cumulative; that is, each new skill builds on those that were previously acquired. All sessions include concentrated practice with the particular skill introduced in that session.

Social Skills Training Scenes

For behavioral rehearsal to take place, a series of scenarios are developed to address each skill that is to be learned. These scenes are used for the role-playing exercise, which is the vehicle through which behavior rehearsal takes place (just as imaginal scenes are the vehicle through which imaginal exposure takes place). Examples of several role-play scenes are presented in Table 8.1.

Problems in Implementing Social Skills Training

One potential problem in SST is that patients are not familiar with behavior rehearsal (role-playing) and initially may not understand the format. A demonstration or two should clarify the purpose of the training, however. A second difficulty is that patients sometimes observe the therapist modeling the scene then attempt to imitate the therapist verbatim. The goal is to encourage patients to individualize their responses so that the words and actions feel comfortable to them.

A third potential problem is the patient's comfort level during the interaction. Behavior rehearsal requires interaction with others even if all aspects of a situation are not detailed clearly. For example, although a particular setting (e.g., you are at the mall and run into an old friend) might be described, the interaction itself evolves as a result of the ongoing role-play. For many patients, rigid cognitive styles do not allow them to interact freely in an unstructured interaction. Therefore, they may hesitate to participate in the behavior rehearsals by, for example, asking numerous questions before starting the interaction, such as, What kind of mall is it? How well do I know this old friend? or What do we have in common? Often, these questions are avoidance tactics or, as noted, reflect the rather rigid personality style frequently seen in those with social anxiety disorder. These types of delay tactics are managed by indicating that all of these details are not necessary and by encouraging the patient to simply begin the interaction.

Although there are some skill deficits that seem to define broadly the behavior of patients with social anxiety disorder, participants in any group will have varying levels of skill. Some will require more instruction and practice than others. In those cases, those who show more skill may be used to assist in the role-plays.

No optimal size for social skills groups has been identified, but it is our practice to limit group size to four or five patients. Even though the size typically is rather small, group members may have varying cultural backgrounds, educational or intellectual levels, and occupations (e.g., unemployed, student, part- or full-time employment). Thus, the context of the skills training (e.g., the role-play scenes) can be modified to reflect personally realistic situations more accurately (e.g., work vs. school). Also, goals should be individualized, depending on the patient background (i.e., difficulty in certain types of social encounters).

Homework

Homework assignments (see Figure 8.5) are an integral part of behavioral treatment and are used with both SST and exposure. The issues to be discussed here pertain to all treatment strategies except when the patient is carrying out exposure without the therapist. The homework assignment should be reasonable, should allow the patient the opportunity to practice the behavior of interest (skill or exposure), and should have a high likelihood of being completed successfully. Initially, therapists usually have to help patients generate homework, but later many patients are able to take on much of this task themselves. We sometimes provide patients with a homework form that details the assignment and assists

HOMEWORK ASSIGNMENT #4

Name: Date:

Identify three potential activities or situations to which you could invite a person to join you:

1.   (easy)

2.   (moderate)

3.   (difficult)

Attend two of these activities and do the following:

1. Initiate a conversation with a familiar person. To maintain the conversation, ask at least two open-ended questions relating to the same topic.

Date completed: Person's name:

Questions asked/topic discussed:

2. Initiate a conversation with a stranger. To maintain the conversation, ask at least two open-ended questions relating to the same topic.

Date completed: Person's name:

Questions asked/topic discussed:

3. Invite someone to join you in an activity.

Date completed: Person's name:

Activity asked person to join you in:

Person's response:

Figure 8.5

in compliance. In Table 8.2, we list sample homework assignments for some of the skills listed in Table 8.1.

Initially, some patients may be reluctant to complete homework assignments, claiming that they did not have time or did not understand

Table 8.2	
Sample Homework Assignments for Social Skills Training Program	
Topic	Homework assignment
Initiating conversation	Initiate a conversation with a familiar person and a stranger.
Maintaining conversation	Initiate a conversation with a familiar person and a stranger. During both conversations, ask at least one open-ended question.
Establishing friendships	Identify three potential activities that you would enjoy. Attend at least two and initiate a conversation in each.
Maintaining friendships	Twice this week, invite someone to join you in an activity.
Assertiveness	Identify a situation in which you need to be assertive. Act on it this week.

the assignment. In the majority of cases, this is avoidance behavior. The noncompletion must be addressed by determining whether the task is too difficult or whether the problem is reluctance because of fear. If necessary, the homework assignment may have to be altered to facilitate completion.

Social Effectiveness Therapy

Social Effectiveness Therapy (SET)[2] is a multicomponent behavioral treatment program specifically designed to decrease social anxiety, improve interpersonal skill, improve social performance (i.e., public speak-

---

[2] *The Social Effectiveness Therapy Treatment Manual* (Turner, Beidel, & Cooley, 1994) is available from Multi-Health Systems, Inc., 65 Overlea Boulevard, Suite 210, Toronto, Ontario, Canada, M4H 1P1, (800) 456-3003.

ing skill), and increase patient participation in social activities. With respect to interpersonal skill, it targets general social functioning as well as some unique problem areas associated with social anxiety disorder. SET incorporates a strategy to help those with social anxiety disorder recognize the inhibitory cocoon that they have constructed and in which they live. The program incorporates the most consistently effective treatment approach (exposure) with an SST component geared specifically to the needs of the patient with social anxiety disorder. SET consists of several components: education, SST, homework assignments, flexibility exercises, exposure, and programmed practice.

Social Effectiveness Therapy includes both individual and group treatment. Group sessions provide patients the opportunity to practice new skills in a relatively safe setting using a variety of interpersonal partners. Thus, in addition to teaching specific skills, the group serves as a social setting, allowing some degree of in vivo exposure (performance) in social situations. Individual sessions are deemed essential for the success of treatment, however. The individual sessions are used to elicit the patient's specific social fear pattern, thereby allowing the program to be tailored to the patient's individual needs. Group and individual sessions run concurrently. Patients come to the clinic twice per week, once for group sessions and once for individual exposure sessions, for 3 months. During the 4th month, there is a once per week individual session. Sessions are 90 minutes in duration. The major components of SET are detailed briefly here and are described more completely in Turner, Beidel, and Cooley (1994). The program is designed to be administered over a 4-month period but can be adjusted easily to meet the needs of individual patients or groups of patients. Thus, we describe the length of treatment as we typically use it, but the length of time for a specific treatment phase is adjustable.

Education

This phase is used to educate patients about the nature of social fears and anxiety and includes a discussion of potential etiological factors.

The patient is thoroughly acquainted with the treatment program and is informed about treatment expectations. This can be done individually or in a group. When groups are used, this session allows patients to become familiar with each other before SST begins. In fact, the new acquaintances in this session might be viewed as the first in a series of steps designed to alter what typically is a rigid and inhibited social living style.

Social Skills Training

SST is implemented as previously described and consists of three phases: social environment awareness, interactional skills enhancement, and presentation skills enhancement. *Social environment awareness* teaches the nuances of when, where, and why one should start and terminate interpersonal interactions. *Interpersonal skills enhancement* addresses the mechanics (verbal and nonverbal) of how to conduct a successful social encounter, targeting unique areas for the patient with social anxiety disorder, such as specific listening exercises and topic transition mastery. The third phase of SST, *presentation skills enhancement,* teaches the mechanics of public speaking, with respect to speech construction and delivery. The goal is to assist the patient in producing well-organized, interesting presentations that will assist in creating an overall positive impression.

Exposure

The second major component of SET is the provision of exposure to the anxiety-producing stimuli. The imaginal as well as in vivo exposure components used in this program are implemented as described previously in this chapter. Imaginal exposure is conducted in 12 sessions during the first 12 weeks of the 16-week treatment program (12 individualized treatment sessions held once per week). Individual sessions are used so that exposure can be directed at the patient's specific fears. In addition, some fears, such as those related to catastrophic results of a failed social interaction, can best be addressed imaginally.

Programmed Practice (In Vivo Exposure)

The last 4 weeks of the 16-week individualized sessions consist of weekly planning of in vivo homework exposure assignments. The therapist and patient meet to develop specific in vivo exposure assignments that the patient will carry out between weekly sessions. The expectation for the scope of social activities will be expanded during these sessions, consistent with the patient's newly acquired social skills and decreased anxiety in these settings. These sessions are used to provide assistance to those who might be reluctant to try out their newly acquired skills, to reinforce independent planning of social encounters, and to stimulate and assist those who need encouragement to plan their own social activities. The emphasis during these sessions is on the patient's assuming control of the therapy. Several exposure assignments are developed each week, and sessions are 90 minutes in length.

Cognitive Restructuring

As we have noted throughout this volume, adults, and perhaps some adolescents, with social anxiety disorder express worry about how others will perceive them. In some instances, this worry may be just an uncomfortable feeling of dread. In other instances, patients report specific cognitions in association with specific situations or tasks. In most cases, these are negative thoughts, such as, "Why bother? I will just make a fool of myself," or "I'll say something stupid and be so embarrassed." Although careful assessment indicates that these thoughts can be eliminated through the use of traditional exposure strategies, many psychologists choose to address these and other negative cognitions directly. Following is a brief description of cognitive restructuring procedures (Heimberg, 1991).

The basic rationale presented to patients is that events do not cause anxiety; it is the thoughts about those events that cause one to be anxious. Therefore, changing thoughts can change emotions (there is no actual empirical support for this rationale, at least none that does not also include an element of exposure). Cognitive restructuring is introduced early in the CBGT program to facilitate acquisition of these skills so that they become part of the exposure simulations and homework assignments. Initial training in cognitive restructuring includes five goals (Heimberg, 1991): (a) reconceptualizing thoughts as hypotheses rather than facts, (b) becoming aware of maladaptive thinking, (c) acquiring skills for identifying cognitive distortions, (d) becoming aware of the connection between maladaptive thoughts and anxiety, and (e) acquiring skills for challenging and changing negative thoughts. These skills are acquired through modeling and homework assignments.

Initially, the therapist models a negative cognition that he or she might have had in a distressful situation (e.g., when giving a presentation). Each thought is examined carefully using the following questions: (a) How would an objective observer view the situation? (b) What is the evidence that the patient's view is the only way to view the situation? and (c) What are alternative views? For example, a negative thought might be, "I'll forget what I want to say." To dispute this thought, the person might say, "In the past, I never forgot what I was going to say, even though I was very nervous. Even if it does not come out perfectly, the important thing is that the audience understands. If they don't understand, they will ask me a question, and I can clarify what I wanted to say." After the therapist models disputing a number of negative thoughts, patients are given some initial practice recognizing their own negative thoughts and disputing them. The patients are given a homework assignment to record all socially distressful situations over the next week and the negative thoughts that accompany these situations.

At the next session, homework is reviewed and the patient is given a list of potential cognitive distortions. Several such lists are available (Burns, 1980; Heimberg, 1991; Persons, 1989). The list in Exhibit 8.3 is from Heimberg (1991). All of these cognitive distortions are discussed with the patient to ensure understanding and relevance to social anxiety disorder.

Exhibit 8.3

Common Cognitive Distortions

All or nothing thinking
Overgeneralizing
Mental filtering
Disqualifying the positive
Jumping to conclusions
Magnifying or minimizing
Catastrophizing
Emotional reasoning
Making "should" statements
Mislabeling
Personalizing

Next, patients participate in a series of exercises designed to teach how to dispute negative thoughts. Patients are given a problematic situation, are asked to generate potential negative thoughts, and then are directed to dispute the negative cognitions (by asking questions such as, "Is that for certain? What evidence exists for that conclusion?"). The final step is to generate more rational responses (thoughts) to replace the negative cognitions. Again, the homework assignment follows the content of the group session and requires patients to monitor and record their (a) negative thoughts in stressful situations, (b) questions used to dispute the negative thoughts, and (c) substituted rational responses.

The ultimate goal of cognitive restructuring is for the patient to acquire a set of cognitive skills that can be applied in distressful social situations. Thus, the final step in cognitive restructuring is for the patient to use these skills whenever he or she feels anxious in social settings. In CBGT, the patient is given numerous group exposure opportunities (called *exposure simulations*) to practice cognitive restructuring. Designing exposure simulations is similar to designing any type of in vivo exposure session and can cover the entire range of situations that elicit distress. Heimberg (1991) noted that, unlike an in vivo exposure session, CBGT exposure simulations can be molded to the exact needs of the individual patient because other group members can serve as the interpersonal partners during the simulation. For example, the patient and other group members may be asked to simulate a work interaction in which colleagues are chatting about the results of the Super Bowl as they stand around the coffee machine. Exposure simulations are 10 minutes in length, and SUDS levels are assessed at 1-minute intervals.

Problems in Implementing Cognitive Restructuring

According to Heimberg (1991), several problems may occur when implementing cognitive restructuring. First, patients might deny the presence of negative cognitions despite high distress, focusing instead on their feelings. Questions such as "What did you think might happen in the situation?" may be useful in eliciting the presence of negative cognitions. Second, some patients may not recognize that their thoughts are distorted or irrational. This may seem inconsistent with a diagnosis of social anxiety disorder inasmuch as the diagnostic criteria require that the patient recognizes that his or her fear is irrational. It is possible, however, that the patient recognizes the fear, but not necessarily the thoughts, as irrational. In such cases, it is recommended that the clinician not try to force the patient to recognize the irrationality of the thoughts. Rather, the patient is encouraged to stop focusing on the thoughts (Persons, 1989). Patients may be encouraged to perform a behavioral experiment to determine whether their predictions actually occur.

A third problem addressed by Heimberg (1991) relates to those patients who do not grasp the core of CBGT (i.e., the cognitive restructuring component). If after repeated attempts the patient still does not understand CBGT's goal or procedures (e.g., thought identification, substitution of positive thoughts for negative ones), clinicians can diminish emphasis on cognitive restructuring and increase attention to the exposure component. A second alternative is to attempt to reduce the complexity of CBGT. For example, rather than a complete cognitive restructuring analysis, patients may be taught a series of simple self-statements to use in the distressful situations.

Other implementation problems include the need to keep the patient on track during the treatment sessions. Heimberg (1991) noted that exposure simulation is the vehicle through which cognitive restructuring occurs. Thus, therapists must not allow patients to delay the simulations with overly detailed explanations of past anxious experiences or detailed and comprehensive lists of all possible automatic thoughts.

Case Study

Thus far, this chapter has focused on reviewing the available literature and discussing the basics of treatment implementation. Next, we present a case example that illustrates how the various procedures were used in the treatment of an adult with generalized social anxiety disorder.[3]

Initial Evaluation

The patient was a 39-year-old, married, African American, female physician who described a long-standing history of becoming "really nervous" in large crowds, especially if the people were unfamiliar. Although unable to recollect the specific onset, she remembered being extremely shy in elementary and junior high school. At social functions, she typically would hide out in the bathroom, feigning illness to avoid social interactions. She reported no close friends or confidants, was unwilling to get involved with people unless certain of being liked, and did not date until after college. She occasionally would consume alcohol before, and frequently during, social events to cope with her discomfort. When in stressful situations, she stuttered. For example, saying her name during introductions, whether to professionals or patients, was particularly

---

[3] This case study from "Culturally Relevant Factors in the Behavioral Treatment of Social Anxiety Disorder: A Case Study," by C. M. Fink, S. M. Turner, and D. C. Beidel, 1996, *Journal of Anxiety Disorders, 10*, pp. 201–209. Copyright 1996 by Elsevier. Reprinted with permission.

Table 8.3

Scores on Self-Report Instruments and Clinical-Rating Scales

Instrument	Pretreatment	Posttreatment	Follow-up
SPAI Difference Score	113	52	55
Brief Social Phobia Rating Scale			
Fear total score	21	2	
Avoidance score	19	2	
Physiological	7	0	
Total score	47	4	
Hamilton Depression Scale	5	0	
Hamilton Anxiety Scale	15	0	
Social Phobia Endstate Functioning Index	0	4	

Note. SPAI = Social Phobia and Anxiety Inventory.

difficult. Consequently, she avoided hospitals (where she would have to speak to other professionals), speaking on the telephone, and introducing herself to others, often being perceived as brusque and somewhat rude.

Assessment

The patient met diagnostic criteria for social anxiety disorder, generalized subtype, and for APD. She complained of depressed mood but did not meet criteria for an affective disorder. Before treatment at our clinic, she received individual therapy and marital therapy in other settings. Although improvements were noted in her marital relationship as a result of marital therapy, no improvement was evidenced in her social-evaluative concerns. She was taking sertraline (75 mg per day) initially, but a withdrawal regimen was begun approximately halfway through behavioral treatment, and she was medication-free at treatment termination.

Self-report, clinician-completed, and behavioral measures were used at pre- and posttreatment. These are presented in Table 8.3. As depicted, the pretreatment assessment scores were consistent with a diagnosis of social anxiety disorder. General anxiety and depression were within normal range of functioning.

Public speaking skill and social skills were assessed through an impromptu speech task and a role-play test. She was only able to speak for 3.5 (out of 10) minutes, and independent evaluators rated her effectiveness during the social interactions as either a 2 or 3 (on a 0–5 point scale), depending on the gender of the role-play partner. Her SUDS rating of distress was 9 (on a 0–10 point scale) during the speech and 5 during the role-play interactions, indicating substantial to very significant distress.

Treatment Goals

A. Reduce anxiety and increase skill in social interactions.
B. Increase social interactions in professional and personal settings.
C. Eliminate avoidance of hospital settings.

Treatment Implementation

Goal A. Reduce anxiety and increase skill in social interactions. Because the patient had the generalized subtype of social anxiety disorder, treatment consisted of SET (Turner, Beidel, & Cooley, 1994). She participated in 12 group SST sessions and 12 individualized imaginal exposure sessions, conducted concurrently with SST using the program described earlier in this chapter. Careful review of all behavioral material indicated that her core fear was that others would view her as incompetent and, in particular, not worthy of being a physician. This fear was most pronounced when the evaluators were older Caucasian male physicians. The individualized exposure scene is depicted in Exhibit 8.4. As indicated, the core fear—that others, particularly older Caucasian men—would discover that she was incompetent, was an integral part of the scene, as were the physical symptoms of distress experienced by the patient during actual encounters.

Goal B. Increase social interactions in professional and personal settings. This was accomplished through the use of in vivo homework assignments

Exhibit 8.4

Imaginal Exposure Scene

It is daily rounds at the Veteran's Administration. Today's even more stressful than usual because the chairman, a White older man, is participating on rounds. The other residents, interns, and medical students, are showing off, quoting from the *New England Journal of Medicine* and all talking at once. The whole time, you are thinking to yourself, "I should say something." You really want to be at your best. The chairman looks around the group and says, "Before we start, why don't we go around the circle and say who we are." You immediately think, "What if the words don't come out?" You quickly glance around and realize that you are in the middle of the circle. You are the only Black person on the team. . . . You can't say your name! You feel hot and begin to sweat. Everyone is looking at you with smug "I knew it" expressions. You really screwed up. Everyone is thinking that the only reason you are in medical school is because you are a Black woman. The department had a certain quota that needed to be filled. Your mouth becomes dry, and you feel nauseous. You feel absolutely stupid, everyone knows that the only reason you got this far is because you are Black. You see the chairman lean to the person next to him and hear him say, "This is what happens when we let a Black girl into the program." Everyone continues to stare at you. You feel incredibly inferior. You know that the only reason you are still in the program is because you are Black. You do not deserve to be a physician, and everybody knows it.

that were initiated after the patient had participated in several imaginal flooding sessions and there was initial evidence of between-session habituation. Homework assignments included the following:

- initiating conversations with coworkers;
- inviting a Caucasian coworker to lunch;

- inviting a Caucasian neighbor to go out to dinner;
- while attending a professional meeting, inviting a Caucasian physician to lunch; and
- inviting her employer, a Caucasian middle-age male physician, to lunch.

Goal C. Eliminate avoidance of hospital settings. Every day for a 10-day period, the patient was to enter a local hospital (which was the location of many distressful encounters in the past and which she currently avoided) and remain there until she experienced a 50% reduction in her distress upon initial entry into the setting (initially this was therapist accompanied). Again, it is important to note that this program was not instituted until the data from the individual exposure sessions showed some degree of between-session habituation.

Treatment Outcome

As depicted in Table 8.3, there was a marked decrease in social anxiety and associated distress. This was evident across self-report measures, and the SPEFI (a composite measure based on the social functioning of individuals without social anxiety disorder) indicated that the patient was functioning at a level comparable to those who did not have social anxiety disorder. In addition, she was able to complete the 10-minute impromptu speech task with a SUDS rating of 3 (on a 0–10 point scale). Her interactions during the role-play test were rated as 5 (on a 0–5 point scale; 5 = *most effective*), and her SUDS rating was either 4 or 2, depending on the gender of the interactional partner. At 4-month follow-up, her SPAI scores were still low. She reported that 1 month after the termination of treatment, she moved to a nearby city and commenced specialty residency training, further indicating that hospitals were no longer problematic for her.

This case study illustrates the use of a multicomponent behavioral strategy to treat severe and generalized social anxiety disorder in an adult patient. There are several aspects of this case that deserve mention.

First, although this woman had achieved a substantial occupational objective—becoming a physician—she still was severely impaired by her social fears. Second, in this particular case, the core fear was her fear of others seeing her as incompetent. There were culturally sensitive aspects to her fear (specifically, that Caucasian men who were in authoritative positions would view her as incompetent). Therefore, the exposure situation had to include these elements. As noted (Fink, Turner, & Beidel, 1996), it is unlikely that the patient would have been able to maintain her long-term treatment gains had this core fear not been extinguished successfully. Additionally, homework assignments played a particularly important role in addressing this fear. Assignments were developed conjointly by the therapist and patient and required some creativity to ensure that the assignments would allow the patient to address elements of the core fear. Also, homework assignments were lagged (i.e., given only after in-session exposure no longer resulted in distress) so that there was a high likelihood of successful completion. Finally, this was a very intensive program and required substantial commitment from the patient to participate in both the twice per week clinic sessions and the additional homework assignments. Most of the assignments could be completed during the course of normal working hours or on the weekends, and thus the time commitment was not overwhelming.

CONCLUSION

Research involving the treatment of social anxiety disorder has progressed rapidly over the past 20 years, and there now is a sufficient body of literature by which to draw some conclusions regarding the efficacy and durability of current behavioral and cognitive–behavioral treatments. In fact, the findings regarding overall efficacy and the key element in these treatments are remarkably consistent. Three strategies (substantive reviews, meta-analyses, and dismantling studies) all indicate that the key ingredient in these interventions is exposure. The efficacy of exposure is so robust that it appears to result in a positive outcome regardless of which variation is used. The most crucial characteristic is that the patient has contact with the distress-producing event for a positive outcome to occur.

One area that has not been examined fully is that of the differential treatment response of social anxiety disorder subtypes. When data from Turner, Beidel, and Jacob (1994) were reanalyzed (Turner, Beidel, Wolff, Spaulding, et al., 1996), all of those patients with specific social anxiety disorder had achieved moderate to high end-state functioning. However, only 33% of those with the generalized subtype had reached this level. This led to the conclusion that for patients with circumscribed social fears (i.e., the specific subtype), exposure alone appears to be sufficient to achieve a positive outcome (Turner, Beidel, Wolff, Spaulding, et al., 1996). For those with the generalized subtype (who constitute the majority of those seen in clinics), however, additional interventions appear to be necessary. In particular, exposure plus the addition of a structured social skills program delivered in a group setting improves outcome for generalized social anxiety disorder (Turner, Beidel, Cooley, Woody, et al., 1994). Skills deficits appear to be prevalent in the generalized subtype because of its earlier onset and long history of social inhibition and withdrawal and possibly because of the overlap in diagnostic criteria with APD. Because of this overlap and the fact that APD and social anxiety disorder can be diagnosed concurrently, many people with generalized social anxiety disorder also have APD.

We have endeavored in this chapter to present the practical side of conducting the major behavioral and cognitive–behavioral interventions used to treat social anxiety disorder, highlighting what we believe to be critical parameters and the common pitfalls faced by clinicians during implementation. As noted, developing and conducting the specific exposure sessions is often straightforward. At other times, considerable resourcefulness is required to develop an appropriate exposure venue. Finally, in addition to consideration of the generalized-specific dimension, other factors such as the presence of comorbid Axis I and II disorders may affect treatment outcome or influence the manner in which treatment is conducted. The few data that exist suggest that individuals with comorbid Axis I or II disorders do benefit from behavioral and cognitive–behavioral treatment but that additional attention to the comorbid conditions will likely be necessary. For example, when severe depression is present, this disorder may need to be addressed before attempting to treat the social anxiety disorder. In other cases, such as when generalized anxiety disorder is present, the order in which these disorders are treated may not be a critical issue. Consideration of each disorder's effect on functional impairment or the patient's general emotional status may be useful in making this type of determination. Clinicians need to remember that some patients will be in need of continued exposure opportunities even after formal intervention has terminated. As noted, the Toastmasters programs, Dale Carnegie classes, or becoming a reader at church often can serve as continued opportunities to further enhance or maintain treatment gains.

9

Behavioral and Cognitive–Behavioral Treatment of Social Anxiety Disorder in Children and Adolescents

Well, my friends told me that when they used to ask my opinion about something, I would always say, "I don't care" or "I don't know." Now when they ask me, I give them my opinion. They said they like me much better now because I say what I think.

—A 10-year-old girl who was asked how she thought she had changed following a 12-week behavioral treatment program for childhood social anxiety disorder

One of the most significant changes since the publication of the first edition of this volume is the increased number of psychosocial treatment studies that have used a carefully diagnosed sample of children with social anxiety disorder. Previously, clinicians relied on studies that described the treatment of shy, socially isolated, or socially withdrawn children. To provide a historical perspective, we review a few illustrative controlled studies involving shy, socially isolated, or socially withdrawn children who were not diagnosed with social anxiety disorder. Then, we present the available treatment outcome data using carefully diagnosed samples of children and adolescents with social anxiety disorder. After these reviews, we describe strategies for the effective implementation of behavioral and cognitive–behavioral treatments. Although we discuss individual behavioral approaches separately, these strategies typically are combined in clinical treatment settings.

EMPIRICAL OUTCOME STUDIES OF SOCIALLY WITHDRAWN AND ISOLATED CHILDREN

As noted throughout this volume, from a social learning perspective, impairment in social functioning may result from a lack of effective social skills, performance inhibition caused by anxiety, or both (Arkowitz, 1981). Most behavioral clinicians assume that socially isolated children have social skill deficits and one method to address these deficiencies is through social skills training (SST) programs. SST is efficacious in increasing social interactions in children with mild to moderate social withdrawal (Schneider & Byrne, 1987; Sheridan, Kratochwill, & Elliott, 1990; Whitehill, Hersen, & Bellack, 1980) as well as shy adolescents (Christoff, Scott, Kelley, Baer, & Kelly, 1985; Jupp & Griffiths, 1990). It is unclear how many children in these samples might have met criteria for social anxiety disorder. Even if a subset did, SST alone would not be expected to produce an optimal treatment outcome because the crucial component of exposure would not be addressed adequately. SST could be an integral component of an overall treatment program, however.

Despite increasing children's social skills, most SST strategies have had limited success in increasing peer acceptance (e.g., Berler, Gross, & Drabman, 1982; Whitehill et al., 1980). Without direct attention to the social fear, even children armed with newly acquired skills will remain inhibited in peer settings. Firmly established patterns of peer neglect may not allow opportunity for the demonstration of new abilities. Thus, such opportunities usually have to be planned as part of the intervention (Finch & Hops, 1982; Paine et al., 1982). One alternative is for the therapist (or the parent) to arrange for social experiences by (a) arranging contingencies to promote social interaction and (b) providing immediate reinforcement when social interactions occur. In school settings, operant strategies and tangible reinforcers (points or prizes) increased interactions in socially isolated children to a level comparable to that of their more sociable peers (Bergsgaard & Larsson, 1984; Guevermont, MacMillan, Shawchuck, & Hansen, 1989). Additionally, studies of socially isolated children have found that SST plus peer-involvement experiences are effective (e.g., Bierman & Furman, 1984; Finch & Hops, 1982; Paine et al., 1982), and peer-pairing procedures (without SST) increased positive social interaction and peer acceptance in socially withdrawn preschoolers (Furman, Rahe, & Hartrup, 1979) and peer-neglected first-and second-grade students (Morris, Messer, & Gross, 1995). Because these young children were not diagnosed with social anxiety disorder, it is unclear how this outcome relates to children with the disorder. It appears, however, that structured peer interactions are a viable component of an overall treatment strategy. Overall, this early literature on shyness indicates that behavioral treatment in the form of operant strategies, SST, and peer pairing appears to be successful in increasing young children's social interactions. Although the heterogeneous nature of these samples precludes drawing direct conclusions for those with childhood social anxiety disorder, findings from these studies formed an important component of interventions developed specifically to treat social anxiety disorder in children.

EMPIRICAL OUTCOME STUDIES OF CHILDREN WITH SOCIAL ANXIETY DISORDER

Initially, outcome data addressing the treatment of social anxiety disorder in children came from larger outcome studies addressing the utility of cognitive–behavioral treatment (CBT) for children with various anxiety disorders (Barrett, 1998; Barrett, Dadds, & Rapee, 1996; Flannery-Schroeder & Kendall, 2000; Kendall, 1994; Manassis et al., 2002; Rapee,

2000; Shortt, Barrett, & Fox, 2001; Silverman, Kurtines, Ginsburg, Weems, Lumpkin, et al., 1999; Silverman, Kurtines, Ginsburg, Weems, Rabian, et al., 1999). Some of the children included in these samples had a primary diagnosis of social anxiety disorder. The results of these investigations indicated that CBT is an efficacious treatment for children with various types of anxiety disorders, and probably for children with social anxiety disorder. One limitation of the extant research base is that in many of the samples, the number of children with a primary diagnosis of social anxiety disorder was limited, and in other instances, results for children with social anxiety disorder were not analyzed separately. For example, 27% of the children in the Barrett et al. (1996) program were diagnosed with social anxiety disorder, but the results were not analyzed separately by specific diagnosis. Thankfully, there now are a number of studies examining behavior therapy and CBT with samples composed solely of children and adolescents with social anxiety disorder.

The first treatment program developed specifically for adolescents with social anxiety disorder (Cognitive–Behavioral Group Therapy for Adolescents [CBGT–A]; Albano, DiBartolo, Heimberg, & Barlow, 1995; Albano, Marten, Holt, Heimberg, & Barlow, 1995) combined procedures used successfully to treat adults with the same disorder (Heimberg, Salzman, Holt, & Blendall, 1993) with the skills development approach for adolescents proposed by Christoff et al. (1985). There are two overall components to CBGT–A, (a) psychoeducation and skills building and (b) behavioral exposure. Each component is 8 weeks in length. During the psychoeducational and skills building phase, children participate in SST, problem-solving training, assertiveness training, and cognitive restructuring. During the second phase, simulated in vivo exposure sessions are introduced. In conjunction with the therapist, each child develops an individual fear hierarchy. Using the hierarchy, children enact items within the session with other children in the group as interpersonal partners. These exposure simulations are 10 minutes in length, and afterward the therapist and group members discuss the positive and negative aspects of the just-completed interaction. For details on the administration of CBGT–A, see Albano, Marten, et al. (1995) and Albano, DiBartolo, et al. (1995). The results of the pilot group (with five adolescents; Albano, Marten, et al., 1995) indicated that 3 months after completion of treatment, social anxiety disorder decreased to subclinical levels for four out of five adolescents. At 1-year follow-up, 4 adolescents were free of any disorder, whereas the fifth had vestiges of social anxiety disorder at a subclinical level. The mean number of negative cognitions during a behavioral assessment decreased, although heightened physiological arousal remained unchanged. In a subsequent comparison of CBGT–A (with or without family involvement) to a wait-list control group, both interventions were efficacious in reducing symptoms of social anxiety disorder, and 70% did not meet diagnostic criteria at posttreatment (Tracey et al., 1998). In another controlled investigation (Hayward et al., 2000), female adolescents with social anxiety disorder were randomized to CBGT–A (without parental involvement) and a no-treatment control group. At posttreatment, 45% of the CBGT–A group no longer met diagnostic criteria, a percentage significantly higher than the 4% rate for the wait-list control group. Residual symptoms of social anxiety disorder remained at posttreatment. At 1-year follow-up, posttreatment differences had disappeared. One possible reason for the attenuated outcome in this investigation was that a number of the adolescents had comorbid depression, and it is unclear how this may have affected treatment outcome or promoted relapse.

Using a sample of children and young adolescents, Spence, Donovan, and Brechman-Toussaint (2000) examined the efficacy of a comprehensive CBT program for social anxiety disorder that included SST, relaxation techniques, social problem solving, positive self-instruction, cognitive challenging, and exposure. In a randomized controlled trial, group CBT with parental involvement (teaching proper modeling, reinforcing the acquisition of children's social skills, and encouraging outside social activities) was compared with group CBT without parental involvement and a wait-list control group. At posttreatment, both treatments were significantly superior to the wait-list control group on a variety of self-report and parental measures. At posttreatment, 87.5% of those in the CBT plus parental involvement group did not meet diagnostic criteria for social anxiety disorder, compared with 58% of those in the CBT with no parental involvement group and 7% of the wait-list control group. The intervention did not affect the number of peer interactions, parental report of peer competence, or independent ratings of assertiveness. Treatment gains were maintained at 6- and 12-month follow-up, and improved social skills were evident at that time for both of the active treatment groups, again suggesting that improvement continues even after the active intervention is completed.

Using solely preadolescent children, a brief (3 weeks for a total of 9 hours) group CBT intervention (education, identification and replacement of negative self-talk, and exposure exercises) was compared with a wait-list control group (Gallagher, Rabian, & McCloskey, 2004). There were no significant decreases on children's self-report of social anxiety at posttreatment, although the groups were significantly different on measures of general anxiety and depression. Parental scores on an anxiety–depression scale decreased, but parental report of social competence did not. At posttreatment, 37% of those in the CBT treatment group who met diagnostic criteria for social anxiety disorder (according to parental report) at pretreatment were without a diagnosis at posttreatment, compared with 0% for the control group. Although this difference was statistically significant, the response rate was only 37% for the treatment group. The most parsimonious explanation is that 3 weeks is an insufficient period of time to remediate social anxiety disorder.

As part of our ongoing research program for social anxiety disorders in children and adolescents, we constructed an intervention program initially directed at preadolescent children (ages 8–12). Our program, called Social Effectiveness Therapy for Children (SET–C; Beidel, Turner, & Morris, 2004), was based on the SET program used successfully with adults but modified substantially to address the developmental stage of the participants. SET–C is a 12-week program consisting of group SST, peer generalization experiences, and individual exposure sessions. Because we believe that there is insufficient evidence for the presence of negative cognitions in preadolescent children (Alfano, Beidel, & Turner, 2002; see chap. 2, this volume), SET–C does not include a cognitive component. In the initial randomized, controlled trial, SET–C was compared with an active, nonspecific intervention designed to reduce test anxiety (Testbusters; Beidel, Turner, & Morris, 2000). At posttreatment, 67% of children who received SET–C no longer met diagnostic criteria for social anxiety disorder, compared with 5% of the Testbusters group. Furthermore, the SET–C group had posttreatment scores that were significantly different from the Testbusters group on measures of social anxiety, general anxiety, social skills, and overall functioning. These results are particularly impressive because this is one of the few studies in which an active treatment (SET–C) was compared with an active, nonspecific intervention (rather than a wait-list control group). Treatment gains from SET–C were maintained 6 months (Beidel, Turner, & Morris, 2000), 3 years (Beidel, Turner, Young, & Paulson, 2005), and 5 years later (Beidel, Turner, & Young, in press). In fact, treatment response rates were higher at each follow-up assessment interval than at posttreatment, indicating that children continue to make improvements even after active treatment is discontinued. It remains unclear whether SET–C will be equally effective for adolescents with social anxiety disorder, although such an investigation currently is underway (Beidel, Turner, Sallee, & Ammerman, 2000).

Two studies have attempted to use parts of the SET–C treatment program to develop interventions considered to be more useful in "typical" treatment settings. Masia and her colleagues (Masia, Klein, Storch, & Corda, 2001) presented pilot data for an intervention that they termed Skills for Academic and Social Success (SASS), which combines truncated versions of the SET–C SST and exposure elements with realistic thinking and relapse prevention components based on a treatment model proposed by Rapee (1998). After 14 group sessions, social anxiety disorder severity ratings decreased significantly from pre- to posttreatment, as did scores on the Liebowitz Social Anxiety Scale for Children and Adolescents and patient ratings on individualized fear hierarchies. There was no significant decrease on the Social Phobia and Anxiety Inventory for Children (SPAI–C), however. These results are promising, but a controlled trial is necessary before drawing firm conclusions. Such a trial is ongoing.

A second modified SET–C program was based on the notion that SET–C is too time and labor intensive for a community outpatient psychiatric clinic. A very small controlled trial (Baer & Garland, 2005) compared a "simplified" version of SET–C to a wait-list control group ($n = 6$ adolescents with social anxiety disorder in each group; 66% in each group were taking medication at the time of the study). The simplified version consisted of twelve 90-minute group sessions consisting of 6 adolescents and 3 group leaders. Each session was divided into two parts: 45 minutes devoted to the SET–C SST (except for one session that was devoted to cognitive strategies to manage anxiety) and 45 minutes for group exposure sessions. In the exposure sessions, the adolescent group was broken down into smaller groups. At posttreatment, 36% of the children in the active intervention no longer met criteria for a diagnosis of social anxiety disorder, compared with 0% of the wait-list control group, a difference that was statistically significant. There were also group differences on self-report measures of social anxiety but not of depression. Although these results indicate that for this very small sample, the modified version of SET–C was superior to a wait-list control group, it should be noted that only 36% of the children were without a diagnosis at posttreatment, a percentage that is substantially lower than that reported for the original SET–C treatment trial (67%; Beidel, Turner, & Morris, 2000). One difference might be that this study used adolescents, and the full SET–C program has yet to be validated as efficacious for an adolescent sample. Given their different stage of physical, emotional, and cognitive development, SET–C may require modification for maximal efficacy with adolescent populations. A second and more likely explanation for the attenuated treatment outcome in this modification is that the program was missing several critical SET–C components (peer generalization, individual exposure sessions). Although attempts to make interventions as time- and labor-efficient as possible are to be lauded, it should not be at the expense of an intervention that is not efficacious for the majority of the patients. As we described in chapters 1 and 2, social anxiety disorder is a severe and chronic condition, with significant immediate and long-term detrimental effects. The goal of developing interventions should be first and foremost to construct a treatment that is efficacious for at least a majority of those with this disorder. We believe that cost-effectiveness should be a secondary, albeit important, consideration.

Comparative and Combination Trials

Increasingly, studies comparing various interventions and the use of combination interventions are beginning to emerge. In a comparative, transcultural trial (Olivares, Garcia-Lopez, Beidel, et al., 2002; Olivares, Garcia-Lopez, Hidalgo, et al., 2002), Spanish adolescents were randomly assigned to traditional cognitive therapy (Olivares, Garcia-Lopez, Beidel, et al., 2002), CBGT–A, a truncated version of SET–C for adolescents, and a wait-list control group. All active treatments were significantly superior to the wait-list control group at posttreatment, and there were few differences among the active interventions with respect to their ability to decrease social phobia symptoms, improve social skills, or enhance self-esteem. Differences between the active treatments and the control group were maintained at 1-year follow-up. One limitation of this study is that there were only about 15 adolescents in each group, but the results are promising, indicating that the interventions are effective across cultural boundaries.

In an open trial, citalopram was combined with psychoeducation for children and adolescents with social anxiety disorder (Chavira &

Stein, 2002). Psychoeducation consisted of an initial education session, instruction in construction of anxiety hierarchies, construction of graduated exposure tasks, teaching basic social skills, cognitive challenging, and relapse prevention procedures. After 12 weeks of treatment, 83.3% of the children and adolescents were judged as improved, consistent with changes on self- and parental reports of social anxiety, depression, and social skills. Although improved, children continued to experience symptoms of social anxiety disorder, and although the outcome is promising, controlled trials are necessary. In fact, two comparative and combination trials are ongoing. In a 4-year multicenter trial for the treatment of anxiety disorders (generalized anxiety disorder, social anxiety disorder, or separation anxiety disorder), CBT (Kendall, 1994) will be compared with fluvoxamine, the combination of fluvoxamine and CBT, or pill placebo (Albano, personal communication, March 31, 2003) throughout a 12-week acute trial, followed by a 6-month treatment maintenance phase. It is unclear how many children with primary social anxiety disorder will be included in the final sample. A second, ongoing two-site trial (Beidel et al., 2004) compares SET–C, fluoxetine, and pill placebo in both children and adolescents with social anxiety disorder. The project will examine the applicability of SET–C to adolescents and determine the long-term (1-year) durability of both active interventions.

TREATMENT IMPLEMENTATION

Developmental considerations must play a role in the specific procedures selected to treat children and adolescents with social anxiety disorder. CBT programs include a cognitive restructuring component. This presumes that children with social anxiety disorder have negative cognitions that contribute to social anxiety and fear. Yet one of the cardinal features of this disorder, as reported by the patients themselves, is an inability to think when they are anxious. Adults with social anxiety disorder frequently characterize their experience as one in which they are flooded with so many thoughts that they are unable to think clearly. Children under age 12 are rarely able to describe having specific thoughts when in the fear-producing situation. A similar argument has been raised regarding the absence of negative cognitions in children and adolescents with panic disorder (Nelles & Barlow, 1988; see the discussion of this issue in chap. 2, this volume).

In chapter 8, we discussed the considerable evidence that exposure is the critical element in the treatment of social anxiety disorder in adults, and the empirical treatment literature suggests that exposure strategies are critical for the efficacious treatment of maladaptive social anxiety in children and adolescents as well. Also, SST (which includes some exposure elements) has been used widely to address social isolation in children. On the basis of the current data, it appears that a combination of exposure and SST is likely to be most effective in addressing social anxiety disorder. Two extant studies (Beidel, Turner, & Morris, 2000; Spence et al., 2000) with children diagnosed with social anxiety disorder support this conclusion. For adolescents, some evidence suggests that cognitive restructuring may be efficacious as well. We now turn to a description of how these treatment strategies are implemented in these populations.

Exposure

As with adults, the most critical part of exposure treatment is understanding all aspects of the fear parameters and, in particular, identification of the core fear. Although adults can often provide sufficient information, this is frequently not the case for children and adolescents. Young children or adolescents may admit to being shy but not be able to clarify further the nature of their fears. Adolescents often refuse to discuss their fears, even when they appear to understand them, because they have not come to treatment willingly and are reluctant to talk to a therapist. Therefore, in many instances, information about the fear's components must be collected from secondary sources, such as parents, teachers,

```
┌─────────────────────────────────────────────────────┐
│                   Exhibit 9.1                        │
├─────────────────────────────────────────────────────┤
```

**Commonly Distressful Situations for Children
With Social Anxiety Disorder**

Answering the teacher's questions
Asking the teacher a question
Reading aloud in class
Physical education class
Taking tests
Interacting with other children (e.g., talking, playing a game, doing
    a school project)
Interacting with adults
Using public bathrooms
Performing in front of others (e.g., dance recitals, sporting events,
    school plays)
Group interactions (e.g., boy or girl scouts, karate class, gymnastics
    lessons, birthday parties)
Eating or drinking in front of others
Ordering food in a restaurant
Answering or talking on the telephone

self-report data, behavioral assessments, or self-monitoring data and clinical conjecture, rather than from direct interview. Such data can be collected using several methods.

The Anxiety Disorders Interview Schedule—Parent Version (ADIS–P) and Anxiety Disorders Interview Schedule for Children—Child Version (ADIS–C; Silverman & Albano, 1995) sections on school and social anxiety disorder contain lists of potential social situations (see Exhibit 9.1). Each situation can be rated for extent of anxiety and avoidance. Although parents may not always be able to provide exact ratings of distress, they often easily identify a broad range of situations.

This identification can be of great assistance when developing exposure situations. Similarly, administration of the SPAI–C (parent or child versions; Beidel, Turner, & Morris, 1995) also helps to identify potentially distressful situations. Additionally, daily diary ratings (see chap. 5, this volume) provide a wealth of information about socially distressful situations that children typically encounter. Any or all of these methods may be useful in determining the parameters of the child's fear.

Once the specific parameters are determined, the clinician must decide how to structure the exposure treatment. Although the same method of exposure used to treat adults (see chap. 8, this volume) can be used with treating children and adolescents, there are a number of factors to consider carefully. Three important decisions regarding how to implement exposure treatment with children include (a) intensity of exposure, (b) mode of exposure, and (c) extent of therapist involvement in the session. Although these factors are important when treating adults, they particularly are important for children. In the ensuing sections, each variable is discussed.

Intensity of Exposure

As noted in chapter 8, exposure can be graduated or intensive. Intensive exposure requires substantial cooperation on the part of the child to enter and remain in the social situation for the appropriate period of time (see the subsequent section on intensive exposure). In addition, the rationale is often difficult for young children to understand, at times resulting in crying or tantrum behaviors. Thus, because of their reluctance or apprehension concerning treatment, a graduated approach often is considered preferable for young children. A graduated approach also helps control the parent's anxiety level, thus avoiding some of the pitfalls of the "Protection Trap" described by Silverman and Kurtines (1996; see chap. 6, this volume). Similarly, children under 12 years old may have difficulty using imagery. Thus, in vivo strategies are used primarily with young children.

Graduated Exposure for Children

Graduated in vivo exposure provides systematic, gradual, and repeated contact with the feared situation. Small amounts of the feared stimuli are presented one step at a time (i.e., hierarchically), and repeated pairings across a number of sessions, using progressively more fearful stimuli, are necessary for efficacious treatment. Attainment of the highest step on the hierarchy with minimal distress is the goal of graduated exposure.

Hierarchy Construction

A graduated approach necessitates the construction of a fear hierarchy. As with adults, the child's assistance in constructing the hierarchy is helpful. When explaining this concept to children, it is often useful to describe the hierarchy as a ladder. For very young children, drawing a picture of a ladder will facilitate understanding. Children (and their parents) should be told that the first part of treatment consists of building a ladder representing their fears. Situations that are less fearful are the bottom rungs of the ladder, whereas those that are more fearful are the highest rungs. Situations or activities are constructed on the basis of the assessment material that outlines the range of the fears and the associated degree of distress.

There are many ways to construct the hierarchy. For example, each situation can be written on an individual index card. Ratings of distress elicited by each situation are made using a Subjective Units of Distress Scale (SUDS). The cards are then ordered to represent the degree of distress elicited. For children, rating scales of 8 or 9 points are most common. Again, the caveat with respect to rating scales noted in chapter 5 is important here. A fear thermometer (e.g., the one depicted in Figure 9.1) or pictures depicting various numerical ratings of distress will assist young children in ordering the hierarchy.

When working with young children, it is recommended that the clinician and the child jointly develop and order the hierarchy. The hierarchy is then reviewed with the parent for accuracy and completeness.

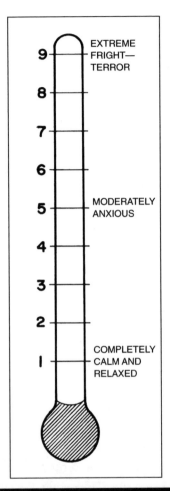

Figure 9.1

Fear thermometer.

Typical hierarchies usually range between 10 and 20 steps (index cards). Because this is a graduated approach, the hierarchy should include situations representing all steps on the SUDS scale. If the review reveals "gaps" in the ladder (i.e., there are situations rated as a 3 and some are rated as a 6, but none rated as 4 or 5), additional items should be constructed. This might be accomplished by varying the scene content of items already in the hierarchy. For example, the item "reading in front of one child" might be rated as a 3, whereas "reading in front of an adult" might be rated as a 6. Therefore, items representing 4 or 5 might be "reading in front of two children" and "reading in front of the babysitter (a teenage girl)," respectively.

An important key to the success of the intervention is that the therapist should not try to impose any type of order on the hierarchy. That is, it is not necessary that the order of the items make sense to the therapist. For some children, reading in front of their best friend may be more anxiety producing than reading in front of an adult. The hierarchy only needs to make sense in terms of representing increasing levels of distress for the child. In other words, maladaptive fear by nature is irrational. Hence, the sequence might not be logical. A hierarchy used for the treatment of a 10-year-old girl with social anxiety disorder is presented in Table 9.1

Implementation of Graduated Exposure

Once the hierarchy is constructed, one or two items are addressed each week. The items may be assigned in session or as homework assignments, depending on their nature. In some cases, an item may be completed in session as well as for homework. Before presenting an item, the child's baseline level of distress is assessed (using either physiological or subjective ratings). As each item is presented, the therapist asks the child to rate current distress using the SUDS scale. Because this is a graduated approach, distress should be low (i.e., 1 or 2 units on the SUDS scale above the child's baseline distress level). Thus, if the child's baseline distress is rated as a 1, exposure to the fearful item should not be rated higher than a 3. The item continues to be presented until the distress rating decreases to baseline. At the completion of the session, the items (or some variation) should be prescribed as a homework assignment to be completed several times during the ensuing week. For example, children who have difficulty greeting strangers may be instructed to answer the telephone at home for the next week. Alternatively, under their

Table 9.1	
Sample Hierarchy for the Treatment of Social Anxiety Disorder	
	SUDS fear rating
Answering a question in class when you know the answer.	1
Eating at a fast-food restaurant.	2
Reading aloud in front of one person; knowing and practicing the material ahead of time.	2
Reading unfamiliar material aloud in front of one person.	3
Writing on the blackboard.	3
Saying hello to a person your age—someone you know but not well.	4
Taking a spelling test on the blackboard.	4
Ordering food in a fast-food restaurant.	4
Making mistakes—tripping in front of someone.	5
Saying hello to an adult whom you know.	5
Reading aloud in front of a group.	6
Being around a group of popular peers but not being required to talk to them.	7
Giving a report in class.	7
Talking to an adult and disclosing information about self.	8
Requesting information from clerks in stores or from the principal.	8
Introducing self to a popular peer.	9
Joining in with a group of peers (e.g., walking to class, playing a game).	9

Note. SUDS = Subjective Units of Distress Scale.

parents' supervision, they might go to the mall and ask questions of unfamiliar store clerks.

As depicted in Table 9.1, some items will most likely occur during school, making it unlikely that the therapist would be present during the exposure session. If the items are assigned solely as homework (i.e., completed outside of the therapy session), the parent and child should be instructed carefully about how to conduct the session, including how long it should last (at least 90 minutes or until distress returns to baseline).

In the case of items such as greeting someone, the child would not necessarily continue to greet the same person for an extended period of time; the child should continue to greet different individuals until the distress dissipates. Thus, a child could be taken to a park or a playground where there are numerous other individuals available to participate in the exposure session.

The following are the steps for implementing graduated exposure:

1. The therapist, in conjunction with the child and the parent, using all of the available assessment data, develops a hierarchy of anxiety-producing situations.
2. One or two items per session are presented (or assigned as homework). Children should be reassured that items farther up the ladder will not be presented until the bottom rungs are successfully completed. The items should elicit only minimal distress, and the child should continue to engage in the situation until that distress has dissipated.
3. Items addressed in the session should be assigned for further practice as homework assignments. If items are completed outside the therapy session, the therapist should provide clear instructions to the parent and child, including the time frame.

Problems in Implementing Graduated Exposure

As noted, situations are ranked from least to most anxiety producing. If the item elicits moderate or high distress, it usually indicates that (a) the initial placement of the item in the hierarchy was incorrect or (b) the item represents too large a step on the ladder from the previous item (i.e., there are rungs missing on the ladder). In the case of the former, the item should be withdrawn and placed farther up the hierarchy. In the case of the latter, the item should be broken down into smaller steps. As discussed earlier, additional items, to fill in the gaps, should be constructed.

The most important potential complication associated with graduated exposure is deriving the hierarchy for a young child, who may have only a limited understanding of the fear. Additionally, parents may recognize a child's distress but not have sufficient understanding to provide all of the necessary fear cues. Often, extremely stressful situations (e.g., SUDS ratings at the top of the hierarchy) are easily identified, as are nonstressful settings. It is the middle items that are the most difficult to identify. Clinicians often need to suggest items that fill in the middle of a hierarchy. Also, an empirical approach can be used to identify relevant items, although this will add to the length of treatment time. Should items not be able to be identified, a graduated approach may not be feasible, and a more intensive alternative should be considered (see the subsequent section on imaginal exposure).

A final consideration is the need for parental involvement. In the majority of cases, children cannot carry out the assignments independently. An exception might be when assignments are carried out in the school setting. In the latter case, only minimal parental involvement is required (e.g., praise when the child completes the task). Other assignments, such as having a friend over to play, inviting a friend to a movie, or eating in a fast food restaurant, require the parent to play an active role in facilitating the item's successful completion. Thus, an important key to successful graduated exposure with children is parental willingness and assistance in carrying out assigned tasks. A number of factors may inhibit active parental participation. For example, parents may not have the physical or economic resources, may be unwilling, or may be impaired by their own social fears. In these cases, there are a few alternatives that might be considered. For parents without physical or economic resources (e.g., they do not own a car) or for those who have severe social fears themselves, constructing all assignments to occur at school is one alternative. In such cases, it may be possible to enlist a guidance counselor or favorite teacher to assist the child with the assignments.

A second, and perhaps better, alternative for those parents who have social fears themselves is to help them enter treatment. Finally, for those parents who are just too busy, the clinician may remind the parent that improperly administered treatment programs are not effective and that they may need to reconsider whether they judge the child's problem to be severe enough to warrant treatment at that time.

Intensive Exposure (Flooding)

The theoretical basis for flooding was discussed in chapter 8. To reiterate briefly, flooding is based on a habituation paradigm, and substantial empirical data demonstrate that repeated exposure to an anxiety-producing situation without the opportunity for escape decreases anxiety (see chap. 8, this volume). Most individuals become so overwhelmed by their anxiety, however, that they cannot wait it out. Rather, they escape or avoid the distressful situation. The goal of intensive exposure (flooding) is to place the children in the fearful situation and help them stay there until the anxiety dissipates.

For older children or adolescents (e.g., age 12 or older) flooding may be the treatment of choice for the same reason that it is for adults (see chap. 8, this volume). Also, flooding may be used when an appropriate hierarchy cannot be constructed or if there is no suitable adult to oversee a gradual exposure program. Rather than a hierarchy, exposure using an intensive (flooding) paradigm means that the child immediately faces the most distressful situation (i.e., the top rung of the ladder). Such situations usually involve performing in front of others, for example, reading, speaking, or writing in front of a group of people. There are subtle differences among these behaviors, and it should not be assumed that just any performance situation will do. Careful assessment is needed to identify the core fear. For example,

> Annie had no difficulty speaking in front of large groups if she had
> a prepared text, but she became quite distressed if she had to speak
> extemporaneously to a group or interact casually with a small group

of children. Her concern was that others would think she was not intelligent, and if she could not prepare in advance, her fears were magnified.

Obviously, Annie had an intense need for perfection as she interpreted it. Thus, presenting the material in the exact way was important to her and to the core fear needed for proper exposure.

Implementing Intensive Exposure (Flooding) Sessions

Constructing the appropriate stimuli for intensive exposure often requires considerable ingenuity on the part of the therapist. Because reading in front of others is a common activity for children and adolescents and a common fear for those with social anxiety disorder, this situation often can be used for intensive exposure. The therapist should keep several children's books on hand, representing various reading levels. This provides ready access to read-aloud material. An alternative is to instruct children to bring in their own school texts; however, children's apprehensions are such that they often forget their book. Having the books on hand prevents the child from escaping the exposure activity.

In the intensive flooding paradigm, in which performance is the critical factor, a child would be given a book and be required to read in front of several audience members (volunteers or undergraduate students) and to keep reading until the anxiety dissipates. In settings where audience members are not readily available, the therapist may take the child to a public place such as a park or a shopping mall, where passersby would hear the child read aloud. Other performance-based exposure activities could include writing spelling words on the board or taking a math test at the blackboard while others observe the performance. At times, the critical factor might revolve around whether the audience was made up of peers or adults, or perhaps authority figures. Also, children who are afraid to join groups of other children could be taken to a beach, playground, or park and be required to interact with other children who are there.

Whatever the situation, the clinician should assess SUDS levels (distress ratings) at least every 10 minutes. If possible, keeping a written record of the distress ratings will help determine patterns of within- and between-session habituation. The therapist must be prepared to deal with initially significant levels of distress elicited by this high-intensity procedure and encourage the child to engage in the exposure setting despite his or her distress. Sometimes providing small rewards throughout the session and a larger reward at completion of the session is helpful. The child (assisted by the therapist) continues to engage in the feared activity for an extended period of time (usually 90 minutes) or ideally until arousal dissipates (within-session habituation; see chap. 8, this volume).

Flooding is not a one-session treatment. Children are exposed to the same distressful situation repeatedly until the situation no longer elicits distress (between-session habituation; see chap. 8, this volume). On average, between 10 and 12 flooding sessions are needed to achieve between-session habituation when treating social anxiety disorder. Figure 9.2 depicts within-session and between-session habituation during an in vivo task for a 10-year-old girl with a severe fear of reading in front of others. Figure 9.3 depicts within-session and between-session habituation during an imaginal task for a 16-year-old boy. For the sake of readability, habituation curves illustrating only several of the sessions are shown.

Many of the problems in implementing intensive in vivo exposure are the same as for intensive imaginal exposure (to be discussed later). Thus, the discussion of problems in implementation is addressed following the presentation of the procedure referred to as imaginal flooding.

Imaginal Versus In Vivo Exposure

An important consideration when implementing exposure with children is whether the stimuli should be presented imaginally or in vivo. Both the graduated and intensive procedures just described used in vivo exposure. Although often preferable, it is sometimes difficult to arrange the in vivo situations, particularly outside of university or specialty clinic

Time to Habituation (In Vivo Task)

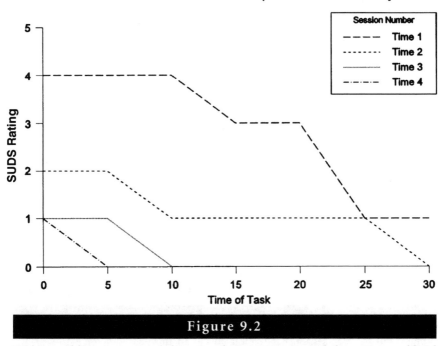

Figure 9.2

Within- and between-session habituation during an in vivo task for a 10-year-old girl with a severe fear of reading in front of others. SUDS = Subjective Units of Distress Scale.

settings. In such cases, imaginal presentation of the distressful situation may be necessary. We do not recommend using imaginal procedures for children under age 10. For older children and adolescents, imaginal exposure may be efficacious and cost-efficient. Furthermore, it allows for exposure to fears that cannot be replicated in vivo.

Imaginal Flooding

As we noted in chapter 8, the key to imaginal exposure is the construction of the imaginal scene. To reiterate briefly, it is crucial that the patient be exposed to the core fear. Those with social anxiety disorder are not afraid of people per se, but they fear that they might do something humiliating or embarrassing in front of others and that the other people

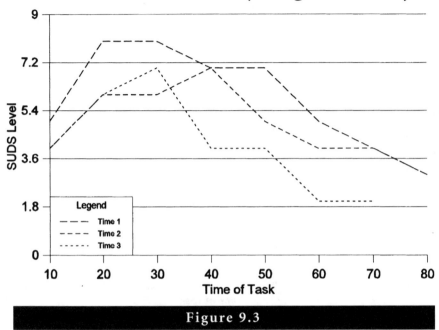

Time To Habituation (Imaginal Task)

Figure 9.3

Within- and between-session habituation during an imaginal task for a 16-year-old boy. SUDS = Subjective Units of Distress Scale.

will think critically of them. Therefore, the imaginal scene must capture this element. Exhibit 9.2 presents two imaginal scenes used in actual treatment cases. The first (Scene 1) is for a 14-year-old boy with a severe fear of reading in front of the class, and the second (Scene 2) is for a 16-year-old boy with generalized social anxiety disorder.

There are several points that should be made about these scenes. First, they include the core fear and depict the child's specific concern. Second, there is no option for the child to cope with the distress or to handle the situation. Because this is a strict habituation paradigm, it is important to make sure the child is exposed to what he or she fears. If allowed to cope, in essence, the child is being allowed to escape or minimize the distress. This is inconsistent with a habituation paradigm.

Exhibit 9.2

Sample Imaginal Flooding Scenes

Scene 1

You are in your English class at school. There are about 25 students in the class. Your class has been studying Shakespeare, and everyone in the class has been taking turns reading aloud. You are really worried about this. You are scared that you might make a fool out of yourself. Your heart is racing, your hands are trembling, you are sweating, and your face feels hot and red. What will you do if the teacher calls on you to read? Everyone will see how nervous you are. Even if they don't, you are likely to mispronounce one of the words and everyone might laugh. No one else has made a mistake. The teacher looks at you and says, "Max, please read the next part aloud." Everyone turns to look at you. They can see how red your face is and how your hands are trembling. You open your mouth to speak, but nothing comes out. You try again and you mispronounce the first word. The guys are all snickering and the girls are smiling. You keep reading, but you keep mispronouncing even the easiest words. Even the teacher is trying hard not to laugh at you. The other kids are whispering, "He doesn't read correctly." The teacher is thinking, "I thought he was smarter than that." Your face is bright red. You feel embarrassed and humiliated.

Exhibit continues

Third, the specific content of the scene is less relevant than the fact that the core fear is captured. Thus, in the first scene in which the adolescent mispronounces words and embarrasses himself in front of others, the scene used a classroom. It could just as easily have been a scene in which the child was reading in front of a church congregation or speaking at a party. To reiterate, the particular scene background is less important than exposure to the specific feared consequences (i.e., the core fear). The procedures for implementing imaginal exposure were presented in chapter 8, and the reader is referred there for details.

Exhibit 9.2 *(Continued)*

Sample Imaginal Flooding Scenes

Scene 2

You are at your locker at school. There are many kids around, but you still feel very lonely. No one talks to you, and you have not been able to talk to anyone either. You think that they are looking at you funny, although you cannot be sure. You feel really nervous. You are sweaty, and your heart is beating fast. They are probably thinking that there is something wrong with you, that they should stay away from you. You just want them to talk to you, to treat you like they treat everyone else. Very close to you are two of your classmates. They are talking about soccer, something you know a lot about. They have not been rude to you in the past, and so you decide that maybe you should talk to them. You inch over toward them, and they do not move away. You think to yourself, "Maybe it will be OK. Maybe they will let me talk to them." You are really nervous. Your heart is pounding, and you can barely get the words out. You are talking so softly you can hardly hear what you are saying. You say something about soccer. They both stop talking and just look at you for a second. They don't really respond to you. They don't ask you anything else, and then they just go back to talking to each other. Once again, you have failed. What's wrong with you that you cannot even say a couple of sentences without getting so nervous that people turn away? You are just a total failure.

Problems in Implementing Intensive Imaginal or In Vivo Exposure

One potential problem using exposure is the failure of the child, adolescent, or perhaps even the parent to understand the treatment rationale. Most adults understand that conquering fear requires facing the anxiety-producing situation, but because children and adolescents initially may be distressed by the procedure, it is important that the rationale be explained carefully and completely. Pictorial illustrations of within-session habituation and between-session habituation often help explain the concepts and goals of intensive exposure. Furthermore, we recommend keeping track of SUDS levels assessed during the treatment sessions and graphing them as illustrated in Figures 9.2 and 9.3. These graphs often are useful to share with children and parents to track the efficacy of the program and to demonstrate progress. Compliance often increases when children and parents see that intensive exposure is having an effect.

Even if they understand the rationale, some children may not have the motivation to participate in this procedure. Children and adolescents usually are brought to a clinic because an adult feels that they have a problem. Thus, they usually are more reluctant and fearful about what treatment will entail. When children are hesitant or noncompliant about participation in treatment, we have found that allowing them some control over the exposure situations engenders their trust and makes them more compliant. Thus, similar to the advice given by March and Mulle (1993) for treatment of children and adolescents with obsessive–compulsive disorder, we advise setting up an agreement (contract) with children. That is, once exposure situations are identified, the child may choose which exposure task to attempt first, and as long as there is continued progress toward the ultimate goal, the therapist and the child jointly decide to move to the next task. With this agreement, children often willingly attempt the first task, and once they are involved in the process, issues of control typically are no longer a problem.

When conducting imaginal exposure, another potential problem is difficulty imagining the scene. As we noted earlier, we do not recommend imaginal exposure for children under age 10, and even some older children and adolescents do not have well-developed cognitive capabilities and thus are not able to imagine the scene. In some cases, simple imagery training (asking the child to practice imagining familiar situations, places, or things) may enhance their abilities. For example, children can practice imagining their bedroom by naming all of its contents and describing them in detail. Similarly, a favorite place or activity can be used. After some practice, a child's imagery capability often improves. In some cases, the child's complaint of not being able to imagine the scene is not because of an inability to imagine but is a way of avoiding the distress associated with a scene. If this happens, the first step is to repeat the rationale for exposure. If this does not eliminate the problem, asking the child to verbalize aloud what he or she is imagining is often effective. Another alternative is to arrange for parents to provide positive reinforcement as a reward for participation. If each strategy is unsuccessful, an in vivo approach might be necessary.

Finally, as noted in chapter 8, children, like adults, may try to minimize distress by attempting to cope during the imaginal procedure. For example, in the second scene in Exhibit 9.2, an adolescent who is attempting to cope may change the scene content such that classmates smile and respond rather than ignore the conversational attempt. Actually, this coping behavior is more common in adults than in children or adolescents, but the older the child or adolescent is, the more likely such a problem will arise. Remediation of this problem is discussed in chapter 8.

Therapist-Accompanied Versus Therapist-Directed Exposure

A final consideration in the implementation of exposure therapy is whether the therapist should accompany the child during in vivo exposure. Our advice is that if at all possible, at least the first several sessions should be therapist accompanied. There are several reasons for this recommendation. First, initial sessions often can reveal additional information about the parameters of the disorder. Second, therapist accompaniment may facilitate compliance. Third, one study that addressed this issue found that clinician-accompanied sessions were more effective than self-exposure for adults with social anxiety disorder (Al-Kubaisy et al., 1992). We recognize that in many settings, therapists may not always be able to leave the clinic to conduct the exposure session. If clinician accompaniment is not an option and the in vivo situation cannot be replicated within the clinic setting, it may be possible to use the parents or some other significant person to conduct the exposure session. In this case, parents or others must be given specific instructions and make a commitment to conduct the exposure session for at least 90 minutes. Furthermore, a practice session in the clinic should be conducted to ensure that the parent or significant person can conduct the session appropriately.

Social Skills Training

As we noted earlier, because SST usually occurs in groups (although individual treatment is possible), it provides a naturalistic exposure session. SST is not formal exposure treatment, however, and cannot take its place. Also, SST is more than just exposure to a group. The goal of SST is to teach children specific skills and provide an opportunity to practice these skills in a controlled setting. As noted in chapter 2, children with social anxiety disorder exhibit specific skills deficits in areas including conversational skills and positive and negative assertion. Exhibit 9.3 presents content areas that we have found lacking in children with social anxiety disorder. In addition, clinicians have noted nonverbal deficits

---

Exhibit 9.3

Content Areas Included in Social Skills Training (SST)

Greetings and introductions
Initiating conversations
Maintaining conversations
Listening skills
Skills for joining groups
Establishing and maintaining friendships
Giving and receiving compliments
Assertiveness with peers
Assertiveness with adults
Telephone skills

such as poor eye contact, low voice volume, and inappropriate vocal tone. This list is not exhaustive but represents difficulties typically encountered.

Elements of Social Skills Training

The primary objective of SST is skills building, not fear reduction. Typically, one behavior (whether verbal or nonverbal) is targeted at each session, but the entire treatment process is cumulative. Nonverbal content skills such as eye contact and voice volume are taught consistently and integrated with the teaching of the content areas. All skills are taught using traditional procedures for SST: instruction, modeling, behavioral rehearsal, feedback, and positive reinforcement. *Instruction* means that the therapist presents the skill to be learned and a rationale for why learning it is important. For example, if the skill is "giving a compliment," children are told that giving compliments is a way to make friends. They are asked to give examples of compliments to assess their understanding of the concept. Then, the therapist models appropriate and inappropriate ways to give compliments. Particularly with younger children, we think it is important to use exaggerated modeling to make the distinctions clear. For example, when modeling how to give a compliment, therapists first could use an extremely aversive vocal tone, no eye contact, and perhaps a low voice volume to demonstrate the wrong way to give a compliment. The therapist follows this by modeling the appropriate way. Children should be questioned regarding differences between the right and wrong ways.

The core of SST, *behavioral rehearsal,* is how the majority of the session time should be spent. Children should be given extensive opportunities to practice the skills. This is usually accomplished by setting up a context in which the behavior can be rehearsed. Although sometimes called role-playing, it is important to remember that the child is not encouraged to play a role. The scene is merely a vehicle through which rehearsal occurs, and the child uses the scene context to practice the skill. The child is instructed to treat the situation as if it were a real social encounter. To continue with the example of giving a compliment, the child may be asked to imagine the following:

> You are sitting in math class. The boy next to you has been studying really hard to improve his grades. The class gets back the most recent test, and he turns to you and says, "I finally got an A!"

The child is to respond to this situation with an appropriate compliment. Because skill acquisition will not occur with a single trial, the child should be provided with several practice opportunities with the same scene and with many additional opportunities using other scenes. After each role-play, the child should be given *corrective feedback* and *positive reinforcement*. Recalling that this is a performance situation and children with social anxiety disorder fear performing in public, it is important to praise the child for any attempt to engage in the rehearsal. Of course, it is also important to point out areas in need of further improvement. Thus, the clinician may respond to the child's attempt as follows:

> Chris, you did very well when you said, "Congratulations, you worked really hard and you deserve an A." I want you to do it again, and this time, I want you to look at me and smile when you say, "Congratulations."

Implementing Social Skills Training

Social skills training can be conducted individually or in small group settings. In the individual setting, the therapist serves as the interpersonal partner in the behavioral rehearsal. Because the therapist then is required to play two roles simultaneously (interpersonal partner and observer of the child's performance), we prefer a group setting whenever possible. This allows one of the other group members to serve as the interpersonal partner, thereby allowing the therapist to concentrate fully on observing the child's performance. In addition, the group setting allows the child the opportunity to practice with a number of children who are representative of his or her peers.

An initial step in conducting SST is taking an inventory of the child's social skills deficits. No widely available self-report measures exist for this purpose, and thus, the clinician must rely on behavioral observation, parental report, the child's report, and clinical observations. The content areas listed in Exhibit 9.3 represent those deficits most commonly encountered in children and adolescents with social anxiety disorder, and clinicians might use this list to assist in an initial inventory.

Once the list of social skills deficits has been constructed, the next step is to construct appropriate scenes to be used in the behavior rehearsal. Some "standard" scenes should be constructed in advance of the session, but the training will be most effective if the child can supply some situations from daily interactions. Thus, there should be a battery of scenes available in case the child does not volunteer any situations; scenes drawn from the child's daily experiences and that tap specific difficulties experienced by the child are most useful.

Ideally, the skill should be presented as described earlier. If an individual format is used, one or two skills should be presented at each session, depending on the child's ability to understand and acquire the particular behaviors. In a group setting, only one content skill per session should be used, thereby allowing each child sufficient practice opportunities. Rehearsal should continue with the same scene until each child has mastered all components. Then, as noted earlier, another scene (requiring each child to practice the same skill) is used.

As we noted with exposure sessions, it is important that the child continue to practice the skill between therapy sessions. Therefore, the therapist must design appropriate homework assignments. This homework should provide the opportunity for continued practice but should not take long to complete (so that the task does not become aversive or a point of contention between parent and child). In addition, these homework assignments serve as generalization experiences, allowing the child to practice the skill outside of the therapist's office and in a variety of natural settings. For example, continuing with the skill of giving

Table 9.2
Generic Homework Assignments for Social Skills Training

Skill	Homework
Greetings and introductions	Smile and say hello to two people you know. Introduce yourself to three new people everyday.
Initiating conversations	Greet a friend and ask a question (each day).
Maintaining conversations	Greet a friend and ask two questions about the same topic each day.
Listening	Ask someone in your class a question. When you get home, write down the answer.
Joining Groups	Ask someone to join you in an activity.
Establishing and maintaining friendships	Telephone a friend each night and talk for 10 minutes.
Giving and receiving compliments	Give two compliments each day.
Being assertive with peers	If possible, be assertive with a peer. If no situation arises, ask two friends to sleep over at your house.
Being assertive with adults	If possible, be assertive with your parents. Otherwise, talk to as many adults as possible.
Using the telephone	Make three telephone calls per day. For example, call pet stores and ask if they sell parakeets.

compliments, the child might be required to give two compliments per day. Children should be given a homework form so that they (and the therapist) can monitor compliance. The assignment should include specific instructions regarding what the child is to do and how to do it. Examples of homework assignments for each skill listed in Exhibit 9.3 are presented in Table 9.2. Clinicians are cautioned that these are "generic" assignments. Homework will be more effective if assignments are tailored to the particular child.

Problems in Implementing Social Skills Training

We noted that children often may be reluctant to rehearse in front of others, particularly in a group setting. We have found that with preadolescent children, small tokens such as stickers often enhance children's motivation to participate. Similarly, for both preadolescent and adolescent children, fast-food coupons or movie passes are substantive motivators. Often, if requested, fast-food restaurants will supply free coupons for french fries (or a similar item), knowing that additional foods will be purchased when the coupon is redeemed. The coupons can be used as a reward for group (or individual) participation.

Another potential problem is noncompliance with homework assignments. There may be several reasons for this refusal. First, it should be determined that the assignment is not too difficult for the child. If it is too difficult, the assignment should be adjusted to make it more likely that the child will be able to accomplish the task successfully. If it is a matter of motivation and not difficulty, simply encouraging the child to complete the task may be insufficient. Rather, it may be necessary for the parent to reinforce the child for the completion of the assignment. Reinforcement need not be expensive. Increased privileges such as a later bedtime or a later curfew for adolescents may be all that is necessary to ensure compliance.

A final potential problem is the transfer of behaviors learned in the office or clinic to other settings. Again, the most effective method to ensure generalization is repeated practice in other group settings. In certain instances, it may be necessary for the parent and therapist to engineer appropriate activities. Parents may have to arrange for another child to visit the house for there to be opportunities to play with other children. Similarly, when the assignment calls for the child to talk to as many adults as possible, parents can assist their children by providing many practice opportunities. For example, children could go into fast-food restaurants and order a meal. They could go into a convenience store and pay for the gas or buy a quart of milk or go into a post office and buy stamps. Generalization opportunities are only as limited as the therapist's creativity and the parent's cooperation.

In our opinion, SST is an integral part of the treatment of social anxiety disorder in children. On the basis of the clinical presentation data in chapter 2, the etiological data in chapter 4, and the adult data in chapters 1 and 8, there is substantial support for the conclusion that those with social anxiety disorder (particularly the generalized subtype) have substantial social skills deficits that require remediation if children are to interact appropriately with others. Although we believe that SST is an integral treatment component, we do not believe that it is sufficient treatment by itself, however. Two meta-analyses of treatment outcome studies with adults (see chap. 8, this volume) indicate that exposure generates the largest effect size. In one of these reports (Taylor, 1996), the effect size for SST alone was found to be inferior to treatments that included exposure. Some reasons for this have been discussed previously. For example, social skills do not generalize "automatically" to nonclinic settings. Even when generalization programs are a part of the intervention, only 21% of the programs produce partial or complete generalization (Chandler, Lubeck, & Fowler, 1992). Although we noted that SST may provide a group setting and, as a result, serve as an exposure situation, it does not include a systematic exposure intervention. Furthermore, as we have stressed several times, exposure therapy must be individualized, exposing the patient to very specific fear cues. Therefore, it is highly unlikely that participating in an SST group would always address each group member's unique fear components. Individualized SST would be even less effective at providing a proper exposure setting. Thus, although SST can be an important aspect of the treatment of social anxiety disorder in children and adolescents, treatment is most effective when combined with some form of exposure, as in the case of SET–C (Beidel, Turner, & Morris, 2004).

Social Effectiveness Therapy for Children[1]

SET–C is a 12-week program during which sessions are conducted twice per week for a total of 24 treatment sessions. Each week the child participates in one SST group session and one individual exposure session. SET–C includes an individualized exposure therapy component that is implemented as previously described in this chapter. For each child, exposure opportunities, either in the clinic or in the child's natural environment, are developed. In addition, the children are given homework assignments geared to the content of the exposure sessions. For example, if a child is fearful of interacting with adults, he or she may be given the assignment to go into 12 stores over the next week and ask questions of adults. Obviously, parental cooperation is a crucial aspect of the success of the homework program.

SET–C also includes a group SST component because studies of the behavioral interactions of children with social anxiety disorder indicate that, compared with their nonanxious peers, these children have poorer social skills and higher levels of observable anxiety (see chap. 2, this volume). Thus, the second weekly session is an SST group. In SET–C, the content of the social skills sessions is geared to the specific deficits known to be present in these children (see section on SST for details of the training procedure and Exhibit 9.3 for the social skills content areas). Finally, a unique aspect of SET–C is the use of a peer-generalization component. This was considered necessary because prior studies with socially withdrawn or isolated children indicated that behaviors acquired in the clinic do not always generalize to other settings without direct intervention. In addition, this component provides opportunities for social learning through the observation of nonanxious peers. Specifically, as part of our SET–C intervention program, we have recruited a group

---

[1] *The Social Effectiveness Therapy Treatment Manual* (Turner, Beidel, & Cooley, 1994) is available from Multi-Health Systems, Inc., 65 Overlea Boulevard, Suite 210, Toronto, Ontario, Canada, M4H 1P1, (800) 456-3003.

of nonanxious peers who serve as peer helpers in the program. After each SST group, the children with social anxiety disorder and the peer helpers go on an outing that lasts for approximately 90 minutes. These activities occur at various places throughout the city, including parks, roller-skating rinks, pizza parlors, bowling alleys, and other popular recreation venues for children. The goal of these outings is to allow the children with social anxiety disorder to practice the skill learned in group in a natural setting and to provide an opportunity to interact with children who are not anxious (i.e., the type of child who usually ignores them). The peer helpers (who are the same age as the children in the treatment group) are selected for their friendly, outgoing nature and their desire to help other children who are shy. They are given minimal instructions and training but are simply told to talk to the shy children, include them in the activity, and help them have fun. Peers do, however, receive instruction in confidentiality issues.

Cognitive Restructuring

Some CBT programs include a component to teach children how to identify and change negative cognitions that might accompany social anxiety disorder. As noted, we have not found evidence of a preponderance of negative cognitions in preadolescent children (Alfano et al., 2002). Such cognitions may, however, be more common in more mature patients, such as adolescents. Cognitive restructuring includes several steps (Kendall, 1994). First, negative thoughts are identified; for example, "She'll never like me, why should I even bother to say hello?" Then rational alternatives are generated; for example, "She always smiles at me, so she probably doesn't hate me," or "Maybe she's just as nervous as I am," or "It's okay to be nervous, everybody's nervous when they meet for the first time." Children then are given practice through behavioral rehearsal or actual exposure sessions whereby they can practice substituting positive thoughts for negative ones. With repeated practice, negative thoughts should cease to occur.

Implementing Cognitive Restructuring

One of the first steps in implementing cognitive restructuring is training the child to recognize automatic negative thoughts. Automatic thoughts are usually considered unrecognized by the individual even though these thoughts can influence behavior. Awareness of unrecognized thoughts is usually accomplished by asking children or adolescents to enter into socially distressful situations and pay attention to what they are thinking. Children are requested to record these thoughts for the next treatment session.

Once identified, the therapist and the patient examine these thoughts and conclusions and determine their veracity. The child is then taught to generate alternative, positive thoughts for these situations. Beidel, Neal, and Lederer (1991) reported that children with social anxiety disorder spontaneously use positive statements to cope with their fears. Thus, children have the innate ability to generate such statements. It is a matter of teaching them to use these statements on a more consistent basis. After the child becomes proficient in generating positive coping statements, the child substitutes positive for negative thoughts. As with traditional exposure or SST, children are assigned homework opportunities to continue to practice the cognitive restructuring task.

Problems in Implementing Cognitive Restructuring

As noted, one difficulty in implementing cognitive restructuring might be the failure of children or adolescents to report the presence of negative cognitions. This might be because young children have not yet achieved a level of cognitive development that allows for the presence of future-oriented cognitions. Furthermore, sometimes children mistake the presence of negative feelings ("I felt very nervous") for negative thoughts ("What if I make a mistake?"). Alternatively, if these thoughts are present but unrecognized or for some reason not reported, there is some indication that children might be trained to become adept at recognizing their

Figure 9.4

Sample cartoon used to help children clarify the nature of negative thoughts.

presence. One strategy advocated by Kendall (1994) that appears helpful in training children to identify and clarify the nature of these negative thoughts is through the use of cartoons and thought bubbles (see Figure 9.4). Children are familiar with cartoons and the use of bubbles to indicate that the character is thinking about something. The exercise entails using a collection of such cartoons illustrating various emotions and asking children to write in the bubble what the character must be thinking. By externalizing the task to the use of cartoon characters and providing a broad range (15–20) of cartoons, we have found that children can become more adept at reporting negative thoughts. As a matter of fact, we have found that when these cartoon bubbles are assigned as homework, children need little encouragement or reinforcement to complete it. The cartoons can also be useful when teaching the substitution of positive coping thoughts for negative ones. In this case, cartoons are altered so that two thought bubbles appear. In the first, the child writes the negative thought. Then in the second, the child constructs a positive coping statement.

We believe that with young children the use of cartoons may be quite beneficial. In addition to possibly teaching children to recognize negative cognitions, the cartoons help to externalize the process. By this we mean that by identifying the negative thoughts of cartoon characters, children can practice the procedure separately from focusing on their own distress. Thus, children can become proficient at the technique before directing it to their own distressing cognitions.

Relaxation Training

We do not view relaxation training alone as an intervention suitable for the treatment of social anxiety disorder. There is no empirical evidence (in either adults or children) to suggest that this procedure, by itself, is efficacious in the treatment of this disorder. Because several CBT programs use relaxation training as part of the treatment protocol, we discuss it briefly here. Relaxation training is an effective strategy to decrease general distress. In children and adolescents, relaxation sessions are generally shorter than for adults (no more than 15–20 minutes) and address fewer muscle groups. We now list some guidelines for the implementation of relaxation training with children and adolescents.

Implementing Relaxation Training

Some children who are noticeably tense and anxious around others often are unable to recognize their physical distress. Using relaxation training effectively requires the recognition that one is tense and anxious and the ability to discriminate between these two states. Thus, before teaching relaxation training, we often engage the children in exercises designed to heighten their awareness of somatic sensations of anxiety. We use the interoceptive conditioning exercises designed by Barlow and colleagues (Barlow, Craske, Cerny, & Klosko, 1989) to illustrate what "bodies can feel like when someone is anxious." Interoceptive exercises include such strategies as running in place for one minute, breathing through a small straw for a minute, and shaking the head from side to side (for details, see Barlow et al., 1989). Children can try the exercise and then discuss with the therapist whether the symptom elicited is similar to what happens to them when they feel anxious.

There are two formalized scripts that have been used to teach relaxation training. The first was a script developed for younger children (Koeppen, 1974). This script addresses cognitive limitations of young children; that is, most relaxation scripts instruct patients to tense and relax various muscle groups. Koeppen's script, recognizing that young children may have difficulty with this type of command, uses images and descriptions of how to tense and relax muscle groups to make the instructions more salient to the child. For example, rather than saying, "Tense the muscles in your right hand by making a fist," the script by Koeppen instructs the child to "Imagine you have a lemon in your right hand and you want to make lemonade. Squeeze the lemon as hard as you can." Although empirical studies are not available, our clinical impression is that young children (age 10 and under) respond positively to this script. Ollendick (as cited in Ollendick & Cerny, 1981) modified this script for use with older children and adolescents. Essentially, Ollendick's modification removes the imagery components and returns the script to simple instructions to tense and relax muscle groups. This latter script is probably most useful for children over age 10.

The child should assume a comfortable position for the session. We tell children to wear play clothes for this session, so that they feel comfortable participating in either the interoceptive or relaxation exercises. Before conducting the actual session, demonstrate the tension-reduction exercises to be assured that the child will understand the task. Instruct the child in a low voice, using a faster tempo when telling the child to tense muscles and a slower tempo when giving instructions to relax. The therapist should make a cassette tape of the first relaxation session, instructing the child to practice relaxation every day at home.

Problems Implementing Relaxation

Few problems exist in implementing relaxation training. Clinicians should explain that relaxation training is a skill, like riding a bicycle, and likewise it will take some time to become proficient. Motivation to practice may be the biggest obstacle to successful implementation. The reinforcement practices discussed earlier would be useful here as well.

Treatment of Selective Mutism

As we noted in chapter 2, selective mutism may be a severe variant of social anxiety disorder. Case descriptions suggest that behavior therapies or combination treatments may be effective, but controlled trials have not been conducted (Albert-Stewart, 1986; Cunningham, Cataldo, Mallion, & Keyes, 1983; Krohn, Weckstein, & Wright, 1992). In addition to social anxiety disorder, children with selective mutism often exhibit defiant and oppositional behaviors (Black & Uhde, 1995; Yeganeh, Beidel, Turner, Pina, & Silverman, 2003; Yeganeh, Beidel, & Turner, 2006) that complicate the clinical presentation and thus the intervention for this disorder. Furthermore, the onset of the difficulty frequently is associated with emotional distress. Therefore, treatment of this disorder must encompass several considerations.

First, the clinician needs to be assured that the refusal to speak has a social-evaluative component. Because a selectively mute child will not, in all likelihood, express such feelings to the therapist, this information will have to be collected from parents or other caretakers with whom the child will communicate and from a behavioral analysis of the situation. Children often express to parents that they are scared or nervous in some situations and that this is why they refuse to speak. Once the behavior is determined to have a social-evaluative component, interventions such as exposure or SET–C may be helpful. These should be developed and conducted as described earlier.

An important consideration for children with this condition is the amount of attention (i.e., positive reinforcement) that parents and other adults give to the negative behavior of not talking. Our clinical experience suggests that children who are selectively mute receive much positive reinforcement for their silence. They get to sit close to their parents, who then translate their whispers or meaningful looks. We have seen some mothers who actually laugh and smile when the child refuses to answer the interviewer's questions or whispers the answer to the mother. In addition, parents can become upset because of their child's defiant behavior and devote substantial attention to it by begging or trying to force the child to talk, making the act of speaking a contest of wills. It is important to understand that even if the attention is negative, it is a form of reinforcement (parents are paying attention to the child) and probably functions to increase the likelihood that the selective mutism will continue. In many cases, it is not only parents who reinforce this negative behavior. For example, in addition to having others respond for her at home, one child with selective mutism in our clinic never responded or asked questions in class, relying instead on classmates to do it for her. In essence, a pervasive pattern of reinforcement for the maladaptive behavior existed.

In cases of selective mutism, a careful behavioral analysis is crucial to fully understand the condition. In particular, it is necessary to identify relevant operant behaviors and develop a plan to address this component. It is important to make parents aware of the negative effects of their current behavior and to teach parents to provide reinforcement when the child speaks rather than when he or she does not speak or uses nonverbal forms of communication. The parent may require formal training in how to differentially reinforce behavior. In some cases, formal contingency management programs might be needed.

Our approach to the treatment of selective mutism is threefold. First, we use a shaping strategy until the child can reliably respond to the therapist and others with audible one-word answers. Second, we use exposure (or a combination of exposure and SST, as in SET–C) as described previously. Parents are encouraged to involve their children in social activities such as scouts, soccer, or dancing lessons, using the parameters described earlier. Third, we enlighten the parents (and train them if necessary) about the role of positive reinforcement and teach the parents how to reinforce appropriate behavior (talking) and extinguish inappropriate behavior (not talking). Thus, parents are instructed that they must stop communicating for the child and translating what the child would like to say. This puts the onus of communication back on the child, where it belongs. Basically, the operant aspects of the behavior are explained to the parent, and the need for effective management of the problem is articulated. The issue of parental reinforcement of mutism is not one that is trivial for the treatment of children with this disorder. The inability of parents to recognize the role their attention plays in maintaining the child's disorder may be specific to the selective mutism or may be merely one aspect of an overall pattern of inadequate parenting skills. In either case, simply pointing out the relationship between the parental attention and the maintenance of selective mutism usually will not be sufficient to alter the behavior. Rather, parents will need direct intervention to change their behavior. In these cases, effective interven-

---

Exhibit 9.4

Sample Graduated Hierarchy for Treatment of Selective Mutism

Whisper aloud to Mom and Dad so that David and Sarah (same-age peers) can hear.

Talk aloud to David.

Talk aloud to David and Sarah together.

Talk aloud to Mom and Dad in front of an unfamiliar adult.

Say one sentence to an unfamiliar adult.

Talk for 2 minutes with an unfamiliar adult (with Mom or Dad in the room).

Talk for 2 minutes with an unfamiliar adult (no parents present).

Say "hello" to a teacher at school—no children present.

Say "hi" to a classmate.

Talk to a teacher in the presence of two children.

Answer a question in front of the class.

---

tion should include a parent management program that includes specific attention to the role of reinforcement in the maintenance of behaviors and that addresses training in differential reinforcement of other behavior (DRO) schedules (e.g., teaching the parent to ignore nonverbal or whispered communications and to respond to the child only when audible words are spoken). If the parental behaviors associated with selective mutism are part of a broader pattern of inadequate parenting skills, a general parent-training program should be implemented. In Exhibit 9.4, we present an exposure hierarchy used to treat selective mutism in a 6-year-old boy. The parents in this case provided positive reinforcement (in the form of special desserts or small toys) for achievement of each step on the hierarchy. The parents (with much difficulty at first) ignored the child's attempt to communicate nonverbally or the child's attempt to force the parent to communicate for him. The program was successful once the parents understood their role. One-year follow-up indicated that treatment gains were maintained.

Case Study

Throughout this chapter, we have described the implementation of procedures for the treatment of social anxiety disorder in children. Now we present a case illustrating the assessment and treatment of a 14-year-old boy with social anxiety disorder and school refusal.

Initial Clinical Interview

Max was a 14-year-old boy who came to the clinic, accompanied by his parents, because of school refusal behavior. Both Max and his parents described a long history of social anxiety and social awkwardness. In addition, Max did not have any friends and participated in few activities (other than soccer) with children his age. Over the past year, his parents had noticed that he had become even more reclusive and concerned about negative evaluation by others. Since the onset of school (2 months previously), he had become increasingly withdrawn. When interviewed, he had not been to school for the past 28 days. He described significant fears in a wide range of social situations, stating that he feared embarrassment and humiliation. In addition to school avoidance, he was afraid to speak or write in front of others, to eat in front of others, or to use public restrooms. In addition, he avoided almost any type of general social interactions, including casual conversations. Max complained of physical symptoms of distress, including heart palpitations, sweating, trembling, and occasional blushing. He had been treated previously at a local mental health clinic with Prozac (20 mg); his response had been poor, however. In addition, he exhibited numerous features of avoidant personality disorder (APD), including no friends, extreme sensitivity to criticism, and an unwillingness to interact with anyone unless he was certain of being liked. The behaviors described at this initial interview were consistent with a diagnosis of severe generalized social anxiety disorder and traits consistent with APD.

Table 9.3

Max's Scores on Self-Report Instruments Assessing Anxiety and Depression

Scale	Scores		
	Pre	Post	Follow-up
State–Trait Anxiety Inventory			
State	31		
Trait	52		
Fear Survey Schedule for Children	42		
Social Phobia and Anxiety Inventory			
Social Phobia subscale	168	120	90
Agoraphobia subscale	27	20	10
Difference score	141	100	80
Beck Depression Inventory	6		

Assessment Phase

After the initial interview, Max was administered the ADIS–C. This interview was conducted for two reasons: first, to confirm the diagnostic impressions of social anxiety disorder and to assess more closely for other anxiety disorders and, second, to begin to collect the behavioral data necessary to construct a treatment plan. The results of the ADIS–C confirmed the initial diagnostic impressions and revealed high levels of distress and avoidance across a broad range of social situations (both public performances and general social interactions). In addition to the ADIS–C, Max completed several self-report inventories. His scores are depicted in Table 9.3. It should be noted that a decision was made, on the basis of Max's age, to administer the SPAI rather than the SPAI–C because the former assesses a broader range of potentially distressful situations with a wider variety of interactional partners.

Scores in Table 9.3 indicate very severe social anxiety disorder as measured by the SPAI. In addition, the STAI–C trait score was high, indicating a tendency to become anxious and worried in a range of situations, a concept known as anxiety proneness. His scores on other measures were in the low to average range, suggesting that he did not have a more generalized anxiety disorder.

Max was instructed in self-monitoring procedures. Because he was avoiding almost all social encounters, however, he reported only minimal distress on a daily basis but virtually no social contact. In other words, the ratings of distress were deceptive because he successfully avoided social interactions. Thus, a decision was made to monitor Max's progress in terms of the number of days he attended school. Finally, a behavioral assessment of Max's social skill was conducted using a similar-age male confederate and several role-play scenes. The assessment revealed that Max had adequate verbal social skills (i.e., he knew what to say in various social situations), but he exhibited poor nonverbal skills (poor eye contact, voice volume, etc.).

Initial Treatment Plan

The initial treatment plan had the following goals:

A. reduce social anxiety and fears of negative evaluation using intensive imaginal and in vivo flooding;
B. return Max to school using a graduated in vivo shaping program;
C. monitor improvement in nonverbal social behaviors as social distress is decreased; and
D. establish social relationships with peers.

Goal A: Reduce social anxiety and fear using intensive flooding procedures. To address the first goal of the treatment program, Max participated in a course of imaginal flooding. The scene was constructed (see Exhibit 9.2, Scene 1, this chapter) to expose him to his core fear of performing poorly in front of others and having others consider him stupid. This scene was presented to Max over the course of six sessions. Blood pressure, pulse rate, and SUDS levels were monitored. There was evidence of within-session and between-session habituation over the course of the six sessions, as depicted in Figure 9.3. At that point, a decision was made to replicate the imaginal scene in vivo, and Max participated in 6 in vivo flooding sessions in which he read aloud to a small audience. Again, within-session and between-session habituation was noted, and Max showed substantial between-session habituation (see Figure 9.3). During this phase, Max was assigned homework, consisting of attending church with his family, accompanying them to restaurants for meals, and keeping up with his schoolwork by participating in the homebound instruction program arranged for him by his parents.

Goals B and D: Return Max to school using a graduated in vivo program and establish social relationships with peers. After achieving between-session habituation in the clinic, the next step was to return Max to the school setting, using the graduated exposure hierarchy that is depicted in the next section. The SUDS ratings (using a 0–100 point scale) reflected Max's judgment about how anxious he would be in each situation.

Max's Graduated Hierarchy

1. Sit in "community program room" located on the school campus but in a building separate from his classes (SUDS 30).
2. Sit in the library, which was in the same building as the school (SUDS 40).
3. Attend one class and spend the rest of the day in the library (SUDS 50).
4. Attend two classes and spend the rest of the day in the library (SUDS 65).
5. Attend the entire morning session and spend the afternoon in the library (SUDS 80).
6. Attend all classes (SUDS 90).
7. Attend all classes and speak to the teacher (SUDS 95).
8. Attend all classes and interact with two peers in each class (SUDS 100).

Max completed each step sequentially and did not advance to the next step until his SUDS level in the previous task did not exceed 20. The entire hierarchy took 25 days to complete. In addition, he was given homework assignments to continue social activities outside of school and to attend his church youth group again. These latter assignments served to increase his social relationships (Goal D).

Goal C: Monitor nonverbal social skills. As Max's social anxiety decreased, there was improvement in his nonverbal social skills concomitant with the lessening of his social fears and avoidance. This improvement was noted both in his interactions with the therapist and by his parents, who often had the opportunity to observe Max interact with peers. Therefore, no additional intervention was considered necessary.

Assessment of Improvement

Figure 9.5 depicts Max's school attendance during the course of treatment and during follow-up. Prozac was discontinued at the end of the active treatment intervention. Although he occasionally still refused to go to school during the immediate posttreatment period, by 6-month follow-up, his only absences were for documented illness.

Case Summary

This case illustration depicts the treatment of a 14-year-old with severe social anxiety disorder and school refusal behavior. Several aspects of this intervention deserve mention. First, Max's parents were very supportive but at the same time very firm. They did not want to reinforce his avoidant behavior and were clear with him that the expectation was that he would return to school as soon as possible. They complied with all aspects of the treatment plan and provided much encouragement for Max to do the same. Thus, this case illustrates a situation in which the parents were a positive asset to treatment, and no intervention in this domain was necessary. Second, although it may be possible in some cases to conduct the graduated and intensive programs concurrently, in Max's case, it was felt that his distress was so severe that he would not

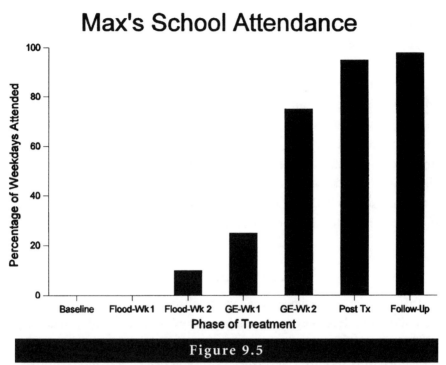

Max's School Attendance

Figure 9.5

Percentage of days that Max attended school on a weekly basis. Flood = imaginal and in vivo flooding. GE = graduated exposure. Post Tx = posttreatment.

be able to make progress on the in vivo hierarchy until his fear had been decreased, although not necessarily eliminated. Third, it was necessary to engage the cooperation of the school in several respects: (a) to provide homebound instruction during the time that Max was not in school so that he did not fall behind in his schoolwork, thus creating another source of distress; and (b) to allow Max to be on the school grounds when school was in session, even though he was not in his classes. In Max's case, school cooperation was easy to obtain. For others, an in-person conference to discuss the nature of the disorder and how the school may assist in the intervention may be necessary.

It is also important to note that Max was not cured at the end of the active intervention program. His posttreatment SPAI difference score had decreased by 40 points (SPAI difference score of 100) but was still in the range of untreated social anxiety disorder. Therefore, although much improved, he continued to score in the range of those who would be considered to have social anxiety disorder. During follow-up, he continued to receive homework assignments to engage in activities with peers. Thus, he was instructed to rejoin the school soccer team and, in the soccer off-season, join one after-school club. In addition, he became involved in youth activities at his church. At 6-month follow-up, he was attending school regularly, had a small circle of friends, and his difference score on the SPAI had dropped another 20 points, reaching the range on the SPAI where those without social anxiety disorder score.

CONCLUSION

In this chapter, we reviewed the available treatment outcome literature on child and adolescent social anxiety disorder. This is still a relatively small literature because interest in childhood social anxiety disorder developed only recently. Nevertheless, several behavioral and cognitive–behavioral treatments show early promise of being successful in treating this disorder. On the basis of the findings from these studies, both SST and exposure strategies seem necessary to overcome social fear and to instigate the development of socially appropriate relationships. All of the behavioral and cognitive–behavioral strategies recently developed for the treatment of social anxiety disorder in children and adolescents include some form of exposure, and several combine exposure and SST. We noted that a particular problem associated with the treatment of children is that in most cases, the decision to seek treatment was not their own. Indeed, the child often does not want to come to the clinic and, in fact, may not feel that there are any problems. Even when young children acknowledge that a problem exists, they may not be able to provide information needed to construct an individualized treatment plan. In such cases, parents, teachers, or significant others become important sources of information needed to establish a diagnosis and to characterize the disorder fully.

We discussed the implementation of each psychological treatment developed specifically for the treatment of social anxiety disorder in children and adolescents, emphasizing procedural issues as well as significant clinical problems that are frequently encountered. In particular, we emphasized the necessity for parental involvement in the assessment and treatment process. Also, teachers and significant others often can provide information that will be useful in establishing a diagnosis and helping to identify or clarify critical parameters associated with the condition.

In addition, we reviewed the syndrome of selective mutism and examined its similarities and dissimilarities with social anxiety disorder. It is clear that there is significant overlap, and we have diagnosed and treated a number of children with selective mutism who also met criteria for social anxiety disorder. In our experience with these children, factors other than social fear frequently are associated with the refusal or inability to speak. The maladaptive behavior pattern seems primarily to be under operant control. Thus, in addition to social anxiety disorder treatment, parent management training, contingency management programs, or both might be needed for effective treatment of this syndrome.

Finally, we have attempted to present details regarding the implementation of these interventions and some of the common pitfalls. Of course, the hierarchies and flooding scenes presented here cannot be used with other children or adolescents and only represent an example of how they might be constructed. They are presented merely as examples of the type of materials that are used in the interventions. The challenge for the clinician is to construct materials that reflect the unique characteristics of each individual child.

Epilogue

Throughout this book, we have addressed the broad spectrum of issues related to social anxiety disorder—its etiology, clinical syndrome, and treatment. Within this broad spectrum, we wanted to devote particular attention to two issues: developmental considerations and a clinician's-eye view of the challenges of diagnosing and treating this disorder.

In discussing developmental considerations, we addressed the clinical manifestation and treatment of social anxiety disorder across the life span—through childhood, adolescence, and adulthood. This examination reveals that although there are many similarities in how social anxiety disorder is manifested, there also are important differences. The core fear of doing something embarrassing or humiliating appears to be consistent across various ages. Even young children endorse the presence of this type of worry, although they may not report it spontaneously. Avoidance also is common across all ages, although sometimes it can be subtle or mislabeled as oppositional behavior. The presence of negative cognitions, however, may be a feature that differentiates the presentation of this disorder in adults and children. In the case of preadolescent children, the presence of such cognitions is rarely found. It might be speculated that these cognitions exist in young children, but, because of their immature stage of cognitive development, they do not have the verbal capacity to express their thoughts. As we have pointed out, however, a hallmark of social anxiety disorder is the often-expressed complaint that when in social encounters, "My mind goes blank" or "I cannot think of anything to say." This would suggest that when in a distressful situation, those with the disorder are so overwhelmed by emotion that they cannot think at all. Thus, we believe that negative cognitions may represent anticipatory worry or retrospective reflection to explain their heightened arousal. Studies designed to address this issue are necessary to understand fully the cognitive dimension of this disorder in adults and children.

A question commonly encountered by those who provide treatment for anxiety disorders (or any disorder for that matter) is "How did I get this way?" The answer is not simple, even though patients wish to hear otherwise. Social anxiety disorder appears to run in families, although it is unclear whether the basis for the familial predisposition is biological, psychological, environmental, or some combination. In our view, it is most likely that some combination of all of these factors is involved in its etiology. Moreover, there may be different pathways. We delineated a number of factors (shyness, behavioral inhibition) that appear to be related to social anxiety disorder. At this time, however, it is unclear whether these constructs represent separate predispositional factors or milder forms of the disorder. Studies conducted during the next decade should further illuminate these relationships.

It is evident that we firmly believe intervention will not be successful unless there is a thorough assessment of the patient's clinical status. This is another area where attention to developmental stage is most important. For example, impromptu speech tasks often are used as part of a behavioral assessment for adults. This task is not relevant (i.e., face valid) for most children, however. In consideration of their developmental stage, reading aloud in front of a group would be more appropriate for children and represent a more valid assessment strategy.

Not only must the assessment materials and measurement strategies be geared to the patient's age, the clinician must understand patient motivational factors as well. That is, adult patients are more likely to comply with self-monitoring forms and other assessment strategies than are young children because the latter usually do not enter treatment of their own volition. Thus, with young children, providing tangible rewards may be necessary to achieve compliance.

Developmental considerations play perhaps their greatest role when it comes to intervention. Not only must the form of the intervention be appropriate for the age of the patient, but additional factors such as comorbid Axis I or II disorders, patient compliance, and the therapist's ability to implement treatment must be considered. For example, Axis II disorders are commonly found in adult patients and present a unique treatment challenge. In contrast, implementing in vivo exposure or homework assignments usually is less difficult with adult patients. Adults usually are able to complete their homework assignments independently. Thus, instructing an adult patient to go out to eat in a restaurant usually requires only the "standard" homework preparation, that is, helping the patient decide on the day and time the assignment will be completed and which restaurant will provide the setting. Giving this same assignment to a child or adolescent requires that parents or other adults be available to transport and stay with the child. The number of schedules that must now be considered has doubled. Additional difficulties arise if parents themselves have an anxiety disorder.

To date, data on treatment maintenance, particularly for the behavioral and cognitive–behavioral treatments for adults, are quite promising. As noted in chapter 7, a substantial number of adult patients who are treated with pharmacological agents appear to relapse when they are switched to placebo or otherwise discontinued from the medication. Thus, although these medications may be useful in the short term, they do not appear to have lasting effects. It is possible, however, that longer term discontinuation schedules or other types of discontinuation strategies (perhaps coupled with cognitive–behavior therapy) may provide more lasting effects.

Short- and long-term follow-up of patients treated with behavioral or cognitive–behavioral therapy indicates that patients maintain and, in some cases, show additional improvement. The most parsimonious explanation for this is that patients continue to apply the skills learned through these interventions and thus enhance their treatment gains. When discharging patients, we always discuss strategies for treatment maintenance. The most obvious recommendation is for patients to continue to place themselves in situations that formerly elicited anxiety. Those with public speaking fears should arrange to continue making presentations in front of groups (such as being a reader at a church), whereas those with more general fears of social interactions should continue to find opportunities (such as adult education classes or community groups) where they can continue to meet and interact with others.

Although no studies have been conducted to determine specifically which factors might enhance treatment maintenance in patients with social anxiety disorder, patients treated for obsessive–compulsive disorder often are prescribed interventions designed to reduce general levels of tension (e.g., relaxation training, exercise, or assertiveness training), all of which may be helpful in decreasing stress and maintaining treatment gains. Particularly for the substantial number of patients with social anxiety disorder who also have generalized anxiety disorder, these interventions might be helpful.

Our second major goal was to attempt to infuse this book with information sufficient to provide a rich clinical perspective on the disorder. We hope that the patient quotes and descriptions illustrate to the reader the challenges faced by those who suffer from the disorder and those who treat them. To further assist clinicians, we have included actual assessment devices and procedures that we have found useful. In addition, we felt that merely providing a description of how treatments are implemented would be insufficient. Thus, we included examples of exposure hierarchies, imaginal flooding scenes, and homework assignments. Our hope is that these actual patient materials illustrate more clearly how these interventions are developed and implemented.

A common comment by those who provide clinical services is that rarely does treatment proceed as described in journal articles or book chapters. We often face similar challenges in our clinical practice. Therefore, we included a discussion of problems and solutions in treatment implementation to illustrate some of the more common problems and how they might be successfully addressed. As illustrated by the contents of this book, social anxiety disorder is a serious, pervasive, chronic, and disabling disorder. We hope this book serves to enlighten the field about the nature and manifestation of this disorder and that our experiences will serve to help other clinicians effectively treat the disorder.

References

Achenbach, T. M. (1985). Assessment of anxiety in children. In A. H. Tuma & J. D. Maser (Eds.), *Anxiety and the anxiety disorders* (pp. 703–734). Hillsdale, NJ: Erlbaum.

Akiskal, H. S. (1985). Anxiety: Definition, relationship to depression and proposal for an integrative model. In A. H. Tuma & J. D. Maser (Eds.), *Anxiety and the anxiety disorders* (pp. 787–797). Hillsdale, NJ: Erlbaum.

Albano, A. M., DiBartolo, P. M., Heimberg, R. G., & Barlow, D. H. (1995). Children and adolescents: Assessment and treatment. In R. G. Heimberg, M. R. Liebowitz, D. A. Hope, & F. R. Schneier (Eds.), *Social phobia: Diagnosis, assessment and treatment* (pp. 387–425). New York: Guilford Press.

Albano, A. M., Marten, P. A., Holt, C. S., Heimberg, R. G., & Barlow, D. H. (1995). Cognitive–behavioral group treatment for social phobia in adolescents. *Journal of Nervous and Mental Disease, 183*, 649–656.

Albert-Stewart, P. (1986). Positive reinforcement in short-term treatment of an electively mute child: A case study. *Psychological Reports, 58*, 571–576.

Alfano, C., Beidel, D. C., & Turner, S. M. (2002). Considering cognition in childhood anxiety disorders: Conceptual, methodological and developmental considerations. *Clinical Psychology Review, 22*, 1209–1238.

Alfano, C. A., Beidel, D. C., & Turner, S. M. (2006). Cognitive correlates of social phobia among children and adolescents. *Journal of Abnormal Child Psychology, 34*, 182–194.

Al-Kubaisy, T., Marks, I. M., Logsdail, S., Marks, I. M. P., Lovell, K., Sungur, M., & Araya, R. (1992). Role of exposure homework in phobia reduction: A controlled study. *Behavior Therapy, 23*, 599–621.

Allgulander, C., Mangano, R., Zhang, J., Dahl, A. A., Lepola, U., Sjödin, I., et al. (2004). Efficacy of Venlafaxine ER in patients with social anxiety disorder: A double-blind, placebo-controlled, parallel-group comparison with paroxetine. *Human Psychopharmacology: Clinical and Experimental, 19,* 387–396.

Alnæs, R., & Torgersen, S. (1999). A 6-year follow-up study of anxiety disorders in psychiatric outpatients. *Nordic Journal of Psychiatry, 53,* 409–416.

Altamura, A. C., Pioli, R., Vitto, M., & Mannu, P. (1999). Venlafaxine in social phobia: A study in selective serotonin reuptake inhibitor non-responders. *International Clinical Psychopharmacology, 14,* 239–245.

American Psychiatric Association. (1980). *Diagnostic and statistical manual of mental disorders* (3rd ed.). Washington, DC: Author.

American Psychiatric Association. (1987). *Diagnostic and statistical manual of mental disorders* (3rd ed., rev.). Washington, DC: Author.

American Psychiatric Association. (1994). *Diagnostic and statistical manual of mental disorders* (4th ed.). Washington, DC: Author.

Amies, P. L., Gelder, M. G., & Shaw, P. M. (1983). Social phobia: A comparative clinical study. *British Journal of Psychiatry, 142,* 174–179.

Anderson, J. C., Williams, S., McGee, R., & Silva, P. A. (1987). *DSM-III* disorders in preadolescent children. *Archives of General Psychiatry, 44,* 69–76.

Anderson, P., Rothbaum, B. O., & Hodges, L. F. (2003). Virtual reality exposure in the treatment of social anxiety. *Cognitive and Behavioral Practice, 10,* 240–247.

Argyropoulos, S. P., Bell, C. J., & Nutt, D. J. (2001). Brain function in social anxiety disorder. *Psychiatric Clinics of North America, 24,* 707–722.

Arkowitz, H. (1981). Assessment of social skills. In M. Hersen & A. S. Bellack (Eds.), *Behavioral assessment* (pp. 296–327). New York: Pergamon.

Asendorpf, J. B. (1990a). Beyond social withdrawal: Shyness, unsociability, and peer avoidance. *Human Development, 33,* 250–259.

Asendorpf, J. B. (1990b). Development of inhibition during childhood: Evidence for situational specificity and a two-factor model. *Developmental Psychology, 26,* 721–730.

Asendorpf, J. B. (1993). Beyond temperament: A two-factorial coping model of the development of inhibition during childhood. In K. H. Rubin & J. B. Asendorpf (Eds.), *Social withdrawal, inhibition, and shyness in childhood* (pp. 265–289). Hillsdale, NJ: Erlbaum.

Atmaca, M., Kuloglu, M., Tezcan, E., & Unal, A. (2002). Efficacy of citalopram and moclobemide in patients with social phobia: Some preliminary findings. *Human Psychopharmacology, Clinical and Experimental, 17*, 401–405.

Attili, G. (1989). Social competence versus emotional security: The link between home relationships and behavior problems at school. In B. H. Schneider, G. Attilli, & J. Nadel (Eds.), *Social competence in developmental perspective* (pp. 293–311). London: Kluwer Academic.

Baer, S., & Garland, J. (2005). Pilot study of community-based cognitive behavioral group therapy for adolescents with social phobia. *Journal of the American Academy of Child and Adolescent Psychiatry, 44*, 258–264.

Baldwin, D., Bobes, J., Stein, D. J., Scharwächter, I., & Faure, M. (1999). Paroxetine in social phobia/social anxiety disorder. *British Journal of Psychiatry, 175*, 120–126.

Bandura, A. (1969). *Principles of behavior modification.* New York: Holt, Rinehart & Winston.

Barlow, D. H., Craske, M. G., Cerny, J. A., & Klosko, J. S. (1989). Behavioral treatment of panic disorder. *Behavior Therapy, 20*, 261–282.

Barrett, P. M. (1998). Evaluation of cognitive–behavioral group treatments for childhood anxiety disorders. *Journal of Clinical Child Psychology, 27*, 459–468.

Barrett, P. M., Dadds, M. R., & Rapee, R. M. (1996). Family treatment of childhood anxiety: A controlled trial. *Journal of Consulting and Clinical Psychology, 64*, 333–342.

Barrett, P. M., Dadds, M. R., Rapee, R. M., & Ryan, S. M. (1996). Family intervention for childhood anxiety: A controlled trial. *Journal of Consulting and Clinical Psychology, 64*, 333–342.

Barrios, B., & O'Dell, S. (1989). Fear and anxieties. In E. J. Mash & R. A. Barkley (Eds.), *Treatment of childhood disorders* (pp. 167–221). New York: Guilford Press.

Bassiony, M. M. (2005). Social anxiety disorder and depression in Saudi Arabia. *Depression and Anxiety, 21*, 90–94.

Beidel, D. C. (1991). Social phobia and overanxious disorder in school-age children. *Journal of the American Academy of Child and Adolescent Psychiatry, 30*, 545–552.

Beidel, D. C., Borden, J. W., Turner, S. M., & Jacob, R. G. (1989). The Social Phobia and Anxiety Inventory: Concurrent validity with a clinic sample. *Behaviour Research and Therapy, 27,* 573–576.

Beidel, D. C., Christ, M. A. G., & Long, P. J. (1991). Somatic complaints in anxious children. *Journal of Abnormal Child Psychology, 19,* 659–670.

Beidel, D. C., & Morris, T. L. (1995). Social phobia. In J. S. March (Ed.), *Anxiety disorders in children and adolescents* (pp. 181–211). New York: Guilford Press.

Beidel, D. C., Neal, A. M., & Lederer, A. S. (1991). The feasibility and validity of a daily diary for the assessment of anxiety in children. *Behavior Therapy, 22,* 505–517.

Beidel, D. C., & Turner, S. M. (1986). A critique of the theoretical bases of cognitive–behavior theories and therapy. *Clinical Psychology Review, 6,* 177–197.

Beidel, D. C., & Turner, S. M. (1988). Comorbidity of test anxiety and other anxiety disorders in children. *Journal of Abnormal Child Psychology, 16,* 275–287.

Beidel, D. C., & Turner, S. M. (1992a). Scoring the Social Phobia and Anxiety Inventory: Comments on Herbert et al. (1991). *Journal of Psychopathology and Behavioral Assessment, 14,* 377–379.

Beidel, D. C., & Turner, S. M. (1992b, October). *Are social phobic children the same as social phobic adults?* Paper presented at the Academy of Child and Adolescent Psychiatry Annual Meeting, Washington, DC.

Beidel, D. C., & Turner, S. M. (1997). At risk for anxiety: I. Psychopathology in the offspring of anxious parents. *Journal of the American Academy of Child and Adolescent Psychiatry, 36,* 918–925.

Beidel, D. C., & Turner, S. M. (1998). *Shy children, phobic adults: The nature and treatment of social phobia.* Washington, DC: American Psychological Association Books.

Beidel, D. C., & Turner, S. M. (2005). *Childhood anxiety disorders: A guide to research and treatment.* New York: Taylor & Francis/Routledge.

Beidel, D. C., Turner, S. M., & Cooley, M. R. (1993). Assessing reliable and clinically significant change in social phobia: Validity of the Social Phobia and Anxiety Inventory. *Behaviour Research and Therapy, 31,* 331–337.

Beidel, D. C., Turner, S. M., & Dancu, C. V. (1985). Physiological, cognitive and behavioral aspects of social anxiety. *Behaviour Research and Therapy, 23*, 109–117.

Beidel, D. C., Turner, S. M., & Fink, C. M. (1996). The assessment of childhood social phobia: Construct, convergent and discriminative validity of the Social Phobia and Anxiety Inventory for Children (SPAI–C). *Psychological Assessment, 8*, 235–240.

Beidel, D. C., Turner, S. M., Hamlin, K., & Morris, T. L. (1998). The Social Phobia and Anxiety Inventory for Children (SPAI–C): External and discriminant validity. *Behavior Therapy, 31*, 75–87.

Beidel, D. C., Turner, S. M., Jacob, R. G., & Cooley, M. R. (1989). Assessment of social phobia: Reliability of an impromptu speech task. *Journal of Anxiety Disorders, 3*, 149–158.

Beidel, D. C., Turner, S. M., & Morris, T. L. (1995). A new inventory to assess childhood social anxiety and phobia: The Social Phobia and Anxiety Inventory for Children. *Psychological Assessment, 7*, 73–79.

Beidel, D. C., Turner, S. M., & Morris, T. L. (1998). *The social phobia and anxiety inventory for children.* Toronto, Ontario, Canada: Multi-Health Systems.

Beidel, D. C., Turner, S. M., & Morris, T. M. (1999). Psychopathology of childhood social phobia. *Journal of the American Academy of Child and Adolescent Psychiatry, 38*, 643–650.

Beidel, D. C., Turner, S. M., & Morris, T. L. (2000). Behavioral treatment of childhood social phobia. *Journal of Consulting and Clinical Psychology, 68*, 1072–1080.

Beidel, D. C., Turner, S. M., & Morris, T. L. (2004). *Social Effectiveness Therapy for Children and Adolescents (SET–C).* Toronto: Multi-Health Systems.

Beidel, D. C., Turner, S. M., Sallee, F. R., & Ammerman, R. T. (2000). Treatment of childhood social phobia. Unpublished manuscript, University of Maryland, College Park.

Beidel, D. C., Turner, S. M., Stanley, M. A., & Dancu, C. V. (1989). The Social Phobia and Anxiety Inventory: Concurrent and external validity. *Behavior Therapy, 20*, 417–427.

Beidel, D. C., Turner, S. M., & Young, B. J. (in press). Social effectiveness therapy for children: Five years later. *Behavior Therapy.*

Beidel, D. C., Turner, S. M., Young, B. J., Ammerman, R. T., Sallee, F. R., & Crosby, L. (in press). Psychopathology of adolescent social phobia. *Journal of Psychopathology and Behavioral Assessment.* Manuscript submitted for publication.

Beidel, D. C., Turner, S. M., Young, B., & Paulson, A. (2005). Social Effectiveness Therapy for Children: Three-year follow-up. *Journal of Consulting and Clinical Psychology, 17,* 721–725.

Bell, C. J., Malizia, A. L., & Nutt, D. J. (1999). The neurology of social phobia. *European Archives of Psychiatry & Clinical Neuroscience, 249*(Suppl. 1), S11–S18.

Bergman, R. L., Piacentini, J., & McCracken, J. T. (2002). Prevalence and description of selective mutism in a school-based sample. *Journal of the American Academy of Child and Adolescent Psychiatry, 41,* 938–946.

Bergsgaard, M. O., & Larsson, E. V. (1984). Increasing social interaction between an isolate first grader and cross-cultural peers. *Psychology in the Schools, 21,* 244–251.

Berler, E. S., Gross, A. M., & Drabman, R. S. (1982). Social skills training with children: Proceed with caution. *Journal of Applied Behavior Analysis, 15,* 41–53.

Biederman, J., Hirshfeld-Becker, D. R., & Rosenbaum, J. F. (2001). Further evidence of association between behavioral inhibition and social anxiety in children. *American Journal of Psychiatry, 158,* 1673–1679.

Birbaumer, N., Grodd, W., Diedrich, O., Klose, U., Erb, M., Lotze, M., et al. (1998). FMRI reveals amygdala activation to human faces in social phobics. *Neuroreport, 9,* 1223–1226.

Birmaher, B., Axelson, D. A., & Monk, K. (2003). Fluoxetine for the treatment of childhood anxiety disorders. *Journal of the American Academy of Child and Adolescent Psychiatry, 42,* 415–423.

Birmaher, B., Waterman, S. G., Ryan, N., Cully, M., Balach, L., Ingram, J., & Brodsky, M. (1994). Fluoxetine for childhood anxiety disorders. *Journal of the American Academy of Child and Adolescent Psychiatry, 33,* 993–999.

Black, B., & Uhde, T. W. (1992). Elective mutism as a variant of social phobia. *Journal of the American Academy of Child and Adolescent Psychiatry, 31,* 1090–1094.

Black, B., & Uhde, T. W. (1994). Treatment of elective mutism with fluoxetine: A double-blind, placebo-controlled study. *Journal of the American Academy of Child and Adolescent Psychiatry, 33,* 1000–1006.

Black, B., & Uhde, T. (1995). Psychiatric characteristics of children with selective mutism: A pilot study. *Journal of the American Academy of Child and Adolescent Psychiatry, 34,* 847–856.

Black, B., Uhde, T. W., & Tancer, M. E. (1992). Fluoxetine for the treatment of social phobia. *Journal of Clinical Psychopharmacology, 12,* 293–295.

Bögels, S. M., & Mansell, W. (2004). Attention processes in the maintenance and treatment of social phobia: Hypervigilance, avoidance and self-focused attention. *Clinical Psychology Review, 24,* 827–856.

Bögels, S. M., van Oosten, A., Muris, P., & Smulders, D. (2001). Familial correlates of social anxiety in children and adolescents. *Behaviour Research and Therapy, 39,* 273–287.

Bögels, S., & Zigterman, D. (2000). Dysfunctional cognitions in children with social phobia, separation anxiety disorder, and generalized anxiety disorder. *Journal of Abnormal Child Psychology, 28,* 205–211.

Bouwer, C., & Stein, D. J. (1998). Use of the selective serotonin reuptake inhibitor citalopram in the treatment of generalized social phobia. *Journal of Affective Disorders, 49,* 79–82.

Bowen, R. C., Cipywnyk, D., D'Arcy, C., & Keegan, D. (1984). Alcoholism, anxiety disorders, and agoraphobia. *Alcoholism: Clinical and Experimental Research, 8,* 8–50.

Brawman-Mintzer, O., Lydiard, R. B., Emmanuel, N., Payeur, R., Johnson, M., Roberts, J., et al. (1993). Psychiatric comorbidity in patients with generalized anxiety disorder. *American Journal of Psychiatry, 150,* 1216–1218.

Bromberg, A. D. (1993). Inhibition and children's experiences of out-of-home care. In K. H. Rubin & J. B. Asendorpf (Eds.), *Social withdrawal, inhibition, and shyness in childhood* (pp. 151–176). Hilldsdale, NJ: Erlbaum.

Brooks, S. J., & Kutcher, S. (2004). The Kutcher Generalized Social Anxiety Disorder Scale for Adolescents: Assessment of its evaluative properties over the course of a 16-week pediatric psychopharmacotherapy trial. *Journal of Child and Adolescent Psychopharmacology, 14,* 273–286.

Brown, E. J., Heimberg, R. G., & Juster, H. R. (1995). Social phobia subtype and avoidant personality disorder: Effect on severity of social phobia, impairment, and outcome of cognitive–behavioral treatment. *Behavior Therapy, 26,* 467–486.

Brown, E. J., Turovsky, J., Heimberg, R. G., Juster, H. R., Brown, T. A., & Barlow, D. H. (1997). Validation of the Social Interaction Anxiety Scale and the Social Phobia Scale across the anxiety disorders. *Psychological Assessment, 9,* 21–27.

Brown, J. B., & Lloyd, H. (1975). A controlled study of children not speaking at school. *Journal of the Association of Workers for Maladjusted Children, 3,* 49–63.

Bruch, M. A. (1989). Familial and developmental antecedents of social phobia: Issues and findings. *Clinical Psychology Review, 9,* 37–47.

Bruch, M. A., Giordano, S., & Pearl, L. (1986). Differences between fearful and self-conscious shy subtypes in background and current adjustment. *Journal of Research in Personality, 20,* 172–186.

Bruch, M. A., & Heimberg, R. G. (1994). Differences in perceptions of parental and personal characteristics between generalized and nongeneralized social phobics. *Journal of Anxiety Disorders, 8,* 155–168.

Bruch, M. A., Heimberg, R. G., Berger, P., & Collins, T. M. (1989). Social phobia and perceptions of early parental and personal characteristics. *Anxiety Research, 2,* 57–63.

Burns, D. D. (1980). *Feeling good: The new mood therapy.* New York: William Morrow & Co., Inc.

Buss, A. H., & Plomin, R. (1984). *Temperament: Early developing personality traits.* Hillsdale, NJ: Erlbaum.

Butler, G., Cullington, A., Munby, M., Amies, P., & Gelder, M. (1984). Exposure and anxiety management in the treatment of social phobia. *Journal of Consulting and Clinical Psychology, 52,* 642–650.

Carpenter, D. J., Lipschitz. A., Fong, R., Krulewicz, S., & Davies, J. (2005, June). *Is it appropriate to combine data from children and adolescents in pediatric MDD clinical trials?* Paper presented at the annual meeting of the National Clinical Drug Evaluation Unit, Boca Raton, FL.

Carrigan, M. H., & Randall, C. L. (2003). Self-medication in social phobia: A review of the alcohol literature. *Addictive Behaviors, 28,* 269–284.

Cartwright-Hatton, S., Tschernitz, N., & Gomersall, H. (2005). Social anxiety in children: Social skills deficit, or cognitive distortion? *Behaviour Research and Therapy, 43,* 131–141.

Caspi, A., Elder, G. H., Jr., & Bem, D. J. (1988). Moving away from the world: Life course patterns of shy children. *Developmental Psychology, 24,* 824–831.

Caster, J., Inderbitzen, H., & Hope, D. (1999). Relationship between youth and parent perceptions of family environment and social anxiety. *Journal of Anxiety Disorders, 13,* 237–251.

Chambless, D. L., Cherney, J., Caputo, G. C., & Rheinstein, B. J. G. (1987). Anxiety disorders and alcoholism: A study with inpatient alcoholics. *Journal of Anxiety Disorders, 1,* 9–40.

Chambless, D. L., & Hope, D. A. (1996). Cognitive approaches to the psychopathology and treatment of social phobia. In P. M. Salkovskis (Ed.), *Frontiers of cognitive therapy* (pp. 345–382). New York: Guilford Press.

Chambless, D. L., Tran, G. Q., & Glass, C. R. (1997). Predictors of response to cognitive–behavioral group therapy for social phobia. *Journal of Anxiety Disorders, 11,* 221–240.

Chandler, L. K., Lubeck, R. C., & Fowler, S. A. (1992). Generalization and maintenance of preschool children's social skills: A critical review and analysis. *Journal of Applied Behavioral Analysis, 25,* 415–428.

Chapman, T. R., Mannuzza, S., & Fyer, A. J. (1995). Epidemiology and family studies of social phobia. In R. G. Heimberg, M. R. Liebowitz, D. A. Hope, & F. R. Schneier (Eds.), *Social phobia: Diagnosis, assessment, and treatment* (pp. 21–40). New York: Guilford Press.

Chavira, D. A., & Stein, M. B. (2002). Combined psychoeducation and treatment with selective serotonin reuptake inhibitors for youth with generalized social anxiety disorder. *Journal of Child and Adolescent Child Psychopharmacology, 12,* 47–54.

Chavira, D. A., Stein, M. B., Bailey, K., & Stein, S. (2003). Parental opinions regarding treatment for social anxiety disorder in youth. *Journal of Developmental and Behavioral Pediatrics, 24,* 315–322.

Chavira, D. A., Stein, M. B., Bailey, K., & Stein, M. T. (2004). Comorbidity of generalized social anxiety disorder and depression in a pediatric primary care sample. *Journal of Affective Disorders, 80,* 163–171.

Chavira, D. A., Stein, M. B., & Malcarne, V. L. (2002). Scrutinizing the relationship between shyness and social phobia. *Journal of Anxiety Disorders, 16,* 585–598.

Cheek, J. M., & Buss, A. H. (1981). Shyness and sociability. *Journal of Personality and Social Psychology, 41,* 330–339.

Christoff, K. A., Scott, W. O. N., Kelley, M. L., Baer, G., & Kelly, J. A. (1985). Social skills and social problem-solving training for shy young adolescents. *Behavior Therapy, 16,* 468–477.

Clark, D. B. (1993, March). *Assessment of social anxiety in adolescents.* Paper presented at the Anxiety Disorders Association of America Annual Convention, Charleston, SC.

Clark, D. B., Turner, S. M., Beidel, D. C., Donovan, J. E., Kirisci, L., & Jacob, R. G. (1994). Reliability and validity of the Social Phobia and Anxiety Inventory for adolescents. *Psychological Assessment, 6,* 135–140.

Clark, D. M. (2001). A cognitive perspective on social phobia. In W. R. Crozier & L. E. Alden (Eds.), *International handbook of social anxiety: Concepts, research and interventions relating to the self and shyness* (pp. 405–430). New York: Wiley.

Clark, D. M., Ehlers, A., McManus, F., Hackman, A., Fennell, M., Campbell, H., Flower, T., Davenport, C., & Louis, B. (2003). Cognitive therapy versus fluoxetine in generalized social phobia: A randomized placebo-controlled trial. *Journal of Consulting and Clinical Psychology, 71,* 1058–1067.

Clark, D. M., & McManus, F. (2002). Information processing in social phobia. *Biological Psychiatry, 51,* 92–100.

Coles, M. E., & Heimberg, R. G. (2002). Memory biases in the anxiety disorders: Current status. *Clinical Psychology Review, 22,* 587–627.

Coles, M. E., & Heimberg, R. G. (2005). Recognition bias for critical faces in social phobia: A replication and extension. *Behaviour Research and Therapy, 43,* 109–120.

Coles, M. E., Turk, C. L., Jindra, L., & Heimberg, R. G. (2004). The path from initial inquiry to initiation of treatment for social anxiety disorder in an anxiety disorders specialty clinic. *Journal of Anxiety Disorders, 18,* 371–383.

Compton, S. N., Grant, P. J., & Chrisman, A. K. (2001). Sertraline in children and adolescents with social anxiety disorder: An open trial. *Journal of the American Academy of Child and Adolescent Psychiatry, 40,* 564–571.

Condren, R. M., O'Neill, A., Ryan, M. C. M., Barrett, P., & Thakore, J. H. (2002). HPA axis response to a psychological stressor in generalised social phobia. *Psychoneuroendeocrinology, 27, 693–703.*

Connor, K. M., Davidson, J. R., Churchill, L. E., Sherwood, A., Foa, E., & Weisler, R. H. (2000). Psychometric properties of the Social Phobia Inventory (SPIN). New self-rating scale. *British Journal of Psychiatry, 176,* 379–386.

Connor, K. M., Kobak, K. A., Churchill, E., Katzelnick, D., & Davidson, J. R. T. (2001). Mini-SPIN: A brief screening assessment for generalized social anxiety disorder. *Depression and Anxiety, 14,* 137–140.

Cook, M., & Mineka, S. (1991). Selective associations in the origins of phobic fears and their implications for behavior therapy. In P. Martin (Ed.), *Handbook of behavior therapy and psychological science: An integrative approach* (pp. 413–434). Elmsford, NY: Pergamon Press.

Cooper, P. J., & Eke, M. (1999). Childhood shyness and maternal social phobia: A community study. *British Journal of Psychiatry, 174,* 439–443.

Craske, M. G. (1991). Phobic fear and panic attacks: The same emotional states triggered by different cues? *Clinical Psychology Review, 11,* 599–620.

Craske, M. G., & Rachman, S. J. (1987). Return of fear: Perceived skill and heart rate responsivity. *British Journal of Clinical Psychology, 26,* 187–199.

Craske, M. G., Rapee, R. M., & Barlow, D. H. (1992). Cognitive–behavioral treatment of panic disorder, agoraphobia, and generalized anxiety disorder. In S. M. Turner, K. S. Calhoun, & H. E. Adams (Eds.), *Handbook of clinical behavior therapy* (2nd ed., pp. 39–66). New York: Wiley.

Cunningham, C. E., Cataldo, M. F., Mallion, C., & Keyes, J. B. (1983). A review and controlled single case evaluation of behavioral approaches to the management of elective mutism. *Child & Family Behavior Therapy, 5,* 25–49.

Dadds, M. R., Barrett, P. M., Rapee, R. M., & Ryan, A. (1996). Family process and child anxiety and aggression: An observational analysis. *Journal of Abnormal Child Psychology, 24,* 715–734.

Daniels, D., & Plomin, R. (1985). Origins of individual differences in infant shyness. *Developmental Psychology, 21,* 118–121.

Darby, W. B., & Schlenker, B. R. (1986). Children's understanding of social anxiety. *Developmental Psychology, 22,* 633–639.

Davidson, J. R. T. (1993, March). *Childhood histories of adult social phobics.* Paper presented at the Anxiety Disorders Association Annual Convention, Charleston, SC.

Davidson, J. R. T. (2003). Pharmacotherapy of social phobia. *Acta Psychiatrica Scandinavia, 108*(Suppl. 417), 65–71.

Davidson, J. R. T., Foa, E. B., Huppert, J. D., Keefe, F. J., Franklin, M. E., Compton, J. S., et al. (2004). Fluoxetine, comprehensive cognitive behavioral therapy, and placebo in generalized social phobia. *Archives of General Psychiatry, 61,* 1005–1013.

Davidson, J. R. T., Ford, S. M., Smith, R. D., & Potts, N. L. S. (1991). Long-term treatment of social phobia with clonazepam. *Journal of Clinical Psychiatry, 52,* 16–20.

Davidson, J. R. T., Potts, N. L. S., Richichi, E. A., Ford, S. M., Krishnan, K. R. R., Smith, R. D., & Wilson, W. (1991). The Brief Social Phobia Scale. *Journal of Clinical Psychiatry, 52,* 48–51.

Davidson, J. R. T., Potts, N., Richichi, E., Krishnan, R., Ford, S. M., Smith, R., & Wilson, W. H. (1993). Treatment of social phobia with clonazepam and placebo. *Journal of Clinical Psychopharmacology, 13,* 423–428.

den Boer, J. A., & Dunner, D. L. (1999). Physician attitudes concerning diagnosis and treatment of social anxiety disorder in Europe and North America. *International Journal of Psychiatry in Clinical Practice, 3*(Suppl. 3), S13–S19.

den Boer, J. A., van Vliet, I. M., & Westenberg, H. G. M. (1994). Recent advances in the psychopharmacology of social phobia. *Progress in Neuro-Psychopharmacology and Biological Psychiatry, 18,* 625–645.

DeWit, D. J., MacDonald, K., & Offord, D. R. (1999). Childhood stress and symptoms of drug dependence in adolescence and early adulthood: Social phobia as a mediator. *American Journal of Orthopsychiatry, 69,* 61–72.

DeWit, D. J., Ogborne, A., Offord, D. R., & MacDonald, K. (1999). Antecedents of the risk of recovery from *DSM–III–R* social phobia. *Psychological Medicine, 29,* 569–582.

Dilsaver, S. C., Qamar, A. B., & Del Medico, V. J. (1992). Secondary social phobia in patients with major depression. *Psychiatry Research, 44,* 33–40.

DiNardo, P. A., Brown, T. A., & Barlow, D. H. (1995). *Anxiety Disorders Interview Schedule for DSM–IV (Lifetime Version).* San Antonio, TX: Psychological Corporation.

Dinnel, D. L., Kleinknecht, R. A., & Tanaka-Matsumi, J. (2002). A cross-cultural comparison of social phobia symptoms. *Journal of Psychopathology and Behavioral Assessment, 24,* 75–84.

Dummit, E. S., III, Klein, R. G., Tancer, N. K., Asche, B., Martin, J., & Fairbanks, J. A. (1997). Systematic assessment of 50 children with selective mutism.

Journal of the American Academy of Child and Adolescent Psychiatry, 36, 653–660.

Edelman, R. E., & Chambless, D. L. (1995). Adherence during sessions and homework in cognitive-behavioral group treatment of social phobia. *Behaviour Research and Therapy, 33,* 573–577.

Elizabeth, J., King, N., & Ollendick, T. H. (2004). Etiology of social anxiety disorder in children and youth. *Behaviour Change, 28,* 162–172.

Elizur, Y., & Perednik, R. (2003). Prevalence and description of selective mutism in immigrant and native families: A controlled study. *Journal of the American Academy of Child and Adolescent Psychiatry, 42,* 1451–1459.

Emmelkamp, P. M. G., Mersch, P. P., Vissia, E., & van der Helm, M. (1985). Social phobia: A comparative evaluation of cognitive and behavioral interventions. *Behaviour Research and Therapy, 23,* 365–369.

Eng, W., Coles, M. E., Heimberg, R. G., & Safren, S. A. (2001). Quality of life following cognitive behavioral treatment for social anxiety disorder: Preliminary findings. *Depression and Anxiety, 13,* 192–193.

Erwin, B. A., Heimberg, R. G., Juster, H., & Mindlin, M. (2002). Comorbid anxiety and mood disorders among persons with social anxiety disorder. *Behaviour Research and Therapy, 40,* 19–35.

Erwin, B. A., Turk, C. L., Heimberg, R. G., Fresco, D. M., & Hantula, D. A. (2004). The Internet: Home to a severe population of individuals with social anxiety disorder? *Journal of Anxiety Disorders, 18,* 629–646.

Essau, C. A., Conradt, J., & Petermann, F. (1999). Frequency and comorbidity of social phobia and social fears in adolescents. *Behaviour Research and Therapy, 37,* 831–843.

Fairbanks, J. M., Pine, D. S., Tancer, N. K, Dummit, E. S., Kentgen, L. M., Martin, J., et al. (1997). Open fluoxetine treatment of mixed anxiety disorders in children and adolescents. *Journal of Child and Adolescent Psychopharmacology, 7,* 17–29.

Fairbrother, N. (2002). The treatment of social phobia—100 years ago. *Behaviour Research and Therapy, 40,* 1291–1304.

Falloon, I. R. H., Lloyd, G. G., & Harpin, R. E. (1981). The treatment of social phobia: Real life rehearsal with nonprofessional therapists. *The Journal of Nervous and Mental Disease, 169,* 180–184.

Fava, G. A., Grandi, S., & Canestrari, R. (1989). Treatment of social phobia by homework exposure. *Psychotherapy and Psychosomatics, 52,* 209–213.

Fedoroff, I. C., & Taylor, S. T. (2001). Psychological and pharmacological treatments of social phobia: A meta-analysis. *Journal of Clinical Psychopharmacology, 21,* 311–324.

Feske, U., & Chambless, D. L. (1995). Cognitive-behavioral versus exposure treatment for social phobia: A meta-analysis. *Behavior Therapy, 26,* 695–720.

Feske, U., Perry, K. J., Chambless, D. L., Renneberg, B., & Goldstein, A. J. (1996). Avoidant personality disorder as a predictor for treatment outcome among generalized social phobics. *Journal of Personality Disorders, 10,* 174–184.

Finch, M., & Hops, H. (1982). Remediation of social withdrawal in young children: Considerations for the practitioner. *Child and Youth Services, 5,* 29–42.

Fink, C. M., Turner, S. M., & Beidel, D. C. (1996). Culturally relevant factors in the behavioral treatment of social phobia: A case study. *Journal of Anxiety Disorders, 10,* 201–209.

Finnie, V., & Russell, A. (1988). Preschool children's social status and their mothers' behavior and knowledge in the supervisory role. *Developmental Psychology, 24,* 789–801.

First, M. B., Gibbon, M., Spitzer, R. L., & Williams, J. B. W. (2002, November). *User's guide for the Structured Clinical Interview for DSM–IV Axis I Disorders— Research Version.* New York: New York State Psychiatric Institute.

First, M. B., Gibbon, M., Spitzer, R., Williams, J., & Benjamin, L. (1997). *Computer-assisted SCID–II for personality disorders.* Washington, DC: American Psychiatric Press.

Flannery-Schroeder, E. C., & Kendall, P. C. (2000). Group and individual cognitive-behavioral treatments for youth with anxiety disorders: A randomized clinical trial. *Cognitive Therapy and Research, 24,* 251–278.

Freeman, J. B., Garcia, A. M., Miller, L. M., Dow, S. P., & Leonard, H. L. (2004). Selective mutism. In T. L. Morris & J. S. March (Eds.), *Anxiety disorders in children and adolescents* (2nd ed.; pp. 280–301). New York: Guilford Press.

Furman, W., Rahe, D. F., & Hartrup, W. W. (1979). Rehabilitation of socially withdrawn preschool children through mixed-age and same-age socialization. *Child Development, 50,* 915–922.

Furmark, T., Tillfors, M., Everz, P. O., Marteinsdottir, I., Gefvert, O., & Fredrikson, M. (1999). Social phobia in the general population: Prevalence and sociodemographic profile. *Social Psychiatry and Psychiatric Epidemiology, 34,* 416–424.

Fyer, A. J., Mannuzza, S., Chapman, T. F., Liebowitz, M. R., & Klein, D. F. (1993). A direct interview family study of social phobia. *Archives of General Psychiatry, 50,* 286–293.

Gallagher, H. M., Rabian, B. A., & McCloskey, M. S. (2004). A brief cognitive–behavioral intervention for social phobia in childhood. *Journal of Anxiety Disorders, 18,* 459–479.

Garcia-Coll, C., Kagan, J., & Reznick, J. S. (1984). Behavioral inhibition in young children. *Child Development, 55,* 1005–1019.

Gauer, G. J. C., Picon, P., Vasconcellos, S. J., Turner, S. M., & Beidel, D. C. (2005). Validation of the Social Phobia and Anxiety Inventory for Children (SPAI–C) in a sample of Brazilian children. *Brazilian Journal of Medical and Biological Research, 38,* 795–800.

Gelernter, C. S., Uhde, T. W., Cimbolic, P., Arnkoff, D. B., Vittone, B. J., Tancer, M. E., & Bartko, J. J. (1991). Cognitive–behavioral and pharmacological treatments of social phobia: A controlled study. *Archives of General Psychiatry, 48,* 938–945.

Ginsburg, G. S., & Silverman, W. K. (1996). Phobic and anxiety disorders in Hispanic and Caucasian youth. *Journal of Anxiety Disorders, 10,* 517–528.

Gökalp, P. G., Tükel, R., Solmaz, D., Demir, T., Kiziltan, E., Demir, D., & Babaŏolu, A. N. (2001). Clinical features and co-morbidity of social phobics in Turkey. *European Psychiatry, 16,* 115–121.

Golwyn, D. H., & Weinstock, R. C. (1990). Phenelzine treatment of elective mutism: A case report. *Journal of Clinical Psychiatry, 51,* 384–385.

Gorman, J. M., & Gorman, L. F. (1987). Drug treatment of social phobia. *Journal of Affective Disorders, 13,* 183–192.

Gorman, J. M., Liebowitz, M. R., Fyer, A. J., Campeas, R., & Klein, D. F. (1985). Treatment of social phobia with atenolol. *Journal of Clinical Psychopharmacology, 5,* 298–301.

Gossard, D., Dennis, C., & DeBusk, R. F. (1984). Use of beta-blocking agents to reduce the stress of presentation at an international cardiology meeting: Results of a survey. *American Journal of Cardiology, 54,* 240–241.

Gould, R. A., Buckminster, S., Pollack, M. H., Otto, M., & Yap, L. (1997). Cognitive–behavioral and pharmacological treatment for social phobia: A meta-analysis. *Clinical Psychology: Science and Practice, 4*, 291–306.

Grayson, J. B., Foa, E. B., & Steketee, G. (1986). Exposure in vivo of obsessive–compulsives under distracting and attention-focusing conditions: Replication and extension. *Behaviour Research and Therapy, 24*, 475–479.

Greco, L. A., & Morris, T. L. (2002). Parental child-rearing style and child social anxiety: Investigation of child perceptions and actual father behavior. *Journal of Psychopathology and Behavioral Assessment, 24*, 259–267.

Greco, L. A., & Morris, T. L. (2005). Factors influencing the link between social anxiety and peer acceptance: Contributions of social skills and close friendships during middle childhood. *Behavior Therapy, 36*, 197–205.

Greist, J. H., Kobak, K. A., Jefferson, J. W., Katzelnick, D. J., & Chene, R. L. (1995). In R. G. Heimberg, M. R. Liebowitz, D. A. Hope, & F. R. Schneier (Eds.), *Social phobia: Diagnosis, assessment, and treatment* (pp. 185–201). New York: Guilford Press.

Guevremont, D. C., MacMillan, V. M., Shawchuck, C. R., & Hansen, D. J. (1989). A peer-mediated intervention with clinic-referred socially isolated girls. *Behavior Modification, 13*, 32–50.

Guy, W. (1976). *ECDEU assessment manual for psychopharmacology.* Rockville, MD: U. S. Department of Health, Education, and Welfare.

Hamilton, M. (1959). The assessment of anxiety states by rating. *British Journal of Medical Psychology, 32*, 50–55.

Hamilton, M. (1960). A rating scale for depression. *Journal of Neurology, Neurosurgery, and Psychiatry, 23*, 56–62.

Hansen, W. B., Collins, L. M., Malotte, C. K., Johnson, C. A., & Fielding, J. E. (1985). Attrition in prevention research. *Journal of Behavioral Medicine, 8*, 261–275.

Hayward, C., Killen, J. D., Kraemer, H. C., & Taylor, C. B. (1998). Linking self-reported childhood behavioral inhibition to adolescent social phobia. *Journal of the American Academy of Child and Adolescent Psychiatry, 37*, 1308–1316.

Hayward, C., Varady, S., Albano, A. M., Thienemann, M., Henderson, L., & Schatzberg, A. F. (2000). Cognitive–behavioral group therapy for social phobia in female adolescents: Results of a pilot study. *Journal of the American Academy of Child and Adolescent Psychiatry, 39*, 721–726.

Heckelman, L. R., & Schneier, F. R. (1995). Diagnostic issues. In R. G. Heimberg, M. R. Liebowitz, D. A. Hope, & F. R. Schneier (Eds.), *Social phobia; Diagnosis, assessment and treatment* (pp. 3–20). New York: Guilford Press.

Heimberg, R. G. (1991). *Cognitive–behavioral treatment of social phobia in a group setting: A treatment manual* (2nd ed.). Unpublished manuscript, State University of New York at Albany.

Heimberg, R. G., Dodge, C. S., Hope, D. A., Kennedy, C. R., Zollo, L., & Becker, R. E. (1990). Cognitive behavioral treatment for social phobia: Comparison with a credible placebo control. *Cognitive Therapy and Research, 14,* 1–23.

Heimberg, R. G., Holt, C. S., Schneier, F. R., Spitzer, R. L., & Liebowitz, M. R. (1993). The issue of subtypes in the diagnosis of social phobia. *Journal of Anxiety Disorders, 7,* 249–269.

Heimberg, R. G., Hope, D. A., Dodge, C. S., & Becker, R. E. (1990). *DSM–III–R* subtypes of social phobia: Comparison of generalized social phobics and public speaking phobics. *Journal of Nervous and Mental Disease, 178,* 172–179.

Heimberg, R. G., Liebowitz, M. R., Hope, D. A., Schneier, F. R., Holt, C. S., Welkowitz, L. A., et al. (1998). Cognitive behavioral group therapy vs phenelzine therapy for social phobia. *Archives of General Psychiatry, 55,* 1133–1141.

Heimberg, R. G., Mueller, G., Holt, C. S., Hope, D. A., & Liebowitz, M. R. (1992). Assessment of anxiety in social interaction and being observed by others: The Social Interaction Anxiety Scale and the Social Phobia Scale. *Behavior Therapy, 23,* 53–73.

Heimberg, R. G., Salzman, D. G., Holt, C. S., & Blendall, K. A. (1993). Cognitive–behavioral group treatment for social phobia: Effectiveness at five year follow-up. *Cognitive Therapy and Research, 17,* 325–339.

Heimberg, R. G., Stein, M. B., Hiripi, E., & Kessler, R. C. (2000). Trends in the prevalence of social phobia in the United States: A synthetic cohort analysis of changes over four decades. *European Psychiatry, 15,* 29–37.

Heinrichs, N., & Hofmann, S. G. (2001). Information processing in social phobia: A critical review. *Clinical Psychology Review, 21,* 751–770.

Heiser, N. A., Turner, S. M., & Beidel, D. C. (2003). Shyness: Relationship to social phobia and other psychiatric disorders. *Behaviour Research and Therapy, 41,* 209–221.

Hembree-Kigin, T. L., & McNeil, C. B. (1995). *Parent–child interaction therapy.* New York: Plenum.

Herbert, J. D., Bellack, A. S., & Hope, D. A. (1991). Concurrent validity of the Social Phobia and Anxiety Inventory. *Journal of Psychopathology and Behavioral Assessment, 13,* 357–368.

Herbert, J. D., Gaudiano, B. A., Rheingold, A. A., Myers, V. H., Dalrymple, K., & Nolan, E. M. (2005). Social skills training augments the effectiveness of cognitive behavioral group therapy for social anxiety disorder. *Behavior Therapy, 36,* 125–138.

Herbert, J. D., Hope, D. A., & Bellack, A. S. (1992). Validity of the distinction between generalized social phobia and avoidant personality disorder. *Journal of Abnormal Psychology, 101,* 332–339.

Herbert, J. D., Rheingold, A. A., Gaudiano, B. A., & Myers, V. H. (2004). Standard versus extended cognitive behavior therapy for social anxiety disorder: A randomized controlled trial. *Behavioral and Cognitive Psychotherapy, 32,* 1–17.

Hersen, M., Bellack, A. S., Himmelhoch, J., & Thase, M. E. (1984). Effects of social skill training, amitriptyline, and psychotherapy in unipolar depressed women. *Behavior Therapy, 15,* 21–40.

Hinde, R. A., & Tamplin, A. (1983). Relations between mother–child interaction and behavior in pre-school children. *British Journal of Developmental Psychology, 1,* 231–257.

Hirshfeld, D. R., Rosenbaum, J. E., Biederman, J., Bolduc, E. A., Faraone, S. V., Snidman, N., et al. (1992). Stable behavioral inhibition and its association with anxiety disorder. *Journal of the American Academy of Child and Adolescent Psychiatry, 31,* 103–111.

Hofmann, S. G. (2004). Cognitive mediation of treatment change in social phobia. *Journal of Consulting and Clinical Psychology, 72,* 392–399.

Hofmann, S. G., Albano, A. M., Heimberg, R. G., Tracey, S., Chorpita, B., & Barlow, D. H. (1999). Subtypes of social phobia in adolescents. *Depression and Anxiety, 9,* 15–18.

Hofmann, S. G., Moscovitch, D. A., Kim, H.-J., & Taylor, A. N. (2004). Changes in self-perception during treatment of social phobia. *Journal of Consulting and Clinical Psychology, 72,* 588–596.

Hofmann, S. G., Newman, M. G., Becker, E., Taylor, C. B., & Roth, W. T. (1995). Social phobia with and without avoidant personality disorder: Preliminary behavior therapy outcome findings. *Journal of Anxiety Disorders, 9,* 427–438.

Hofmann, S. G., Newman, M. G., Ehlers, A., & Roth, W. T. (1995). Psychophysiological differences between subgroups of social phobia. *Journal of Abnormal Psychology, 104,* 224–231.

Holt, C. S., Heimberg, R. G., & Hope, D. A. (1992). Avoidant personality disorder and the generalized subtype of social phobia. *Journal of Abnormal Psychology, 101,* 318–325.

Holt, C. S., Heimberg, R. G., Hope, D. A., & Liebowitz, M. R. (1992). Situational domains of social phobia. *Journal of Anxiety Disorders, 6,* 63–77.

Hope, D. A., Heimberg, R. G., & Bruch, M. A. (1995). Dismantling cognitive–behavioral group therapy for social phobia. *Behaviour Research and Therapy, 33,* 637–650.

Hope, D. A., Herbert, J. D., & White, C. (1995). Social phobia subtype, avoidant personality disorder, and psychotherapy outcome. *Cognitive Therapy and Research, 19,* 339–417.

Hughes, I. (2002). A cognitive therapy model of social anxiety problems: Potential limits on its effectiveness? *Psychology and Psychotherapy: Theory, Research and Practice, 75,* 411–435.

Hummel, R. M., & Gross, A. M. (2001). Socially anxious children: An observational study of parent–child interaction. *Child & Family Behavior Therapy, 23,* 19–41.

Huppert, J. D., Franklin, M. E., Foa, E. B., & Davidson, J. R. T. (2003). Study refusal and exclusion from a randomized treatment study of generalized social phobia. *Journal of Anxiety Disorders, 17,* 683–693.

Hymel, S., Rubin, K. H., Rowden, L., & LeMare, L. (1990). Children's peer relationships: Longitudinal prediction of internalizing and externalizing problems from middle to late childhood. *Child Development, 61,* 2004–2021.

Ihenaga, K., Kiriike, N., Matasuyama, M., Oishi, S., Kaneko, K., & Yamagami, S. (1996, August). *Phobic and anxiety symptoms in preadolescent and adolescent children.* Paper presented at the World Congress of Psychiatry, Madrid, Spain.

Inderbitzen-Nolan, H., Davies, C. A., & McKeon, N. D. (2004). Investigating the construct validity of the SPAI–C: Comparing the sensitivity and specificity of the SPAI–C and the SAS–A. *Journal of Anxiety Disorders, 18,* 547–560.

Ishiyama, F. I. (1984). Shyness: Anxious social sensitivity and self-isolating tendency. *Adolescence, 19,* 903–911.

Jefferson, J. W. (2001). Benzodiazepines and anticonvulsants for social phobia (social anxiety disorder). *Journal of Clinical Psychiatry, 62*(Suppl. 1), 50–53.

Jerremalm, A., Jansson, L., & Öst, L. G. (1986). Cognitive and physiological reactivity and the effects of different behavioral methods in the treatment of social phobia. *Behaviour Research and Therapy, 24,* 171–180.

Jupp, J. J., & Griffiths, M. D. (1990). Self-concept changes in shy, socially isolated adolescents following social skills training emphasising role plays. *Australian Psychologist, 25,* 165–177.

Juster, H. R., Heimberg, R. G., & Engelberg, B. (1995). Self selection and sample selection in a treatment study of social phobia. *Behaviour Research and Therapy, 33,* 321–324.

Kagan, J., Arcus, D., Snidman, N., Feng, W. Y., Hendler, J., & Greene, S. (1994). Reactivity in infants: A cross-national comparison. *Developmental Psychology, 30,* 342–345.

Kagan, J., Reznick, J. S., & Snidman, N. (1987). The physiology and psychology of behavioral inhibition in children. *Child Development, 58,* 1459–1473.

Kashani, J. H., & Orvaschel, H. (1990). A community study of anxiety in children and adolescents. *American Journal of Psychiatry, 147,* 313–318.

Kearney, C. A., & Silverman, W. K. (1990). A preliminary analysis of a functional model of assessment and treatment for school refusal behavior. *Behavior Modification, 14,* 340–366.

Keller, M. B. (2003). The lifelong course of social anxiety disorder: A clinical perspective. *Acta Psychiatrica Scandinavia, 108*(Suppl. 417), 85–94.

Kendall, P. C. (1994). Treating anxiety disorders in children: Results of a randomized clinical trial. *Journal of Consulting and Clinical Psychology, 62,* 100–110.

Kendler, K. S., Neale, M. C., Kessler, R. C., Heath, A. C., & Eaves, L. J. (1992). The genetic epidemiology of phobias in women: The interrelationship of agoraphobia, social phobia, situational phobia, and simple phobia. *Archives of General Psychiatry, 49,* 273–281.

Kerr, M., Lambert, W. W., & Bem, D. J. (1996). Life course sequelae of childhood shyness in Sweden: Comparison with the United States. *Developmental Psychology, 32,* 1100–1105.

Kessler, R. C. (2003). The impairments caused by social phobia in the general population: Implications for intervention. *Acta Psychiatrica Scandinavica, 108*(Suppl. 417), 19–27

Kessler, R. C., Birnbaum, H., Demler, O., Falloon, I. R. H., Gagnon, E., Guyer, M., et al. (2005). The prevalence and correlates of nonaffective psychosis in the National Comorbidity Survey Replication (NCS–R). *Biological Psychiatry, 58,* 668–676.

Khan, A., Leventhal, R. M., Khan, S., & Brown, W. A. (2002). Suicide risk in patients with anxiety disorders: a meta-analysis of the FDA database. *Journal of Affective Disorders, 68,* 183–190.

Kobak, K. A., Greist, J. H., Jefferson, J. W., & Katzelnick, D. J. (2002). Fluoxetine in social phobia: A double-blind, placebo-controlled pilot study. *Journal of Clinical Psychopharmacology, 22,* 257–262.

Koeppen, A. S. (1974). Relaxation training for children. *School Guidance and Counseling, 9,* 521–528.

Kopp, S., & Gillberg, C. (1997). Selective mutism: A population-based study: A research note. *Journal of Child Psychology and Psychiatry, 38,* 257–262.

Krohn, D. D., Weckstein, S. M., & Wright, H. L. (1992). A study of the effectiveness of a specific treatment for elective mutism. *Journal of the American Academy of Child and Adolescent Psychiatry, 31,* 711–718.

Kushner, M. G., Sher, K. J., & Beitman, B. D. (1990). The relation between alcohol problems and the anxiety disorders. *American Journal of Psychiatry, 147,* 685–695.

Kutcher, S., Reiter, S., & Gardner, D. (1995). Pharmacotherapy: Approaches and applications. In J. S. March (Ed.), *Anxiety disorders in children and adolescents* (pp. 341–385). New York: Guilford Press.

Ladd, G. W. (1981). Effectiveness of a social learning method for enhancing children's social interaction and peer acceptance. *Child Development, 52,* 171–178.

Ladd, G. W., & Goiter, B. S. (1988). Parents' management of preschoolers' peer relations: Is it related to children's social competence? *Developmental Psychology, 24,* 109–117.

Lader, M. H. (1967). Palmer skin conductance measures in anxiety and phobic states. *Journal of Psychosomatic Research, 11,* 271–281.

Lader, M., Stender, K., Bürger, V., & Nil, R. (2004). Efficacy and tolerability of excitalopram in 12- and 24-week treatment of social anxiety disorder: Randomised, double-blind, placebo-controlled, fixed-dose study. *Depression and Anxiety, 19,* 241–248.

LaGreca, A. M., Dandes, S. K., Wick, P., Shaw, K., & Stone, W. L. (1988). Development of the Social Anxiety Scale for Children: Reliability and concurrent validity. *Journal of Clinical Child Psychology, 17,* 84–91.

LaGreca, A. M., & Stone, W. L. (1993). Social Anxiety Scale for Children—Revised: Factor structure and concurrent validity. *Journal of Clinical Child Psychology, 22,* 17–27.

Lang, P. J. (1968). Fear reduction and fear behavior: Problems in treating a construct. In J. M. Shlien (Ed.), *The structure of emotion* (pp. 18–30). Seattle, WA: Hogrefe & Huber.

Last, C. G., Hersen, M., Kazdin, A. E., Finkelstein, R., & Strauss, C. C. (1987). Comparison of *DSM–III* separation anxiety disorder and overanxious disorder: Demographic characteristics and patterns of comorbidity. *Journal of the American Academy of Child and Adolescent Psychiatry, 26,* 527–531.

Last, C. G., Hersen, M., Kazdin, A., Finkelstein, R., & Strauss, C. C. (1991). Anxiety disorders in children and their families. *Archives of General Psychiatry, 48,* 928–937.

Last, C. G., Perrin, S., Hersen, M., & Kazdin, A. E. (1992). *DSM–III–R* anxiety disorders in children: Sociodemographic and clinical characteristics. *Journal of the American Academy of Child and Adolescent Psychiatry, 31,* 928–934.

Last, C. G., & Strauss, C. C. (1990). School refusal in anxiety disordered children and adolescents. *Journal of the American Academy of Child and Adolescent Psychiatry, 29,* 31–35.

Last, C. G., Strauss, C. C., & Francis, G. (1987). Comorbidity among childhood anxiety disorders. *Journal of Nervous and Mental Disease, 175,* 726–730.

Lecrubier, Y., Wittchen, H. U., Faravelli, C., Bobes, J., Patel, A., & Knapp, M. (2000). A European perspective on social anxiety disorder. *European Psychiatry, 15,* 5–16.

Lepine, J. P., & Lellouch, J. (1995). Classification and epidemiology of social phobia. *European Archives of Psychiatry and Clinical Neuroscience, 244,* 290–296.

Lepine, J. P., & Pelissolo, A. (2000). Why take social anxiety disorder seriously? *Depression and Anxiety, 11,* 87–92.

Levin, A. P., Saoud, J., Strauman, T., & Gorman, J. (1993). Responses of generalized and discrete social phobics during public speaking. *Journal of Affective Disorders, 7,* 207–221.

Liberman, R. P., King, L. W., DeRisi, W. J., & McCann, M. (1975). *Personal effectiveness: Guiding people to assert themselves and improve their social skills.* Champaign, IL: Research Press.

Lieb, R., Wittchen, H. U., Höfler, M., Fuetsch, M., Stein, M. B., & Merikangas, K. R. (2000). Parental psychopathology, parenting, styles, and the risk of social phobia in offspring. *Archives of General Psychiatry, 57,* 859–866.

Liebowitz, M. R. (1987). Social phobia. *Modern Problems in Pharmacopsychiatry, 22,* 141–173.

Liebowitz, M. R., DeMartinis, N. A., Weihs, K., Londborg, P. D., Smith, W. T., Chung, H., et al. (2003). Efficacy of sertraline in severe generalized social anxiety disorder: Results of a double-blind, placebo-controlled study. *Journal of Clinical Psychiatry, 64,* 785–792.

Liebowitz, M. R., Gelenberg, A. J., & Munjack, D. (2005). Venlafaxine extended release vs. placebo and paroxetine in social anxiety disorder. *Archives of General Psychiatry, 62,* 190–198.

Liebowitz, M. R., Gorman, J. M., Fyer, A. J., Campeas, R., Levin, A., Davies, S., & Klein, D. (1985). Psychopharmacological treatment of social phobia. *Psychopharmacology Bulletin, 21,* 610–614.

Liebowitz, M. R., Gorman, J. M., Fyer, A. J., & Klein, D. F. (1985). Social phobia: Review of a neglected anxiety disorder. *Archives of General Psychiatry, 42,* 729–736.

Liebowitz, M. R., Heimberg, R. G., Schneier, F. R., Hope, D. A., Davies, S., Holt, C. S., et al. (1999). Cognitive–behavioral group therapy versus phenelzine in social phobia: Long-term outcome. *Depression and Anxiety, 10,* 89–98.

Liebowitz, M. R., & Marshall, R. D. (1995). Pharmacological treatments: Clinical applications. In R. G. Heimberg, M. R. Liebowitz, D. A. Hope, & F. R. Schneier (Eds.), *Social phobia: Diagnosis, assessment, and treatment* (pp. 366–383). New York: Guilford Press.

Liebowitz, M. R., Quitkin, F. M., Stewart, J. W., McGrath, P. J., Harrison, W., Rabkin, J., et al. (1984). Phenelzine vs. imipramine in atypical depression: A preliminary report. *Archives of General Psychiatry, 41,* 669–677.

Liebowitz, M. R., Schneier, R., Campeas, R., Hollander, E., Hatterer, J., Fyer, A., et al. (1992). Phenelzine vs. atenolol in social phobia. *Archives of General Psychiatry, 49,* 290–300.

Lucock, M., & Salkovskis, P. M. (1988). Cognitive factors in social anxiety and its treatment. *Behaviour Research and Therapy, 26,* 297–302.

Lundh, L., & Öst, L. (1996). Recognition bias for critical faces in social phobics. *Behaviour Research and Therapy, 34,* 787–794.

Lydiard, R. B., Larraia, M. X., Howell, E. F., & Ballenger, J. C. (1988). Alprazolam in social phobia. *Journal of Clinical Psychopharmacology, 49,* 17–19.

MacDonald, K. (1987). Parent–child physical play with rejected, neglected, and popular boys. *Developmental Psychology, 5,* 705–711.

Mahr, G. C., & Torosian, T. (1999). Anxiety and social phobia in stuttering. *Journal of Fluency Disorders, 24,* 119–126.

Mancini, C., Van Amerigen, M., Szatmari, P., Fugere, C., & Boyle, M. (1996). A high-risk pilot study of the children of adults with social phobia. *Journal of the American Academy of Child and Adolescent Psychiatry, 35,* 1511–1517.

Manassis, K., Fung, D. E., Tannock, R., Sloman, L., Fisenbaum, L., & McInnes, A. (2003). Characterizing selective mutism: Is it more than social anxiety? *Depression and Anxiety, 18,* 153–161.

Manassis, K., Mendlowitz, S. L., Scapillato, D., Avery, D., Fiksenbaum, L., Freire, M., et al. (2002). Group and individual cognitive–behavioral therapy for childhood anxiety disorders: A randomized trial. *Journal of the American Academy of Child and Adolescent Psychiatry, 41,* 1423–1430.

Mannuzza, S., Fyer, A. J., Liebowitz, M. R., & Klein, D. F. (1990). Delineating the boundaries of social phobia: Its relationship to panic disorder and agoraphobia. *Journal of Anxiety Disorders, 4,* 41–59.

Mannuzza, S., Schneier, F. R., Chapman, T. F., Liebowitz, M. R., Klein, D. F., & Fyer, A. J. (1995). Generalized social phobia: Reliability and validity. *Archives of General Psychiatry, 52,* 230–237.

March, J., & Mulle, K. (1993). *"How I ran OCD off my land": A cognitive–behavioral program for the treatment of obsessive–compulsive disorder in children and adolescents.* Unpublished manuscript, Duke University.

Marks, I. M. (1970). The classification of phobic disorders. *British Journal of Psychiatry, 116,* 377–386.

Marks, I. M. (1985). Behavioral psychotherapy for anxiety disorders. *Psychiatric Clinics of North America, 8,* 25–35.

Marks, I. M., & Gelder, M. G. (1966). Different ages of onset in varieties of phobia. *American Journal of Psychiatry, 123,* 218–221.

Masia, C. L., Hofmann, S. G., Klein, R. G., & Liebowitz, M. R. (1999). *The Liebowitz Social Anxiety Scale for Children and Adolescents (LSAS–CA).* Available from Carrie L. Masia, PhD, NYU Child Study Center, 215 Lexington Avenue, New York, NY 10016.

Masia, C. L., Klein, R. G., Storch, E. A., & Corda, B. (2001). School-based behavioral treatment for social anxiety disorder in adolescents: Results of a pilot study. *Journal of the American Academy of Child and Adolescent Psychiatry, 40,* 780–786.

Mattick, R. P., & Clarke, J. C. (1989). *Development and validation of measures of social phobia scrutiny fear and social interaction anxiety.* Unpublished manuscript.

Mattick, R. P., & Peters, L. (1988). Treatment of severe social phobia: Effects of guided exposure with and without cognitive restructuring. *Journal of Consulting and Clinical Psychology, 56,* 251–260.

Mattick, R. P., Peters, L., & Clarke, J. C. (1989). Exposure and cognitive restructuring for severe social phobia: A controlled study. *Behavior Therapy, 20,* 3–23.

McGee, R., Feehan, M., Williams, S., Partridge, F., Silva, P. A., & Kelley, J. (1990). DSM–III disorders in a large sample of adolescents. *Journal of the American Academy of Child and Adolescent Psychiatry, 29,* 611–619.

McNeil, D. W., Ries, B. J., Taylor, L. J., Boone, M. L., Carter, L. E., Turk, C. L., et al. (1995). Comparison of social phobia subtypes using Stroop tests. *Journal of Anxiety Disorders, 9,* 47–57.

McNeil, D. W., Ries, B. J., & Turk, C. L. (1995). Behavioral assessment: Self-report, physiology, and overt behavior. In R. G. Heimberg, M. R. Liebowitz, D. A. Hope, & F. R. Schneier (Eds.), *Social phobia: Diagnosis, assessment and treatment* (pp. 202–231). New York: Guilford Press.

Melfsen, S., & Florin, I. (2002). Do socially anxious children show deficits in classifying facial expressions of emotions? *Journal of Nonverbal Behavior, 26,* 109–126.

Merikangas, K. R., & Angst, J. (1995). Comorbidity and social anxiety disorder: Evidence from clinical, epidemiologic, and genetic studies. *European Archives of Psychiatry and Clinical Neuroscience, 244,* 297–303.

Merikangas, K. R., Avenevoli, S., Acharyya, S., Zhang, H., & Angst, J. (2002). The spectrum of social phobia in the Zurich cohort study of young adults. *Biological Psychiatry, 51,* 81–91.

Merikangas, K. R., Lieb, R., Wittchen, H. U., & Avenevoli, S. (2003). Family and high-risk studies of social anxiety disorder. *Acta Psychiatrica Scandinavia, 108*(Suppl. 417), 28–37.

Mersch, P. P. A. (1995). The treatment of social phobia: The differential effectiveness of exposure in vivo and an integration of exposure in vivo, rational emotive therapy and social skills training. *Behaviour Research and Therapy, 33,* 259–269.

Mersch, P. P. A., Emmelkamp, P. M. G., Bögels, S., & van der Helm, J. (1989). Social phobia: Individual response patterns and the effects of behavioral and cognitive interventions. *Behaviour Research and Therapy, 27,* 421–434.

Mersch, P. P. A., Emmelkamp, P. M. G., & Lips, C. (1991). Social phobia: Individual response patterns and the long-term effects of behavioral and cognitive interventions. A follow-up study. *Behaviour Research and Therapy, 29,* 357–362.

Mersch, P. P. A., Jansen, M. A., & Arntz, A. (1995). Social phobia and personality disorder: Severity of complaint and treatment effectiveness. *Journal of Personality Disorders, 9,* 143–159.

Messer, S. C., & Beidel, D. C. (1994). Psychological correlates of childhood anxiety disorders. *Journal of the American Academy of Child and Adolescent Psychiatry, 33,* 975–983.

Mineka, S. (1987). A primate model of phobic fears. In H. Eysenck & I. Martin (Eds.), *Theoretical foundations of behavior therapy* (pp. 87–111). New York: Plenum Press.

Mineka, S., & Cook, M. (1988). Social learning and the acquisition of snake fear in monkeys. In T. Zentall & G. Galef (Eds.), *Comparative social learning* (pp. 51–73). Hillsdale, NJ: Erlbaum.

Mineka, S., & Zinbarg, R. (1991). Animal models of psychopathology. In C. E. Walker (Ed.), *Clinical psychology: Historical and research foundations* (pp. 51–86). New York: Plenum Press.

Mineka, S., & Zinbarg, R. (1995). Conditioning and ethological models of social phobia. In R. G. Heimberg, M. R. Liebowitz, D. A. Hope, & F. R. Schneier (Eds.), *Social phobia: Diagnosis, assessment, and treatment* (pp. 134–162). New York: Guilford Press.

Mogg, K., Philippot, P., & Bradley, B. P. (2004). Selective attention to angry faces in clinical social phobia. *Journal of Abnormal Psychology, 113,* 160–165.

Morris, T. L. (2004). Social development. In T. L. Morris & J. S. March (Eds.), *Anxiety disorders in children and adolescents* (2nd ed., pp. 59–70). New York: Guilford Press.

Morris, T. L., Hirshfeld-Becker, D. R., Henin, A., & Storch, E. A. (2004). Developmentally sensitive assessment of social anxiety. *Cognitive and Behavioral Practice, 11,* 13–28.

Morris, T. L., & Masia, C. L. (1998). Psychometric evaluation of the Social Phobia and Anxiety Inventory for Children: Concurrent validity and normative data. *Journal of Clinical Child Psychology, 27,* 452–458.

Morris, T. L., Messer, S. C., & Gross, A. M. (1995). Enhancement of the social interaction and status of neglected children: A peer-pairing approach. *Journal of Clinical Child Psychology, 24,* 11–20.

Moutier, C. Y., & Stein, M. B. (2001). The biological basis of social phobia. In S. G. Hofmann & P. M. DiBartolo (Eds.), *From social anxiety to social phobia: Multiple perspectives* (pp. 179–199). Needham Heights, MA: Allyn & Bacon.

Mowrer, O. H. (1947). On the dual nature of learning: A re-interpretation of "conditioning" and "problem-solving." *Harvard Educational Review, 17,* 102–148.

Mullaney, J. A., & Trippett, C. J. (1979). Alcohol dependence and phobias: Clinicial description and relevance. *British Journal of Psychiatry, 135,* 565–573.

Munjack, D., Baltazar, P., Bohn, P., Cabe, D., & Appleton, A. (1990). Clonazepam in the treatment of social phobia: A pilot study. *Journal of Clinical Psychiatry, 51,* 35–40.

Neftel, K. A., Adler, R. H., Kappell, L., Rossi, M., Dolder, M., Kaser, H. E., et al. (1982). Stage fright in musicians: A model illustrating the effects of beta-blockers. *Psychosomatic Medicine, 44,* 461–469.

Nelles, W. B., & Barlow, D. H. (1988). Do children panic? *Clinical Psychology Review, 8,* 359–372.

Newman, M. G., Hofmann, S. G., Trabert, W., Roth, X., & Taylor, C. B. (1994). Does behavioral treatment of social phobia lead to cognitive changes? *Behavior Therapy, 25,* 503–517.

Noyes, R., Jr., Crowe, R. R., Harris, E. L., Hamra, B. J., McChesney, C. M., & Chaudhry, D. R. (1986). Relationship between panic disorder and agoraphobia: A family study. *Archives of General Psychiatry, 43,* 227–233.

Olfson, M., Guardino, M., Struening E., Schneier, F. R., Hellman, F., & Klein, D. F. (2000). Barriers to treatment of social anxiety. *American Journal of Psychiatry, 157,* 521–527.

Olivares, J., Garcia-Lopez, L. J., Beidel, D. C., Turner, S. M., Albano, A. M., & Hidalgo, M. D. (2002). Results at long-term among three psychological treatments for adolescents with generalized social phobia (I): Statistical significance. *Psicologia Conductual, 10,* 147–164.

Olivares, J., Garcia-Lopez, L. J., & Hidalgo, M. D. (2001). The Social Phobia Scale and the Social Interaction Anxiety Scale: Factor structure and reliability in a Spanish-speaking population. *Journal of Psychoeducational Assessment, 39,* 69–80.

Olivares, J., Garcia-Lopez, L. J., Hidalgo, M. D., LaGreca, A. M., Turner, S. M., & Beidel, D. C. (2002). A pilot study on normative data for two social anxiety measures: The Social Phobia and Anxiety Inventory and the Social Anxiety Scale for Adolescents. *International Journal of Clinical and Health Psychology, 2,* 467–476.

Ollendick, T. H., & Cerny, J. A. (1981). *Clinical behavior therapy with children.* New York: Plenum Press.

Ontiveros, A., & Fontaine, R. (1990). Social phobia and clonazepam. *Canadian Journal of Psychiatry, 35,* 439–441.

Oosterbaan, D. B., van Balkom, A. J. L. M., Spinhoven, P., & van Dyck, R. (2001). The placebo response in social phobia. *Journal of Psychopharmacology, 15,* 199–203.

Öst, L. G. (1985). Ways of acquiring phobias and outcome of behavioral treatments. *Behaviour Research and Therapy, 23,* 683–689.

Öst, L. G. (1987). Age of onset in different phobias. *Journal of Abnormal Psychology, 96,* 223–229.

Öst, L. G., & Hughdahl, K. (1981). Acquisition of phobias and anxiety response patterns in clinic patients. *Behaviour Research and Therapy, 16,* 439–447.

Otto, M. W., Pollack, M. H., Gould, R. A., Worthington, J. J., McArdle, E. T., & Rosenbaum, J. F. (2000). A comparison of the efficacy of clonazepam and cognitive–behavioral group therapy for the treatment of social phobia. *Journal of Anxiety Disorders, 14,* 345–358.

Otto, M. W., Pollack, M. H., Maki, K. M., Gould, R. A., Worthigton, J. J., Smoller, J. W., & Rosenbaum, J. F. (2001). Childhood history of anxiety disorders among adults with social phobia: Rates, correlates, and comparisons with patients with panic disorder. *Depression and Anxiety, 14,* 209–213.

Paine, S. C., Hops, H., Walker, H. M., Greenwood, C. R., Fleischman, D. H., & Guild, J. J. (1982). Repeated treatment effects: A study maintaining behavior change in socially withdrawn children. *Behavior Modification, 6,* 171–199.

Pande, A. C., Davidson, J. R. T., Jefferson, J. W., Janney, C. A., Katzelnick, D. J., et al. (1999). Treatment of social phobia with gabapentin: A placebo-controlled study. *Journal of Clinical Psychopharmacology, 19,* 341–348.

Parke, R. D., & Bhavnagri, N. P. (1989). Parents as managers of children's peer relationships. In D. Belle (Ed.), *Children's social networks and social supports* (pp. 241–259). New York: Wiley.

Perrin, S., & Last, C. G. (1993, March). *Comorbidity of social phobia and other anxiety disorders in children.* Paper presented at the Annual Convention of the Association for Advancement of Behavior Therapy, Charleston, SC.

Persons, J. B. (1989). *Cognitive therapy in practice: A case formulation approach.* New York: Norton.

Pollard, C. A., & Henderson, J. G. (1988). Four types of social phobia in a community sample. *Journal of Nervous and Mental Disease, 176,* 440–445.

Potts, N. L. S., & Davidson, J. R. T. (1995). Pharmacological treatments: Literature review. In R. G. Heimberg, M. R. Liebowitz, D. A. Hope, & F. R. Schneier (Eds.), *Social phobia: Diagnosis, assessment and treatment* (pp. 334–365). New York: Guilford Press.

Putallaz, M., & Heflin, A. H. (1990). Parent–child interaction. In S. R. Asher & J. C. Coie (Eds.), *Children's status in the peer group* (pp. 189–216). New York: Cambridge University Press.

Radke-Yarrow, M., & Zahn-Waxler, C. (1986). The role of familial factors in the development of prosocial behavior: Research findings and questions. In D. Olweus, J. Block, & M. Radke-Yarrow (Eds.), *Development of antisocial and prosocial behavior: Research, theories, and issues* (pp. 207–233). Orlando, FL: Academic Press.

Rao, P., Beidel, D. C., & Turner, S. M. (2006). Developmental aspects of social anxiety disorder. Unpublished manuscript, University of Maryland, College Park.

Rapee, R. M. (1995). Descriptive psychopathology of social phobia. In R. G. Heimberg, M. R. Liebowitz, D. A. Hope, & F. R. Schneier (Eds.), *Social phobia: Diagnosis, assessment and treatment* (pp. 41–66). New York: Guilford Press.

Rapee, R. M. (1998). *Overcoming shyness and social phobia: A step-by-step guide.* North Bergen, NJ: Bookmart Press.

Rapee, R. M. (2000). Group treatment of children with anxiety disorders: Outcome and predictors of treatment response. *Australian Journal of Psychology, 52,* 125–129.

Rapee, R. M., Brown, T. A., Antony, M. A., & Barlow, D. H. (1992). Response to hyperventilation and inhalation of 5.5% carbon dioxide-enriched air across the *DSM–III–R* anxiety disorders. *Journal of Abnormal Psychology, 101,* 538–552.

Reich, J., & Yates, W. (1988a). Family history of psychiatric disorders in social phobia. *Comprehensive Psychiatry, 29,* 72–75.

Reich, J., & Yates, W. (1988b). A pilot study of treatment of social phobia with alprazolam. *American Journal of Psychiatry, 145,* 590–594.

Reiter, S. R., Pollack, M. H., Rosenbaum, J. F., & Cohen, L. S. (1990). Clonazepam for the treatment of social phobia. *Journal of Clinical Psychiatry, 51,* 470–472.

Renfry, G. S. (1992). Cognitive–behavior therapy and the Native American client. *Behavior Therapy, 23,* 321–340.

Reznick, J. S., Kagan, J., Sniderman, N., Gersten, M., Boak, K., & Rosenberg, A. (1986). Inhibited and uninhibited children: A follow-up study. *Child Development, 57,* 660–680.

Rickels, K., Mangano, R., & Khan, A. (2004). A double-blind, placebo-controlled study of a flexible dose of venlafaxine ER in adult outpatients with generalized social anxiety disorder. *Journal of Clinicial Psychopharmacology, 24,* 488–496.

Rinck, M., & Becker, E. S. (2005). A comparison of attentional biases and memory biases in women with social phobia and major depression. *Journal of Abnormal Psychology, 114,* 62–74.

Roberson-Nay, R., Beidel, D. C., Turner, S. M., & Strong, D. (2006). *The SPAI–23.* Unpublished manuscript, University of Maryland, College Park.

Rodebaugh, T. L., Holaway, R. M., & Heimberg, R. G. (2004). The treatment of social anxiety disorder. *Clinical Psychology Review, 24,* 883–908.

Rosenbaum, J. F., Biederman, J., Bolduc, E. A., Hirshfeld, D. R., Faraone, S. V., & Kagan, J. (1992). Comorbidity of parental anxiety disorders as risk for childhood-onset anxiety in inhibited children. *American Journal of Psychiatry, 149,* 475–481.

Rosenbaum, J. F., Biederman, J., Gersten, M., Hirshfeld, D. R., Meminger, S. R., Herman, J. B., et al. (1988). Behavioral inhibition in children of parents with panic disorder and agoraphobia. *Archives of General Psychiatry, 45,* 463–470.

Rosenbaum, J. F., Biederman, J., Hirshfeld, D. R., Bolduc, E. A., & Chaloff, J. (1991). Behavioral inhibition in children: A possible precursor to panic disorder or social phobia. *Journal of Clinical Psychiatry, 52*(Suppl.), 5–9.

Rubin, K. H., & Asendorpf, J. B. (1993). Social withdrawal, inhibition, and shyness in childhood: Conceptual and definitional issues. In K. H. Rubin & J. B. Asendorpf (Eds.), *Social withdrawal, inhibition, and shyness in childhood* (pp. 3–17). Hillsdale, NJ: Erlbaum.

Rubin, K. H., LeMare, L. J., & Lollis, S. (1990). Social withdrawal in childhood: Developmental pathways to peer rejection. In S. R. Asher & J. D. Coie (Eds.), *Peer rejection in childhood* (pp. 217–249). New York: Cambridge University Press.

Rubin, K. H., & Mills, R. S. L. (1988). The many faces of social isolation in childhood. *Journal of Consulting and Clinical Psychology, 56,* 916–924.

RUPP Anxiety Study Group. (2002). Treatment of pediatric anxiety disorders: An open-label extension of the Research Units on Pediatric Psychopharmacology Anxiety Study. *Journal of Child and Adolescent Psychopharmacology, 12,* 175–188.

Russo, M. E., & Beidel, D. C. (1994). Comorbidity of childhood anxiety and externalizing disorders: Prevalence, characteristics, and validation issues. *Clinical Psychology Review, 3,* 199–221.

Scarr, S. (1969). Social introversion as a heritable response. *Child Development, 40,* 813–822.

Schmidt, L. A., & Schulkin, J. (1999). *Extreme fear, shyness, and social phobia: Origins, biological mechanisms, and clinical outcomes.* New York: Oxford University Press.

Schneider, B. H., & Byrne, B. M. (1987). Individualizing social skills training for behavior-disordered children. *Journal of Consulting and Clinical Psychology, 55,* 444–445.

Schneier, F. R., Barnes, L. F., Albert, S. M., & Louis, E. D. (2001). Characteristics of social phobia among persons with essential tremor. *Journal of Clinical Psychiatry, 62,* 367–372.

Schneier, F. R., Blanco, C., Campeas, R., Lewis-Fernandez, R., Liu, S.-H., Marshall, R., et al. (2003). Citalopram treatment of social anxiety disorder with comorbid major depression. *Depression and Anxiety, 17,* 191–196.

Schneier, F. R., Chin, S. J., Hollander, E., & Liebowitz, M. R. (1992). Fluoxetine in social phobia. *Journal of Clinical Psychopharmacology, 12,* 62–63.

Schneier, F. R., Johnson, J., Hornig, C. D., Liebowitz, M. R., & Weissman, M. M. (1992). Social phobia: Comorbidity and morbidity in an epidemiologic sample. *Archives of General Psychiatry, 49,* 282–288.

Schneier, F. R., Liebowitz, M. R., Abi-Dargham, A., Zea-Ponce, Y., Lin, S. H., & Laruelle, M. (2000). Low dopamine D_2-receptor binding potential in social phobia. *American Journal of Psychiatry, 157,* 457–459.

Schneier, F. R., Martin, L. Y., Liebowitz, M. R., Gorman, J. M., & Fyer, A. J. (1989). Alcohol abuse in social phobia. *Journal of Anxiety Disorders, 3,* 15–23.

Schneier, F. R., Spitzer, R. L., Gibbon, M., Fyer, A. J., & Liebowitz, M. R. (1991). The relationship of social phobia subtypes and avoidant personality disorder. *Comprehensive Psychiatry, 32,* 496–502.

Scholing, A., & Emmelkamp, P. M. G. (1993a). Cognitive and behavioural treatments for fear of blushing, sweating or trembling. *Behaviour Research and Therapy, 31,* 155–170.

Scholing, A., & Emmelkamp, P. M. G. (1993b). Exposure with and without cognitive therapy for generalized social phobia: Effects of individual and group treatment. *Behaviour Research and Therapy, 31,* 155–170.

Scholing, A., & Emmelkamp, P. M. G. (1996). Treatment of generalized social phobia: Results at long-term follow-up. *Behaviour Research and Therapy, 34,* 447–452.

Schuckit, M. A., Tipp, J. E., Bucholz, K. K., Nurnberger, J. I., Jr., Hesselbrock, V. M., Crowe, R. R., & Kramer, J. (1997). The life-time rates of three major mood disorders and four major anxiety disorders in alcoholics and controls. *Addiction, 92,* 1289–1304.

Schwartz, C. E., Snidman, N., & Kagan, J. (1999). Adolescent social anxiety as an outcome of inhibited temperament in childhood. *Journal of the American Academy of Child and Adolescent Psychiatry, 38,* 1008–1015.

Schwartz, C. E., Wright, C. I., Shin, L. M., Kagan, J., & Rauch, S. L. (2003, June 20). Inhibited and uninhibited infants "grown up": Adult amygdalar response to novelty. *Science, 300,* 1952–1953.

Shaffer, D., Fisher, P., Dulcan, M. K., Piacentini, J., Schwab-Stone, M. E., Lahye, B. B., et al. (1996). The NIMH Diagnostic Interview Schedule for Children Version 2.3 (DISC–2.3): Description, acceptability, prevalence rates, and performance in the MECA study. *Journal of the American Academy of Child and Adolescent Psychiatry, 35,* 865–872.

Sheehan, D. V., Lecrubier, Y., Sheehan, K. H., Amorim. P., Janavs. J., Weiller, E., et al. (1998). The Mini-International Neuropsychiatric Interview (M.I.N.I.): The development and validation of a structured diagnostic psychiatric interview for *DSM–IV* and ICD–10. *Journal of Clinical Psychiatry, 59*(Suppl. 20), 22–33.

Sheridan, S. M., Kratochwill, T. R., & Elliott, S. N. (1990). Behavioral consultation with parents and teachers: Delivering treatment for socially withdrawn children at home and school. *School Psychology Review, 19,* 33–52.

Shortt, A. L., Barrett, P. M., & Fox, T. L. (2001). Evaluating the FRIENDS program: A cognitive–behavioral group treatment for anxious children and their parents. *Journal of Clinical Child Psychology, 30,* 525–535.

Silverman, W. K., & Albano, A. M. (1995). *Anxiety Disorders Interview Schedule for Children.* San Antonio, TX: Psychological Corporation.

Silverman, W. K., & Kurtines, W. M. (1996). *Anxiety and phobic disorders: A pragmatic approach.* New York: Plenum Press.

Silverman, W. K., Kurtines, W. M., Ginsburg, G. S., Weems, C. F., Lumpkin, P. W., & Carmichael, D. H. (1999). Treating anxiety disorders in children with group cognitive–behavioral therapy: A randomized clinical trial. *Journal of Consulting and Clinical Psychology, 67,* 995–1003.

Silverman, W. K., Kurtines, W. M., Ginsburg, G. S., Weems, C. F., Rabian, B., & Serafini, L. T. (1999). Contingency management, self-control, and education support in the treatment of childhood phobic disorders: A randomized clinical trial. *Journal of Consulting and Clinical Psychology, 67,* 675–687.

Simeon, J. G., & Ferguson, H. B. (1987). Alprazolam effects in children with anxiety disorders. *Canadian Journal of Psychiatry, 32,* 570–574.

Simeon, J. G., Ferguson, H. B., Knott, V., Roberts, N., Gautheir, B., Dubois, C., & Wiggins, D. (1992). Clinical, cognitive, and neuropsychological effects of alprazolam in children and adolescents with overanxious disorder and avoidant disorders. *Journal of the American Academy of Child and Adolescent Psychiatry, 31,* 29–33.

Simon, N. M., Otto, M. W., Korbly, N. B., Peters, P. K. M., Nicolaou, D. C., & Pollack, M. H. (2002). Quality of life in social anxiety disorder compared with panic disorder and the general population. *Psychiatric Services, 53,* 714–718.

Simonian, S. J., Beidel, D. C., Turner, S. M., Berkes, J. L., & Long, J. H. (2001). Recognition of facial affect by children and adolescents diagnosed with social phobia. *Child Psychiatry and Human Development, 32,* 137–145.

Simpson, H. B., Schneier, F. R., Campeas, R. B., Marshall, R. D., Fallon, B. A., Davies, S., et al. (1998). Imipramine in the treatment of social phobia. *Journal of Clinical Psychopharmacology, 18,* 132–135.

Skre, I., Onstad, S., Torgersen, S., Lygren, S., & Kringlen, E. (1993). A twin study of *DSM–III–R* anxiety disorders. *Acta Psychiatrica Scandinavica, 88,* 85–92.

Smail, P., Stockwell, T., Canter, S., & Hodgson, R. (1984). Alcohol dependence and phobic anxiety states. I. A prevalence study. *British Journal of Psychiatry, 144,* 53–57.

Spence, S. H., Donovan, C., & Brechman-Toussaint, M. (1999). Social skills, social outcomes, and cognitive features of childhood social phobia. *Journal of Abnormal Psychology, 108,* 211–221.

Spence, S. H., Donovan, C., & Brechman-Toussaint, M. (2000). The treatment of childhood social phobia: The effectiveness of a social skills training-based, cognitive–behavioral intervention, with and without parental involvement. *Journal of Child Psychology and Psychiatry, 41,* 713–726.

Stein, D. J., Berk, M., Els, C., Emsley, R. A., Gittelson, L., Wilson, D., et al. (1999). A double-blind placebo-controlled trial of paroxetine in the management of social phobia (social anxiety disorder) in South Africa. *South African Medical Journal, 89,* 402–406.

Stein, D. J., Stein, M. B., Pitts, C. D., Kumar, R., & Hunter, B. (2002). Predictors of response to pharmacotherapy in social anxiety disorder: An analysis of 3 placebo-controlled paroxetine trials. *Journal of Clinical Psychiatry, 63,* 152–155.

Stein, D. J., Versiani, M., Hair, T., & Kumar, R. (2002). Efficacy of paroxetine for relapse prevention in social anxiety disorder. *Archives of General Psychiatry, 59,* 1111–1118.

Stein, D. J., Westenberg, H. G. M., Yang, H., Li, D., & Barbato, L. M. (2003). Flovoxamine CR in the long-term treatment of social anxiety disorder: The 12- to 24-week extension phase of a multicentre, randomized, placebo-controlled trial. *International Journal of Neuropsychopharmacology, 6,* 317–323.

Stein, M. B., Chartier, M. J., Hazen, A. L., Kozak, M. V., Tancer, M. E., Lander, S., et al. (1998). A direct-interview family study of generalized social phobia. *American Journal of Psychiatry, 155,* 90–97.

Stein, M. B., Chavira, D. A., & Jang, K. L. (2001). Bringing up bashful baby. *Psychiatric Clinics of North America, 24,* 661–675.

Stein, M. B., Fyer, A. J., Davidson, J. R. T., Pollack, M. H., & Wiita, B. (1999). Fluvoxamine treatment of social phobia (social anxiety disorder): A double-blind, placebo-controlled study. *American Journal of Psychiatry, 156,* 756–760.

Stein, M. B., Goldin, P. R., Sareen J., Eyler-Zorrilla, L. T., & Brown, G. G. (2002). Increased amygdala activation to angry and contemptuous faces in generalized social phobia. *Archives of General Psychiatry, 59,* 1027–1034.

Stein, M. B., Liebowitz, M. R., Lydiard, B., Pitts, C. D., Bushness, W., & Gergel, I. (1998). Paroexetine treatment of generalized social phobia (social anxiety disorder). *Journal of the American Medical Association, 280,* 708–713.

Stein, M. B., Pollack, M. H., Bystritsky, A., Kelsey, J. E., & Mangano, R. M. (2005). Efficacy of low and higher dose extended-release venlafaxine in generalized social anxiety disorder: A 6-month randomized controlled trial. *Psychopharmacology, 177,* 280–288.

Stein, M. B., Walker, J. R., & Forde, D. R. (1994). Setting diagnostic thresholds for social phobia: Considerations from a community survey of social anxiety. *American Journal of Psychiatry, 151,* 408–412.

Stemberger, R. T., Turner, S. M., Beidel, D. C., & Calhoun, K. S. (1995). Social phobia: An analysis of possible developmental factors. *Journal of Abnormal Psychology, 104,* 526–531.

Storch, E. A., Masia, C. L., Pincus, D., Klein, R., & Liebowitz, M. (2001, March). *Initial psychometric properties of the Liebowitz Social Anxiety Scale for Children and Adolescents.* Poster presented at the annual meeting of the Anxiety Disorders of America Association, Atlanta, GA.

Storch, E. A., Masia-Warner, C., Dent, H. C., Roberti, J. W., & Fisher, P. H. (2004). Psychometric evaluation of the Social Anxiety Scale for Adolescents and the

Social Phobia and Anxiety Inventory for Children: Construct validity and normative data. *Journal of Anxiety Disorders, 18,* 665–679.

Strauss, C. C., Lahey, B. B., Frick, P., Frame, C. L., & Hynd, G. W. (1988). Peer social status of children with anxiety disorders. *Journal of Consulting and Clinical Psychology, 56,* 137–141.

Strauss, C. C., & Last, C. G. (1993). Social and simple phobias in children. *Journal of Anxiety Disorders, 1,* 141–152.

Stravynski, A., Lamontagne, Y., & Lavallee, Y. J. (1986). Clinical phobias and avoidant personality disorder among alcoholics admitted to an alcoholism rehabilitation setting. *Canadian Journal of Psychiatry, 31,* 714–719.

Stravynski, A., Marks, I., & Yule, W. (1982). Social skills problems in neurotic outpatients: Social skills training with and without cognitive modification. *Archives of General Psychiatry, 39,* 1378–1385.

Tancer, M. E. (1993). Neurobiology of social phobia. *Journal of Clinical Psychiatry, 54,* 26–30.

Tancer, M. E., Mailman, R. B., Stein, M. B., Mason, G. A., Carson, S. W., & Golden, R. N. (1994–1995). Neuroendocrine responsivity in monoaminergic system probes in generalized social phobia. *Anxiety, 1,* 216–223.

Taylor, S. (1996). Meta-analysis of cognitive–behavioral treatments for social phobia. *Behavior Therapy and Experimental Psychiatry, 27,* 1–9.

Tharwani, H. M., & Davidson, J. R. T. (2001). Symptomatic and functional assessment of social anxiety disorder in adults. *Psychiatric Clinics of North America, 24,* 643–659.

Thomas, A., & Chess, S. (1977). *Temperament and development.* New York: Brunner/Mazel.

Tillfors, M., Furmark, T., Ekselius, L., & Fredrikson, M. (2001). Social phobia and avoidant personality disorder as related to parental history of social anxiety: A general population study. *Behaviour Research and Therapy, 39,* 289–298.

Tillfors, M., Furmark, T., Marteinsdottir, I., Fischer, H., Possiota, A., Långström, B., & Fredrikson. M. (2001). Cerebral blood flow in subjects with social phobia during stressful speaking tasks: A PET study. *American Journal of Psychiatry, 158,* 1220–1226.

Torgersen, S. (1983). Genetic factors in the anxiety disorders. *Archives of General Psychiatry, 40,* 1085–1089.

Tracey, S. A., Mattis, S. G., Chorpita, B. F., Albano, A. M., Heimberg, R. G., & Barlow, D. H. (1998, November). *Cognitive–behavioral group treatment of social phobia in adolescents: Preliminary examination of the contribution of parental involvement.* Presented at the Annual Meeting of the Association for Advancement of Behavior Therapy, Washington, DC.

Tse, W. S., & Bond, A. J. (2002). Serotonergic intervention affects both social dominance and affiliative behaviour. *Psychopharmacology, 161,* 324–330.

Tupler, L. A., Davidson, J. R., Smith, R. D., Lazeyras, F., Charles, H. C., & Krishnan, K. R. (1997). A repeat proton magnetic resonance spectroscopy study in social phobia. *Biological Psychiatry, 42,* 419–424.

Turner, S. M., & Beidel, D. C. (1989). Social phobia: Clinical syndrome, diagnosis and comorbidity. *Clinical Psychology Review, 9,* 3–18.

Turner, S. M., & Beidel, D. C. (2002). *Social phobia: Assessment and treatment of social skill.* Unpublished manuscript, University of Maryland, College Park.

Turner, S. M., Beidel, D. C., Borden, J. W., Stanley, M. R., & Jacob, R. G. (1991). Social phobia: Axis I and Axis II correlates. *Journal of Abnormal Psychology, 100,* 102–106.

Turner, S. M., Beidel, D. C., & Cooley, M. R. (1994). *Social Effectiveness Therapy: A program for overcoming social anxiety and social phobia.* Toronto, Ontario, Canada: Multi-Health Systems.

Turner, S. M., Beidel, D. C., Cooley, M. R., Woody, S. R., & Messer, S. C. (1994). A multicomponent behavioral treatment for social phobia: Social Effectiveness Therapy. *Behaviour Research and Therapy, 32,* 381–390.

Turner, S. M., Beidel, D. C., & Cooley-Quille, M. R. (1995). Two year follow-up of social phobics treated with Social Effectiveness Therapy. *Behaviour Research and Therapy, 33,* 553–556.

Turner, S. M., Beidel, D. C., & Costello, A. (1987). Psychopathology in the offspring of anxiety disorders patients. *Journal of Consulting and Clinical Psychology, 55,* 229–235.

Turner, S. M., Beidel, D. C., Dancu, C. V., & Keys, D. J. (1986). Psychopathology of social phobia and comparison to avoidant personality disorder. *Journal of Abnormal Psychology, 95,* 389–394.

Turner, S. M., Beidel, D. C., Dancu, C. V., & Stanley, M. A. (1989). An empirically derived inventory to measure social fears and anxiety: The Social Phobia and

Anxiety Inventory. *Psychological Assessment: A Journal of Consulting and Clinical Psychology, 1,* 35–40.

Turner, S. M., Beidel, D. C., & Epstein, L. H. (1991). Vulnerability and risk for anxiety disorders. *Journal of Anxiety Disorders, 5,* 151–166.

Turner, S. M., Beidel, D. C., & Jacob, R. G. (1994). Social phobia: A comparison of behavior therapy and atenolol. *Journal of Consulting and Clinical Psychology, 62,* 350–358.

Turner, S. M., Beidel, D. C., & Larkin, K. T. (1986). Situational determinants of social anxiety in clinic and non-clinic samples: Physiological and cognitive correlates. *Journal of Consulting and Clinical Psychology, 54,* 523–527.

Turner, S. M., Beidel, D. C., Long, P. J., & Greenhouse, J. (1992). Reduction of fear in social phobics: An examination of extinction patterns. *Behavior Therapy, 23,* 389–403.

Turner, S. M., Beidel, D. C., & Roberson-Nay, R. (2005). Offspring of anxious parents: Reactivity, habituation, and anxiety-proneness. *Behaviour Research and Therapy, 43,* 1263–1279.

Turner, S. M., Beidel, D. C., Roberson-Nay, R., & Tervo, K. (2003). Parenting behaviors in parents with anxiety disorders. *Behaviour Research and Therapy, 41,* 541–554.

Turner, S. M., Beidel, D. C., & Townsley, R. M. (1990). Social phobia: Relationship to shyness. *Behaviour Research and Therapy, 28,* 497–505.

Turner, S. M., Beidel, D. C., & Townsley, R. M. (1992). Social phobia: A comparison of specific and generalized subtypes and avoidant personality disorder. *Journal of Abnormal Psychology, 101,* 326–331.

Turner, S. M., Beidel, D. C., & Wolff, P. L. (1996). Is behavioral inhibition related to the anxiety disorders? *Clinical Psychology Review, 16,* 157–172.

Turner, S. M., Beidel, D. C., Wolff, P. L., Spaulding, S., & Jacob, R. G. (1996). Clinical features affecting treatment outcome in social phobia. *Behaviour Research and Therapy, 34,* 795–804.

Turner, S. M., Cooley-Quille, M. R., & Beidel, D. C. (1995). Behavioral and pharmacological treatment of social phobia: Long-term outcome. In M. Mavissakalian & R. Prien (Eds.), *Anxiety disorders: Psychological and pharmacological treatment* (pp. 343–371). Washington, DC: American Psychiatric Press.

Turner, S. M., Johnson, M. R., Beidel, D. C., Heiser, N. A., & Lydiard, R. B. (2003). The Social Thoughts and Beliefs Scale: A new inventory for assessing cognitions in social phobia. *Psychological Assessment, 15,* 384–391.

Turner, S. M., Stanley, M. A., Beidel, D. C., & Bond, L. (1989). The Social Phobia and Anxiety Inventory: Construct validity. *Journal of Psychopathology and Behavioral Assessment, 11,* 221–234.

Van Ameringen, M., Mancini, C., Pipe, B., Oakman, J., & Bennett, M. (2004). An open trial of topiramate in the treatment of generalized social phobia. *Journal of Clinical Psychiatry, 65,* 1674–1678.

Van Ameringen, M. V., Mancini, C., & Streiner, D. L. (1993). Fluoxetine efficacy in social phobia. *Journal of Clinical Psychiatry, 54,* 27–32.

Van Ameringen, M., Mancini, C., & Streiner, D. (1994). Social disability in anxiety disorders. *Neuropsychopharmacology, 10*(Suppl. 3), 615S.

van Dam-Baggen, R., & Kraaimaat, F. W. (2000a). Social skills training in two subtypes of psychiatric inpatients with generalized social phobia. *Scandinavian Journal of Behavior Therapy, 29,* 14–21.

van Dam-Baggen, R., & Kraaimaat, F. (2000b). Group social skills training or cognitive group therapy as the clinical treatment of choice for generalized social phobia? *Journal of Anxiety Disorders, 14,* 437–451.

van der Linden, G., Stein, D. J., & van Balkom, A. J. L. M. (2000). The efficacy of the selective serotonin reuptake inhibitors for social anxiety disorder (social phobia): A meta-analysis of randomized controlled trials. *Journal of Clinical Psychopharmacology, 15*(Suppl. 2), S15–S23.

Velosa, J. F., & Riddle, M. A. (2000). Pharmacologic treatment of anxiety disorders in children and adolescents. *Psychopharmacology, 9,* 119–133.

Vernberg, E. M., Abwender, D. A., Ewell, K. K., & Beery, S. H. (1992). Social anxiety and peer relationships in early adolescence: A prospective analysis. *Journal of Clinical Child Psychology, 21,* 189–196.

Versiani, M., Nardi, A. E., Mundim, E. D., Alves, A. B., Liebowitz, M. R., & Amrein, R. (1992). Pharmacotherapy of social phobia: A controlled study with moclobemide and phenelzine. *British Journal of Psychiatry, 161,* 353–360.

Viesselman, J. O., Yaylayan, S., Weller, E. B., & Weller, R. A. (1993). Antidysthymic drugs (antidepressants and antimanics). In J. S. Werry & M. G. Aman (Eds.),

Practitioner's guide to psychoactive drugs for children and adolescents (pp. 239–268). New York: Plenum Press.

Vythilingum, B., Stein, D. J., & Soifer, S. (2002). Is "shy bladder syndrome" a subtype of social anxiety disorder? *Depression and Anxiety, 16,* 84–87.

Wacker, H. R., Mullejans, R., Klein, K. H., & Battegay, R. (1992). Identification of cases of anxiety disorders and affective disorders in the community according to *ICD–10* and *DSM–III–R* using the Composite International Diagnostic Interview (CIDI). *International Journal of Methods in Psychiatric Research, 2,* 91–100.

Wagner, K. D., Ray, B., Stein, M. B., Carpenter, D. J., Perera, P., Gee, M., et al. (2004). A multicenter, randomized, double-blind, placebo-controlled trial of paroxetine in children and adolescents with social anxiety disorder. *Archives of General Psychiatry, 61,* 1153–1162.

Warren, S. L., Huston, L., Egeland, B., & Sroufe, L. A. (1997). Child and adolescent anxiety disorders and early attachment. *Journal of the American Academy of Child and Adolescent Psychiatry, 36,* 637–644.

Watson, J. B., & Rayner, R. (1920). Conditioned emotional reactions. *Journal of Experimental Psychology, 3,* 1–14.

Weissman, M. M., Leckman, J. F., Merikangas, K. R., Gammon, G. D., & Prusoff, B. A. (1984). Depression and anxiety disorders in parents and children. *Archives of General Psychiatry, 41,* 845–852.

Whitehill, M. B., Hersen, M., & Bellack, A. S. (1980). Conversation skills training for socially isolated children. *Behaviour Research and Therapy, 18,* 217–225.

Wilson, J. K., & Rapee, R. M. (2005). The interpretation of negative social events in social phobia: Changes during treatment and relationship to outcome. *Behaviour Research and Therapy, 43,* 373–389.

Wittchen, H. U., Stein, M., & Kessler, R. C. (1999). Social fears and social phobia in a community sample of adolescents and young adults: prevalence, risk factors and comorbidity. *Psychological Medicine, 29,* 309–323.

Wlazlo, Z., Schroeder-Hartwig, K., Hand, I., Kaiser, G., & Munchau, N. (1990). Exposure in vivo vs. social skills training for social phobia: Long-term outcome and differential effects. *Behaviour Research and Therapy, 28,* 181–193.

Woody, S. R., & Adessky, R. S. (2002). Therapeutic alliance, group cohesion, and homework compliance during cognitive–behavioral group treatment for social phobia. *Behavior Therapy, 33,* 5–27.

Yeganeh, R., Beidel, D. C., & Turner, S. M. (2006). Selective mutism: More than social anxiety? *Depression and Anxiety, 23,* 117–123.

Yeganeh, R., Beidel, D. C., Turner, S. M., Pina, A. A., & Silverman, W. K. (2003). Clinical distinctions between selective mutism and social phobia: An investigation of childhood psychopathology. *Journal of the American Academy of Child and Adolescent Psychiatry, 42,* 1069–1075.

Young, B. J., Beidel, D. C., Turner, S. M., Ammerman, R. T., McGraw, K., & Coaston, S. C. (in press). Pretreatment attrition and childhood social phobia: parent concerns about medication. *Journal of Anxiety Disorders.*

Zaider, T. I., & Heimberg, R. G. (2003). Non-pharmacologic treatments for social anxiety disorder. *Acta Psychiatrica Scandinavia, 108,* 72–84.

Zhang, W., Ross, J., & Davidson, J. R. T. (2004). Social anxiety disorder in callers to the Anxiety Disorders Association of America. *Depression and Anxiety, 20,* 101–106.

Zitrin, C. M., Klein, D. F., Woerner, M. G., & Ross, D. (1983). Treatment of phobias: A comparison of imipramine and placebo. *Archives of General Psychiatry, 40,* 125–138.

Author Index

Subject Index

Core fear(s), *continued*
  in case study, 255, 258
  in children, 271, 284, 315
    identification of, 280–281
    in sample scene, 285
  exposure revelation of, 231
  failure to incorporate, 232
Crisis situations, 156
Cultural norms, 87

Dale Carnegie classes, 260
Defiant behaviors. *See* Oppositional
    defiant disorder
Depression
  and combination of medication,
    199
  and paroxetine, 190–191
  and passive isolation in children,
    49
  and school refusal, 71
  and shyness, 111
  and social anxiety disorder, 20,
    34, 37–38, 63
    and citalopram, 180
    and outcome of behavioral or
      cognitive–behavioral
      treatment, 219–220
    and subtype differences, 25
    treatment for, 162, 163, 260
  in youth, 62, 74–75
Developmental considerations
  in assessment, 316
  for childhood social anxiety
    disorder, 48–50, 61
  and diagnostic considerations,
    15
  in treatment, 317
Diagnosis
  cultural nuance in, 89
  and self-monitoring procedures,
    139

of social anxiety disorder in
    adults, 12–17
of social anxiety disorder in
    children, 50–55, 79–80,
    83
See also Assessment of social
    anxiety disorder
*Diagnostic and Statistical Manual of
    Mental Disorders, Third
    Edition (DSM–III)*, 3, 4, 12,
    32, 84, 145
*Diagnostic and Statistical Manual of
    Mental Disorders, Third
    Edition, Revised (DSM–III–R)*,
    4–5, 82, 85, 217
*Diagnostic and Statistical Manual of
    Mental Disorders, Fourth
    Edition (DSM–IV)*, 5, 13, 14,
    51, 53, 54, 70, 73, 74, 83, 85,
    128
Diaries, of children, 57
Differential diagnosis
  in adults, 33–35, 39–40
    and avoidant personality
      disorder, 40–41, 43
    and depression, 37–38
    and generalized anxiety
      disorders, 36–37
    and medical conditions, 38–39
    and obsessive–compulsive
      personality disorder, 37,
      41–43
    and panic disorder, 35–36
    and paranoid personality
      disorder, 43–44
    and schizoid personality
      disorder, 44–45
  in children and adolescents, 70
    and depression, 74–75
    and externalizing disorders,
      75–77, 79

About the Authors

Deborah C. Beidel, PhD, is the author or coauthor of more than 180 journal articles, book chapters, and books, primarily in the area of anxiety disorders. She has served on the editorial boards of numerous psychological journals including the *Journal of Consulting and Clinical Psychology*, the *Journal of Abnormal Child Psychology*, and *Behavior Therapy*. She has chaired the Anxiety Disorders Association of America Children's Task Force and the National Institute of Mental Health Child and Adolescent Psychosocial Research Consortium. Currently, she is the chair of the American Psychological Association Division 12 (Society of Clinical Psychology) task force on science and practice. Dr. Beidel was the recipient of the 1990 New Researcher Award from the Association for Advancement of Behavior Therapy and the 1995 recipient of the Distinguished Educator Award from the Association of Medical School Psychologists. She is a diplomate of the American Board of Professional Psychology in both clinical and behavioral psychology. Currently, she is professor of psychiatry; director of research in child psychiatry; and director of the Anxiety, Stress, and Trauma Research Network at Pennsylvania State University College of Medicine/Hershey Medical Center in Hershey.

Samuel M. Turner, PhD, authored or coauthored more than 200 journal articles, book chapters, and books, mostly on anxiety disorders. He served as associate editor-in-chief of the *American Psychologist* and on the editorial boards of numerous psychological journals including the *Journal of Consulting and Clinical Psychology*, *Behavior Therapy*, and *Behaviour Research and Therapy*. In addition, he served on numerous national committees and panels including the Extramural Scientific Advisory Board of the National Institute of Mental Health. Dr. Turner was the 1997 recipient of the American Psychological Association's award for Distinguished Contribution to Professional Knowledge and the 1997 award recipient for Distinguished Contribution to Research from the Association of Medical School Psychologists. He held diplomates from the American Board of Professional Psychology in clinical and behavioral psychology. At the time of his death in 2005, he was professor of psychology and codirector of the Maryland Center for Anxiety Disorders at the University of Maryland in College Park.